TALKING PICTURES

By the same author

The Matter of Mandrake
The Hounds of Sparta
Tales of the Redundance Kind
End Product
A Series of Defeats
To Nick a Good Body
The Hollywood Greats
The Movie Greats
Have a Nice Day
Sticky Wicket
The Film Greats

TALKING PICTURES

Barry Norman

ARROW BOOKS

Arrow Books Limited
20 Vauxhall Bridge Road, London SW1V 2SA

An imprint of Random Century Group

London   Melbourne   Sydney   Auckland
Johannesburg and agencies throughout
the world

First published by Hodder and Stoughton 1987

Arrow edition 1991

© Barry Norman 1987

Printed and bound in Great Britain by
Butler & Tanner Ltd, Frome and London

ISBN 0 09 964830 X

CONTENTS

Preface
7

One The Coming of Sound
9

Two The Studio System
31

Three Hollywood and Sex
73

Four Hollywood Goes to War
105

Five Hollywood and Crime
143

Six Hollywood and Politics
177

Seven The B Movie
229

Eight The Western
251

Nine The Decline of the Studios
287

Ten Hollywood Now
307

Index
337

In the compiling and writing of this book, and indeed of the BBC television documentaries which spawned it, I owe a special debt of thanks and gratitude to the following: Judy Lindsay, the overall producer of the TV series, David Jeffcock and Michael Parker, both of whom toiled day and night without ever seeming to pause for sleep, Ian Kiel, Robin Lough, Andrew Gosling and Janina Kolodziej who, apart from all her other duties as the production assistant, had to do all the driving and shouldered this task without complaint – well, more or less. My deepest thanks to all of you.

PREFACE

What follows in this book is not and does not purport to be a comprehensive history of Hollywood since the introduction of sound. To tell such a tale would take not one volume but several.

Instead, what I offer here – as in the BBC television series on which the book is based – is an investigation of various aspects of Hollywood since 1927 when *The Jazz Singer* revolutionised the movie industry. Well, I say "based" on the TV series but in fact this is an extension of it. A TV documentary, as I keep telling my colleagues to the point of tedium, is the equivalent of a 2,500–3,000 word magazine article, heavily illustrated. There is, consequently, a limit to the amount of verbal information it can impart. The same, of course, is true of a book but to a much lesser extent. In both you have to select, discard and, eventually, stop somewhere – but a book offers a far wider degree of choice.

So this is not simply the book of the TV series, though it owes its inspiration and its very existence to it. Both represent a distillation of considerably more than 100 interviews, conducted in such places as London, Hollywood, New York, San Francisco, Athens and Rome. The interviewees ranged in age from the ninety-five-year-old Hal Roach, producer of the Laurel and Hardy films, to Molly Ringwald, who was a couple of days short of her nineteenth birthday when I talked to her.

These conversations, spread over a period of two years, left me sometimes delighted and invigorated, sometimes irritated (usually by actors or actresses, who refused to address themselves to the questions and instead took the opportunity of delivering unsolicited and unwanted versions of their autobiographies), sometimes saddened (when the ravages of age became only too apparent in people I had long admired) – and with one tangible souvenir, Jamie Lee Curtis's hair grip which she left in my hotel bedroom. No, no, wait – it wasn't like that at all. I interviewed her in my hotel bedroom on Sunset Boulevard, chaperoned by a camera crew of four and at least three members of the production team.

One further point, and it's a sort of apology: in the following pages you will notice that films are usually ascribed to their directors, John Ford's *Stagecoach*, for example. The purists won't like that; actually, I don't like it and the scriptwriter, William Goldman, positively hates it. He said: 'When attribution is given to a film, as in Steven Spielberg's *The Color Purple*, it's madness. It would make perfect sense if there were a bunch of other "Color Purples" and you were trying to be precise as to which one you were talking about, like whose performance of Beethoven's 5th are we talking about. But to give attribution to a director as if he wrote it is loony-tunes time and anybody who's ever been around a movie set knows that the director is at the mercy of the star, at the mercy of the studio, at the mercy of the cameraman – everybody's at everybody else's mercy in a movie. And to single out anyone, whether it's the director or the star or the screenwriter, is foolishness. Basically, movies are a group activity but no one wants to know that. We all want to think the stars are cute and the directors are terrific and make up all the visuals. But if the directors do the visuals, why do you pay a cameraman 10,000 dollars a week, which is what a top cameraman gets now? It's because they're worth it, not because they say "yessir" to the director.' He blamed the French, the leaders of the *nouvelle vague* such as Godard and Truffaut, for the current cult of the director but in the end, he said, 'even they admitted it was a lot of crap anyway'.

Well, of course, he's quite right. But, you ask, if I agree with all that why do I still attribute films to the director alone? Because it's more convenient, that's why; it's a label, if you like, a sort of shorthand. It saves time and space and makes for easy identification. It helps me and I hope it helps you. Nevertheless, I suppose I should apologise to all the producers, stars, writers, cinematographers, editors, hairdressers, key grips, best boys and transport captains who might feel, indignantly, that any particular film was actually *their* film. All right, I do so apologise – but not very contritely.

THE COMING OF SOUND

On 6 October 1927 Warner Brothers held the premiere of their latest film, *The Jazz Singer*, in New York and promptly revolutionised the entire motion picture industry. The movie – a Jewish tale of a cantor's son, Al Jolson, who prefers show business to his father's calling, thus provoking much parental dismay – was hardly powerful enough in itself to stand the film business on its ear; it was by no means bad but equally it was by no means exceptional.

What in fact caused the sensation was that during the picture Jolson and others in the cast were actually heard to speak and indeed Jolson delivered the first immortal line in the movies – 'Wait a minute, you ain't heard nothin' yet!' As a brief, pungent statement to usher in the era of the talking picture it was certainly apt enough but not quite as amazingly prophetic as it might seem now. For a start it was a catch-phrase that Jolson had been using on stage for years. And besides, a quick look through the history of the cinema from the late nineteenth century onwards shows that talkies were bound to come sooner or later and it could well be argued that they came later than they might have done.

From the beginning there had always been sound in the cinema – the so-called silent films were shown to a musical accompaniment – but what had been lacking until the later 1920s was the human voice. That and a system whereby sound and image could be perfectly synchronised, an idea which was patented (in theory anyway) by the Lumière Brothers as far back as 1896. Even before that, however, Thomas Edison and his assistant W. K. Laurie Dickson had experimented with a system that linked Edison's motion picture machine, the Kinetoscope, to his phonograph. The result, called the Kinetophone, used a kind of stethoscope to provide sound accompaniment to moving pictures for the individual spectator. Other more advanced systems were developed in various parts of the world in the ensuing years – a patent for a sound system using a photoelectric cell was issued in 1900 – but for the first two decades of this century all were too clumsy to have any real commercial application.

For some time Europe held the edge in these experiments and had it not been for the First World War (when Britain, France and Germany had rather more pressing matters on their minds) the talking picture as a form of mass entertainment might possibly have been a European invention. What effect that would have had on Hollywood and the development of film as an art form is difficult to say. Probably not much, in fact; America was always quicker to spot the commercial possibilities of the movies, to decide what the bulk of the audience really wanted to see (not art as a rule) and to invest its money accordingly. In any event, by the 1920s the most significant work towards the introduction of sound pictures was taking place in the USA. At the start of the decade individuals such as Lee de Forest and companies like Western Electric, Bell Telephones and General Electric were vying with each other to demonstrate their sound techniques. By 1925 Fox had installed de Forest's Photofilm system in a few of its theatres but public response was apathetic and the equipment was swiftly removed, although two years later the system itself was integrated into Fox's own Movietone process.

In the end Warners were the most emphatic pioneers for no more lofty reason than financial desperation. Unlike its main competitors the studio had not invested widely in theatres of its own and as a result its films tended to be shown on the minor circuits with a consequent cash flow problem. Faced with an economic crisis, Warners acquired the Vitagraph Company and its small chain of thirty-four American and Canadian cinemas and, using Western Electric apparatus, gambled on the introduction of sound.

Hal Wallis who, for many years, was the studio's head of production, said that the "visionary" among the four brothers Warner was Sam, who unlike Harry, Albert and Jack, regarded sound as the signpost to the future. But initially even Sam's vision was limited to the use of music, for when the studio's Vitaphone System was launched in 1926 the first half of the programme consisted of a number of musical shorts featuring the Metropolitan Opera Company of New York and the second half was a full-length drama, *Don Juan* starring John Barrymore and Mary Astor, in which again the sound was restricted to music. Even so, *Don Juan* was a breakthrough – the first feature film with synchronised sound.

Not all the brothers, however, seemed to grasp the full implications of the revolution they had just launched. As Jack Warner records in his autobiography, Sam said: 'Don't forget, you can have actors talk, too.' To which Harry replied, testily: 'Who the hell wants to hear actors talk?'

Eventually, of course, everyone did and perhaps the most significant aspect of that evening of 6 August 1926, when *Don Juan* had its premiere, was the showing of a very short picture in which Will H. Hays, president of the Motion Picture Producers and Distributors of America, was heard to congratulate Warners, Western Electric and Bell Telephones for making it possible for him to speak directly from the screen to the audience. Not that, at the time, many people took much notice. The critics were impressed by the cinema's latest display of magic but on the whole the public was not. The response was warm rather than ecstatic and although *Don Juan* did well at the box office, encouraging Warners to make more films with synchronised sound, the studio showed a financial loss that year.

In this, though, it was not alone, for in 1926 the silent movie industry was suffering a slump because of the enormous impact that radio was beginning to make. On 15 November that year, for example, the broadcast of the Jack Dempsey–Gene Tunney fight attracted an audience of fifty million listeners. Such figures, along with the interest that Warners' Vitaphone shorts had aroused, caused the other major studios to turn their attentions to sound but with reservations. In February 1927, the five most important companies – MGM, Universal, First National, Paramount and Producers Distributing Corporation – jointly agreed to what amounted to a "wait and see" policy, in part because at the time there were several sound systems on the market and they were unsure how things would shake down. Apart from Warners, who had the exclusive rights to Vitaphone, only the Fox Film Corporation, under its President William Fox, was immediately interested in investing in sound.

Fox, an ambitious and very wealthy man, bought the rights to a rival sound system, renamed it Movietone and started to make newsreels, beginning with a four-minute recording of West Point cadets marching. But the newsreel came properly into its own some three weeks later, on 20 May 1927, when Charles Lindbergh set off on his solo flight to Paris and by the evening of the same day the Movietone coverage of his departure was shown in a cinema.

Even so, it was Warners who again made the next momentous move. As Hal Wallis said: 'They were in difficulties then and for some time after. It was always a race to raise money for the week's payroll. But they were a young company *vis-à-vis* Paramount and Metro and they were always looking for new things. They had to come up with unusual and important advances to be recognised.'

Well, the next important and unusual advance was *The Jazz Singer* and that was indeed a risk. In those days the cost of installing sound equipment in a theatre could be as much as 25,000 dollars and even by the end of 1927 only about 200 American cinemas were so equipped. Many of those had only made the change because Harry Warner, by now converted to brother Sam's view, had proved an effective evangelist.

But despite his efforts and the modest success of more than 100 Vitaphone shorts and a couple of features with musical effects, Warners were in the red and badly in need of a hit when they went into production with *The Jazz Singer*.

This had started out as a successful stage play, starring George Jessel, and when Warners bought the film rights for 30,000 dollars they had Jessel in mind to re-create his role as the cantor's son on screen. But Jessel over-reached himself. When he learned that songs were to be added in the film he asked – on the advice of his friend Eddie Cantor – for an extra recording fee. Warners said No – and promptly offered the role to Cantor, leading one to speculate on what kind of a friend he really was to Mr Jessel. No, perhaps that's unfair because in fact Cantor turned the part down, whether because he, too, had asked more than he was offered or because he felt that Jessel, who had been extremely popular in the stage version, was too hard an act to follow, is difficult to say. Quite possibly he felt, as did many others, that talking pictures would prove to be only a passing fad anyway.

In the end the visionary himself, Sam Warner, suggested they cast Al Jolson, who had appeared in the touring version of the play, and Jolson accepted, ironically demanding and receiving nearly twice as much as Jessel had wanted – 75,000 dollars. On the other hand, he was generally regarded as twice the star that Jessel was, so perhaps his greater remuneration was only reasonable.

The Jazz Singer took four months to shoot at a cost, sizeable for the time, of half a million dollars and apart from four talking segments, wherein Jolson also sang, it was free of dialogue. Nevertheless, when it opened at the Warner Theatre the public response was rapturous; the first night audience rose from its collective bottom to its collective feet to applaud the sound – and especially the talking – sequences. Unhappily, Sam Warner, he who had made it all possible, was not there to see himself and his vision vindicated. Twenty-four hours before the premiere he died in a California hospital of a cerebral haemorrhage brought on, in brother Jack's view, by the strain involved in bringing *The Jazz Singer* to the screen. His brothers also missed the first night for they had hurried by train from New York to be with Sam before he died but they certainly read of their film's success in the Press next day.

In particular perhaps as they leafed through their newspaper clippings they came across this piece by one Welford Beaton in *The Film Spectator*: 'The Jazz Singer* definitely establishes the fact that talking pictures are imminent. Everyone in Hollywood can rise up and declare that they are not and it will not alter the fact. If I were an actor with a squeaky voice I would worry.'

Well, actors – and actresses – with squeaky voices would indeed soon begin to worry and with very good cause. But why should everyone in Hollywood rise up and declare that talking pictures were not imminent? Simply because Hollywood (the Warners and Fox apart) did not want talking pictures to be imminent. The big film companies owned cinema chains and converting those to sound could, as we have seen, be a very expensive business; they also owned studios which, though perfectly geared to the manufacture of silent pictures, would be rendered obsolete by the introduction of talkies or "talkers" as they were known in those early days. Then, too, there was the question of the backlog of so far unreleased silent films which everyone had been turning out – what future would they have if the public was encouraged too quickly to expect sound? Lastly, and just as important as anything else, there was the potential loss of the lucrative foreign markets. A silent picture was universal; it had no nationality. But a sound picture, and certainly a talking picture, could only be shown with advantage in a country that spoke its language of origin.

The cinema problem alone was awe-inspiring. Between them seven of the companies, including Paramount, MGM and First National, owned about 1,550 theatres. Converting them, at a cost of 25,000 dollars each, would not leave a whole lot of change from 40 million. Nor would the rebuilding of the studio sound stages be much cheaper, for this entailed the tearing down of the glass and plywood structures which had hitherto sufficed and replacing them with bricks and mortar. (Indeed, in the eighteen months between June 1928 and the end of 1929 the industry spent 37 million dollars on this work.)

But when *The Jazz Singer* opened all this expenditure lay in the future and at that time the opponents of sound, those speaking from a position of vested interest in silent movies, found unusual and rather surprising support among the intellectuals. Even Eisenstein had his doubts about the innovation, doubts which were perhaps expressed most cogently by the British critic and film maker Paul Rotha who said that sound films 'are to be resented' because 'they are harmful and detrimental to public culture'. Pardon? Well, I think what he was driving at was this: 'The sole aim of the producers is financial gain', an extraordinarily naive claim it seems to me. When was financial gain *not* one of the paramount interests of film makers?

But from whatever direction opposition came the doubters were rapidly overtaken by events. Very soon it became clear that the public interest in *The Jazz Singer* meant that every Hollywood studio, however reluctant, would have to invest in sound if it was to survive. A silent version of the film, to be shown in unconverted cinemas, was no great success but by January 1928 Warners could take out a full page advert in *Variety* to boast that the talkie was 'playing to one million people a week'.

And that perhaps was the turning point. Until then the studio had still been hedging its bets. In November 1927 Warners announced a forthcoming programme of twenty-six silents and twelve talkies for they were still afraid that the novelty might wear off and were wondering how much dialogue an audience could take in one film. Such doubts, however, were resolved in July of 1928 with the opening of *The Lights of New York*, a coarse and extremely indifferent gangster movie, which is remembered now only for the historical fact that it was the first all-talking picture and the audience liked it for that reason. The *New York Times* described it as 'seven reels of speech'.

Once more Warner Brothers had led the way but now their rivals were not so far behind. Soon after *The Lights of New York* opened Paramount came up with its own first all-talkie, *Interference*, and the trend was established. By the following year cinemas throughout the United States were installing sound systems and around seventy-five per cent of all films made included at least some sound. The revolution begun on 6 October 1927 was already pretty well complete.

And yet the critics, especially those who feared that the coming of dialogue pictures would detract from the art of the cinema, were not entirely wrong. Even while *The Jazz Singer* was being made, across the Atlantic in France Abel Gance was putting the finishing touches to his epic silent film, *Napoleon*, a picture whose fluidity, power, grace and visual imagery have rarely, if ever, been surpassed since and weren't remotely approached by the early talkies. The fact is that the introduction of sound added one dimension to films but took away another – movement. Quite apart from being on the whole badly acted, with dialogue ponderously and portentously spoken, the early talkies were virtually static and for this the system was to blame.

While he was directing those early musical shorts in Brooklyn, Sam Warner discovered that the microphones were so sensitive to sound that he and his technicians had to take their shoes off when they moved around the stage. Even the faint whirr of the camera was picked up and reproduced on the sound track with the result that the camera was banished to a soundproof booth and there it remained, stationary, for some time. This led to dialogue scenes being shot mostly in a single close-up, sometimes in a two-shot; hardly ever were there three or more people on screen together. The (concealed) microphones were as stationary as the cameras and there simply was not enough room around them for more than a couple of actors at a time.

But apart from the camera noise there were other extraneous sounds to be eliminated somehow and various methods, not all of them ingenious, were devised to do so. At Paramount, as the writer-director Joseph L. Mankiewicz recalled, 'they had no sound stages, so they stripped the props department of miles of carpeting and

Above: The start of it all – Jolson. *The Jazz Singer* and 'You ain't heard nothin' yet'

Left: Garbo and Gilbert – the most notable survivor and the most notable casualty of the coming of sound

Right: 'If I were an actor with a squeaky voice I would worry.' Unless, presumably, the good Professor Feuchtinger was around

"From Now On—
VOICE
Will be the factor in picking
Movie Stars"

Jacqueline Logan

"Anyone who thinks at all can see how important a good voice will be in the movies from now on, and what a deciding factor it will be in picking stars for various parts.

I rejoice in the coming of the Talking Movies as an added outlet for the expression of artistic acting and I realize the importance of developing and training the voice to the utmost degree.

With vocal mastery comes poise, confidence and commanding personality. For these things all those who aspire to stardom should labor with all their hearts."

Jacqueline Logan

I Guarantee to Improve
Your Voice 100%

Mail coupon below at once—and learn how with my wonderful NEW Silent Method of Voice Culture, I actually **guarantee** to improve your voice at least 100% or refund you every penny. Think what this means—especially now with the great demand the Talking Movie has made for men and women with rich, compelling voices. Movie Directors **are** now seeking—NOT just pretty faces and nice figures—but FINE VOICES! Practically all the big stars are taking voice culture. See what Jacqueline Logan says in her letter shown above. Here is YOUR one big chance—the chance you've been longing for—to really get into the movies—write me at once and let me show you how you can develop a rich, compelling, commanding voice. But don't delay—mail coupon NOW!

Voice Book—FREE!

Mail coupon now and without any cost or obligation on your part I will immediately send you my wonderful voice book—"*Physical Voice Culture*" telling all about my *guaranteed* NEW Silent Method of Voice Culture. Take the first step now toward the voice you've longed for—the movie chance you've hoped for—*mail this coupon!*

Prof. E. Feuchtinger, PERFECT VOICE INSTITUTE,
Dept. 12-68 1922 Sunnyside Avenue, Chicago

used that to line the walls of the silent stages.' Not surprisingly that wasn't entirely effective and so in the early days most talking pictures were made at night. They would start shooting, Mankiewicz said, at 5 p.m. 'because that way we'd miss the noise of the traffic going by on Melrose Avenue.' And they would work through until 3 a.m. 'It was a very makeshift operation for quite a while with the microphones being hidden in the flowers and that sort of thing and the camera installed in a little square box.'

The cinematographer William Clothier, who was a camera assistant when sound came, had vividly unpleasant memories of that "little square box". To begin with, he said, it wasn't a box at all – 'It was a booth, which was ten feet tall and eight feet wide. We'd set two cameras on a table in there. Then we got around to the blimp, which was four foot wide and six foot long and was carried around. You shot through a lot of optical glass and it took four men to move the camera two inches. We were inside the blimp or the booth and it was hotter than the Devil in there. Oh yeah, you'd just sweat. It'd be hell, especially in the summertime with all the lights going and being enclosed in that booth. There were four people in there. We had two cameras with an operator and an assistant on each and the cameramen were outside the booth, watching the action.'

At first the film stages and the recording studios were rigidly separated. Some Warner Brothers' pictures, for instance, were shot at the Burbank studio while the sound was recorded several miles away on Sunset Boulevard in Hollywood, being conveyed there by a telephone link up. And, as at Paramount, filming was done by night when the streets were quiet. The result of all this, as Joe Mankiewicz said, was that the sound man 'was *the* boss. Whether the scene was beautifully played or not he was the one who had to approve the takes.' The boss? No, said Douglas Fairbanks Jr, who was eighteen when the talkies arrived, the sound man was more than that. 'He was a magician. Nobody understood what he was up to, so he could get away with all sorts of things. He was like Merlin, or the Wizard of Oz and a bit of a faker in some ways because he was experimenting himself at that time.' And he was powerful, too – a man to be respected, feared and placated. Esther Ralston, who was known in the 20s as "the American Venus" largely because she had been in a silent film of that name, remembered making *The Wheel of Life* with Richard Dix in 1929 and Dix pointing to the sound man and saying, 'See that guy up there? You better be nice to him or he'll make a baritone out of you and a soprano out of me.'

Sound changed everything, including the atmosphere on the set. In the silent days people would wander onto the stage, even while filming was in progress, and laugh and chat and generally disport themselves as though nothing was going on at all. And the actors would have live music on tap to help them portray the right emotions. The German-born character actor Fritz Feld had a quartet of violins, piano and cello playing La Marseillaise to make him cry. Buddy Rogers, a leading man of the 20s and 30s who later became more famous as the husband of Mary Pickford, preferred four violins to get him in the mood for a love scene. But with sound such aids were impossible. No music, no visitors, locked doors. Fairbanks said: 'At first it was just hell, physically I mean. They had to use a lot of light, lighting for four or five cameras at the same time. This was at a period when they had two different kinds of lights and it was very, very hot. You had to be careful to lock every door; you couldn't have any air coming in because that made a hissing sound; fans would make noise; and there was no air conditioning, of course. And so you just wilted. After each scene they'd have to open all the doors and let everybody get a breath of air and cool off a bit. Then they'd lock everything up and do it again . . .' The director (according to Buddy Rogers) would say, 'Oh, please are you ready, sound man?' and then (according to the director Fred Zinnemann, who began in Hollywood as an extra on *All Quiet on the Western Front*) the arguments would break out. 'We had constant fights between the sound man and the cameraman because there were complaints that the microphone got in the way of the lights and we spent five minutes hearing these arguments before we could shoot. There was a lot of bad blood . . .'

Even on location filming the new technology changed everything. In the silent days William Clothier worked at a small studio on Poverty Row, an area just off Sunset Boulevard where films (mostly westerns) were made so cheaply that even to call them "low budget" would give them a financial dignity they did not deserve. In the mornings he would walk to the studio, pick up a car, put the camera equipment in the back seat, stop off in Hollywood to collect a couple of cowboy actors, stop again to buy eight box lunches (at 25 cents each) from a purveyor of such things named Pauline and drive to the location some ten miles or so out of town. 'We had eight, ten people in the whole company, including the actors. Plus we'd have a couple of horses, of course, but we'd pick them up from a local farmer. Then when sound came in, Good Lord, we'd leave the studio with fifteen trucks and limousines and buses and we'd have more drivers than we used to have people in the picture . . . And the budgets went up. I remember shooting western films, I think we used to shoot a picture in six days for about 3,000, 4,000 dollars including the actors' pay. When sound came in budgets zoomed to 200,000 dollars for a picture, 500,000 dollars . . .'

Sometimes, in desperation, they would put up barrage balloons to keep the aeroplanes away because outdoors, as much as indoors, the sound man was boss, magician, dictator and he remained that way until the advent of the boom microphone, for the invention of which practically every early Hollywood director is modestly prepared to take full credit.

But until the boom came along, static cameras and static microphones made inevitably for extremely static films and it was not until 1929 that easy movement returned to the cinema. The man principally responsible for releasing the camera from bondage was Rouben Mamoulian, an Armenian-born stage director who had made a great reputation on Broadway in the 1920s and was hired by Paramount to direct *Applause*, a tear-jerking melodrama about a vaudeville star, Helen Morgan, who loses the love of her daughter. Mamoulian, who had never made a film before, took talking pictures a considerable step forward with this, his first production.

And not a moment too soon. Though cinema audiences had increased markedly since the introduction of sound, the populace was already beginning to grow restless because of the slowness, lack of action and stage-bound nature of most of the films.

Many of the stories were indeed bought straight from the theatre and became known as "teacup dramas" on account of the fact that nobody in them ever seemed to do much except talk and drink tea. As Mamoulian said: 'The studios wanted dialogue. So they would buy a play and keep it as it was and film it with three cameras, each in a bungalow. And the director and the cameraman and the focus puller would have to get in there, in those little bungalows, with the camera. They'd have two close-ups and one medium shot and the result was a photographed stage play.'

Mamoulian was not impressed with any of this but wisely, in view of his total lack of experience in film making, decided to spend some time around the Astoria Studios in New York studying the methods of other directors before embarking upon a picture of his own.

He observed, he asked questions, he learned what to do and, just as importantly, what not to do and when finally he felt ready to start work the first thing he suggested was moving those bungalows in which the cameras dwelt. That was his first problem . . . 'They said, "No, they're tough to move, very difficult," and the camera-man said, "You can't do it."' Walking around this obstacle for the moment, Mamoulian then put forward the notion of recording the sound on two tracks instead of one. The response was the same . . . 'The sound man said, "It's impossible; it's never been done; we can't do it." In other words they turned down everything I wanted to do. And that went on for three days. Finally I went upstairs to the Great Moguls and I said, "Now look, am I a director or am I an office boy? Nobody listens to me; they won't do anything I want."'

The Great Moguls called in the cameraman and the sound man who both said, as they had before, that what the director wanted could not be done, adding triumphantly what is normally the clincher in any argument over film production: 'All we're trying to do is save the studio money.' But for once the Great Moguls were unmoved and said: 'Well, look, Mr Mamoulian is the director – you do what he asks.'

With the lines of demarcation thus officially drawn, the first question posed by the cameraman, George Folsey, was where he should put the cameras. Mamoulian replied, to everyone's astonishment, that there would be only one camera. They were shooting a bedroom scene at the time and what he wanted was the whole thing done on one shot, starting in long-shot and moving into close-up – or, to put it another way, what he wanted, as Folsey pointed out, was the impossible: the camera in its bungalow was simply too heavy to move.

And it was then that Mamoulian came up with a brilliant idea which, like most brilliant ideas, was stunningly simple. He said, 'Look, will you get some people and ask them to put little rollers on this bungalow. And then get six strong men and have them move it in and out and here and there.' And so it was done and so movement returned to the camera.

(Mamoulian may well have been the first director to have this idea but around the same time others were working independently towards the same end. William Wyler, for instance, claims to have devised moving shots by putting the padded camera box on rails while he was making a western called *Hell's Heroes*. His film, however, was made a little later than Mamoulian's, although there is no suggestion that Wyler simply pinched the idea. Apart from anything else, he was filming in the west while Mamoulian was in the east, in New York, and communications between the two coasts were not as fast or as frequent as they are now.)

Still, on the day he liberated the camera Mamoulian said he went home exhausted and full of doubt about what he had done and fearful that tomorrow would be his last day at Paramount. But when he returned to the studio the doorman, who normally refused to recognise that he was of any importance at all and would invariably greet him with a belligerent, 'Hey, where do you think you're going?', sprang forward to open his taxi door with a respectful, 'Good morning to you, Mr Mamoulian, sir.' The director had barely recovered from this traumatic experience and was still wondering what it might portend when his assistant explained all. The Great Moguls, Adolph Zukor and Jesse Lasky Sr, had seen the rushes of the bedroom scene and were entranced. 'Whatever Mamoulian wants,' they had said, 'give it to him.'

With the camera again able to wander about – even if it did have to be shoved along by six men built like Arnold Schwarzenegger – Mamoulian felt strong enough to tackle what he considered the next great problem of talking pictures: the limitations imposed by having a single sound track. 'I said, "If you can do that with the camera, why shouldn't we be able to use the sound in a similarly imaginative way?" So, in one scene for instance Helen Morgan sings a lullaby, or rather she sings one of her burlesque songs as if it were a lullaby, to put her daughter to sleep. The daughter takes a rosary from under her pillow and says a prayer. Well now obviously neither in life nor on the stage could you hear both because a whisper and a loud song don't go together. And that's when I said, "Look, let's record the prayer on one channel and the song on another channel and we'll control both and that way we'll have two sound channels." And, of course, it worked out – luckily – and after that everybody was using multi-channel sound.'

When Zukor and Lasky saw the finished film they were overwhelmed with admiration both for it and for Mamoulian's innovations. 'They made speeches about how wonderful *Applause* was and said I should rest for two weeks and then come back and they would give me the most marvellous contract.'

In those two weeks, however, *Applause* opened to enthusiastic reviews but hardly any box office. There were no stars in it and in those days stars were what the public wanted above all. It was, therefore, not two weeks but twelve months later before Zukor and Lasky contacted him again, thus indicating that the general feeling in Hollywood then as now was that while art may be all very well for them as likes that sort of thing the only true measure of a film's merit is the number of decibels it generates at the cash register.

On the other hand, Mamoulian was at least called back eventually – to direct *City Streets*, a gangland melodrama starring Sylvia Sidney and Gary Cooper. Interestingly, although a year had gone by since *Applause* had shown what could be done with the available film and sound equipment by an imaginative director, Mamoulian's (or Wyler's) techniques had not yet been widely copied. Miss Sidney, who was then twenty and making only her second film, accepted them as the norm

Left: A silent movie stage with piano and violin to set the mood. And, by contrast (below left), an early sound stage. No music but boxes to house the cameras – 'It was hotter than the Devil in there'
Right: Pola Negri listening to a playback of her voice test. She may have liked it but nobody else did much
Below right: Dietrich with Rouben Mamoulian, the man who released the camera from bondage
Below: Helen Morgan in *Applause*, the film in which Mamoulian introduced the double sound track

because 'I didn't know any better that it was extremely unusual for him to have a camera on a trolley.'

City Streets was not a particularly good picture but it was important because of another of the director's innovations, the use of subjective sound. 'For the first time I used audible thoughts over a silent close-up. Now again everybody said, "This is crazy. Cooper isn't here in the scene, she's alone in her bed and you can hear Cooper talking in her thoughts."' Once more the sceptics were proved wrong; the scene of Miss Sidney alone in bed and remembering what Cooper had said to her was one of the most effective in the film, introducing a technique which, as Mamoulian said, has since become pretty well overdone.

(Actually, Mamoulian's claim to have been the first to use subjective sound is open to challenge. Two years earlier John Ford had done much the same thing in a short called *Napoleon's Banner* when he had used the sound track to express Napoleon's thoughts as he moved around, thereby becoming one of the earliest directors to take the talking picture out of doors.)

However, for his next idea which he introduced in his third film, *Dr Jekyll and Mr Hyde*, Mamoulian probably can take the innovator's credit – the use of the subjective camera. The star of what is still the best screen version of that story was Fredric March but occasionally the camera stood in for him.

Mamoulian said: 'I don't believe in experimentation for its own sake. But if you want something, dramatically, that the means you have cannot achieve then you invent something new. In this case I thought how strongly it would involve the audience if they, and not just the man there on the screen, were in the process of transformation themselves. For that I said I would have to establish the camera now and then as being Dr Jekyll or Mr Hyde and I had to do it right away because you have to put your terms, the rules of the game, to the audience immediately. Once you establish that, you see, they're with you. That's why I started with the camera being Dr Jekyll in the whole first reel.'

For all his ingenuity, however, for all his achievements in extending the frontiers of talking pictures it was not Mamoulian who made the first classic film of the sound era. That honour fell to Lewis Milestone, the director of *All Quiet on the Western Front*. The subject of course, life and death in the trenches during the First World War, was a natural for the cinema but what made it outstanding was Milestone's highly individual use of sound and picture. He was not as inventive as Mamoulian but like Mamoulian he refused to be dominated or restricted in his camera movements by the tyranny of the microphone which he used, unusually at that time, to record natural sound and snatches of overheard conversation. The result was not simply a very powerful film, for which Milestone won the Academy Award for best director, but one with much greater fluidity than was common in 1930.

1930 was also notable for Greta Garbo's first sound film, *Anna Christie*, which was widely advertised with the thrilling slogan (thrilling, that is, to those who found the topic of vital interest) – "Garbo Talks!" The picture itself was no great landmark in the history of the cinema but its novelty – Garbo finally giving utterance – does reflect the ambivalent feelings that Hollywood still had, three years after *The Jazz Singer*, towards talking pictures.

Since the advent of sound Garbo had made seven films, all of them silent, in the last of which, *The Kiss*, the cast also featured Lew Ayres who, a little later, was to star in *All Quiet on the Western Front*. *The Kiss* was made in 1929 by which time, as Lew Ayres said, 'Sound was on its way. There was no doubt about that. Garbo had held back because sound had been very detrimental to many of the stars of the silent era. They may not have spoken well or their voices were not what the public expected. And Garbo was very fearful, I think – and so was the company. She was *the* big star at that time and MGM was very concerned. She held off because she had a deep accent, as we all know, and rather a deep, throaty quality to her voice and I guess the studio was apprehensive.'

But if she were to continue as *the* big star Garbo, like everyone else, had to make the switch to sound films eventually. (The only person to hold out with any success against the talkies was Chaplin, who was not heard to speak on film until *Modern Times* in 1936 and then what he uttered was, deliberately, gibberish.)

Garbo, however, may have been wiser than she knew not to rush into talkies too quickly. By 1930 the quality of sound reproduction, which had been extremely rough in the early days, had improved considerably, so that when she delivered her first line: 'Gimme a vhisky with ginger ale on the side and don't be stingy, baby', the audience heard her loud and clear and were delighted. One critic described her voice as "rich, full, voluptuous, limpid, incredibly throaty, smoky and sonorous", somehow leading one to suspect that he rather liked it.

Encouraged by this response she promptly went on to make a German version of *Anna Christie*, which was the practice then. (She also made a Swedish version, which she preferred.) The two main methods by which Hollywood was trying to hold on to its international market were, firstly, to take out world patents on the most effective sound systems, thus making it difficult for other countries to compete and, secondly, by making foreign language versions of its films. And these were full versions – not simply dubbed or subtitled. Mostly the movies were reproduced only in French, German and Spanish but some were made in as many as fifteen different languages. It was a cumbersome and costly process and was fairly quickly abandoned.

But now that Garbo had, triumphantly, made the big leap into the new era there could no longer be any doubt that the talking picture had come to stay, even though Hollywood was still not entirely happy about it. Sylvia Sidney recalled that when she arrived there from the New York stage in 1929 everyone told her gloomily: 'The golden age of Hollywood is finished. Now we have a very unglamorous Hollywood because of all you people who've come from Broadway to do films.'

Financially, in fact, the golden age was yet to come but certainly an epoch had ended. One effect of sound was to put greater power than ever into the hands of the major studios and their head offices in New York. Another was to cause the eclipse of many actors and actresses who had been among the biggest stars in the world.

The German Emil Jannings who in 1927/8 had won the very first Academy Award for best actor for his performances in two silent films, *The Way of all Flesh* and *The Last Command*, was among the most notable casualties. Knowing his English to be less than perfect he went back to Germany to make his talking debut, in his native tongue, in *The Blue Angel* with Marlene Dietrich. (That didn't work out too well, as a matter of fact, because she totally overshadowed him in the picture.)

Another who failed satisfactorily to make the transition was Clara Bow, the famous "It Girl" of the 1920s. She was to have starred in *City Streets* but according to Sylvia Sidney: 'Mamoulian was brought to California to coach and train her because she was terrified of talking pictures. And they'd been rehearsing about two weeks, I think, when they realised she was going to have a nervous breakdown and they couldn't possibly start a film with her. They were going to shelve the whole movie until Mamoulian said, "Well, there's a girl just arrived from New York whom you could use . . ."' That girl, of course, was Miss Sidney. Clara Bow, who was only twenty-two when sound came in, did in fact go on to make a number of talkies but never to any great effect. Her stardom ended with the silent film.

Much the same fate befell Appolonia Chalupek, aka Pola Negri, who was still appearing in films into the 1960s but whose fame as a smouldering sexpot rests entirely on her work in silent pictures. Many of her contemporaries fared no better. Dolores Costello, for example, lost most of her credibility when, in her first talkie *Tenderloin*, she was heard to say: 'Merthy, merthy, have you no thithter of your own?' Mind you, she did continue to appear in films but the old magic seemed to have gone somehow. Norma Talmadge, still only thirty-four with the coming of sound but already a veteran since childhood of twenty years in silents, made the transition quite well in her first talkie, *New York City Nights* in 1929, in which her Brooklyn accent was quite acceptable. But when she brought the same accent to her role of Madame Du Barry in *Woman of Passion* the following year the audiences were not so tolerant. Her sister Constance, who was equally famous, sent her a cable: 'Leave them while you're looking good and thank God for the trust funds Momma set up.' Norma took the advice and so, incidentally, did Constance herself.

The most famous victim of all, though, was John Gilbert, who fell quite horrendously by the wayside. He had been among the very biggest of silent stars, the male equivalent of Garbo with whom he had co-starred in a number of films, but sound virtually saw the end of him. The usual reason given for his fall was that, as was the case with many of his contemporaries, his voice was inadequate. But, at worst, that was only part of the story, the main problem being that he was trouble to have around. He was an alcoholic who had fallen foul of the studio boss, Louis B. Mayer, whom he had frequently insulted and with whom, so it is said, he even came to blows. The occasion, according to legend, was Gilbert's wedding to which Garbo had been invited but which she failed to attend. When Gilbert complained about her absence Mayer suggested he should be satisfied with having slept with her, whereupon the bridegroom walloped him.

There is one school of thought that says Mayer hated Gilbert so much that he deliberately had the sound distorted on *His Glorious Night*, the 1929 film that was supposed to mark the great star's breakthrough into talkies. Whether this was true or not, Gilbert's voice did come as a laughable surprise to the audience, being lighter than they had expected. But maybe what really caused them to snigger were the words he was called upon to utter. 'I love you, I love you, I love you,' he declared passionately, while kissing his leading lady from fingertip to shoulder (a moment parodied later by Gene Kelly in *Singin' in the Rain*). This kind of stuff may have been fine in silents but it was rightly thought to be over the top in a talking picture. *His Glorious Night* was a flop and so was *Redemption*, which Gilbert had made earlier but which had been held back because it was thought, correctly, to be so bad.

What adds fuel to the accusation against Mayer – put forward by, among others, Gilbert's daughter Beatrice – is that in his few subsequent sound films the actor was revealed to have a rather pleasant voice, not nearly as high-pitched as it sounds in *His Glorious Night*. Now it might seem far-fetched to suggest that Mayer, the head of MGM, would deliberately seek to destroy the career of his studio's leading leading man, especially as Gilbert was only thirty-two in 1929. There is indeed no concrete evidence that Mayer did anything of the kind but the rumour persists to this day, possibly because other factors were involved apart from personal animosity. Gilbert had just signed a new million-dollars-a-year, three year contract and MGM, having second thoughts, asked him to take a salary cut. Gilbert refused. In those circumstances it's not impossible that Mayer might have thought it a shrewd, long-term tactical move to shake the star's confidence a bit and make him more biddable. If so it didn't work. Gilbert completed his contract at the originally negotiated price. But after one or two more unimpressive talkies MGM seemed to lose interest in him entirely, with the result that a somewhat querulous advertisement appeared one day in the trade papers: 'Metro-Goldwyn-Mayer will neither release me from my contract nor offer me work. Signed John Gilbert.'

That had no discernible effect whatsoever and when the contract expired in 1932 MGM released him, although they did recall him soon afterwards to co-star with Greta Garbo, his erstwhile lover, in *Queen Christina*. But that piece of casting had more to do with Garbo than with the studio. Her love affair with Gilbert was over but she seems to have remained fond of him until the end, so fond in fact that before Gilbert was signed to appear in *Queen Christina* she had declined to appear opposite any one of Franchot Tone, Leslie Howard, Nils Asther, Bruce Cabot and Laurence Olivier. She wanted Gilbert and she got him but the attempt to rehabilitate his career was a failure. The audience loved her, hated him. Thereafter he made one more film, *The Captain Loves the Sea*, for Columbia and in 1936 at the age of thirty-eight he quite literally drank himself to death, although the official cause of his demise was tactfully attributed to a heart attack. (Hollywood, frugal as ever, did not waste Gilbert's tragi-dramatic story but used him as the model for the fading, alcoholic actor in *A Star is Born* in 1937.)

In all this the case for Mayer is argued by Samuel Marx, who was the head of MGM's script department at the time. He categorically disputed any suggestion of evil-doing on Mayer's part, although he did not blame Gilbert's daughter for 'wanting to alibi the things that happened to him'. He said 'I knew John Gilbert. I heard him talk. He had a voice like David Niven, which was wonderful for David Niven but wrong for John Gilbert. Mr Mayer was the greatest, most practical motion picture man to run a studio whom I have ever known. He was a marvellous administrator. The last thing he would have done, no matter what his personal feelings, was try to ruin a star, because that star meant millions of dollars.'

Against that, however, there is the testimony of Douglas Fairbanks Jr who also knew John Gilbert and said his voice was "quite adequate". As Fairbanks saw it, 'he was a very fine actor, good personality, but he was having a row with Louis B. Mayer and, according to old stories I've heard and read, it became part of MGM's policy to ruin his career because he wouldn't sign the contract they wanted him to sign. So they spread the word that audiences were laughing at his voice. I don't believe they were, actually. I think people went in expecting to laugh and did so. Because in addition to that I'm told they even manipulated the sound and gave him a different register from that of his own voice... A lot of tricks were done to him. That's the story I've heard and I'm inclined to believe it's true because so many people were in the studio at that time and they said that's what happened.'

Yet if Gilbert's was the most spectacular tumble from grace there were others which must, to the victims, have been just as painful. The exquisite Louise Brooks went quickly from stardom to serving behind a counter at Macy's department store, her voice too having been found unsuitable. In fact, she was dubbed by Margaret Livingstone in the first known instance of a star's voice being replaced by that of someone else. Mae Murray who, at one time, had been not only a star but the wife of some obscure European prince, was arrested for vagrancy after being discovered sleeping on a bench in New York's Central Park.

But many of the old stars survived to go on to glory in the talkies. Some did so by assiduous use of the multitude of voice, singing and dialogue coaches who came streaming into Hollywood with the arrival of sound. Others, like Ronald Colman, went on to even greater fame because whatever it was that talking pictures needed they had in abundance. Nevertheless, for all of them the transition period was nerve-wracking. Buddy Rogers, for instance, had gone straight from university to the Paramount talent school and had never really been called upon to act in his life. Certainly, he said, 'We never thought we'd be called upon to act with our voices... We always knew the dialogue would be changed because they had special writers for that. I'd play a love scene with a girl and I'd say, "Oh gee, you're not looking so good. Where did you go last night?" and the caption writer would change that to, "Darling, you look beautiful..." We had no voice whatsoever.'

But then came sound and, as Rogers was preparing to make *Wings* with his friends Gary Cooper and Richard Arlen, the word came through that John Gilbert's voice had been tried and found wanting. 'Gilbert the great lover, who had played opposite Garbo and Shearer and all of them...' Panic. 'We said, "Hey, what's going on here?" We were told that only one voice in a thousand would register for the movies and Cooper said, "Heck, I don't know whether I have a voice or not." We were truly worried...' One morning they arrived at Paramount to discover that a new sound stage had been built and all the contract stars were going in, one by one, to find out whether they had a voice or not. 'One day they took Wallace Beery in there and we waited and watched outside, Gary Cooper and I, for four or five hours and all of a sudden the door opened and a little boy ran out and said, "He has a voice! Wally Beery can talk! Isn't that great?" It was that serious that Cooper and Dick Arlen and Jack Oakie and I made a pledge that if one of us didn't have a voice we'd each give ten per cent of our salaries to him as long as we lived.'

But that was not the end of their problems. All right, they might each have a voice, but could they act? The old flamboyant and meaningless gestures which had served so well in silent pictures looked absurd when accompanied by dialogue. Dialogue itself was something new: they'd never had to learn any of that before. 'All we had to do was just say something and this caption writer would make up charming, amusing things after he saw the film. We didn't have to be funny or dramatic – it was all up to the man who wrote the captions.'

Some silent stars, like Garbo and Mary Pickford, stepmother of Douglas Fairbanks Jr, held back from the new-fangled talkies. 'With Mary,' said Fairbanks, 'I think it was a desire to preserve an image which she was able to project more pointedly in the silent days. The minute she talked she'd come down to earth, so to speak, make herself more realistic. Before, she was a little unreal, something beyond the tangible . . . She was such a big star that she didn't have to do anything at all except what she wanted to do.' Pickford's career never really prospered in the sound era – she was, after all, thirty-four when it came in, knocking on a bit to be "America's Sweetheart" – but it's worth remembering that she did win the Academy Award for her first talking picture, *Coquette*, in 1929.

Douglas Fairbanks Sr, on the other hand, had virtually no truck whatsoever with this new-fangled gimmick. He did make a few sound movies but with no great enthusiasm. 'He was a unique rebel,' his son said. 'He was all for everybody else making sound films; he loved watching the development of them and he would remark with enthusiasm on the new ideas that were coming in. But rather like his partner and great friend, Chaplin, he didn't want to participate himself. Although he had been a classic actor originally, had begun in the theatre and had been a star on Broadway for many years . . . he did not think his own style, which was largely mime, was suitable for talking pictures. *The Thief of Baghdad* is almost a ballet . . . Chaplin also thought his medium was the silent film and that it was an art form of its own, something quite separate . . . It was the difference between oil painting and water colours . . . So [my father] made three or four films and then stopped because he just didn't like doing it any more.'

Well, it was a new age and the new stars had learned their trade far more than the people they succeeded not in silent pictures but in the theatre. The old idols were soon replaced by the likes of Spencer Tracy, Edward G. Robinson and Humphrey Bogart and, at MGM, the vacancy left by John Gilbert was filled by Clark Gable. Between these newcomers and old Hollywood there often existed something very close to animosity. Among the existing stars who had never been on the stage, whose only experience had been miming in silent films there was, said Douglas Fairbanks Jr, 'Concern, anxiety, a great deal of resentment and jealousy of those who came on from the theatre and were challenging them, threatening their jobs . . . Sides were taken and some bitter words exchanged . . . I can remember that quite vividly.'

For their own part the new people from the east coast 'tended to be rather arrogant, looking down their noses at these mere film people'. And the mere film people, said Sam Marx, hated all the interlopers, not just the actors but the writers as well. 'They were called "eastern scribblers" by the local columnists. They were invaders, they were absolutely undesirable. And to a great extent they didn't like the silent people either who, they thought, were ignoramuses.'

And the combination of the invaders and the ignoramuses, existing at first in an atmosphere of mutual suspicion, changed the very image of the movie star. In the silent days, said Esther Ralston, the stars were regarded as 'Something not quite of this earth . . . We were gods, goddesses, we were something inspirational, something that doesn't exist now.' Putting it a little differently, Douglas Fairbanks Jr said they were looked upon, these old stars, as creatures of fantasy. 'They weren't really quite human, semi-godlike, a form of American aristocracy, you might say, or another species of human that came down from outer space. But they were quickly to be discarded when another favourite came along . . .' Yet while they were the favourites – for three years, maybe four; the public life of a top star was not reckoned to be much more than that – 'They were far better-known than the stars of today. By comparison there aren't any stars today in the same sense. The phrase "superstar" is frankly to my mind abused compared with what they were in those days. Superstars then, like Mary Pickford and my father, or Charlie Chaplin and others were superstars who could not be duplicated today . . .'

So when the movies learned to speak and a language barrier was erected, the stars not only lost the international audiences that made the likes of Chaplin household (or possibly huthold) names in the depths of Africa or China, they also fell from their celestial perches. They spoke and they had accents, therefore they were human. You knew they didn't come from heaven – they came from Kansas or Texas or New Jersey. As Esther Ralston had it: 'They were more earthy or, shall we say, more real.'

Now, too, the rules of the game had changed. Whereas in the heyday of the silent movies the very biggest stars had exercised enormous power, henceforth it was the studios who would have and would use the muscle. For a brief period in the early twenties the 'lunatics', it was said, 'had taken over the asylum'. The most formidable example of this was the formation by Chaplin, Pickford, Fairbanks and D. W. Griffith of United Artists in 1919. They were later joined by Norma Talmadge, John Barrymore, Gloria Swanson and Buster Keaton. But of all that lustrous array only Chaplin was to survive as a truly important star after the introduction of sound. From that point on the sheer economics of the industry led inevitably to the studio system and, by extension, to the dubbing of Beverly Hills as "the most luxurious slave quarters in the world".

At such a time of turmoil when, more than ever before, neither new nor old Hollywood could be sure how long the fame, the money and the stardom would last, there was an understandable degree of uncertainty among the actors. Ralph Bellamy remembered meeting the newly arrived Clark Gable in a restaurant while they were making *The Secret Six* at MGM. Gable said: 'What do you think of this place?'

Above: Garbo talks!
'Gimme a vhisky . . . and
don't be stingy, baby'
Right: Lew Ayres in the
first classic film of the
sound era, *All Quiet on
the Western Front*

Bellamy replied frankly that he didn't know yet, for he too was new in Hollywood, having just come in by rail on the Santa Fe Chief. Gable said: 'I just got 11,000 dollars for playing a heavy in a western – 11,000 dollars. No actor is worth that. I got myself a room in a house at the top of Vine Street, I got a second-hand Ford and I'm not buying anything you can't put on the Chief because this isn't going to last.' Bellamy said that was the first time he had heard the expression but I doubt if Gable had coined it. 'Never buy anything you can't put on the Chief,' was a catchphrase among the immigrants from the east coast. And, after all, their caution was justified.

For evidence of that you have only to look at the subsequent careers of the pioneers of talking pictures. In an ideal world, no doubt, they would all have gone on to even more spectacular triumphs but in fact they did not. Al Jolson, who was forty-one when *The Jazz Singer* appeared, made only thirteen more films (the most notable of them his second, *The Singing Fool* in 1928) before he died in 1950 and his screen fame rests on those first two pictures plus his impersonation by Larry Parks in *The Jolson Story* in 1949, for which Jolson himself provided the singing voice. (George Jessel, who priced himself out of history, had a much fuller career than the man who replaced him, as did Eddie Cantor.) Alan Crosland, the director of both *The Jazz Singer* and its predecessor, *Don Juan*, died in 1936 aged forty-two without ever again making much of an impact in the cinema.

Rouben Mamoulian, the great early innovator, made only sixteen films before ending his career on a depressing note by being replaced as director of *Cleopatra* in 1962. But in 1935 he had been a pioneer once more when he directed the first Technicolor film, *Becky Sharp*. In any case he was never greatly enamoured of the movies and preferred to work in the theatre where he enjoyed a high and richly deserved reputation. In 1986 he was living in Beverly Hills in an elegant house whose equally elegant furniture and curtains had been pretty well destroyed by the multitude of Persian cats which he cheerfully allowed to live there with him on terms of complete equality.

Lewis Milestone went on to direct numerous films before his death in 1980 but his masterpiece remains *All Quiet on the Western Front*, which he made when he was thirty-five. Much the same may be said of Lew Ayres, who at the age of seventy-eight was living comfortably on the fringes of Beverly Hills and still made cameo appearances, mostly in TV series. His curriculum vitae includes well over sixty films, including the creation on screen of the character of Dr Kildare. But nothing he ever did afterwards quite matched the impact of his performance in *All Quiet* . . . Of that success he said: 'It's too bad it didn't come a little later in my life because I was so green that I wasn't truly able to handle the position it catapulted me into. I've had a roller-coaster career ever since.'

Of all the people involved in those first momentous and significant talking pictures of the period 1927–30 those who went on to the longest, most glorious and virtually uninterrupted careers were probably Mickey Mouse, who made his talking debut in *Steamboat Willie* in 1928, and Jack Warner who, with his brothers, was responsible for the talkie phenomenon in the first place. But then Jack Warner was neither a director nor an actor – he was the head of a studio.

THE STUDIO SYSTEM

It was Richard Rowland, the head of Metro (before a series of mergers had converted it into Metro-Goldwyn-Mayer) who, on hearing of the formation of United Artists in 1919, delivered the famous line: 'The lunatics have taken over the asylum.' The original lunatics were Chaplin, Pickford, Fairbanks and Griffith, soon to be joined by both the Talmadge sisters, Swanson, John Barrymore and Keaton, with Joe Schenck imported to run the business side of things.

In Hollywood at that time the idea of actors controlling their own destinies was considered preposterous and, in fact, United Artists did not begin to operate with true effectiveness until long after the original founders had departed. But ... the lunatics taking over the asylum? Well, yes and no. Actually, the lunatics – the stars – had been if not in control then at least immensely influential for the past decade.

In the early years of the century cinema actors and actresses had been anonymous, being known to audiences simply as "The Biograph Girl" or, in the case of Mary Pickford, "The Girl with the Curls". This was deliberate policy on the part of the Motion Picture Patents Company which ran the infant industry and which suspected, rightly as it turned out, that once the stars were named and became famous they would demand more money. But around 1908, Carl Laemmle, seeking publicity for his own company, denied a rumour – which he had started in the first place – that his "Imp Girl", Florence Lawrence, had been killed in a car crash. The result of this little stunt certainly made Florence Lawrence's pictures more popular but it also had the effect of causing rival companies to identify their casts, too, and by 1909 the California-based Bank of America was already advancing small loans to film makers on the strength of the star names they could offer. What's more, the Motion Picture Patents Company was swiftly proved right – the stars did want more money, *lots* more money.

Thus the stick that Laemmle had taken in hand merely to tickle up his competitors turned into a kind of demonic rod that beat not only them but himself as well. The star was born. (To Laemmle, too, as a matter of fact, goes much of the credit or, if you prefer, blame for introducing another custom that has often been the bane of Hollywood – nepotism. As the jingle put it, 'Uncle Carl Laemmle has a very large faemmle' and, at one time or another, he had pretty well all of them on his payroll.)

By the 1920s the stars were not only internationally famous but, in some cases, amazingly rich. Pickford and Chaplin – and later Swanson – were earning more than a million dollars a year and they, along with others, could virtually write their own contracts and exercise a considerable degree of power over the production of their films. Some of them (Gloria Swanson, for example, who was billed by her studio as "the second woman to make a million dollars – and the first to spend it") flaunted their wealth to the general delight of the public but not their bosses.

The advent of star-power meant that the moguls were virtually being held to ransom and there was not a lot they could do about it, although Paramount countered the demands of the actors with Cecil B. de Mille's "All Star Pictures", which actually meant no stars at all except the flamboyant director himself. But otherwise the best they could manage to do was to import large numbers of European stars who, having more modest aspirations, were prepared to work for less money than their American counterparts. This worked to some extent but even so by the end of the 1920s the million-dollars-a-year salary was by no means uncommon.

What put the moguls back in control was, first, the coming of sound and then the Depression. The arrival of talking pictures left most of the companies strapped for cash after the enormous cost of converting studios and cinemas and also induced panic among the silent stars, many of whom were unable to make the transition. Even those who could were faced by another threat from the influx of theatre-trained actors who, like European movie stars, were also prepared to accept a lower scale of pay.

Nor was that all for now everyone, established or not, had to pass the sound test which, in the hands of a canny mogul – and all the moguls were nothing if not canny – could be an awesome weapon. They could shatter a well-paid star's confidence by refusing to grant a test at all on the grounds that his/her voice was so obviously inadequate that there was little point. Or, if a test were made, it could easily be rigged to make the actor sound like Donald Duck (although Donald Duck wasn't actually about in those days).

With the lunatics thus driven back into a corner (from which they would not really escape until the 1950s) the studios enjoyed a brief period of prosperity – until the Depression came along. At first the public curiosity engendered by these new-fangled talkies had kept the box offices busy enough to cause Wall Street to talk of the cinema as a "Depression-proof industry" but this illusion was shattered in 1931.

In that year Warner Brothers, who had made profits of 17 million dollars in 1929 and 7 million dollars in 1930, lost nearly 8 million dollars; Fox went from a profit of 9 million dollars in 1930 to a loss of 3 million dollars; RKO's 1930 surplus of 3 million dollars became a 1931 deficit of 5.6 million; Paramount stayed fairly comfortably in the black but nevertheless its profits fell from 18 to 6 million (and in 1932 the company returned a loss of 21 million dollars). Only MGM, with a 1931 profit of 12 million dollars, emerged relatively unscathed. Not that any of this can have come as a great surprise for the signs had been there for anyone to see. In 1929 average weekly cinema attendances in the USA had been 110 million; in 1930 the figure fell to 80 million and in 1932 it dropped to 50 million.

In the first few years of the decade the financial slump continued with catastrophic effects. Paramount went into bankruptcy and Universal and RKO into receivership. Warners, losing a further total of 20 million dollars in 1932 and 1933, were struggling to survive, as were Columbia and United Artists. Fox underwent massive internal reorganisation. Yet for some, especially the actors, it took a while for the Depression to bite. Buddy Rogers said: 'The only time I was successful or making money was in those years, the Depression years. I didn't know what was going on. Room mates from my college would come out and I'd see them selling oranges and apples on the street corners . . . They were brilliant students. There was a Depression on but it hadn't hit me yet . . . I was driving a nice car and, as I look back now, it makes me sad because people would scratch their initials on my car. Naturally some of them were hungry and maybe there wasn't milk in the house or meat but I couldn't understand it at that moment.'

Eventually, though, even the actors understood it. In March 1933 President Franklin D. Roosevelt announced an unwelcome bank holiday – the banks, he said, would cease dealing for a while. In Hollywood, as elsewhere, this caused panic. Rogers said: 'The Bank of America closed down in Beverly Hills. All of us had our money there. I remember all of us rushing down to the bank, Dietrich, Wallace Beery, all of us banging on the doors – "Let us in, let us in." They wouldn't let us in for twelve days. I had about 30 dollars in my pocket and I had no idea whether the bank would ever open again . . .'

In this emergency MGM could just about manage to pay its people in cash but other studios could not. Universal suspended all contracts. Fox simply told its staff that it couldn't pay up and that was that. At this stage the entire industry was on the point of total collapse. What to do, what to do? Well, the moguls got together and asked the American Academy of Motion Picture Arts and Sciences to mediate. The Academy had been formed in 1927, with the well-known altruist Louis B. Mayer among the founding fathers. Its function was to be 'an alliance of the creative elite of Hollywood, to provide a forum for the exchange of ideas, to create a bureau of standards for the industry and to act as mediator in disputes among various groups involved in film production'. (The Academy Award, or Oscar, was added as an afterthought.)

The establishment of the Academy was widely interpreted by Hollywood cynics as a crafty move to protect the bosses and forestall unionisation and the cynics, as alas is often the case, were not entirely wrong because the various writers', directors' and actors' unions were fobbed off for several years. In any event cynicism did not seem entirely out of place in March 1933, when the Academy, having mediated, came up with a recommendation that all studio employees, however lofty or lowly, should take a fifty per cent salary cut for eight weeks. Sam Marx said: 'All the studios promised – and I don't believe any of them sustained the promise – that they would give the money back when better times came along. As it is, MGM kept the cut over a period of about six weeks. Most of the studios went eight or ten weeks.'

It was an impassioned Mayer who, in a series of speeches each said to be worthy of an Oscar in any year, urged this financial sacrifice on his own astonished work-force. The electricians and the carpenters were not impressed. Possibly they knew already that he could weep whenever he wanted to and could – and did – give an alarming impersonation of a man in the throes of a terminal heart attack when it suited his purposes. Anyway, they turned him down, arguing that while a star might not miss half his income a lower paid artisan certainly would. With the actors, who had been summoned to a meeting in the studio's number one projection theatre, he had greater success. Marx said: 'Mayer came in with about a three days' stubble of beard and tear-stained eyes and a helpless look to him. He almost couldn't get the words out. He just stood in front of this group of writers, actors and some directors and looked around helplessly until someone said, "We know why we're here, Mr Mayer..." I'm reasonably sure it was Freddie Bartholomew, the child actor of his day, who said, "I'm the youngest person in the room and I'll take the cut, Mr Mayer..."' And so the MGM actors, like actors in every other studio, took the cut and were not happy about it feeling that, as was usual then and is indeed still usual today, the highly paid artists were being blamed for all the industry's problems.

Sam Marx believed this episode was ultimately disastrous for the studios because it precipitated the formation of the various craft guilds, people banding together to ensure that nothing similar could happen again. But it certainly gave everyone a fright. Driving home the advantage they had gained the studios tried to manipulate Roosevelt's National Industrial Recovery Act, which became law in June that year, to their own ends. In drafting their "Code of Fair Competition for the Motion Picture Industry" the companies suggested, reasonably in their view, that star raiding among studios should be barred, the activities of agents should be curbed and the salaries of creative artists should be limited. It was a nice try but it didn't work. The Screen Writers' Guild (formed in April 1933) and the Screen Actors' Guild (formed in June) bombarded Washington with telegrams and threatened to strike. The result was that when the Code of Fair Competition was signed into law on 27 November, the more outrageous provisions were excluded. But even so it endorsed and even strengthened the major companies' monopoly of manufacture, distribution and exhibition and, in effect, left the studios more powerful than before.

As for the companies which had been most financially stricken in the early part of the decade, the intervention of the banks and in some cases a series of mergers enabled them to rise phoenix-like – albeit somewhat singed and still gently smouldering – from the ashes and very soon Hollywood revolved around what were to be known as the eight majors: MGM, Warners, 20th Century-Fox, Paramount, Columbia, Universal, United Artists and RKO. By now the studio system and with it the star system were firmly established, although it was the studios who manipulated the stars. They did this by means of the seven-year contract with its fiendishly clever option and suspension clauses. The option clause, exercisable only by the studios, meant that every six or twelve months, depending upon what had been agreed, the bosses could decide whether or not they wanted the contract to continue. Thus an actor's seven-year contract would in fact only run seven years if all the options were taken up. This in itself was bad enough but there was worse to come because if it so desired a studio could, by invoking and applying the suspension clause, make a contract run indefinitely. What this meant was that if a star proved recalcitrant – behaving perhaps in public in a way that was objectionable to the studio or turning down a part that was offered without just cause (the studios democratically taking it upon themselves to decide what was or was not just cause) – he/she could be suspended without pay until the guilt was deemed to have been expurgated. And then – and herein lay the true glory of the suspension clause – the time during which the star had been suspended was added on to the end of the contract. Thus an actor who had been suspended for a total of eighteen months during his seven-year deal could (again only if the studio wished it) be forced to serve eight and a half years before being released.

Now this might not have been intolerable if the stars had been given any kind of control over the parts they played or the films they appeared in but, except in a few rare cases, they were not. They were told what to do and they were obliged to do it. With hindsight it's surprising that they agreed to such terms in the first place but when the seven-year contract was introduced the actors were not yet organised and, besides, the insecurity of the Depression years allied to the fierce competition offered by the invasion of young hopefuls from the theatre left them with very little muscle to exercise.

Ah yes, but what if you were suspended? You could always take other work couldn't you – appear on radio or the stage, do vaudeville or cabaret? Well, no you couldn't because your contract forbade you to do anything at all without the studio's permission. As Joan Fontaine said, a suspended actor wasn't even allowed to take a job behind the counter in a department store. So then the trick was to avoid suspension but something apparently as simple as that was not always possible even for the most biddable star. To quote Joan Fontaine again: 'If the studio didn't have a script ready for you they would send you one that they knew you would turn down. Well, they could send you the dictionary or the telephone book and you would have to turn it down and you would be suspended. That meant they didn't have to pay you at all until they submitted something else to you. Meanwhile, the children had to go to school and the bills had to be paid and it was terrible tyranny because the actor had to capitulate . . .' In that way her seven-year contract with David Selznick eventually lasted a full decade.

Surely, though, there was some escape clause. Suppose that you, a star, were so utterly determined to get out of what you felt to be an unfair contract that you deliberately offended your studio mogul (easily the most effective way to have yourself fired) and he therefore refused to exercise his option the next time it came up. You might, as a result, be unemployed but this could only be temporary. You were still, after all a star and Hollywood at its peak was turning out close to 800 films a year – of one kind or another – so another studio was bound to snap you up, wasn't it? Well, no, it wasn't. Before you could even grab the phone to call the next mogul of your choice the word would have gone around that you were trouble. As Joan Fontaine said of Louis Mayer: 'He could hire and fire and insult and, oh, he could do anything he chose. He could even ostracise you if you didn't do what he said. He could call up other studio heads and say, "Don't hire so and so because they're on my blacklist." You could really be out if he didn't like you.'

Esther Ralston, the American Venus, discovered this to her cost. At MGM in the early 30s she was Mayer's "white-haired girl" and she looked upon him as "a nice old grandfather''. But one night in the Brown Derby restaurant dear old granddad made a pass at her. She fobbed him off smartly but the next morning she was called into his office. She went in thinking all was forgiven and forgotten and trilling a cheery, 'Good morning, Mr Mayer.' Whereupon the wolf in granddad's clothing revealed his teeth. 'Siddown,' he said (or possibly snarled). 'You sing your songs, you smart ass. You think you'll get away with it, you think you're pretty smart, don't you? Well, I'll blackball you. You'll never get another picture in any studio in town...' And so on. Miss Ralston returned to her dressing-room to have a weep, knowing that her days at MGM were over. And so they were. She wasn't fired or blackballed – but she was loaned out to Universal for thirteen straight pictures and... 'That was the end of my career as a star.'

Sometimes, if you were big enough, you could rebel and get away with it. In 1932, for instance, Garbo walked out on MGM and went home to Sweden because she had been offered only 7,000 dollars a week against the 10,000 she wanted. Garbo won. In the same year James Cagney left Warner Brothers arguing that he was worth more than the 1,000 dollars a week they were paying him. The Academy was called in to mediate and finally Warners took him back at a salary of 1,750 dollars a week. But on the whole, once a studio had you under contract you were hooked, gaffed and landed. In the late 1930s Cagney rebelled again, claiming this time that he was overworked because Warners had made him appear in five films in a year instead of the agreed four. Invoking one of the clauses in his contract that appeared to work to his advantage, he swept out claiming the studio was in breach of their agreement having billed Pat O'Brien above him in *Devil Dogs of the Air*. (To rub a little salt into the wound Cagney added, as a by the way, that the story 'had no reason for being filmed under any circumstances'.) Warners took him to court and in the meantime Cagney made two films for an independent company, Grand National. As it turned out his gesture was doubly unsuccessful. Warners won the legal action and the independent pictures fared badly at the box office, not least because the brothers Warner were able to stop them getting mass distribution. Uncowed but knowing when he was licked, Cagney returned to the fold.

Studio control, however, extended even further than the fundamental decision as to whether a star could work and when and for whom. It practically covered his entire life. A star was expected to live up to the image the studio had created for him – to buy a bigger house, build a swimming pool, employ a butler and maids. He might argue that he couldn't afford all this; never mind, said the studio, we'll lend you the money. And it did, thus plunging him into its debt and ensuring that he was unlikely to emulate the Garbos and Cagneys by walking out on them, because now he couldn't afford to.

Nor was that all. The moguls instructed their contract players on how to dress and behave in public and on whom they could or could not be seen with or even marry. Mayer once ordered Ann Rutherford not to see John Garfield any more because he was too old for her. Goodbye, Mr Garfield. Evelyn Keyes, under contract to Cecil B. de Mille, had a date or two with Anthony Quinn. De Mille summoned her and said: 'Don't you dare go out with that half breed again.' (Not that it matters but

Mr Quinn was not actually a half breed; he was Irish-Mexican. And anyway he had the last laugh by marrying de Mille's daughter.) But ... goodbye, Mr Quinn. Mayer told June Allyson not to marry Dick Powell, whom he considered a has-been, and when she ignored him refused to speak to her for months, only relenting when Powell's next film re-established him as a star.

Even as late as the 1950s the studios were still organising the private lives of their players. Mamie van Doren, who was under contract to Universal, where they were trying to present her as a rival to Marilyn Monroe, was instructed to go out with Rock Hudson. 'I didn't want to,' she said, 'but it was really required. It was part of the business of becoming a name. You used other actors to get your name in a magazine, to get your picture taken.' In this case, actually, Universal had an ulterior motive. Hudson was the young romantic lead of the moment but a rumour – well-founded, as we now know – was going about that he was homosexual and so a "romance" was invented between him and Miss van Doren. 'I think they used me to make people say, "Well, if he's going out with *her* he certainly isn't gay."'

What was also "really required" was that once a film was released its stars should go on personal appearance tours throughout the country to publicise it. Whether they wanted to do any such thing was beside the point: they had to. Mamie van Doren recalled that 'I used to go out into middle America after I finished a movie, way out into the boondocks. It was unbelievable – it was exhausting – but that's how you became known in those days... You had to go out and sign autographs and it got very wearying, very.' Sometimes it was more than just wearying, it could become frightening. The young Sylvia Sidney, under contract to B. P. Schulberg at Paramount in the early 30s, said: 'I told Mr Schulberg that there should be a school for young people like myself. We should have some training as to the kind of exposure we would get. I was totally unprepared for it and handled it very badly. Today I can laugh at it but at the time it seemed to be almost a mutilation of my personal being. People I didn't know ... flying down the street after me and mobbing me and stuff like that. It just absolutely unhinged me.' Her reaction to being so unhinged was to behave badly towards the fans. 'I ran, I screamed "Don't touch me!" and then they'd yell at me. I remember one time I did this in New York and they said, "We're never gonna see your movies again!"'

Well, it could be argued that making personal appearances and being mobbed by sometimes terrifying crowds goes with the territory if you're a star in whatever medium. But as Cornel Wilde, who was on contract to Warners, pointed out: 'The demands on the successful actor of the moment were endless. I had very little time off. Every time one of my movies came out I went on tours, went to New York, did radio interviews and all kinds of things. I literally had no time to myself. I was married then to Patricia Knight and we had a little daughter about a year old and I hardly ever saw them.'

Ah yes, you might say, but think of the money they were earning. Well, the money was not necessarily all that good. Or, at least, it was variable. The stars might be pulling down a fortune every week but the young contract players usually began on a pittance. Robert Wagner started at Fox in 1950 on 75 dollars a week (about 55

Above: Sylvia Sidney, who was told that people like her had destroyed the old, glamorous Hollywood
Left: Esther Ralston "the American Venus", who was Mayer's favourite until "nice old grandfather" made a pass
Above right: L.B. Mayer, "nice old grandfather", spurned pass-maker and friend of presidents, in this case Herbert Hoover
Right: James Cagney kissing and making up with (from the left) Frank Capra, Darryl Zanuck and Jack Warner after his little contractual difficulties

dollars take home pay); MGM signed Janet Leigh in 1947 for 50 dollars a week and for this she had to change her name from Jeannette Morrison; Jane Russell was signed by Howard Hughes to star in *The Outlaw* in 1943 for 50 dollars a week and for a couple of years afterwards did very little except publicity stunts, going about in low-cut blouses looking "mean, moody and magnificent". Women, in fact, always had the worst deal when it came to promoting films. Anne Baxter, who moved from one studio to another, was called upon to pose for cheesecake pictures wherever she went. 'They had a can of stuff they called "Sex". It was Vaseline and you rubbed it on your shoulders to make them gleam . . . and, oh my God, really you felt ridiculous. But what were you going to do? It was, "Wet your lips, honey, and suck in your tummy and look sultry and think a smile and . . ." Well, there you were. Oh dear. But you had to do it.'

No doubt people in other trades have to do even less agreeable things but nevertheless it must have been a touch dehumanising. And these, remember, were the experiences of people who were already stars or at least on the way to becoming stars. What could happen to them earlier, before they had actually been signed by a studio, was even more debilitating.

Cornel Wilde recalled that when he was still working in the theatre the head of casting for Warner Brothers arrived in New York to look over young potential leading men. 'He interviewed me, along with 150 others, and I remember that interview because it was so outstandingly rude and humiliating. We were all gathered in a big waiting room and a nice young lady would call out our names and we'd march down the corridor to where there was a door open. I saw some who would go in and stay two minutes and others who would start to move in and recoil, as if they'd been poked in the belly with a spear. They were all crushed; they'd walk out broken. And finally it was my turn and I get to the door and I see a man, standing behind a desk, with a very fat Hitler moustache. He had one hand on top of the desk and as I entered he went like this . . .' Mr Wilde made a dismissive gesture with his hand to illustrate what the man with the fat Hitler moustache had done . . . 'And that was my interview.'

But was that typical? Yes, he said, pretty well – and that was how young contract players were also treated in those days, the 1940s. 'It was awful. Once the actor made it, of course, everybody fawned and kneeled and bowed and whatever. But the men in power, especially the little men in power, were rude, insulting – I mean, just awful.'

The big men in power could also behave badly, though. After fifteen films – including *A Song to Remember*, in which he played Chopin, haemorrhaged all over the piano keys and became an instant star – Cornel Wilde was cast to star in *Forever Amber* at 20th Century-Fox by Darryl F. Zanuck, the studio boss. Zanuck, said Mr Wilde, 'had his human frailties. He'd get very hooked on some little doll and she'd be promoted immediately to roles she wasn't ready for. You know there were two versions of *Forever Amber*? I was in the first version with Peggy Cummins, who later became a very good actress; a pretty little gal, English girl. At that time she was too young for the role, too inexperienced and she played the whole thing with about two expressions. Everybody on the set knew that it was impossible, except Zanuck. But after thirty-nine days of shooting he finally gave in and had all of it burned – the negative, everything – so that nobody would have a record of his big mistake.' A year passed and then, with a new script, a new director and a new producer, Zanuck was ready to start again.

'He had Linda Darnell to play Amber. She was not ideal but she was a heck of a lot better than Peggy Cummins. She was experienced, she was beautiful and very nice, a very nice person. And again I was supposed to play Bruce Carlton. I was willing to play it but my marriage was falling apart because I was always working – I hardly saw my wife, as I said before – and I wanted two months off to go to Hawaii and have a vacation with her and get things back to normal. But they wouldn't give it to me. So I said, "Well, my marriage comes first and I won't do the picture," and I took off – we went to Hawaii. My agent flew over to tell me what the studio would do to me if I didn't make the picture and Zanuck asked me to come in as a personal favour – whatever that meant – to do the part; you know, for *his* sake. Why? Why for his sake? But the New York office was after him and they insisted that he deliver me in the role, the public was expecting it and so forth. I refused – and he was furious. He set out to get me and he did. For years they gave me down-graded pictures, little foreign pictures in black and white . . . That vendetta went on for years.'

And it went on despite the fact that Wilde did eventually agree to appear in *Forever Amber*. But before he did so, while he was still arguing, he was placed on suspension. 'They took away my beautiful star dressing-room on the lot and started putting out unpleasant publicity. And, of course, I was getting no salary. Then, as soon as I agreed to do the part, I got my dressing-room back and started getting my salary again.'

All that, then, was one side of the coin that was "the studio system" – that and the kind of meticulous attention to detail which reached its zenith (or nadir) at MGM where, in the main production office, they solemnly charted the menstrual periods of every actress under contract so that they could shoot around each lady when she was inconvenienced. The men didn't escape minor degradation either. Clark Gable, for instance, had all his teeth removed at the behest of Louis Mayer, who felt that false ones would look better. From an aesthetic point of view he was probably right but from a personal point of view I should imagine that natural teeth, however crooked or even stained, would be preferable for the wearer. (Joseph L. Mankiewicz said that at one period Mayer developed an obsession about teeth and tried to persuade everybody on contract to have them ripped out.)

But . . . every coin has two sides and the obverse side of this one was perhaps not so bad. The moguls may have believed that "there are three types of people in Hollywood: men, women and actors" and treated the latter, of whatever sex, as children, raging egoists, nitwits or social and emotional incompetents but they took care of them. The paternalism exercised by the studios was not always benevolent but mostly it was.

The movies, said Joseph Kennedy, who dabbled in them and also fathered the future President of the USA, 'is the only industry where the assets pick up their hats every afternoon and go home'. And though the assets may have felt that the homes they went to, usually in Beverly Hills, were 'the most luxurious slave quarters in the world' they went to them without a care. If the swimming pool or the tennis court needed repairs, if the roof leaked, the plumbing went wrong or the wiring was faulty the studio would have it seen to. Even at work they were cosseted. MGM, as an example, had a special restaurant where every day the best food available in Hollywood was served, free, to the stars, thus leading to the belief that MGM was the only place in the world where you could get 5,000 dollars a week and all found.

Dore Schary, who briefly succeeded Louis Mayer as head of MGM, said to me once that it was nonsense to describe contract artists as chattels except in the sense that, being under contract, they could be placed on suspension. 'But even when that happened,' he said, 'the studios would be around after a while to make sure the stars weren't really in trouble, weren't injuring themselves. They'd be offered another deal, another contract. The studios really looked after them.'

And indeed they did. The moguls could, and frequently would, rent stars for whom they had no immediate use to another studio at a profit of which the stars received nothing. (MGM lent Clark Gable to Columbia in this way as a form of punishment because, for once, he had been making mild waves. Columbia put him in *It Happened One Night* and Gable won his only Oscar and returned to MGM a bigger star than he had been before. Metro did very well out of the deal; Gable received nothing except a good role and an Academy Award.)

But against that those same studios would tend their assets with meticulous, and sometimes even loving, care. To paraphrase William Holden in *Sunset Boulevard*, Frankenstein and My Fair Lady are really the same story since each deals with the moulding of raw material to create something different. Hollywood was in the business of refining Eliza Doolittles.

An example of this was Ava Gardner who, aged sixteen, was tested at MGM by the director George Sidney. At that time, Sidney said, she was to put it mildly raw, being a product of a poor background in the deep south, almost unaware of what shoes were for and the possessor of an incomprehensible accent. But MGM recognised her innate talent, signed her, groomed her and, at the behest of Louis Mayer, tested her again when she was seventeen and then when she was eighteen because what the studio was interested in was not so much her immediate possibilities as her long-term potential and it was content to wait for that to develop.

As the director Richard Brooks put it: 'There was very little that a star ever did that was not under the supervision of the studio – especially for the women. The studios brought them along, groomed them, even educated them. They organised their social life, became involved in their medical life, their health problems, their babies if they were having any or their abortions if they were having any.'

And if they were in any kind of trouble that could bring them into conflict with the law, the studio was able to help out there, too. Each company had what amounted to a studio police chief whose job was to make contact with – and keep sweet – the various law enforcement agencies. 'The studios,' as Dore Schary said, delicately, 'had friends in the police department.' What that meant was that if a star was involved in a motoring accident when drunk (e.g. Clark Gable) or created a public disturbance when drunk (e.g. Spencer Tracy) or was involved in a potential scandal when caught in the wrong bedroom (e.g. lots of people) the studio's "friends" in the police department would quietly make sure that nobody ever appeared in court and no names were mentioned in the newspapers. There was no bribery involved, said the delicate Dore Schary, but 'gifts might be exchanged'. At Fox in his time there, said Don Ameche, there was a man whose job was to 'sit by the phone from 7 o'clock at night until 7 o'clock in the morning to handle any distress signals that came in. That was his job and I'm sure he did a lot for a lot of people because there was much shenanigans going on then ... traffic violations or maybe getting in a brawl somewhere, breaking up a nightclub or restaurant – something like that. Most of that never got near the papers.'

The studios, said Sam Marx, 'had tremendous power. The city of Los Angeles owed a lot to the movie industry and the mayor of the city, or the governor of the state for that matter, or the head of police were all constant visitors to the studios and had their pictures taken with the stars as a means of publicising themselves for a future election day And that would be the reason why scandals were played down as much as possible. When they did get out of hand there was nothing much to be done about it, of course, but generally I would say there were more scandals around Hollywood that nobody ever heard of than those they did.'

When in 1932 Paul Bern, the husband of Jean Harlow, shot himself, Louis Mayer and his head of publicity Howard Strickling were called to the scene before the police. And, according to Sam Marx, who was also there at the time, Mayer picked up Bern's suicide note and was about to take it away and destroy it until Strickling pointed out that the absence of same might point strongly to Harlow having murdered her husband. If it had served his purpose, Marx said, Mayer would not have thought twice about destroying such vital evidence. 'But that was comparatively minor compared with what else he could do. Don't forget at that period in his life he was one of the most powerful men in the world. He was a close friend of the president, Herbert Hoover, his income was constantly publicised as the greatest weekly salary in the United States ... Certainly he was a powerful man.'

Thus the stars were almost totally controlled by the studios who, when you look back from this distance in time, might be thought to have pulled off what amounts to a gigantic confidence trick. Because the studios' success, the success of the entire industry, was predicated on stars. They were what the public wanted; without them, especially in the 30s and 40s, the appeal of the cinema would have been minimal. But perhaps the studios were right to treat them as not very bright children because it was not until the 1950s that the stars began to realise how much power they had.

The trick, which the moguls practised so well, was to keep the big names always just a little bit nervous. For instance, an uppity star might come in one day – and this happened to Mario Lanza – and find someone in the next dressing-room wearing a costume identical to his own and apparently learning the same lines. At the very least it must have made Lanza pause to think. When Tab Hunter was the bobby-sox idol of the 50s he went on suspension for a while because he had turned down a role. When he returned somebody at the studio pointed out a young man across the way.

'Do you see him? Huh? Do you see him? Who does he remind you of?' Hunter said: 'Who? I don't know... What are you talking about?' And the other man said: 'Doesn't he remind you of a young Tab Hunter?' The message was clear: there would always be an eager replacement waiting in the wings and the studios were ever on the lookout for one. 'The first time I was ever plonked into a make-up chair at MGM,' said Greer Garson, 'the head of make-up looked me over and said, "Well, who is she? Is she Garbo? Hardly. Is she Jeanette MacDonald? Hardly. Is she Norma Shearer?" I said "Couldn't I just be Greer Garson?"' Well, yes finally they did allow her to be just Greer Garson but the point was that she, like the others to whom she had been compared and found wanting, was what MGM called "a lady actress", which is to say that she was earmarked to play ladies rather than girls or broads or whores or whatever. And it was always useful to have plenty of lady actresses around just in case one of the more established lady actresses grew stroppy.

Yet, time and again, it was the stars – not the films themselves, nor the writers and directors – who pulled the studios out of trouble. In 1932/3 when Paramount was in dire straits the success of Mae West's pictures came to the rescue and in 1937 Deanna Durbin's films did the same for Universal.

It was, though, MGM above all who realised the value of the stars. "More stars than there are in Heaven," it boasted erroneously but impressively of its contract list. And it helped itself overcome the slump of the early 30s with films like *Grand Hotel* which, in 1932, starred not only Garbo and John Barrymore but also Lionel Barrymore, Joan Crawford and Wallace Beery. The next year *Dinner at Eight* included Jean Harlow, John Barrymore, Wallace Beery, Marie Dressler and Billie Burke and *Night Flight* featured Gable, Robert Montgomery, Myrna Loy, both male Barrymores and Helen Hayes. The public eventually tired of these star-studded epics, preferring to concentrate its attentions on perhaps two or three celestial names, but the star principle which had pertained in the silent era and had, briefly, been abandoned at the beginning of the talkies when new and lesser-known names had flooded in from the theatre, had been re-established.

And as the Depression eased and Hollywood began to settle down under its eight main hierarchies – or, as Joe Mankiewicz described them, "medieval baronies" – each studio developed its own hallmark. MGM was the ritzy establishment, the home of glitz and glamour, of the musical and the American Dream. MGM movies peddled optimism and the belief that nothing was impossible. In them a shopgirl could work behind a counter in Woolworths but still live in a penthouse flat. And she would invariably end up marrying a millionaire. The films of MGM were full of beautiful people, beautifully dressed, beautifully staged and beautifully photographed. But thanks to Irving Thalberg who, whether or not he was the genius many people thought him to be, was certainly a man who believed that dignity and seriousness were not necessarily alien to films, the studio also had a policy of producing quality pictures, whose intention was not merely to win financial rewards on a vast scale but to remind everyone that the cinema could also be art. The 1936 *Romeo and Juliet* starring Norma Shearer and Leslie Howard – both horribly miscast, incidentally – is a case in point. (Actually, the casting could have been even more dreadful: according to Sam Marx, Thalberg wanted Gable to play Romeo but even Gable, not exactly the brightest of men, decided that that was too much.) This theme might have been developed more strongly if Thalberg had not died of pneumonia in 1936 at the age of thirty-seven, although his desire to make what he called "intelligent films" was not always supported by Mayer. Despite the MGM motto, "art for art's sake" never had much appeal for Mayer. Marx remembered him coming out of a successful sneak preview of *San Francisco* – 'which was a wow. It had Gable, Tracy and Jeanette MacDonald; it had a fabulous earthquake . . .' – beaming and thanking everyone and saying, 'Now there's *my* idea of a prestige picture.'

Yet, whether you believed prestige was about star-crossed lovers or a convulsion of the earth's surface in northern California, MGM was the place to be. 'It was,' said the director George Sidney, 'Camelot. It was the Emerald City, a kingdom of magic, a world within a world. Everything was there – food, dentistry, all your physical problems attended to. There was any kind of person you needed – someone to fix your watch, to fix your toe nails, to teach you to speak French, to duel, to sing, to dance, to speak English, to speak American . . . There were always specialists at MGM at that time. They were striving for perfection. It was a great land, it was a way of life and we kept together very clannishly. The studios were families and the families were run by a father figure and Louis B. Mayer was a father image. Because he was there you felt Big Daddy was there and you had a back-up, you had protection.' As for Thalberg, the production chief, well he wasn't Big Daddy but . . . 'He was very, very important because he was a literate man and he was trying to improve the quality. That's what he was after . . . He went out and hired the finest writers from all over the world and did everything to bring English-speaking literacy into films. He was a very, very strong influence . . .'

Warner Brothers was another matter. It was known as "a writers' studio" and early in the 1930s its head of production, Darryl Zanuck, later to run 20th Century-Fox, proclaimed that henceforth the studio would concentrate on social issues – exposé films, gangster stories, pictures dealing with injustices against "little people". To quote George Sidney again: 'People always said that if there were no newspapers Jack Warner wouldn't have a studio. He'd just take today's headlines and, bingo, he'd have the picture being made tomorrow.' Yet, in essence, MGM and Warners were not entirely different. At Metro, Sidney said, each film was a star vehicle. 'They figured they would make two Garbo pictures, two Gable pictures, a Tracy picture, a Harlow picture and at the beginning of the year they would figure out a whole programme of pictures. They'd put the names of the stars in one list and then they started matching films to them. They'd say, Well, Gable could be in *Test Pilot*, Gable could be in this, Robert Montgomery could be in that and they were shuffling a deck . . . The star was the complete draw.' Jack Warner also knew the value of such glitteringly celebrated names but . . . 'He took people that you'd never think would be movie stars – Jimmy Cagney, Edward G. Robinson, Humphrey Bogart, Georgie Raft: a strange kind of group. Yet he'd bounce that off with one of the most beautiful men we've ever had in Hollywood, Errol Flynn. That was his way of doing it. MGM did it with beautiful women and beautiful men.'

It was, however, at Warners and not at MGM that the Hollywood ground rules were swiftly established. In 1932 Jack Warner and Darryl Zanuck issued a statement declaring that from then on no actor or actress would be given any kind of say in any kind of aspect of a film's production. And they meant it. In 1936 Bette Davis was so dissatisfied with the workload and "inferior roles" that Warners imposed upon her that she fled to England to break her contract. The studio pursued her relentlessly through the English courts and won a breach of contract decision against her. But it must be said that when Miss Davis returned, full of trepidation, to Hollywood, Jack Warner paid her legal costs and offered her a better selection of scripts in the future, being no doubt satisfied that while, in this instance, he could offer the carrot rather than the stick the basic principle of studio autonomy had been upheld.

Perhaps – though probably not – he was also concerned by the fact that the court case had publicly exposed the near slavelike conditions of the stars. For example, under the terms of her contract Miss Davis could be forced to make a personal appearance at the Republican Convention even though she was herself a Democrat. Furthermore, she was not allowed to divorce her husband for three years without studio permission and the publicity clause meant that the studio could insist on her appearing in product advertisements and that a drawing of her, semi-nude, could be used to promote a film. And indeed things did not change all that much when, after the legal action, she returned to Warners. Certainly she was treated more seriously as an actress but otherwise the studio's grip on her activities was not greatly eased and after she won the Oscar for *Jezebel* in 1938 she was on suspension for almost a year.

Broadly speaking what, contractually, applied to Bette Davis also applied to other stars. But on the whole and throughout the years of the studio system women were treated, and paid, less well than men. There were, of course, exceptions. In 1936 at MGM Claudette Colbert was reputed to be the highest-salaried individual in America on 302,000 dollars a year. Against that, and taking only a few examples at random, in 1932 when Cagney was dissatisfied with 1,000 dollars a week, Joan Blondell was rubbing along on 250 dollars and in 1939, by which time Cagney's wages had risen to 12,500 dollars a week and Paul Muni's to 11,500, Warners' highest-paid female star, Bette Davis, was on 4,000 dollars a week. Eight years later Miss Davis's pay had risen to 328,000 dollars a year, making her allegedly the highest-salaried woman in the USA – a nice enough income, to be sure, but still some way short of the annual increment of 467,361 dollars that made Humphrey Bogart America's best-salaried man.

Nor was that all. Except in the case of the biggest stars – the likes of Garbo, Crawford, Davis, Hepburn – a woman's career was much shorter than a man's. Indeed, unless she had managed to achieve what would now be called "superstar" status, she could easily be finished at thirty or very soon afterwards. Sylvia Sidney, for instance, made twenty-four films between 1929 and 1941 by which time she was thirty-one; she has been in only ten or so since then. At thirty, she said, you were 'Done. Done. Done. You became a character person right away. You played mothers and frumpy parts. There was no sex, no sex at all.' So Hollywood was less interested in women than in girls – why? 'Because,' she said, 'I guess men are.'

That being so (and I daresay it is) things were especially hard for actresses who were renowned mostly for their beauty. Virginia Mayo, signed by Samuel Goldwyn in 1944, was hailed by Louella Parsons, doyenne of the gossip columnists, as the prettiest girl to arrive in Hollywood for years. Miss Mayo was delighted at the time because at least she had been noticed and her career was under way. But later the Parsons description of her became more of a millstone than a flattering label, for attention was continually devoted more to her physical appearance than to her acting ability. Serious parts were hard to come by; she was thought of mostly as the pretty girl in a number of Danny Kaye comedies. And when she did play a dramatic role (in *The Best Years of our Lives*) and played it well, it made no real difference. She was back in a comedy next time out. 'To this present day,' she said, the present day then being the summer of 1985, 'I'm still noted for being good-looking instead of for being an actress. I don't like that.'

After five years with Goldwyn she went to Warners and hung on there until 1959, at which point she was given the choice of appearing with Randolph Scott in a western, which she really hated, called *Westbound* or being placed on suspension. Under protest she made the film because she felt that the choice was no choice. 'It was the end of my contract and they were trying to squeeze me out. They did that to all the actors who were on the way out. It was a very dirty way to treat people but they did it.' Yes, but why was she on the way out? She was still undoubtedly a star but she was also thirty-nine and though as good-looking as ever she could no longer play a girl.

Mamie van Doren, who was really only a star of B pictures and was regarded as an out and out sexpot, lasted for less time than Miss Mayo. Although today her old films, such as *Teacher's Pet* (1958), have something of a cult following in America and she is still making pictures, her initial career was over almost before it had begun. She was discovered first by Howard Hughes, who was then running RKO studios among his many other enterprises. 'It started when he saw my picture in a paper. I was sixteen and he liked 'em nice and young. So he had his casting director at RKO call me . . .' The roles she was given were not exactly demanding. In one film, *Jet Pilot*, with John Wayne she played a WAAC and had one of the shortest speaking parts on record. 'Look!' she cried.

Hughes, she said, was "a very eccentric man" who wore white gloves at lunch and usually needed a shave. 'One afternoon he asked me if I was a virgin and I said, "You'll never know".' Sometimes he would pick her up with her mother in an old Chevrolet and take them to Palm Springs – 'and, ah, that's about it.' Their relationship was purely professional then, was it? Miss van Doren laughed, said, 'Ah, it was professional, I guess,' and laughed again.

Well, anyway, Hughes gave her a start but then she moved on to Universal, aged twenty and quite spectacular to look at. 'I don't think the studio executives there quite knew what to do with a blossoming young, aspiring, sexy actress. They were really dedicated to exploitation. I had great aspirations as an actress but when they looked at me they saw this blonde hair and they really made me into a dumb blonde.'

True, they put her through a kind of grooming process, sending her to what she called their "talent school", where she was taught to ride and fence and was given elocution lessons. But most studios did that with their young contract players. 'The minute I got to Paramount,' Sterling Hayden said, 'they gave me a drama coach. They attached a wrestler to me, to make sure I behaved myself and got home and didn't drink too much. I had a voice coach and . . . it was so ridiculous. I had to train with the wrestler in the Paramount gym. But they paid on Thursdays and there were plenty of girls around.' Well, chacun à son goût . . . Hayden stayed at Paramount for the money and the girls; van Doren stayed at Universal because she wanted to act and welcomed the encouragement to watch established stars (Joan Crawford, for example) who happened to be filming there. 'It was marvellous for youngsters. I mean, you were really getting the bulk of what you wanted to know about acting.'

Nevertheless, what all this led to was simply more dumb blonde roles. 'Every time there was a dumb blonde part I was it. In that era, the 50s, and at Universal especially women were second bananas to the men. There were Rock Hudson, Jeff Chandler, Tony Curtis . . . Those were your three male stars – there were no female stars. I watch television now and I see an interview with, like, Glenn Ford and people like that and they say, "People who put down those big leaders of the studios, they're talking like they've got a bubblehead because without those studio bosses it couldn't have happened." Well, they [the Glenn Fords etc.] weren't women. They got the roles, the macho parts, and sure it was great for some of them but not for all of us.'

For Miss van Doren it was far from being great – "pretty good" is probably about as close as it came – and by the beginning of the 1960s it was virtually over, partly because a more natural, less obviously voluptuous look was becoming fashionable for women but also because . . . 'Let me tell you something: when you reached thirty in those days you were finished. I mean, a woman was not wanted after she reached thirty. You had to get a contract before you were twenty or they didn't want you. They wanted young girls with childish minds and they dressed you up like you were forty years old . . . It's really unbelievable how they made you look older but they wanted you very young. And when you got to thirty you were too old.'

Well, as I said, Miss van Doren was never really a star but it probably wouldn't have helped much if she had been. Anne Baxter was a star and the winner, in 1946, of the Oscar for best supporting actress for her performance in *The Razor's Edge*. She signed a contract with David O. Selznick in 1940 when she was seventeen but twenty years, forty-odd films, one Academy Award and another Academy nomination (for *All About Eve* in 1950) later her career as a Hollywood leading lady was over. As Leslie Halliwell remarks tersely in *The Filmgoer's Companion* after 1960 she "found the going got tough". And it got tough because actresses in Hollywood were "second-class citizens" and anyway she had passed the dreaded age of thirty. 'I left at thirty-six and a half and at forty you played grandmothers. At forty you'd dried up; at forty-five there was nothing for you. Older or younger – yes. But this time [between thirty and forty-five] which should have been the filet mignon of one's life was a no-woman's land, believe me.'

Of course, after a brief period of marriage and semi-retirement in Australia she made films again, many films, but the roles were harder to find. And not only for her –

Left: The initial breakthrough: *Don Juan*, the first feature film with synchronised sound
Below: Jolson – 'You ain't heard nothin' yet'

Above: Warner Brothers indifferent gangster talkie *Lights of New York* – "seven reels of speech"
Right: Paramount's first talkie *Interference*

Husband and wife Douglas
Fairbanks Sr and Mary Pickford,
silent "superstars" and two of the
founders of United Artists in
1919. She won an Oscar for her
first sound movie but never really
made it in the talkies

Marlene DIETRICH in "*Angel*"

Produced and Directed by

ERNST LUBITSCH

Left: Dietrich – 'You had to explain things to her and you had to light her properly'
Right: Joan Crawford in 1930 – one of the first and most durable of the stars of the sound era
Below: *Gold Diggers of 1935*, one of the Busby Berkeley films which helped revive the musical

Garbo in *Camille*. No matter
how you photographed her, said
Rouben Mamoulian, she always
looked beautiful

even the superstars had trouble. 'Bette [Davis] thought she was through at 41 when the script for *All About Eve* came. Imagine that. She did. She told me that. And the script miraculously appeared because Claudette [Colbert] couldn't do it. And this gave Bette's career an enormous momentum. Now Crawford also managed but they did it, she and Bette, because they were determined, they knew how to fight.'

But once begun the fight, for status and position, never ended. Vincent Sherman recalled directing *Goodbye My Fancy* with Joan Crawford in 1951 when she was forty-five. 'Jack Warner called me one day and said, "I don't want any more close-ups of Crawford." I said, "Why not?" He said, "Well, she's getting too old for close-ups." I said, "But I can't make close-ups of the other people and not make them of her. She's too smart for that. She'll soon start raising hell about it." He said, "That's how I want it. I'm running the studio." Well, I ignored him and I did the close-ups and at the end of it one of his assistants said to me, "Mr Warner was very disappointed you didn't follow his instructions."'

One law for the men; another for the "second-class citizens". Nobody, to my knowledge, ever said that Gable or Cooper or Tracy or Wayne were too old for close-ups.

Another hazard for women – oh yes, they had plenty to contend with – was the casting couch. Mamie van Doren knew about it in the 50s – the smooth, or maybe not so smooth, approach from the director who'd found the ideal role for a certain toothsome actress and wondered whether she would like to talk about it in his office at . . . 'Oh, I don't know: six, six-thirty. When the studio's quiet, you know?'

'Yeah,' she said, 'it has happened to me. I'm not gonna tell you the outcome, obviously . . . I didn't do too much, did I? Or I didn't do the right thing.' Another of those bewildering enigmatic laughs of hers.

But the casting couch probably came into existence at about the same time as the first movie was made and with it came a tendency to regard actresses as consumer goods, studio executives for the use of. In the 1920s Esther Ralston – though not molested herself, having four brothers to protect her and being known unofficially as "Miss Alaska" – was aware of young women gaining entrée to the studios and thinking, 'Well, if I have to be nice to the casting director, I'll have to be nice, I suppose.' And in the 1930s Joan Fontaine said the studios always had a stable of girls around who were known as "the availables". Young contract players were also expected to be available at times. Miss Fontaine said: 'I was once asked to go on location with a lot of exhibitors. I was eighteen or whatever and my mother went with me and sat at my table and all of them came around and said, "Get rid of her." I said, "Well, she *is* my mother." And my mother said, "All right, Joan, it's time for bed." And there were knocks on the door . . . And when I got back to RKO I was called in by the head of the publicity department who said, "You've been very uncooperative. I mean, you've not been kind. The whole reason you were up there was to be gracious to all those businessmen . . ."' Miss Fontaine went home, nonplussed, and told her mum and mum, a lady clearly who was never less than plussed, went up to the studio and had several sharp words with the head of publicity whereafter her daughter was never again requested to be "gracious" to visiting businessmen. Going on into the

40s and the 50s Janet Leigh, on loan from MGM, had similar trouble at RKO, only this time with the head of the studio himself, Howard Hughes. 'He was not an unkind man,' she said, giving the impression of one choosing her words carefully, 'but he had odd ways of working and did mix, er, let's say business with pleasure and I just had no desire or feeling for that. So it was a constant kind of struggle – not struggle physically but I mean to elude all of his arrangements and, um, it was a pain . . .'

Evelyn Keyes said that at parties, at dinner tables and in their offices, producers and directors would sit around and compare notes on the desirability and, in some cases, the known sexual expertise of various women on the lot. Having found and sampled a good thing they were – being all chaps together – generously prepared to pass it on to their friends. The fact that men talked like this did not in itself, of course, mean that actresses were obliged to sleep with them but the pressures that were put upon women to be sexually compliant could be fierce.

Evelyn Keyes was once chased around a hotel suite – 'around the chairs, around the couch . . .' – by an amorous director who, when it became clear that he was more likely to run himself into a heart attack than into her bed, threatened to ruin her career. He didn't manage that but, since she was working with him at the time, 'he rather tortured me on the set'. Well, that kind of approach was, as Miss Keyes put it, 'on the lower level, the quickie. And studios often signed young girls for six months, paid them the minimum and expected them to be available.' But girls who accepted that kind of contract usually found themselves discarded at the end of it. 'Just going to bed with somebody, I mean walking into the office and making out on the couch – no, that wouldn't get you a job.' What might do the trick, however, was if a producer or director 'found a young lady attractive and really liked her. That could get her roles. But that was a little different. That's not a quickie, that's an involvement. I won't go so far as to say love – an involvement.'

But even if your arrangement went way beyond the quickie or even an involvement and love itself had loomed up there was still an element of menace. When Evelyn Keyes was under contract to Columbia, Harry Cohn, the head of the studio, threatened to "freeze" her career because she rebuffed him. 'He talked of leaving his wife and marrying me. He wanted a love affair. You know, if I could do certain things over I certainly would look at that differently now. But then I got indignant and said, "How dare you!" and made an enemy. I mean, there must have been a better way to handle it. I did it badly.' Cohn, scorned and as good – or as bad – as his word, did freeze her career. 'I didn't get certain parts that I wanted, that I asked for. I'd get the same level of parts that I'd had before.'

On the other hand the shrewd use of a sexual reputation, even if it was undeserved, could be most helpful to an actress. Anne Baxter, under contract to Darryl Zanuck at Fox, coveted the rather racy role of Sophie in *The Razor's Edge*. No chance. To Zanuck there were only two kinds of women – "librarians" and "broads". Miss Baxter, he said, was a librarian; Sophie was a broad. Yet one morning, to the great astonishment of herself and her agents, the studio called to say, 'We'd like to test Anne.' And having been tested the librarian was deemed to have been a disguised broad all the time and was cast as Sophie. Five years later she discovered how this had come about. A friend of hers, Gregory Ratoff, one of Zanuck's producers, had procured her the role by means of a judicious lie. He had no knowledge, in the Biblical sense, of Miss Baxter whatever but . . . 'He was a gambling pal of Mr Zanuck. I always suspected that's one reason Mr Zanuck made him a producer, so he could afford to pay his gambling debts. Anyway, he had Zanuck's ear and he was down at Palm Springs with him and Darryl was smoking his cigar in his bikini and saying, "What are we going to do about this Sophie business?" and Greg said, "What about Anne Baxter?" Zanuck said, "No, she's a cold potato." Greg said, "Darryl, I have had it. It's maaarvellous!" Well, of course, Zanuck dropped his cigar; he couldn't believe it. But he thought it was awfully funny and said, "Go ahead test her." And then I got the part. Isn't that terrible?'

Zanuck's arbitrary division of women into two distinct categories may not necessarily have been widespread in Hollywood but typecasting, which is what it amounted to, was. A studio would decide on a certain persona for an actor or actress and roles would be tailored to fit it. The players might occasionally resent this and attempt to break the mould but in general typecasting, which meant the audience knew pretty well what to expect from any given performer, was an important ingredient in the building of a star. Sometimes the persona, or image, was decided upon at once – Greer Garson for instance was destined from the start to play what MGM was pleased to call "lady parts". Sometimes it took a little longer. Clark Gable, in his day the acknowledged "King of Hollywood" and, along with John Wayne, probably the biggest star there ever was arrived at MGM when the studio contained more actresses than actors and there was a need for people to play opposite all those leading ladies. Consequently, in his first year at Metro Gable appeared in fourteen pictures, paired with Shearer, Crawford (three times) Marion Davies and Garbo, among others. At that stage his screen persona was still being developed, so he played a minister (opposite Davies in *Polly of the Circus*), a Salvation Army officer (opposite Crawford in *Laughing Sinners*), a prig (opposite Garbo in the dreadful *Susan Lennox, Her Fall and Rise*) and an utter cad in *Night Nurse*, which starred Barbara Stanwyck and Joan Blondell. In *A Free Soul* he slapped Norma Shearer around and struck gold – *that* was the Gable the public wanted. Howard Hawks once said that Gable played a kind of heavy, a heavy with a grin, and that was what the people loved. So there he was – the rugged, all-American good guy with just enough of a hint of nastiness to wallop a woman should the occasion demand. And having been decked out with that image he was most reluctant to abandon it. Irving Thalberg had a devil of a job persuading him to play Fletcher Christian in *Mutiny on the Bounty* – 'I talk like an Ohio miner,' Gable said. 'I'm not going to talk like a British seaman of 200 years ago.' And he refused at first to weep when called upon to do so in *Gone With the Wind* on the grounds that weeping was both unmanly and, more important, unGable.

Of course, there were times when persona-building, or person-changing, foundered on account of the performer's stubbornness. Howard Hughes acquired Janet Leigh as an unsophisticated ingenue from MGM and tried to transform her into a sex symbol, somewhat in the Jane Russell mould. Though she did later acquire

Above left: Garbo and
Gable in *Susan Lennox . . .*
one of the films that
helped establish the King
of Hollywood
Above: Gary Cooper with
Jean Arthur in *Mr Deeds
Goes to Town*, a prime
example of Capra on the
side of the little man
Left: Vivien Leigh signs
to play Scarlett O'Hara to
the obvious satisfaction
of David Selznick, Leslie
Howard and Olivia de
Havilland
Right: Bette Davis in
Jezebel. She won an
Oscar for her role and
was then suspended for
nearly a year

a more mature and sophisticated image, Miss Leigh resented Hughes's efforts at the time and eventually he abandoned them after she threw a telephone at him. Actually, the telephone throwing was the climax of an argument about some contractual matter but it did give Hughes an inkling that this was not a lady to mess about with. When Miss Leigh's image did change it was because she had grown older and nobody can be an ingenue for ever, just as nobody can be a bobby-sox idol for ever. Both Robert Wagner and Tab Hunter started out as bobby-sox idols, all clean-cut and bright-eyed and grinning with what looked like sixty-four teeth apiece. Hunter didn't particularly like being a bobby-sox idol although, looking back on that time from the age of fifty-four, he said: 'It was nice in a way. There's something kind of bittersweet about the naivety of the 50s and early 60s.' Wagner, on the other hand, enjoyed it immensely. 'I loved it. I thought it was great. It was terrific.... I was involved in a couple of bizarre publicity stunts. I was asked to take Jayne Mansfield to a premiere or they paired you up with somebody else but that never bothered me very much. The only time they really got me a bit upset was when they had me romantically involved with the leading lady; Terry Moore was one. They had us *married* virtually ... But it didn't really make very much difference. They wrap fish in it the next day, you know what I'm saying?' Besides, you can't be a bobby-sox idol when you're much over twenty and both Wagner and Hunter were finally able to throw off this label and emerge as more mature actors.

Ralph Bellamy, by contrast, never did outgrow his image and indeed it drove him out of Hollywood. Riffling idly through a script in the office of a friend at Warner Brothers one day he came upon a list and description of the proposed characters. Against one of them, the note said: 'A naive but charming fellow from the south west – a typical Ralph Bellamy part.' Mr Bellamy was so appalled at being thus pigeon-holed that he immediately went back to the New York stage and didn't return to Hollywood for ten years.

But along with the persona, the build-up, the grooming and the exposure, an actor needed something more if he were to metamorphose into a star. Talent? Well, yes, though if you look at some of the stars it clearly wasn't all that essential. No, what he also needed was luck and timing and this was exemplified in Gable's career. He went to MGM in 1930, precisely the time when the studio was anxiously seeking a top leading man to replace John Gilbert. And he was, or anyway gave the impression of being, archetypically American, which was extremely important. The coming of sound had given the movies a voice and that voice spoke increasingly in an American accent because the bulk of the audience was to be found in the USA. In 1936, for example, America had 18,192 cinemas, compared with Germany's 5,273, Britain's 4,960 and Italy's 4,800. (Russia had nearly 35,000 but Russia had never been a very lucrative market for American films.)

In the silent days movies, even Hollywood movies, had had no particular nationality; now they did – for the most part they were American and they tended to be set more and more in the American idiom, being littered with brassy, wise-cracking showgirls, New York and Chicago gangsters and good ol' honest, upright country boys like Gary Cooper, Henry Fonda and James Stewart. The new kind of star, tailored to fit the new kind of picture, was very different from the old regime. The silent stars were gods and goddesses who dwelt on Olympus ("ivory-towered" was George Sidney's description); their successors were more recognisably mortal. They were, as stars always had been and are still, the closest thing America has to royalty or a peerage but theirs was a democratic royalty – anyone given good looks, a bit of talent and a lot of luck could join. So truck drivers, waitresses, bell hops and beauty queens flooded into Hollywood and some of them became stars.

But how well they were treated depended on the studio that signed them. They all suffered the seven-year contract with the one-way options and the "hangman's noose" of the suspension clause but in more general terms the kind of personal treatment they were given had much to do with whoever was running the studio. At MGM, under Mayer and Thalberg, the stars were valued more than anywhere else. It was Thalberg who devised the all-star pictures of the early 30s and although he was relieved of his duties as head of production after a heart attack in 1933 (he later returned to run his own production unit until his death in 1936) the studio's attitude was well-established. Everyone on the lot was urged to regard himself as part of one big, happy family – though the degree of happiness depended on whether or not you upset Louis Mayer. If you were careless enough to do that he would plead with you, weep at you, rail at you, pretend to have some kind of anguished fit or seizure and, if none of that worked, fire you. Greer Garson would sometimes refuse to accept a role offered by another executive but she never said no to L.B. 'Mr Mayer was the beating heart of MGM . . . His birthday was a big fiesta for us. Judy Garland sang, Jeanette MacDonald sang, Mickey Rooney clowned and we cheered and cheered. We had an enormous birthday cake for him and almost everybody had something to say. There was a strong air of paternalism and it was genuine.' The birthday of Mayer, a childhood immigrant from Minsk, was actually a double celebration because it fell on 4 July, a date arbitrarily chosen by himself. Sam Marx said that Mayer never knew his real date of birth and picked Independence Day because he and so many of the other immigrant movie moguls (Goldwyn and Laemmle, for instance) 'were trying to prove they were great Americans because they had become Americans and hadn't started out that way.'

Still, Mickey Rooney clowning to celebrate Mayer's (and only incidentally America's) birthday may have done so with a certain bitterness in his heart. When Eddie Bracken joined the studio in 1940 after a great Broadway success he discovered that he was being paid some 2,500 dollars a week while his idol and one of the biggest stars in Hollywood, the said M. Rooney, was only on about 750 dollars. Paternalism and exploitation could often stroll arm-in-arm in happy companionship. Bracken also believed that from the time of Wallace Reid (the silent actor who died of drug addiction in 1923) onwards there was a notorious MGM doctor who treated many of the studio's stars with uppers and downers to make them alert on the set and help them sleep at night. In this context Judy Garland's name particularly is often mentioned but Bracken said the same treatment was given to Reid and Gable among others. Both Rooney and Joe Mankiewicz have denied this story to me, arguing that Mayer would have gone crazy if he thought anyone was getting any of his stars hooked on drugs. But there is no doubt that Garland was so hooked and it's at least possible that she became so because a studio doctor had prescribed amphetamines and the like for her at a time when little was known about the side effects of such stimulants and tranquillisers.

Paramount, according to Buddy Rogers who spent several years there, was another "family" studio. 'Everyone was a friend. It was like your brother, your sister, your uncle, your aunt. We were all under contract, we were all getting paid; we were all getting paid to love each other . . . We'd go on the stage and make the first take and the director would say, "Buddy, great! That's just great!" Well, he loved me because we were under contract, we were like brothers.' True, this was in the earlier years of talking pictures and later things changed. 'Independent production came in and people said, "You're not a family. You must shape up, you must do this, do that . . ." But it was like a fraternity the first few years.'

At Fox things were different. Not a lot of fraternity there and, as at Warners, the emphasis was on the story rather than the star. Anne Baxter found Darryl Zanuck a fairly visible presence to the writers, directors and producers but not, in her experience, to the actors. She rarely saw him on set and gained the impression that 'there was a large moat around his office. I think I was in it exactly once in my life. My mother and I were ushered in, almost stumbled in on the thick carpet, and miles away there was this desk piled with stuff and (peeping above it) this messy little hair and a cigar. And he said, "We're gonna do great things with you, right?" And that was it . . . I never was in that office again.' Robert Wagner found him more accessible. 'You were very much aware of his presence all the time,' he said. 'He was a dynamic human being. He cared very much about the picture business, cared about his people . . . He *was* the studio; he made the decisions. He was a tyrannical man – a lot of anger, a lot of humour, a lot of every kind of emotion you could experience but you knew where it was coming from; it wasn't hidden.'

Naturally none of the studios neglected its stars but the extent to which each looked after them was a matter of degree. The protection and cosseting that were common at MGM were not practised at Fox, nor at Warners either. Being under contract there, said George Raft once, was "like being in Alcatraz". Carroll Baker remembered Jack Warner as 'a bit of a buffoon really. He always thought of himself as a comedian and he was very bad. I mean, his jokes were legendary they were so awful. And he also did a tap dance. He did everything but talk seriously.' He could, however, be serious enough – and hard enough – when it suited his purposes. Virginia Mayo said: 'At Warner Brothers we were made to toe the line. We were never allowed to be late. Jack Warner kept a record of the first take in the morning and at what hour it was in the can. And he kept a record of each individual: if you made a mistake and the take had to be done over, that went on your record. If you goofed, that was a black mark . . .' And if you collected a lot of black marks? 'I suppose your option would not be picked up.'

Well, that must have been alarming – it's always alarming to work against a background of fear and threats. But the threat was there wherever you were employed, less obvious at MGM perhaps, more so at Warners and Columbia where the head of the studio, Harry Cohn, was in the words of Evelyn Keyes 'a tyrant. That was *his* studio – the Kingdom of Cohn. He owned Columbia and therefore everybody in it.'

To Miss Keyes, who had great affection for him, Cohn was "a diamond in the rough", which is perhaps a gentler way of saying, as other people did, that he was a foul-mouthed, hectoring bully. In the kingdom of Cohn the subjects had no privacy for the monarch installed hidden microphones so that he could hear whatever was being said in the studio (especially anything uncomplimentary to himself) and since bugging people is only partially effective he also ran a string of informers to identify the malcontents and dissidents. The producer Pandro S. Berman once said that if Louis Mayer could woo you from another studio he valued you; if Cohn could do the same thing he felt contempt for you. 'He figured that if you were foolish enough to make a deal with him, you couldn't be any good.' This habit of riding roughshod over his subjects and their feelings is exemplified by Cohn's treatment of the writer Budd Schulberg (son of B. P. Schulberg, one of Hollywood's founders). Columbia was to film Schulberg's novel *The Harder They Fall*, an exposé of boxing racketeers, and the producer Jerry Wald wanted the author to write the screenplay. Schulberg was agreeable and the details were discussed on a three-way telephone call between the writer, at his home in New Hope, Pennsylvania, and Cohn and Wald in Hollywood.

Wald asked him, formally, to write the script and Schulberg said: 'Fine but I'd like to write it here, where I'm talking from.' At this point Cohn broke in, saying: 'No, no. My writers are on the lot, in my studio nine to five. I don't have writers out in wherever-the-hell place you are – Nohope, Pennsylvania.' And that was the end of it. Schulberg wrote an adaptation of the novel but somebody else wrote the screenplay – at Columbia Studios and not in Nohope, Pennsylvania.

Cohn was probably the most feared and hated man in Hollywood – which is saying a lot – and of all the moguls he was the one who interfered most in production, quarrelling so often with stars, producers and directors that the staff turnover at Columbia was the highest in the industry. For years he was known as "Harry the Horror", a nickname he lost only when Ben Hecht redubbed him "White Fang". And yet . . . It was Cohn who allowed and encouraged Frank Capra to make some of the best and most socially conscious films to come out of Hollywood in the 1930s and 40s. Films like *Mr Deeds Goes to Town* and *Mr Smith Goes to Washington* may have been sentimental comedy-dramas but they espoused the cause of the common man against bureaucracy at a time when Hollywood in general was more concerned with escapism.

Cohn may have been the toughest of the Hollywood moguls but it was a case of primus inter pares: they were all tough, ulcer-givers rather than ulcer-sufferers. And, above all, they loved films. Nearly all of them had come to Hollywood from unexpected directions; they had originally been furriers, glove salesmen and the like but, to quote Richard Brooks, they would 'hug those cans of film as if they were personal pints of blood'. And this was true even in the case of those who knew little about the process of film-making. Of Jack Warner, Hal Wallis said that 'he kept out of the making of the pictures. I don't know whether he read a script or not but he couldn't edit a script or cut a film. He made pictures with a gut feeling.' (Certainly he didn't appear to read books. When he bought the screen rights of *Anthony Adverse* someone in the studio asked: 'Have you read it?' And Warner replied: 'Read it? Hell, I can't even lift it.')

The received opinion of almost all the moguls is that they were monsters and maybe they were. But as Evelyn Keyes said of Harry Cohn: 'First of all, to be the head of something you have to have a drive. I mean, you can't be a nice person. You know? That doesn't mean you have to be an evil person either but you have to punch your way, you have to be strong. So everybody's not gonna love you. Harry knew everybody wasn't going to love him; he'd resigned himself to that.' Yet the indications are that he had done more than simply resign himself to being everybody's least favourite Hollywood mogul – he seemed even to encourage and enjoy his reputation as a mean, hard character. 'Harry did wonderful things. But he didn't want anyone to know. If he did anything nice, if he helped somebody with money, he wouldn't tell. He'd probably say something nasty about that person.'

And again he shared with his fellow tycoons a passion for films. 'He had a screening room off his office and I had the pleasure, and I put it that way, to be in there once in a while when the day's rushes would come up and he'd say, "Come with me; sit there." To see Harry Cohn's face as he watched his film was a pleasure. It was a love, that's what it was – love.'

So there they were, these disparate but similar characters – the moguls. The studios controlled the stars and the moguls controlled the studios. But who controlled the moguls? The answer is: head office in New York. In the public view the studio bosses were the monarchs of the industry but it was the viziers and chamberlains lurking behind the thrones – the money men in their offices in Manhattan – who really held the power. The film business is a neat example of the tail wagging the dog. The films themselves were the dog and therefore they were the important element, right? No, wrong. It was the tail – distribution and exhibition – which represented the most important elements and they were run by head office. It was not Jack Warner in Hollywood but brothers Harry and Albert in New York, not Harry Cohn, the head of the studio, but brother Jack, running administration and sales, not Louis Mayer but Nick Schenck in Manhattan who held the purse strings.

Joseph L. Mankiewicz explained it like this: 'The mythology which is slowly but surely gelling into a sort of history of Hollywood is that of the all-powerful major studios with ruthless men at the head who were endowed with this incredible power. But they were not at all men of incredible power; they were the heads of factories which were built out there in the West and run from the East, where their owners lay. The studio heads did what they were told to do – "We want so many films from you this year." All the fun lies in talking about Louis Mayer did this and Louis Mayer did that but Louis Mayer fought throughout his life to acquire some power. In the end he was fired by his bosses in New York when they thought he was no longer any use to them... For example, Loew's Incorporated owned the factory called Metro-Goldwyn-Mayer. The Fox Theatre chain, an enormous theatre chain, owned 20th Century-Fox. These boards of directors met in New York and that's where the power lay for anything of real importance. Certainly if somebody had been caught raping someone, the head of the studio would get the head of the studio cops to square it with the police but that kind of power is gossip column power.

'However, if Clark Gable's contract were coming up for renewal, New York would send out to Louis B. Mayer a statement, very official, which proved conclusively to anyone who examined it that Loew's had lost a lot of money that year. And this paper would be the one that Louis Mayer had in his desk drawer when Gable came in to talk contract and more money and he'd show it to Clark Gable and before he could make a deal with Clark Gable he had to have the okay from the people in New York. That's why in every studio head's office there was always a little cupboard in which there was a private telephone. And he'd say, "Excuse me a minute; I have to go and wash my hands," and he'd go into the cupboard and he was really talking to New York ... Mayer was powerful in the sense that he had a very short fuse; he was a very quick-tempered man, who could fly into rages. And he had power in a very parochial sense, yes – but only on the lot.'

This convenient system whereby the same parent company owned the factory in which the products were made, the distribution chain which moved them to the point of sale and the cinemas where they were sold and exhibited to the public was – as we shall discover later – eventually to be destroyed, leaving the studios isolated and increasingly weak. But it was this monopoly which made up the strength of the studio system, a system which was constantly criticised and deplored in its time but about which those who once felt they had suffered under it are now much inclined to temper their views.

Joe Mankiewicz again: 'Never in my life would I have thought I could say what I'm about to say now, which is that having grown up, professionally as it were, with the Harry Cohns and the Louis Mayers and the Darryl Zanucks and the Nick Schencks and the Warner brothers ... Well, compared with the people today they were like the Medici as I look back ... The major studios seemed to be able to produce some pretty damned good films and some pretty damned good people.'

And then, too, they offered – give or take the one-sided contracts – security. As Sylvia Sidney put it: 'You finished one film Saturday night, you started another one Monday ... If you wanted to be in movies there were only those big organisations, those big studios ... I think a lot of people were carried over the years because they had to produce so many films, they had to fill those theatres. So there were a lot of secondary stars who maintained stardom who, let's say, today wouldn't make it.' There was also, as George Sidney said, the question of the studios' interest in the development of individuals. 'They were interested to discover what would George Sidney be at twenty-five or forty, what would Lana Turner's career be like, what would Gable's, what would Tracy's ... They were running a business, they were servicing the world. The world had a big appetite and they were a big restaurant and they were serving the food up.'

For everyone there was a comforting sense of continuity – of employment, of build-up, of opportunity. If the last film didn't work the next one might and there would, for most people anyway, always be a next one. Vincent Sherman said: 'When

Ava Gardner, signed by
MGM at sixteen and
groomed for stardom at
twenty-one

you have the means of production, distribution and exhibition all owned by the same company you've got an industry. You had big lists of contract writers, contract producers, contract directors, contract stars so in that sense it was very efficient. I thought it was great. Although I was one of those who used to say, "Wouldn't it be nice if we could do so and so and didn't have to worry about the studio", I'm not so sure that the break up achieved any great progress. I thought the old studio system was pretty damn good. Maybe those were the golden days of Hollywood, you know, because when you got a script you went to work on it, you didn't have to worry about how or where to raise the money or who was going to be in it because you had a bank of stars to choose from. Today I find that, well, the people who are running the studios are not what I call exactly picture-makers or creators: they're more business-men – lawyers, accountants, promoters and so forth . . . The moguls, they grew up with the business; they started with two-reelers and they took all kinds of short cuts and they loved film. They came here young men, immigrants mostly, they had that dream of America and they put that dream into their films . . . They expressed the American ideal, I think, and they built a tremendous industry.'

Well, the colour of nostalgia is rose, the colour indeed of the spectacles through which people tend to look back at the past. Even Budd Schulberg, whose Hollywood experiences were not always of the happiest, thinks now with mild regret of the old studio system. In his time he was extremely critical of those moguls, not just Harry Cohn but also Louis Mayer who, when Schulberg wrote *What Makes Sammy Run*, a scathing insight into the mores and politics of Hollywood, tried to have him run out of town for disloyalty. 'He said I'd never work there again. In a way I was blacklisted before there was a blacklist.' But now, well now . . . 'Without any question it was not as bad as I thought at the time. As I look back I think even of men like Harry Cohn, whom I couldn't stand, who would give people their head. They were bigger gamblers. They didn't say, "Well, let's test the market," and make complicated examinations à la all the computerised big business methods of today, trying to find out in advance something you absolutely cannot find out. I don't care how scientific you get, you'll never be able to read the public's mind and tell what kind of pictures they want to see. But in those days they didn't worry about testing the water: they went on their hunches. They were gamblers and they rolled the dice and as I look back on them I begin to feel a certain nostalgia which, I must say, I never had before.'

Even Stanley Kramer, always one of the most independent-minded of pro-ducers, acknowledges regret at the passing of the system. 'I dealt with some of the real heavies of all time and by heavies I mean villains. I don't want to blast their memories but, I mean, Harry Cohn was a tough feller, Jack Warner was a tough feller, Louis Mayer was no angel. But what I miss, what they represented in the studio system, was a bringing together of talent . . . There was an aura and there was talent and I miss that. There's none of that now, none of it. There are no stars comparatively. How many could you name – half a dozen? – who are part of the tradition. But there used to be 180 stars.'

In a sense, of course, stars who had been under contract to one studio for a long time became more or less institutionalised. Anne Baxter left Fox after fourteen years and 'it was like jumping into an empty pool. I was afraid. I'd been under that lovely umbrella – it was like belonging to something. It's like leaving home or leaving a marriage that wasn't entirely happy – it's still scary.'

One of the criticisms most frequently levelled at the old system was that it led to each studio developing its own consistent house style and stamping out originality. To an extent that was true – each studio did have its own style: an MGM picture was unmistakably an MGM picture, just as the kind of *film noir* that Warner Brothers produced could not easily be matched elsewhere. But again the old, so-called slaves of the system are inclined to rally to its defence. The director Edward Dmytryk said: 'How much originality do you see today? We made a lot of crap in those days, just as they do today but I think we made a slightly larger percentage of good stuff because we were allowed to. If a studio made sixty pictures a year, they averaged out. It could afford to make what they used to call "prestige pictures". They could afford to make three or four prestige films a year, even if they lost money. They'd make it back on all the other stuff. You don't have that today . . .'

What Dmytryk believed film makers miss nowadays is the continuity. 'I could get a contract at Fox and I knew that, well, I had at least five, six, seven years to go and I could plan my thing. I could say, "No, I don't want to do this film and yes, I want to do that one," and I wasn't worried if I was finishing a film and didn't have another to start on. You know, not only directors and actors but everybody – that's the great illness they go through today, even the very successful ones. Take Michael Caine. He's a millionaire. He finishes one film and three days later he's saying, "Jesus Christ, I'm outa work. I gotta work." Richard Burton was like that – "I gotta make a film" (it didn't matter what it was), "I gotta make a film." We didn't have to do that in those days. We could plan ahead and we didn't have to worry about money. If the studio and I agreed on a film I wanted to make – say, *The Caine Mutiny* or *The Young Lions* – they said, "We'll finance it up to this point." I knew I had the money, I didn't have to worry about whether it was coming. And I knew, we all knew, that I didn't have to worry about the thing when it was released, or not too much. We knew it wasn't going to be a desperate flop or whatever. But today everything is a gamble.' (They knew it wouldn't be a desperate flop because even if it turned out very badly, the studio would simply put it together with a guaranteed hit – the latest Gable picture perhaps – and foist it on the exhibitors as an obligatory double bill.)

Today, too, the opportunities for the would-be stars are strictly limited. But under the studio system there were the screen tests – plentiful, regular and, said George Sidney, "very, very important", because stars were the industry's life blood and Mayer particularly felt there could never be too many of them. And if an actor failed one screen test he could always have another elsewhere. Sidney found one young man who impressed him and put him in a test with a girl in whom MGM were interested. 'The next day the studio said, "Why'd you use a midget? That man you used in the test, he's a midget." I said, "No, but listen he's strong, he's . . . and he's blond . . ." and the studio said, "There can be no blond leading men. That is the law." So the test went over to Paramount and Frank Tuttle, who was directing a film there, said, "This is the man I want," and his name was Alan Ladd.' (Ladd wasn't actually a midget but he was very short and he did, literally, have to stand on a box when playing scenes with tall leading ladies.) Sidney also made a test of a girl from Texas called 'Clara-Lou something. And they said, "Ahh, she's too sexy. We don't want that kind of thing here," and the test went over to Warner Brothers and someone decided to call her "The Oomph Girl" and that was Ann Sheridan. There are many stories like that. Marilyn Monroe was at practically every studio in this town and no one said, "Wait a minute, there's a quality there..."' Well, somebody did eventually, of course, but only perhaps because there was a studio system, a large output of films and a constant need for new faces. Can we really be sure that a girl like Monroe, who drifted unwanted – except physically – from studio to studio would one day become a star under present conditions?

Oh, naturally, there were drawbacks even in that golden age. For a start, a year's contract only meant forty weeks pay, not fifty-two. If you were on, say, 1,000 dollars a week you earned 40,000 dollars a year, not 52,000. And there are certain aspects of the studio system which some people now praise and would like to recapture that are deeply deplored by others. Cornel Wilde said: 'The policy at Warner Brothers was that if you were being paid, you worked no matter what and that was a very big shock to me.' It was the "no matter what" not the necessity to work that shocked him. Mr Wilde had gone to Hollywood from the theatre, having been plucked out of a production in which he was playing Tybalt to Laurence Olivier's Romeo and Vivien Leigh's Juliet and so perhaps he had loftier ideas than the average young movie actor. Besides he had been made attractive promises that were never kept. 'Warners told me that, confidentially (though it wasn't confidential at all) they were having trouble with John Garfield, who was a big star, and that they saw in me a taller, better-looking John Garfield. They felt that I could do any role he could plus others that he couldn't do – like Shakespeare. And then they made up with Garfield and all the things that might have happened didn't happen. They just used me as they did every other actor in any role that I could possibly play – because I was being paid.'

It was tough at Warners, he said – very difficult. And it would have been the same at Columbia. 'They wanted you to do what they thought was commercial and that was that.' Like so many other actors he felt he would have been much better off at Fox or, best of all, at MGM. Indeed, after Warners dropped him he found it *was* much the same at Columbia and that despite the fact that they took him on when no other studio would. 'I was turned down by everyone. I was told I couldn't be a leading man, that I looked too dangerous, my skin was too yellow and my hair was too curly.' Eventually Fox signed him and lent him out to Columbia to make *A Song to Remember* which he remembers with affection because, although it was universally derided by the critics, it did make him a star and increased his fan mail from 300 to 10,000 letters a month. It also brought him an Oscar nomination as best actor. But Columbia, he said, like Warners made the films they believed would bring in the most money and while he was there he was usually typecast in period pieces.

Well, the studio system, like any other, had its advantages and its disadvantages but what it did achieve, incontrovertibly, was the creation of Hollywood as the movie capital of the world. And when a combination of anti-trust laws and economic circumstances brought about the destruction of the studio system and with it the star system, it landed a blow from which the film industry has never really recovered. The past always has a tendency to look more attractive the further away you move from it but those who now look back on the Hollywood of the 1930s, 40s and early 50s with nostalgia and regret for its passing are certainly looking back on what, for all its faults, was indeed a golden age for film makers; an age which perhaps could only have existed when it did and which can never come again.

Mamie van Doren and Rock Hudson. 'If he's going out with *her* he can't be gay'

THREE

HOLLYWOOD AND SEX

The cinema discovered sex at about the same time as it discovered the moving picture, although in the first context "discovered" is perhaps a little strong since there is considerable evidence that the human race in general had known quite a lot about sex for some while. But what the cinema discovered (or rather rediscovered for this, too, had certainly been well-known to writers and popular entertainers) was that sex equals cash at the box office, a fact swiftly demonstrated to the infant movie industry.

At an early board meeting of the Biograph Company in the 1890s it was revealed that while, on one particular day, certain films of a moral and uplifting nature had taken sums comfortably in excess of 20 cents and the story of a ballet dancer had soared through the one-dollar barrier, a picture entitled *Girl Climbing Tree* – an accurate description because climbing a tree was all she did, plots being rather basic in those days – had earned all of 3 dollars and 65 cents. This announcement led one of the assembled directors to remark thoughtfully: 'I think we'd better have some more of the *Girl Climbing Tree* kind.'

And so they did and so did all their competitors. Indeed, one of the best-known of early films was *The Kiss*, the main feature of which was one May Irwin inhaling a kiss through the soup-strainer moustache of John C. Rice. Even spicier offerings were soon to follow; *How Bridget Served the Salad Undressed* (Bridget, you understand, being a serving wench a touch slow on the uptake) and *Dolorita's Passion Dance* attracted much enthusiastic appreciation. But through the ages Sex's constant companion has been Censorship, a glum, cadaverous fellow dressed in black, for ever shaking his head and sucking his teeth in sharp disapproval of his more skittish partner's behaviour and the cinema was not long to be free of his attentions. No sooner had Dolorita attempted to follow up her passion dance with a "Houchi Kouchi" than the traditional blue pencil made its appearance. *Dolorita's Houchi Kouchi* was banned and around 1903 an even more extraordinary fate befell a certain Fatima, whose belly dance when seen in peepshow form was apparently deemed acceptable but when projected and enlarged beyond lifesize was thought to pose a moral danger to the populace. Censorship decreed that a white, fence-like superimposition should cover the screen, or certainly the offending belly. This is one of the earliest examples of the dottiness of censorship because in fact what this superimposition did was to highlight Fatima's navel.

Nevertheless, it was already becoming clear that henceforth the light footsteps of sex in the movies would be rendered a great deal less light by the censor's ball and chain. What were also emerging, even then, were the patterns – the motifs – that would dominate the censorship question right up to the present day. Especially in the earlier years films were essentially a working-class entertainment and it has always been the self-imposed duty of the upper and middle classes to protect the lower orders from their own base instincts. Thus, while it hardly needed saying that neither Dolorita's "Houchi Kouchi" nor Fatima's belly dance could possibly corrupt the educated or the well-born they would certainly inflame servants, labourers, shop girls and the like to unimaginable lust. Bad enough if such things were viewed in private but they were not – they were shown in public places of entertainment, often to quite large gatherings of people, where depravity, it was argued, could spread like an epidemic. Even something as innocuous as *The Kiss* was thought, in some quarters, to place the onlooker in peril.

And as censorship started in the movies so it was to continue, doggedly protecting people who, for the most part, deeply resented that protection. In such circumstances it was inevitable that the sex film would continue to thrive and just as inevitable that it would be under constant attack. The protected carried on giving their approval to pictures like *The Flatiron Building on a Windy Day*, which afforded tantalising glimpses of ladies' knickers, and to a series of risqué imports from foreign parts, especially France where, as all America knew, nobody ever thought about anything except sex. And the protectors continued to strike back. In 1907 Chicago passed the first legislation dealing specifically with motion pictures; in 1909 New York actually went so far as to close its nickelodeons; in the same year the film industry, realising that a little togetherness was necessary in the face of the onslaught, formed the National Board of Censorship of Motion Pictures. Its aim was to forestall external censorship legislation and in that it was the ancestor of all other such industry watchdogs from the Hays and Production Codes to the Classification categories of the late 1960s.

Despite all these goings-on, however, sex in the movies began to get seamier and in 1913 the first American exploitation picture appeared – *Traffic in Souls*, an exposé of the white slave trade much inspired by the success of imported Danish films on the same subject. It was an immediate box office success and was therefore swiftly imitated. Then, a logical progression I suppose from stories about brothels, came a number of films dealing with syphilis, the forerunner being *Damaged Goods*, which artfully made itself respectable by being accompanied by an earnest lecture on the subject from a medical man. Abortion was also given its place in the limelight in such productions as *Where are My Children?* and *Motherhood*.

All those films would seem pretty innocuous today but in their time they caused grave concern to the guardians of morality and indeed to the law. In a crucial decision in 1915, the Supreme Court, ruling against the Mutual Film Corporation, decided that 'the exhibition of motion pictures is a business, pure and simple' and in so deciding deprived films of the protection of the First Amendment, which guaranteed freedom of speech. What that meant was that the cinema was precluded from the liberty afforded to the press, literature and the stage and that movies were liable to *prior restraint* from local censorship boards. This situation, which prevailed until the

1950s, virtually excluded films in America from any consideration as art and, after the Second World War, proved a severe handicap to movie makers who wished to tackle weightier and more mature subjects.

In the second decade of the century, however, the industry – undeterred by the Supreme Court – proceeded to creep up on sex from a different direction and in 1915 the vamp was introduced in the person of one Theodosia Goodman, a tailor's daughter from Cincinnati. Not that the movie audience knew her as such. To them plump, Jewish Miss Goodman was presented as equally plump Theda Bara, the daughter – would you believe? – of an Arabian princess from the Nile, a femme fatale born under the shadow of the Sphinx and weaned on the blood of vipers. (To have made her as well-rounded as she became vipers' blood must be packed with calories.) The fact that her screen name was an anagram of Arab Death probably served only to add to the mystery and the exoticism. The figure of the vamp owed her origin partly to a painting by Philip Burne-Jones and partly to Kipling's poem "The Vampire" – 'A fool there was and he made his prayer (Even as you and I!), To a rag and bone and a hank of hair . . .' That poem inspired a successful Broadway play which, in turn, became Theda Bara's first (and, to be honest, only) smash hit movie, *A Fool There Was*. In it, she played a woman of enormous sexual power and, of course, because American girls couldn't possibly be so wicked, foreign extraction who treated men with disdain and contempt and humiliated her married lover in front of his wife and family with the deathless line, 'Kiss me, my fool.'

The most significant outcome of that film was that it caused the producer, William Fox, to form his own company which in the fullness of time became 20th Century-Fox. Otherwise, it spawned as all lucrative films do a number of imitators but none of them lasted long and, come to that, neither did Miss Bara. Her career was virtually over by 1920 and so was that of the vamp. One great problem was the insurmountable difficulty of reconciling the seductive, almost evil, screen image with the faithful, home-loving body that the public insisted their stars should be in private life.

Even so the vamp's moody, broody, heavy-lidded gaze became a stereotype of female sexuality in the cinema and remained that way for decades. There's really not a lot of difference between Theda Bara's slow burn from half-closed eyes and the steamy pout of Jane Russell in *The Outlaw* and, later, Marilyn Monroe in a million publicity stills.

However, running concurrently with the vamp there appeared a more sophisticated kind of sex in the movies. The cinemas were now beginning to attract the middle classes and nickelodeons were being replaced by loftier creations called picture palaces. Foremost among the film makers pandering to this more knowing audience was Cecil B. de Mille who had discovered, with a picture called *The Cheat* in 1916, that there was a lot of mileage to be extracted from the notion of a nice girl pretending to be a vamp. The advantages of this were enormous: given proper reasons – the winning back of a reluctant spouse, perhaps – the heroine, or hero, could get up to all kinds of naughty things so long as in the end (the very end) it could be thought that they hadn't really enjoyed themselves. This massive hypocrisy pleased-the audiences and somehow seemed to satisfy the censors. In a series of films (*Old Wives for New* and *Forbidden Fruit*, for example) stretching into the 1920s de Mille, while pretending to deplore the immorality of the Jazz Age, was able to provide unlimited titillation while, at the same time, introducing hitherto undreamed of luxury to the screen – actresses (Gloria Swanson in particular) draped in exotically revealing creations, bedrooms done up like something out of a high-class bordello and bathrooms: bathrooms as big as ballrooms, bathrooms with huge sunken tubs and handmaidens hanging around with warm towels. It cannot be said that de Mille actually invented the bathroom but at a time when not everybody had such things he instilled in the populace at large a yearning to own one.

De Mille, though, was not without his rivals. Ernst Lubitsch and Erich von Stroheim came from Germany to give, if anything, an even more wicked edge to sophisticated sex. And they, especially von Stroheim, got away with it by exploiting the American conviction that Europeans were altogether sexier and more decadent than anyone reared in the good old US of A could ever wet-dream of being. And given the premise that all this adultery, fetishism and all-round depravity was going on in Europe, a continent lost to any hope of redemption anyway, von Stroheim was able to rattle along for some time without let or hindrance, both as director and – playing the irresistible lover – as actor. In *Queen Kelly* (which, for financial reasons and the disenchantment of the star, was never finished) he had Gloria Swanson remove her knickers and throw them at an army officer, who picked them up and caressed his face with them, the kind of gesture which later would not be permitted for several decades. And in another film von Stroheim himself is seen to sniff lustily at his own middle finger, an action which is never explained but which does lead the audience to wonder idly where that finger might have been.

Another equally passionate but on the whole purer kind of sex was peddled by Rudolph Valentino who dealt in dreams, specifically women's dreams of being swept off their feet and carried away (preferably into a desert) by an archetypal Latin lover. Men didn't think much of Valentino, regarding him as unfair competition. But women treated him with a kind of unbridled, hysterical adulation that would not be equalled until the emergence of the Beatles. When he died in 1926 his funeral was the occasion for scenes of unparalleled frightfulness with screaming, sobbing women fighting to get even a glimpse of the proceedings. To men, John Gilbert was a more acceptable screen lover; to start with he was an American and besides he didn't go in for all that sweeping and carrying off. But even about him they had their doubts and in fact it was not until the sound era and the rise of Clark Gable that there arrived a screen hero whom men could admire as much as women did. But then sound changed many things and it could be argued that Valentino died at exactly the right time because the chances are that he would never have survived in talkies.

Meanwhile, the New Woman had appeared on the scene, women having been given the vote and consequently greater freedom in 1919. And in her wake came the Jazz Baby, the flapper (exemplified by Colleen Moore) and the "It Girl" (Clara Bow). What they had in common was a desire to overthrow the old conventions and introduce a single moral standard for men and women. The likes of Gloria Swanson

Theda Bara, the original vamp, doing a heavy-lidded moody in *The Soul of Bhudda*
Inset: It looks no more than a friendly peck these days. But in 1896 *The Kiss* caused a positive scandal

and Joan Crawford were also part of this movement, creating a startling new image of fast-living young women, who smoked and drank and flirted. And significantly the women they portrayed doing these things were often working-class girls: manicurists, waitresses, usherettes. In the past only middle-class women were allowed to enjoy themselves in films. Even so, the Jazz Baby was not permitted to go too far; if she did there had to be a scene in the final reel in which she apologised brokenly for her misdemeanours, received the gracious forgiveness of her father and probably promised to marry the boy next door. Later on as the euphoria of the Jazz Age passed and the grimmer reality of the Depression settled in, "chorus girls" would not get off so lightly. But then "chorus girl" was often a euphemism for prostitute and in the cinema prostitutes had to pay the price.

On the whole sex and sex appeal provided the prime motif of Hollywood films in the 1920s but while this was good for the box office it had unwanted and unforeseen side effects, for Hollywood itself came to be seen as a place of iniquity. And this view was reinforced by a series of scandals – the suicide in 1920 of Olive Thomas, Mary Pickford's sister-in-law; the unsolved murder of the director William Desmond Taylor in 1922, in which Mary Miles Minter and Mabel Normand were said to be implicated; the revelation after his death that Wallace Reid had been a drug addict. And, of course, most sensational of all was the Fatty Arbuckle case, a gross miscarriage of justice in which the fat comedian was charged with the manslaughter, during a weekend party in 1921 which may or may not have been a drunken orgy, of a starlet named Virginia Rappe. The case went to court three times and in the third trial Arbuckle was acquitted and exonerated. He should never have been charged in the first place – but a small consolation that was because, acquittal and exoneration or not, he was railroaded out of the business, a scapegoat offered up by Hollywood to appease the forces of moral disapproval.

These and other scandals involving sex and drugs had thrown the industry into a mild panic, fearing that their affairs might come under the scrutiny of a federal investigation. So to ward off any such danger Hollywood appointed Will H. Hays as a kind of commissar to help them clean up their act. In the Harding administration, Hays had been Postmaster General; he was a skilled lobbyist and organiser and he took his job – essentially to be the industry's mouthpiece in Washington and with the press – very seriously indeed. He believed firmly in the movies as mass entertainment and disapproved of anything unsuitable for a family audience. In his acceptance speech he urged the industry to take the same care as any clergyman or teacher of that 'virgin thing, that sacred thing, that unmarked slate – the mind of a child'. And everyone said "Hear, hear" to that because who the hell was making films for children anyway? In the appointment of Hays, as in much else to do with Hollywood, there was a marked decree of hypocrisy. On both sides, I fancy. Because although Hays, prompted by the William Desmond Taylor murder, introduced the famed (or notorious) "morality clause" into contracts and initially demanded that books, scripts and screenplays should be submitted to his office for approval before they could be filmed, he soon began to back down. The approval of scripts proved unworkable and in 1927 he replaced that notion with a list of Do's and Don'ts, which was sufficiently vague to allow smart writers and directors to pay it lip service and little more. In 1930 the list of guidelines was formalised into the Hays Office Code but that had very little effect either. Certainly in those early days the chief accomplishment of the Hays Office was that by presenting itself as Hollywood's own self-censoring body it prevented a number of communities from setting up censorship boards of their own. And it was the multiplicity of these local censoring boards, all with different standards of what was and was not acceptable, that provided the industry with its biggest bugbear.

Still, censorship was having some degree of effect, however much the rules were bent, possibly because it was a fairly simple business that did not amount to very much more than general exhortations to film makers not to show crime sympatheti- cally, to uphold the sanctity of marriage and to avoid explicitly treating of sex or "low forms of sex relationships". But the stronger producers in particular could circum- vent any or all of these rules if eighty-five minutes of screentime sin were followed by five minutes of redemption. Typically, the main sufferers were not those who exploited sex and violence but the people who laboured under the misapprehension that the cinema was serious and important and so sought to tackle serious and important matters. D. W. Griffith was a prime example. Labour pains were censored from *Way Down East*, and *The White Rose* was banned in a few states because of its theme of a hypocritical clergyman seducing an orphan. For the most part Hays could head off that kind of state intervention but equally, once he became established he was most unlikely to let such bothersome subjects reach the screen anyway. Practi- cally from the start the censors and guardians of our morals have considered the cinema to be at its most dangerous when it's at its most serious.

If one were to seek an encapsulation of the Hays Office credo it could perhaps be best found in the advice given by one writer, Herman Mankiewicz, to another, Ben Hecht, on the latter's arrival in Hollywood in 1927: 'In a movie . . . the hero, as well as the heroine, has to be a virgin. The villain can lay anybody he wants, have as much fun as he wants, cheating and stealing, getting rich and whipping the servants. But you have to shoot him in the end.' Hecht, taking this to heart, determined that as far as possible he would concentrate on writing films about villains because it seemed more honest.

The arrival, almost simultaneously, of sound and the Depression, made the Mankiewicz dictum even more valid. The aftermath of the Wall Street crash had understandably changed the mood of the nation; Jazz Age frivolity no longer seemed quite appropriate somehow; life was real and life was earnest and the movies began to reflect that. To some extent they were influenced by the new influx to Hollywood of writers attracted by the possibilities of talking pictures – journalists, novelists, playwrights who, in their previous works, had never been bound by the charming but, alas, Utopian notion that virtue is always rewarded and crime doesn't pay. They learned, though. Yes, they were able to inject a gritty realism into the films of the early thirties – up to a point, Lord Copper; for the hero was still a virgin and the heavy had to be shot in the end.

But in a variety of other ways it was possible to circumvent the Hays Code: there was an increase of brutality and violence in such gangster movies as *Public Enemy* and *Scarface*; a fair bit of horizontal lovemaking went on; preparations for bed were lingered over; cinematically taboo activities such as extra-marital shenanigans and prostitution (either overt or covert in pictures like *Faithless*, *Back Street* and *Call Her Savage*, had a tendency to crop up rather more often than Mr Hays would have liked; and comedies were still taking a frank approach to sex.

Of course the moralists disapproved but the climate of opinion was not in their favour. The mood throughout the country was one of cynicism and even despair; moviegoers were not interested in palliatives and placebos – they wanted films that mirrored their own plight, their own frustrations. At the tail end of the Jazz Age films showed prostitution as a means whereby girls could get their share of the good life, a shortcut to the American Dream. But by the early thirties taking to the streets had become a last, desperate way to earn a living. In 1930 twenty per cent of America's ten million working women were unemployed but in one in six urban families the only wage-earners were women – and they were paid sixty per cent less than men anyway. For a good many of them sex for sale was a necessary sideline and as in life, so in the movies. Abandoned or unmarried mothers making ends meet in the oldest profession known to mankind began to make an appearance on the screen. In *Blonde Venus*, Dietrich takes her baby with her onto the streets, an ill-advised move one would have thought, and in *Faithless* Tallulah Bankhead, her lover dead, dashes out and propositions the first man she meets. The censors and the moralists didn't like any of this but how could they argue that such films were likely to deprave and corrupt when, to a large extent, they were merely reporting on what was happening throughout the country? Well, actually, they did so argue in newspaper editorials and the like but not at first to any great effect. Nor, until the repeal of the Volstead Act, were they able to persuade cinema audiences to join them in deploring the frequent depiction of gangsters as rather glamorous figures. The public, always more sensible than politicians, had known from the start that Prohibition was a nonsense and tended to regard bootleggers not as villains but as public benefactors performing a vital social service.

The early 1930s, with the mood and content of films undergoing a radical change and the studios – like every other business in America – struggling to survive, were indeed a turbulent time. With the Valentinos and the Gilberts either dead or swept aside, Clark Gable emerged as the epitome of the all-American male, a man of rugged sexuality not to be trifled with by anyone of either sex. The image of Gable, carefully fostered by MGM, was the image of "the regular guy", one who was just as happy when out hunting and fishing with the boys as when he was having his will of some luscious, melting female. And he was remarkably open-handed in his treatment of women. Tramps and heiresses came alike to him; he greeted them all with the same lop-sided grin, handled them (physically as well as metaphorically) with rough and ready charm and was not above slapping them around if, in his opinion, they had stepped out of line. There was nothing smooth about Gable the screen lover, nor could he be socially classified. In the egalitarian society of America he was just as acceptable when manhandling the lofty Norma Shearer in *A Free Soul*, playing the chauffeur in *Night Nurse,* cavorting with the bold and brassy Jean Harlow in the bath scene in *Red Dust,* playing the reporter wooing wealthy and well-born Claudette Colbert in *It Happened One Night* or, as Rhett Butler, telling wilful Vivien Leigh that frankly, his dear, he didn't give a damn. In the new realism of the early thirties Gable was, as Norma Shearer said, "a new kind of man" and though his appeal was frankly sexual, MGM saw to it that it was so carefully projected as not to cause offence.

On the distaff side, female sexuality was on offer from a variety of sources – Crawford, Stanwyck (though really their time was yet to come), Shearer, Colbert . . . But the Queen of them all was still Garbo who was, and remains, the outstanding woman star in the history of the cinema. Her contribution to sex was a noble spirituality; she suffered a lot (and Hays and his Code approved of that). And when men set out to woo her they really had to work at it – they had to be pretty keen, too, because her attitude usually seemed to suggest from the start that no good could possibly come of all this and more often than not she was right. The overwhelming impression I have of Garbo pictures is one of loss, her loss. Two scenes from *Queen Christina* sum it all up. The first is when remembering her three nights of passion with John Gilbert – nights which, of course, will never be repeated – she goes through the room touching everything to implant it all for ever in her memory. (Rouben Mamoulian, who directed her in that film, made her move to a metronome to catch the right rhythm.) And the second is at the end when she sails away, staring out to sea, giving a very fair impression of the figurehead on a sloop. By design the expression of her face was one of – nothing. Mamoulian said: 'For weeks I couldn't solve the ending and then it came to me. When Garbo said to me, "What do I act at the end?", I said, "You come to the front and you act nothing, because no matter what you act you'll split the audience. If you smile they'll say, 'What on earth is she smiling at?' If you cry, they'll say 'What a weak woman'. No matter what you do there'll be a fragmentation of the audience but what we want at the end is to have the whole audience with us, as one." And I said "The only way to do it is you walk up, you stay there, you think of nothing, you don't blink, you become a mask and let every spectator write his own feelings in. Then you can't go wrong, because they are the authors." And that's what she did.' Even Louis Mayer was convinced and that wasn't easy because Mayer was essentially a happy-ending man. Garbo was, by common consent, great but she was not always popular at the box office, suffering spirituality not being everybody's cup of tea. But on the other hand her brand of subtle sex kept her away from trouble with the censors until, ironically, the very end of her career when her last film, *Two-Faced Woman,* was condemned by the Catholic Legion of Decency in 1941. It was a ludicrous story anyway in which she played a ski instructress who pretended to be her own twin sister to revive the flagging affections of her husband. *Time* magazine said of it: 'It is almost as shocking as seeing your mother drunk.' Not surprisingly it flopped at the box office and Garbo promptly retired, being financially cushioned by shrewd investments which had left her untouched by the Depression.

The failure of the film was the accepted reason for Garbo's retirement but Dore Schary, once head of MGM, had another version. Garbo was thirty-six when she made *Two-Faced Woman* and the cinematographer, Joseph Ruttenberg, was fifty-two. The Schary story, as he told it to me, went like this: one day Garbo, the director George Cukor and various acolytes went into the studio viewing theatre to have a look at the rushes. When they had finished, Garbo said: 'What on earth is the matter with Joseph? He makes me look so awful!' There was a moment's tactful silence and then somebody said. 'Well, Greta, Joseph's getting older, you know . . .' Garbo took the hint.

Rouben Mamoulian also directed (in *Song of Songs*, 1933) the other great European sex goddess of the time, Marlene Dietrich. Of Garbo he said: 'She was blessed with the most cinematic face that ever was. I was making tests of her because I wanted to know how to light her and no matter what I did, the result was beautiful. So I told Bill Daniels (Garbo's favourite lighting cameraman), I said. "Let's try and ruin it." So we photographed her with incredible lights, this way, that way . . . But no matter what you do, that face is beautiful. People see more in it than actually is there. It's one of those miraculous things. Also, she was very intuitive.' By contrast, Dietrich he thought was 'a great trouper, very logical, very reasoning. You had to explain things to her and you had to light her properly.' What was special about her, he said, was "the image, her personality". Dietrich, of course, had arrived in America sizzling hot on the strength of her performance as Lola-Lola in *The Blue Angel*. Her screen image was much raunchier than Garbo's, far more that of the blatant femme fatale but possibly because she was pointed in the wrong direction by her pet director Joseph von Sternberg and others, or possibly for fear of offending the Code, she never quite made the impact in Hollywood that she might have done. She had the most amazing legs and an intriguing touch of sexual ambivalence – in her first American film, *Morocco*, in which she co-starred with Gary Cooper, she kisses another girl on the lips while attired in full masculine evening dress of top hat and tails. Well, this was dangerous stuff in 1930; possibly too dangerous because while it helped to win, and retain, for her the abiding devotion of the homosexual audience she nevertheless toned down her act considerably after that and her career was drifting nowhere in particular until it was revived by her role as the archetypal golden-hearted tart in *Destry Rides Again* in 1939.

Of the American sexpots in those early thirties the most spectacular was the ill-fated Jean Harlow, who died in 1937 aged twenty-six. On screen she was flashy and tarty, the original platinum blonde. (It was said that she even dyed her pubic hair that shade, possibly in the interests of providing a uniform colour scheme but possibly, too, because she was alleged not to bother with underwear and didn't want a kind of five o'clock shadow peeping through.) Off screen, she was entirely different – though still platinum blonde – and was, in fact, one of the best-liked stars in Hollywood; the news of her death was greeted by a two-minute silence in almost every studio. But her great forté as an actress was to make sex funny and comedy sexy and in that she was the direct forerunner of Marilyn Monroe.

In many ways, however, the most significant actress of that time was Mae West. Three things conspired to bring about an end to the somewhat laissez-faire relationship the film industry had enjoyed with the censor since the announcement of the

Hays Office Code in 1930: Roosevelt's New Deal which called for an end to despair and cynicism and more or less insisted upon a new mood of hope and idealism; the publication of a best-selling book, *Our Movie-Made Children* in 1933, which pointed out for the first time (certainly the first time in a serious, quasi-sociological manner) that films did have an impact and an effect on people, especially on the young and impressionable and this effect, being often adverse, could lead them to reject traditional values; and Mae West.

In 1933 Paramount was in the hands of the receiver and all seemed lost. Then along came Mae West, selling sex with the subtlety of a fairground barker. She was already forty-one, no age now when the sex symbols of TV are nearly all in the old boiler bracket but positively ancient in an age in which generally speaking, women were thought to be dried up at thirty. Her first film for Paramount was *Night After Night*, notable for such exchanges as: 'Goodness, what lovely diamonds.' – 'Goodness had nothing to do with it, honey.' (The punchline, of course, is delivered by Miss West.) But the pictures that literally saved the company and kept it in business were *She Done Him Wrong* and *I'm No Angel*. The poster for the latter contained the line 'hitting the high spots of lusty entertainment'. When Adolph Zukor read that he summoned the studio publicity man, Arthur Mayer, and complained about the word "lusty". Mayer explained, ingenuously, that it derived from the German "lustig", meaning "merry", "jolly", "amusing" and the like. Zukor listened patiently, sighed and said: 'Mayer, one look at that dame's tits and I know what the word "lusty" means.'

And so did the censor. And the censor didn't like it. Actually, he didn't like anything much about Mae West: he didn't like the way she parodied sex with her outrageously padded bosom and hips; he didn't like the way she made fun of it and particularly the hypocrisy surrounding it; he didn't like the fact that she represented the sort of woman who actively enjoyed sex in exactly the way a man might; he didn't like her air of independence, assurance and equality; and perhaps he particularly disliked the fact that unlike other naughty girls/women in films she never seemed to have to get married in the last reel.

John Bright, one of her two co-writers on the screenplay of *She Done Him Wrong* (adapted from Mae West's own Broadway hit *Diamond Lil*) didn't like her much either but for different reasons. In the first place, he said, she claimed the credit for all the best lines, even when they were his. 'I had to say to her, "Now, as you said ..." and then I'd give her one of my own lines and she believed it was hers. She was an astonishing person in many ways. She made no bones about her sex life, which consisted of musclemen and black prizefighters ...' Mind you, he did acknowledge that at least some of the memorable West gags were her own work – 'She had a talent for the one-liner.' He admitted, too, that it was her 'astonishing personality that made the film a hit – a hit, not a work of art'. He got on well with her, he said, but they argued every day and she threw him off the picture as he was writing the last scene of the script, a script which in its own way was a work of art since the Hays Office passed it – on paper – with blessings and only grew livid when it saw the result on celluloid.

'Now the cat was out of the bag,' Bright said. 'The innuendoes the film was

83

replete with were not manifest on paper. It was the reading she gave which was obscene . . . She made sex accepted for its own sake with no nonsense or bullshit. Her personality was a celebration of sexuality. She was a pioneer in this respect.'

It would be too much to suggest that Mae West alone was responsible for the moral backlash that was evident in 1933 and 1934 but the unflinching boldness of her films and her screen persona had not passed unnoticed. In any event this backlash effectively finished her career, though John Bright believed there were other reasons for the brevity of her movie stardom. 'I told the head of the studio that if he allowed her to have a free hand with the director, the writer and the stooges she had around her her tenure in Hollywood would be a total of five pictures. This came about.' Well, not quite. Between 1932 and 1943 she actually made ten films. But why was Bright convinced she wouldn't last? Because she wouldn't take advice, he said, and 'because she picked stooges, yes-men, to do her bidding. She wanted to be the big cheese, she wanted to make stooges out of everybody.' Whether or not this was so, it was censorship that, as it were, de-sexed her in the later films and it may be that, for the Hays Office, she was simply the last straw arriving as she did with or in the wake of a spate of films that dealt with prostitution, adultery, premarital sex (*Trouble in Paradise*, 1933), ménages à trois (*Design For Living*, also 1933), skinny dipping (Dolores Del Rio in *Bird of Paradise*, 1932) and the early musicals of Busby Berkeley (*Gold Diggers of 1933*, *Footlight Parade*, *Fashions of 1934*) which revealed unprecedented and much appreciated acreages of female skin.

The Roman Catholics were the first into action, forming the Legion of Decency in late 1933 and proclaiming on their placards: 'An admission to an Indecent Movie is a ticket to hell' – by implication a one-way ticket at that. Well, ten million Catholics pledged to keep away from "indecent movies" and by extension hell was a pretty heavy threat, especially as other religious groups took similar action although without promising quite such dire consequences for frequenting naughty pictures. As ever when faced by the prospect of external censorship the film industry hobbled swiftly into action and introduced some of its own. In 1934 the Breen Office was established to revive the more or less neglected Motion Picture Code of 1930 under a Production Code Administration headed by Joseph Ignatius Breen. The idea of scripts having to be submitted to the censor had not worked under Hays but now it did – for now there was a Seal of Approval to be won. So first the script and then the finished film was shown to the Breen Office and only with that stern body's approval could the seal be gained. Without this nod of consent a movie could only be released by a member of the Motion Picture Producers' Association at the cost of a 25,000 dollar fine. Since all the important theatres were controlled by members of the MPPA, in other words the major companies, no important film was shown without a seal until Otto Preminger's *The Moon is Blue* in 1953.

Meanwhile the Legion of Decency cleared up any doubts about the kind of film that would send its spectators directly to hell without passing "Go" and collecting their £200 by announcing its own classification system which ran the gamut from A (morally unobjectionable for general patronage) to C (condemned – as, presumably, would be the audience). Not to be outdone the Breen Office spelled out its own

Production Code – a mind-boggling list of prohibitions, both vague and specific, which forbade any film to be made which might lower the moral standards of those who saw it ... throw the sympathy of the audience on to the side of sin, crime or wrong-doing ... refer to sex perversion, white slavery, miscegenation, abortion, scenes of childbirth or passion (this latter apparently being particularly harmful to the young and – here follows the Code's own italics – *criminal classes*) and impure love (thus precluding everything except marriage, since impure love was stated to be "outside divine law").

Enough, you think? Ah, but wait. Breen has barely got into his stride yet. Take bedrooms, for example: the depiction of these had to be governed by "good taste and delicacy" because 'certain places are so closely and thoroughly associated with sexual sin that their use must be carefully limited'. Double beds were out for a start and so was any suggestion that a husband might sit on his wife's bed unless he had both feet on the ground. What about kissing then? Kissing was all right, wasn't it? Well, yes, up to a point and so long as it didn't last too long. Eight seconds, Breen thought, was about right for a kiss and even then both participants had to be standing up or anyway definitely not horizontal or anywhere near a bed. Oh, and by the way, if they weren't married to each other not only did they have to abide by all those rules but they mustn't allow their legs to touch under a table.

Is that it, then? No, not quite. You couldn't show naked children – you couldn't even show naked animals, not if there was a danger that someone might catch a glimpse of their sexual organs. And so it went on ... God only knows what frightful images must have been pulsating away in the minds of the people responsible for all this nonsense.

What's more, in practice the Code was often even barmier than it was in theory.

As an example let's return to Garbo and *Two-Faced Woman*. To win back her husband, Melvyn Douglas, she pretends to be her own, sexier sister and with this supposed sister Douglas falls in love. Well, so what? Whoever she may pretend to be she is still his wife and the film has already made it clear that they're married. Ah yes, said the Code, but Douglas doesn't know that this second Garbo is actually the first Garbo in disguise so he *thinks* he's committing adultery. Well now, we can't have that. So the Breen Office insisted on the insertion of a telephone call very early on to inform Douglas of the plot. Thus he is never in doubt: he knows all along that both Garbos are the same Garbo. But the Legion of Decency condemned the whole thing anyway.

Sometimes, too, in their eagerness not to upset the Roman Catholics the Breen Office came on with a religious fury that would have turned Calvin pale and caused a hell-fire preacher to tell them to ease up a bit. In one script, for instance, they wouldn't allow a fallen woman to repent and lead a good life: she had to be seen to *fail* to lead a good life, thus denying the very possibility of redemption and never mind what Christ may have said on the subject.

Now if the industry had stuck rigidly to all these rules it wouldn't have been possible to make anything much sexier or more violent than *Rebecca of Sunnybrook Farm* but, of course, they didn't. They found their own ways to treat taboo subjects

Left: Cecil B. de Mille's *Forbidden Fruit* showing "naughty" Agnes Ayres and her supposedly hidden companion
Below: A naughty touch of sexual ambivalence – Marlene Dietrich in topper and tails in *Morocco*

Left: Clark Gable and Norma Shearer in one of the gentler scenes from *A Free Soul*
Right: The censor disapproved of Mae West. Other men didn't
Inset right: Some of the revealing outfits from Busby Berkeley's *Gold Diggers of 1933*

in such a manner as to circumvent the Code and, perhaps surprisingly, they were not always and not altogether unhappy about censorship. 'I'll tell you something that might sound strange to you,' said Rouben Mamoulian, 'but occasionally I didn't mind it and I'll tell you why: because when the censor objects to something it makes you think and suddenly you invent a different way of doing it that is much more interesting, much more erotic and can't be censored.'

He cited, as an example, the difficulties he encountered in 1948 when he was directing *Summer Holiday*, a musical version of Eugene O'Neill's *Ah Wilderness*. In particular there was the scene in which the boy, Mickey Rooney, having just returned from an encounter with a prostitute is lectured by his father, Walter Huston, on the dangers of disease. The Breen Office was horrified . . . 'You must cut this where it says "naked", cut this where it says "disease", cut this where it says . . .' Mamoulian said: 'But that's O'Neill. My God, he's the greatest living American playwright!' It made no difference – until Mamoulian had an inspiration and seizing the script said: 'Look, I'll tell you what I'll do: I'll cut out the second half of every sentence.' Now the Breen Office was horrified for a different reason. 'You don't have to go that far,' they said, 'that's O'Neill!'

'Oh, I'd like to,' said Mamoulian, 'I'd like to have you completely satisfied. I don't know whether O'Neill will like it but that's what I'll do.' And he did. And as he pointed out to me, by condensing the script he changed the whole emphasis of the scene, making it comic rather than serious and showing the father being embarrassed, not the son. 'It hits home,' he said. 'Much more interesting than a lecture on sex. So sometimes censorship helped.'

A similar point was made by the director Edward Dmytryk, who now lectures at the film school at the University of Southern California. The depiction of violence was banned under the Code just as strenuously as the depiction of sex, which made for difficulties when, in 1944, Dmytryk was making the thriller *Murder My Sweet* in which Dick Powell played Philip Marlowe. The restrictions, he said, called for more subtlety, more ingenuity, as for instance in a scene in which Powell had to hit a guard over the head. This could not be shown as one continuous action; instead the director had to cut it up into a series of separate shots – one in which Powell was seen swinging the traditional blunt instrument, another in which something is seen to hit the guard on the head, then Powell again, the guard again and so on. But as Dmytryk said: 'Is there any doubt in your mind that he hit him on the head, even though you don't see him do it and you don't see blood splashing all over everything? It's the same with sex scenes. For me, it's a helluva lot better if you do them subtly. Sex is a wonderful thing but a private thing and the minute it becomes public it's no longer wonderful. I don't want to be made a voyeur against my will. I don't want to walk into a picture and see writhing bodies all over the place. To me they're funny but not that funny. You know? It's not that I'm against writhing bodies; I'm just against looking at somebody else's. I think there was much more . . . almost satisfaction out of suggestiveness than there is in the overt things that are done today. So all the Code did was make us think: how can we get this effect, how can we get that effect without doing it so openly that the Breen Office says, "No, you can't."'

Joe Mankiewicz, as rebellious a man as ever took up residence in Hollywood, declared forthrightly that 'The censorship was stupid, all censorship always is. It also said in that [Breen] list that when the door opens to a bathroom it's understood that no toilet will be visible. And the public must have thought that until 1955 or so America had no toilets. God knows where they did it . . .'

And yet, and yet . . . 'As Lubitsch pointed out to me one day it also made you rather ingenious.' (That word again). Mankiewicz said: 'You had to think of ways around it and I've said often enough that Mr Lubitsch could direct a young lady walking up to a door and reaching for the doorknob and deciding whether or not to go in and then walk away and come back and go in quickly. And he'd stay on that doorknob with his camera and there'd be more sex emanating from that particular bit of business than in all the writhing and intertwining genitals that they're turning out by the hundreds today.'

Censorship a good thing then? No, not exactly. In *All About Eve* for example, there was a scene in which somebody was called upon to say: 'What a story! Everything but the bloodhounds snapping at her arse.' Mankiewicz said: 'That's what it should have been – "arse". But . . . "arse is out". I said, "All right, let's have her say 'butt'." No – "butt" is out. I went through about a dozen always more innocent, more vague, more vapid, more meaningless synonyms for "arse" and finally I wound up with "rear end" . . .'

And then there were the physical restrictions. 'In a kissing scene you could only have the lips together for eight seconds,' said George Sidney. 'Well, that's kind of short shrift. And you had to come out of the kiss with the lips sealed, so I'd be shooting a scene with a script girl holding up her stop watch to show me five, six, seven. . . . "Out! OK, break, break, break, keep the lips together . . ." Then, as a person who did a lot of musicals, the annexation of the navel was a big problem because you couldn't expose a navel. So you had a beautiful costume and up the centre would be some piece of buckram or something and when the girls were dancing they'd be stuck with this. Finally, we got freedom of the navel which was a very, very big thing.'

In 1947 Sidney directed Spencer Tracy and Lana Turner in *Cass Timberlane* and . . . 'There was a scene in her bedroom just before she was about to go to the hospital and have a baby and I played it, I thought, very beautifully. He sat at the end of her bed and talked to his wife about oh, what shall we name the child, you know – a nice warm scene, lovely music, fireplace, snow outside, the whole mess. The censorship said, "You can't do it. A man can't sit on a bed with a lady." I said. "That's no lady, that's his wife", the old joke. I said "It's his *wife*; she's about to give birth." But no, we couldn't do it. They made us go back and made Spencer sit in a chair opposite the bed.'

Even elderly parties were not immune from this prohibition. In his script for *How Green Was My Valley* in 1941, the writer Philip Dunne had an aged miner and his equally aged wife clambering into bed together as they discussed their son's education. But, no. A bed suggested sex and even geriatric sex – or perhaps especially geriatric sex – was anathema to the censors. 'We had to restage the scene in the kitchen,' Dunne said. Five years later in *The Late George Apley*, he wrote a discussion between Apley and wife about a book their daughter had been reading. What's it about, asks the wife. 'Well,' says Apley. 'I shall have to use a word I've never used in your presence. It seems to be largely a book about sex.' To which Mrs Apley replies: 'How could you write a whole book about that?' Quite a funny exchange but ... 'Right away they said, "Sex is out",' said Dunne. 'But I was prepared. I said, "OK, the word's out. Next question." They said, "Wait a minute. What do you mean? Aren't you going to put up a fight?" I said, "No, no. I'll take your word on it." They said, "What are you going to do – cut the scene?" I said, "No. Obviously he'll have to whisper something in her ear. So she'll say, 'What's the book about?' and he'll say, 'I'll have to use a word I've never used in your presence,' and whisper in her ear." Well, they thought for a minute and said, "OK. You get your way. Sex stays in"....'

It's easy enough, I think, to feel that a mind – or, in the case of the Breen Office, a whole group of minds – that can see evil and a tendency to corrupt in the mere mention of such words as sex, arse, bastard (which was even excised from Laurence Olivier's *Henry V*), virgin (acceptable when referring, say, to territory but verboten when applied to a woman), damn, God (except when used in direct communication with the Deity) and such mild terms of abuse as jerk or punk is itself corrupt. But the eternal problem with censorship is that once it starts it never knows when to stop. The very question: "Censorship or not?" has been debated fiercely enough through the ages without any clear resolution and the rider: "Well, if censorship then how much?" is equally insoluble. The brand that was imposed upon Hollywood and by extension every other country that wished to sell its films to America from the mid-1930s onwards looks now to have been absurdly puritanical. Yet for reasons other than the fact that it caused movie makers to exercise their wits in order to slide around it, it was not altogether unwelcome.

The general impression put about at the time was that this censorship had been nobly self-imposed by the industry but this was by no means entirely true. Self-imposed perhaps – but from necessity rather than nobility. As Joe Mankiewicz said: 'It was very simple. There were forty-eight states at the time. That meant forty-eight state censorship boards. Each state had a censorship board for every major town and even smaller towns. So you could send out a print of a film and have it chopped up by forty-eight different censor boards – to begin with. Then, for instance, within the state of Illinois you had not only the state censor board, you had the Chicago censor board and the censor boards of every small town, and they would cut your film to pieces. Now apart from that we had the Legion of Decency, which was far and away the worst because what happened would be that a priest in, ah, Long Branch, New Jersey, wouldn't like a film and he'd get up and say, "Anyone who goes to see that film has committed a mortal sin and faces excommunication." So the Hays Office, or Breen Office, served a very healthy purpose in terms of the sanity of picture makers because to send a film out and leave it to the mercy of any church group that declared itself to be the censorship board for a particular town or village anywhere from Dorset to Wyoming would have been disaster. Finally, somebody had the sense to say, "Look, why don't we get together and draw up a list of what you people want and what we can live with so that our films won't be butchered?" That way everything was at least collated, so that you could send a film out having committed the idiocies yourself rather than have it cut behind somebody's grocery store.'

Besides, if a message – of violence or all-consuming passion – could no longer be stated, it could at least be implied by means of innuendo, nuance and suggestion. True, this tended to mean that although a taboo subject could still be dealt with it couldn't be dealt with honestly but even so given talented writers, directors and cast the implicit could be just as effective as the explicit. In *Casablanca*, for instance, nobody needed to see Humphrey Bogart and Ingrid Bergman naked on a bed to know that during their time together in Paris they had done rather more than exchange butterfly kisses. Similarly, the (unstated) sexuality between John Garfield and Lana Turner in the 1946 version of *The Postman Always Rings Twice* was hardly less obvious than that between Jack Nicholson and Jessica Lange in the 1982 remake when virtually nothing was left to the imagination.

What this new sophisticated approach to forbidden subjects needed was sophisticated, grown-up players and in the late 1930s Hollywood had them in abundance – William Powell and Myrna Loy in "The Thin Man" series, which was noted for its verbal innuendo; Garbo in *Ninotchka*; Katharine Hepburn and Cary Grant in *Bringing Up Baby*; Grant again (once) and Constance Bennett three times in the "Topper" series; Clark Gable and Claudette Colbert in *It Happened One Night* and many more. Not entirely by coincidence, I suspect, the leading actresses of the 1930s played women and not girls. On screen sexual nudge-nudge can be amusing when purveyed by adults; in the hands of juveniles it is frequently embarrassing.

In the war years the emphasis on woman as opposed to girl continued. The pin-up girls of the American forces were not the big breasted but barely weaned adolescents of today's *Playboy* centrefolds or page three of the *Sun*. They were, rather, Betty Grable, who was already twenty-four when America joined the war or Ann Sheridan, the "Oomph girl", who was twenty-five, or Lana Turner, who was twenty-one. Their appeal was different, too – they were enticing without giving the least hint that they might be available. Even the most popular piece of cheesecake of the Second World War, Betty Grable (the "all-American floosie" as the critic Richard Schickel described her) was invariably presented in an impenetrable one-piece bathing suit that looked as if it could only be removed by a second party with the aid of a hammer and chisel. In wartime sex and the approach to sex undergo a dramatic change. Conventions such as steady courtship and long engagements are thrust impatiently to one side and people grab what they can when they can. But the Code and the Legion and their fellow censorship boards were still there to ensure that the decencies were observed. By the simple expedient of wearing a sweater a couple of sizes too small Lana Turner may have been able to hint strongly at the delights that lay under the wool but those delights themselves were never on display; Grable was armoured from armpit to thigh and even male pin-ups, the beefcake boys, were obliged to shave their chests, since it was well known that a touch of hair on a manly torso was calculated to drive female onlookers into transports of lust.

On screen, too, the Code did not relax its vigilance. Adultery might be suggested in such films as *The Maltese Falcon* and later *Double Indemnity* and *The Lady from Shanghai* but it was never specifically mentioned so that the guilty parties must in the end face retribution for a sin which they had never been seen to commit and of which they had never openly been accused. This must have caused great bafflement in the slower-witted members of the audience. But then one of the by-products of censorship is that the viewer must learn to read between the lines – how else could anyone have recognised the homosexual relationship between Sydney Greenstreet and Elisha Cook Jr in *The Maltese Falcon*?

With many of the male stars away – in some cases actually fighting, in others merely poncing around in flash uniforms – the war years offered splendid opportunities for actresses, especially as cinema audiences were predominantly female and, what's more, composed largely of working females. So now Crawford, Davis and Stanwyck came into their own and newer, younger stars arose to replace the stalwarts of the 1930s. It was the time of Grable, Sheridan and Turner, of Gene Tierney and Ingrid Bergman, of Betty Hutton, Joan Fontaine and, later, Lauren Bacall. Of these Turner and Bacall most obviously represented the traditional, slinky, bad (or anyway naughty) girl and yet it was the apparently demure Ingrid Bergman who aroused the wrath and condemnation of the moralists and censors, although the cause of their displeasure was what she did off-screen rather than on.

In 1948 it was revealed that, though already married to someone else, she was having an affair with the Italian director Roberto Rossellini and was with child by him. Ingrid Bergman – the nunlike Ingrid Bergman, she who had indeed taken the wimple in *The Bells of St Mary's*. Hollywood and all of America could hardly believe that such iniquity was possible and so with righteous indignation and magnificent hypocrisy the nation rose and drummed her out, never effectively to allow her to return until 1956. Apart from anything else this was a splendid example of double standards – one for men, another for women. For when in 1942 Errol Flynn was brought to trial on two charges of statutory rape the publicity did his reputation no end of good and vastly increased the box office receipts of his then current film, *Gentleman Jim*.

In some ways, however, the treatment of Ingrid Bergman was the last great backlash of the moral indignation movement. Although the Legion of Decency and Cardinal Spellman would continue to fulminate against sex in the movies for some time (Mamie van Doren was a particular target: 'They reacted as though I was contributing to the delinquency of minors if I even passed a schoolhouse') the edifice was beginning to wobble. America's breast fixation, epitomised by the attention paid to Lana Turner, became particularly apparent when Howard Hughes starred a pair of them in *The Outlaw*. They were, of course, attached to Jane Russell and vast acreages of them were on display. When the film was made in 1941 the Breen Office gave it a Seal of Approval after certain cuts were made but the first night audience laughed it off the screen because the story, about an encounter between Billy the Kid and Doc Holliday, was pretty awful and the mammaries were the only true points of interest. Hughes promptly withdrew the picture, restored the cuts, launched a steamy advertising campaign – "Mean, Moody, Magnificent" and "Two good reasons to see Jane Russell . . .", for example – and relaunched it, sealless, in 1943. In the cinemas where it was allowed to play it did such good business that it was reshaped again, regained its seal and cleaned up on the major circuits. But it was not widely shown until 1950.

What caused the censorship trouble and the withdrawal of the seal in 1943 was, in Jane Russell's opinion, a scene in which, wearing a low-cut blouse, she had to lean over a bed containing the ailing Billy the Kid and pull the covers up. 'I'm leaning over the bed and the camera was right across from me so there was too much cleavage. Greg Toland, the cameraman, said, "We're gonna have to change that angle, boss," and he changed it and we shot it again. Well, in the final cut Howard wanted that scene [the way it was shot the first time] but there was no excuse for it, no rhyme or reason. He just wanted to break the ban and they [the censors] weren't going to allow him to, so it just went on and on.' Originally *The Outlaw* was to have been directed by Howard Hawks but he demanded the kind of overall artistic control of the film that Hughes, the producer, was never about to give him. So Hawks left and Hughes took over, which was almost certainly a mistake. Miss Russell said: 'He knew what he wanted but he didn't know how to tell you how to do it. So we had many, many takes. It was nothing to have thirty-five takes on a very simple little scene. And then when Doc Holliday is finally in his grave and Billy is saying a few words he did 102 takes so that Howard could have 102 choices.'

But apart from the censorial uproar, the condemnation by the League of Decency and the threat of excommunication for anyone who went to see what Bob Hope once described as "the two and only Jane Russell", *The Outlaw* also provided a piece of Hollywood folklore. To give the impression that his star's magnificent chest could defy the laws of gravity and remain pert and upright untrammelled by support, Hughes employed his knowledge of aerodynamics (he was, after all, a skilled engineer) to design a special seamless bra for her and, so the story goes, she wore it throughout the film. In fact, she said, she never wore it at all. 'It was ridiculous – it went down the back and around the waist and it was very uncomfortable. So I threw it under the couch and the wardrobe girl said, "Oh no, I'm gonna get fired." I said, "Shut up. It'll be all right," and I put on my own bra and put Kleenex over the seams and I went out and Howard took a look and said, "Okay" and went right ahead and he never knew the difference.'

In the end *The Outlaw* made a great deal of money for Howard Hughes but for those who wished to see sex portrayed on the screen in an honest, adult manner it was a retrograde step, most of Hollywood arguing that if infantile titillation and big knockers paid off, why bother to be serious about the subject. On the other hand it had shown that the power of the seal could be broken, that films could be successful without official approval, a fact which Otto Preminger emphatically underlined in 1953 when the Breen Office refused to give the nod to *The Moon is Blue* because the script contained such disgusting words as "virgin", "mistress" and "seduction". Preminger made it anyway as an independent production and released it with a C (for condemned) rating from the Legion and proved, more forcibly than *The Outlaw* had done, that even in those circumstances a film could do enormously well at the box office. At last cracks were beginning to appear in the foundations of the Production Code and the Legion of Decency and they widened considerably three years later with the appearance of *Baby Doll*, an adaptation written and directed by Elia Kazan of the play by Tennessee Williams. This was a much more serious, and therefore dangerous, subject than either *The Outlaw* or *The Moon is Blue*, the tale of a raunchy child bride (Carroll Baker), of deceit and adultery. Cardinal Spellman reacted in his usual Pavlovian manner by forbidding his congregation to see it "under pain of sin" and in predominantly Roman Catholic areas the box office undoubtedly suffered. But not elsewhere – thus indicating that the Legion of Decency no longer exerted universal influence and could bring rather less muscle to bear in its relationship with the studios.

Carroll Baker said that the wrath of the Legion and the fulminations from the pulpit came as a great shock to all concerned with the film. 'We had never expected such a thing. As a matter of fact at the first previews the humour came through, we had great laughs and even great reviews. Then suddenly when we were banned by the Catholic church everybody sort of took a turnaround and started to find things that they thought were licentious in the film.' What caused the banning, she discovered (though not until some years later), was the fact that in the script Baby Doll, aged nineteen, is given in marriage by her father to Archie Lee (Karl Malden) on the understanding that there should be no consummation until her twentieth birthday. The randy Archie Lee is so overheated by the presence in his home of this sultry but untouchable nymphet that he drills holes in her bedroom wall so that he can look at her. 'That was all very funny,' said Miss Baker. 'But the Catholic church said it was a sin. They felt it was highly immoral that the marriage wasn't consummated. Cardinal Spellman stood up in St Patrick's Cathedral in New York and said it was immoral – in dress, in speech; he just laid everything on it.' Happily, he stopped short of denouncing Miss Baker herself and, in fact, the Catholic church in Italy didn't even bother to denounce even the film. 'It played there perfectly happily,' she said. One other significant point: according to Miss Baker the Breen Office had passed the film without first consulting the Legion of Decency, to the latter's great indignation. 'So they sort of said, "Okay, this is it. Now we're going to show you, we're going to make an example of this picture."' In fact, of course, they did not succeed and the Legion's attacks served only to show that its power was lessening.

This is not, by any means, to suggest that henceforth sex would always be treated intelligently and in a grown-up manner in the movies. Far from it. Generally speaking the films of the 50s suggested that sex was a pastime for adolescents only and anyway stopped a long way short of actual intercourse. This was the era of the teenybopper idols – Tony Curtis, Troy Donahue, Rock Hudson, an assortment of Hunters (Tab and Jeff), for instance, on the male side and on the distaff side such well-scrubbed, gleaming examples of American youth as Natalie Wood, Jane Powell, Debbie Reynolds and Doris Day, she who invented virginity. Robert Wagner looked back on those bobby-sox films as a product of the time. 'A lot's happened since then. Morals have changed, morality has changed. But that was the time of the boy next door. There was a great innocence about the movies.' More than innocence, Tab Hunter said – 'There was a naivety about them, which I thought was very endearing. You know, Rock Hudson carrying Doris Day down Fifth Avenue wrapped in blankets. They were kind of simple and nice and sweet.' He did not delude himself that such pictures reflected life as it really was but, 'There was a sort of mystery about films; there was also a mystery about actors and actresses.' Now it's different ... 'Now I know what such and such an actress's favourite foods are, where she dines, what kind of car she drives, all the different people she's living with, how many babies she has.' The loss of that mystery may, in fact, have much to do with the decline in popularity of the cinema itself. When stars were remote beings about whom little was known except what the studios wanted people to know, they were exciting figures, larger than life. When they chose to step down from that pedestal, announce that they were actors first and only film stars irrelevantly, appear in public in old jeans and sweat shirts, publicise their abortions and illegitimate children (sometimes in such cases you wonder whether the actress, steadfastly refusing to name the father of her child, has any clear idea who the father might be), they may have become freer but they lost the magic the big screen had conferred upon them and were no longer any more impressive than the diminutive figures who appeared nightly and less than twelve inches tall on the family TV screen. There was a mystery about sex, too, in those 1950s films, the climax of any relationship being an eight-second kiss with lips clamped firmly together. 'They were really quite restrictive,' Tab Hunter said. 'They'd tell you if your hand was going a little too low or something like that. It was all what I call the "superficial school". Now what people want is real people in real situations but I love leaving some things to the imagination. I think that's so exciting; it can be very intriguing and really whets your appetite.'

To a large extent the emphasis placed at that time on youth and youthful romance was economic. In the postwar years teenagers had stopped going to the cinema, preferring to stay at home or baby-sit (a 750 million dollars a year industry by the late 1940s), listening to the radio or gramophone. So films were concocted to lure them back and a new audience was created, an audience of twelve to twenty-four year-olds and to a large extent – even more in the 1980s than in the 1950s – this has dominated the cinema ever since, to the detriment of serious film makers. True, a number of pictures, starting perhaps with the 1946 *Duel in the Sun*, which had Jennifer Jones as a sultry half-breed causing ructions between Gregory Peck and Joseph Cotten, and including Marlon Brando and Vivien Leigh in *A Streetcar Named Desire*, sought to indicate that sex – an even more advanced form of sex than heavy breathing and inconsequential groping – was possible between people of such advanced ages as twenty-five plus. But on the whole this eternally popular human activity was reduced to a matter of male adolescents yearning after voluptuous sex symbols or the girl next door, and the girl next door grimly keeping her knees together and her honour intact until desire could be sanctified by marriage.

Among those sex symbols, inevitably perhaps after the rumpus surrounding their early films, were Jane Russell and Carroll Baker, each of whom found herself typecast, despite all efforts to resist, in steamy films which attracted censorship

Marilyn Monroe – a
devastating combination
of youthful innocence,
vulnerability and
sexuality
Left: "Mean, moody and
magnificent" Jane
Russell in *The Outlaw*
Below left: Rock Hudson
and Doris Day, the boy
next door and "she who
invented virginity"

problems – Russell in *The French Line* and *The Revolt of Mamie Stover*; Baker in *The Chapman Report*. For Miss Russell this was ironic, since she is the most devoutly Christian of movie stars, and for Miss Baker, deeply irritating, since she believed that in a sense *Baby Doll* had ruined her life. 'I'm still called Baby Doll. I mean, it's like my middle name. I wouldn't mind so much if, like Marlene Dietrich, it had been *The Blue Angel* or something. But there's something about being called Baby Doll, particularly now I'm a grandmother ... You know, if I take my little grandson somewhere and they call me Baby Doll I'm not going to like that very much.' (To underline her point: the night after I had talked to her I had dinner with a Hollywood executive. 'Who did you see today?' he asked. 'Carroll Baker,' I said. 'Oh,' he said. 'Baby Doll ...').

The greatest sex symbol of them all, however, was Marilyn Monroe; indeed she is incomparably the greatest female star of the last forty years. For the purposes of her time and the mood of the movies in her time she had everything: she was undoubtedly a fully developed woman but she had a childlike quality; she exuded sexuality but she also had innocence. The on-screen Monroe (and possibly the off-screen one as well) was not the manipulator of her own desirability but the victim of it and as such she aroused the sympathy of women as well as the longing of men. In an age culminating in the era of the mini-skirt, in which women in films and in life were valued – and were urged to believe they were valued – almost exclusively in terms of their physical attraction, Monroe epitomised femininity. In many of her films, especially the earlier ones, she was either a possession (a crooked lawyer's moll in *The Asphalt Jungle*, a theatre critic's plaything in *All about Eve*), an object of fantasy (*The Seven Year Itch*) or a prize to be won (*Some Like It Hot*). Only perhaps in *Bus Stop* and *The Misfits* was much concession made to the fact that beneath the sex symbol there lurked a human being whose hopes and fears and dreams were not altogether unlike those of a man. But on the whole she and her imitators and rivals were treated as trinkets, objects, sexual toys and that can be destructive, as Carroll Baker became aware.

'At certain moments,' she said, 'I really did think the evil eye was on me. I really felt that there was this wave of dislike and that people wanted to see me dead. There was a tremendous jealousy because after Marilyn Monroe I was the one who was getting all of that – what was supposed to be – desirable publicity, not necessarily desirable for me but if you are the sex symbol then you get the lion's share of the publicity and nobody wants to be photographed with you because you're going to get more attention than they are. Nobody wants to be seen with you. The jealousy was so tremendous that I always felt that when I had troubles there were a lot of people who felt very gleeful about it. Listen, I was on the *Queen Mary* when I heard about Marilyn Monroe's death and my husband and I were devastated. But there were other Hollywood people aboard who were not at all unhappy about it. As a matter of fact a very famous actress said, "Oh well, we all knew this was coming, didn't we? She was so unstable and, well, we didn't really lose anything for the community, did we?"' Monroe, said Miss Baker, had never properly been accepted in that Holly-wood community. 'They thought she was pretty outrageous when she first began.

She did things like not wear a bra and she had this reputation of being a calendar girl and they just thought, Well, she's not one of us.' And because she was "not one of us" she was treated with a hostility of which, Carroll Baker was sure, she was totally aware. 'Sometimes I used to see Marilyn at parties where she came in so open and vulnerable – she had an enormous vulnerability. She used to come in so lovely and so open and you would see people say things to her or she sensed that this was the moment when someone was going to say something and she absolutely defocused. She just sort of took herself out of the place she was in.'

The more adult treatment of sex in the movies took a small step forward in 1951 with *From Here to Eternity* in which Deborah Kerr was allowed to play a mature, adulterous woman whose love-making on the beach with Burt Lancaster led if not to the earth moving then at least to waves crashing. Fred Zinnemann, who directed the film, said: 'Everybody was really nervous about that scene on the beach. But the Breen Office passed it; they asked for a cut of about six feet, which was all right.' Thus encouraged by the granting of a little more freedom films began to signal ever more clearly that an act of sexual intercourse had taken place – rockets soaring rudely upwards to illustrate the congress of Cary Grant and Grace Kelly in *To Catch a Thief* (1956) and a train plunging into a tunnel and emerging tooting triumphantly to leave us in no doubt about what that same Cary Grant and Eva Marie Saint had been up to in *North by Northwest* (1959). Both films, of course, directed by Alfred Hitchcock. Gradually sex and extravagant spectacle were becoming the cinema's main defensive weapon against television. If sex could still only be hinted at – albeit with an ever more lubricious wink – in films, it was hardly even acknowledged on TV. And once the illicit lovers were allowed pretty well to get away with it in *From Here to Eternity*, the way was clear to extend the frontiers ever further.

By 1960 even prostitution was winning official approval: *Butterfield 8* gained an Oscar for Elizabeth Taylor and *Never on a Sunday* won a nomination for Melina Mercouri. Soon afterwards *Breakfast at Tiffany's* and *Irma La Douce* attempted to cash in on that success. In 1962 homosexuality cropped up in *Advise and Consent* and a touch of lesbianism in *A Walk on the Wild Side*. Four years earlier in *Cat on a Hot Tin Roof*, said the screenwriter and ultimate director Richard Brooks, they were forbidden even to mention the word "homosexuality", which rather defeated the purpose since that was what the story was about. Brooks said: 'George Cukor, who was originally going to be the director, said if he couldn't make it the way the play was done he would withdraw and he did.' Finally and, to be fair, more at MGM's insistence than that of the censors, the plot was changed so that the Paul Newman character was no longer a homosexual but a young athlete who had never really discovered his manhood. But in the end, to ensure that we were all aware that he had finally grasped the essential difference between men and women, a pillow is thrown on to the bed to be followed, we can assume with confidence, by Mr Newman and Elizabeth Taylor. MGM's reason for this ending, said Brooks, was that a film which co-starred Newman and Taylor and did not bring them both together would be hooted off the screen. Brooks thought the studio was probably right. But if homo-sexuality had become acceptable (or had at least been admitted) by 1962, castration had not. In Tennessee Williams' play, *Sweet Bird of Youth*, the handsome young gigolo is ultimately castrated. In the screen version, again written and directed by Brooks, he simply has his face drastically rearranged, so that he is no longer pretty. Brooks did not actually want either ending; instead he wanted a final shot of the gigolo, Paul Newman again, being dumped at sea from a garbage scow but the studio would not let him shoot it so he left, never to return for twenty years.

In 1966 Sidney Lumet made *The Pawnbroker* in which naked breasts appeared for the first time. They were, admittedly, black breasts and therefore in that still racially prejudiced era probably not regarded as being nearly as provocative as white ones but they were certainly naked. What's more even the Code office agreed that the showing of same was, in the context, "vital" and "valid". Naturally the Legion disagreed and slapped its usual C certificate on the film but by now nobody was really taking the Legion very seriously. Between 1963 and 1965 it had condemned thirty-eight films, more than half of them from major studios, without much bothering anybody and, possibly dispirited, in 1967 it gave up being the Legion of Decency and became instead the National Catholic Office for Motion Pictures, in which guise it devoted itself to protecting children rather than adults.

Also in 1966 there was Michelangelo Antonioni's *Blow Up*, a baffling picture irritatingly hard to follow which nevertheless featured a great deal of nudity and treated sex with a frankness hitherto unseen in American cinemas. It was, needless to say, very successful. So now Hollywood itself plunged enthusiastically into the sex movie. Two things in particular enabled it to do so: first, in 1952, an attempt to ban *The Miracle*, an Italian picture in which a peasant woman believes her baby was fathered by St Joseph, had been taken to the Supreme Court which, overthrowing the 1915 judgment against Mutual, ruled that films were indeed a serious medium and therefore guaranteed freedom of speech under the First Amendment. (The director of *The Miracle* was, ironically, that same Roberto Rossellini who in popular belief had debauched the saintly Ingrid Bergman.) And secondly, in 1966 the Code itself was extensively revised to accept, for the first time, the principle that matters of contention should be judged in the context of the entire film and not in isolation. Pressing home this advantage, the industry pushed through a new classification, SMA – Suitable for Mature Audiences – which was introduced in 1967 specifically to allow *Who's Afraid of Virginia Woolf?* to bandy some choice four-letter words about. This was supposed to be a one off, applicable to *Virginia Woolf* only but, Hollywood knowing a good thing when it saw one, by the following year almost half the films released by the majors were SMA. And in 1968 with a sigh of resignation the Motion Picture Association of America – which embraced the Breen Office and the Code – introduced a classification system: G (general audience), M (mature audience), R (people over eighteen) and X (only for those over twenty-one). In 1970 this was changed again, M becoming GP (general patronage) and later still PG (parental guidance), R allowing admission to people under seventeen if accompanied by an adult and X for those over seventeen. Other changes have taken place more recently but the significance of the early classification system and its modifications was that now, at last, the sex film was freely available to people of seventeen and over, the most lucrative market of all. Since then the cinema has not looked back; some would say that it has rarely looked up either, its gaze being firmly fixed midway between its navel and its knees.

The man chiefly responsible for introducing the classification, or rating, system was Jack Valenti, the president since 1966 of the Motion Picture Association of America. It became necessary to do so, he said, because 'our society was going through a radical, revisionary change'. The old Hays/Breen Office with its list of do's and don'ts was 'thoroughly out of place in a society that was changing rapidly. Moreover I think creative directors and producers were straining to make films with more candour than we were able to do before.' This mature, philosophical thinking, however, was not the main reason for the change. Much more urgent was what is known as the "Dallas Classification Case". The Supreme Court had decreed that it was legal for state and local communities to inaugurate their own classification systems. 'If that had taken place,' said Valenti, 'we would have had chaos in the marketplace – 200, or 300 rating boards around the country, each of them imprisoning a film in a kind of rating that might not be suitable for the community next door.' So faced with this threat – and, you understand, bearing in mind the needs of creative producers and directors – the MPA plunged into a round of meetings with film makers, religious and political leaders and came up with a rating system mutually agreeable to all. Valenti also said that he had found the Seal of Approval constricting. 'I wanted two simple objectives. One, the screen should be free: no one should tell a creative director/writer/producer/actor what kind of film he ought to make. And second, we ought to redeem our obligations to the parents of this country. We could at least give them some advance, cautionary warning about a film so that they – not us – could make judgments about what films their children could see.' So the Rating Board is not in any sense a censorship board? 'Absolutely not,' he said. The board might advise but it did not force anybody to cut anything. 'The decision to edit is the producers' and directors' responsibility, not ours.'

The old Production Code, he thought, was much more deeply involved in film making than the Rating Board is. 'If you didn't get a Seal of Approval it was like a stigma, like a fungus on the face of your film, and you might be denied a lot of play dates. Indeed, under the old Code my two predecessors [Hays and Breen] would see to it that your film could not be distributed by the companies in the Motion Picture Association. So it was a pretty unrelenting kind of stricture.' He himself by contrast had issued 'very stern orders that the rating board is not to get involved in the editing process'. Certainly it would advise on what cuts or changes might be made to alter a film's rating but then it was up to the film maker to decide whether the changes would be beneficial or not. 'We do not insist on it; we do not choose to be involved; we do not censor; we do not ban.' But then he didn't seem to feel that except as a guide to parents ratings meant much anyway. According to what he called "Valenti's Rule" there was no evidence at all of a connection between a film's rating and its box office take. But this seems, to say the least, a touch naive. With the bulk of today's cinema audience in America being in its early and middle teens, an X certificate, for example, would be about as welcome to most film makers as a second ulcer.

Whatever the rights and wrongs of that argument there is no doubt that the introduction of the rating system has had its effect. Since 1967 the landmarks in sexual licence have come thick and fast. As *The Graduate* (1967) Dustin Hoffman was seen to be wearing underpants while in bed with his mother's best friend; two years later in *John and Mary* he had realised what an encumbrance this garment could be and had discarded it. In 1968 *The Sergeant* and *The Detective* dealt quite openly with homosexuality without raising a murmur of protest; in 1969 *Goodbye Columbus* introduced the condom and the jock strap; in 1970 *The Boys in the Band* treated homosexuality not only openly but also sympathetically; Oliver Reed and Alan Bates wrestled each other nude in *Women in Love* and *Catch 22* gave us a full frontal of Paula Prentiss, while in *Myra Breckinridge* Raquel Welch raped a male actor with a dildo. Could there be anything left to depict? Well, yes, there could. In 1971 *Straw Dogs* especially explored the uneasy connection of sex and violence and in 1972 *Last Tango in Paris* introduced us to male-female buggery (with the aid of half a pound of best butter) while fellatio very nearly – but not quite – was given public approbation in *Deep Throat*.

To these and many other films dealing blatantly with sex added protection was given by another Supreme Court ruling in 1974 in a case brought against *Carnal Knowledge*, a Mike Nichols picture starring Jack Nicholson about one man's infinitely varied but finally sated sexual adventures. Ruling against the state of Georgia, the court decided that a film's obscenity could only be judged by the standards of the community in which it was shown and that in this instance *Carnal Knowledge* was not obscene enough to lose its protection under the First Amendment. (From this I suppose we must conclude that there is very little obscenity in Georgia or, alternatively, that practically everything is regarded as obscene in Georgia.)

What the new freedom of the cinema has meant, in theory at least, is that sex and its attendant problems can now be treated in a totally grown-up manner. In practice this has not happened very often. Far too frequently the relaxed rules have led to the inclusion of nude and sex scenes for their own sake, whether or not they have any relevance to the plot. And, as a matter of social interest, they have enabled the cinema to reveal that the American fixation has shifted far south of the breast – cunnilingus has been commonplace (though strongly implied rather than shown) since Laurence Harvey practised it on Julie Christie in the British production *Darling* in 1965. Actually, for those on the alert for that sort of thing it was depicted much earlier – in Joseph H. Lewis's 1955 crime thriller, *The Big Combo*, which included a love scene wherein Richard Conte made his way slowly down a young woman's body and vanished out of the bottom frame. Lewis was hastily summoned to the Breen Office where he was told the scene would have to be cut. 'Why?' he asked. 'I don't understand what you gentlemen mean.' The gentlemen eyed him suspiciously and said: 'Well, when Conte is there with her and kissing her, he kisses her here and here and there and there and then where the hell does he go?' And Lewis replied with great innocence: 'How the hell do I know where he went? Maybe he went for a cup of coffee.' They were not satisfied with this explanation and expostulated further until, with well-simulated fury, Lewis accused them of having filthy minds and wondered how they dared have the effrontery to approach a director in this manner. 'And they apologised to me,' he said, 'and left the sequence in.'

Hollywood's fascination with the female breast has not, of course, faded away simply because total nudity is now permitted. As one producer put it, 'The American male goes for the bust. He just thinks busts are something wonderful . . . In the 50s it was the big bust that got them. To me, at that time, it was the most alluring, forbidden part of a female's body. Today tastes have gone down to the rear and those parts of the body you didn't see that much of in those days and weren't that attractive. It was a fixation. Styles change. But I still think the bust is a big plus for a girl but the big ones are more or less kind of out.'

In the 1950s, however, the big ones – veritable whoppers – were very much in. For a brief time the screenwriter George Axelrod (who scripted among other things *The Seven Year Itch*, *Breakfast at Tiffany's* and *The Manchurian Candidate*) had Jayne Mansfield under personal contract and made a short screen test of her, the climax of which came with her rubbing one of her breasts gently against the camera. It wasn't, I hasten to add, an official test but Axelrod had it shown on what he called the "Bel Air circuit". He said: 'Those were producers and high level people in Hollywood who had their own projection rooms and no after dinner conversation and therefore showed movies every night. So I had this shown as a sort of selected short subject and within five days they hired her.' What that rapid success emphasised, he thought, was that in the 50s the bust 'was the only available sex object. You weren't, under any conditions, allowed by the censors to get into anybody's knickers.' On the other hand you could, just, show knickers. Marilyn Monroe revealed hers in 1955 in the famous subway grating scene in *The Seven Year Itch*, when the air coming up from the subway blew her skirt over her head. 'We didn't know,' said Axelrod, 'that the guy who was running the wind machine below would become over-excited, which is what he did and made the picture another 20 million dollars.' The Breen Office had no objection to the knickers but it did insist on the excision of the line of dialogue in which Monroe said: 'Oh, this breeze is so nice, I feel so sorry for you with your hot pants.' Later Axelrod was grateful, and quite rightly, that the censors made them cut the line.

After 1965, however, actresses – like Miss Christie in *Darling* – quite often gave the impression of not even wearing knickers. At least one assumes she wasn't for how else could Mr Harvey have done what he quite obviously did? Miss Christie won the Academy Award for that picture and so simulated cunnilingus and simulated fellatio, too, became respectable. But sexual freedom/licence/licentiousness has also had far more disturbing side effects: in the 1970s in particular there was a spate of films, mostly of very poor quality, in which women were used almost entirely as victims, people to be brutalised, raped and otherwise sexually abused. Pictures like Michael Winner's *Death Wish* (1974), which included a scene of appalling brutality being inflicted on Charles Bronson's screen wife and daughter, set the trend. Winner, and those who imitated him ever more crudely, might argue that it was necessary to show such horror in order that the audience could understand and sympathise with the later vengeful behaviour of Bronson or whoever. But whether you are prepared to accept this argument or not – and I am not because I believe that implicit, or off-screen, violence is much more horrifying to anyone with a modicum of imagination than anything filmed in gory close-up – it was noticeable that it was always women, never men, who were victimised. Fortunately, by the mid-1980s even this phase appeared to have passed and it is perhaps significant that in *Death Wish 3* it was the murder of a *male* friend and not of his wife, daughter or maid that persuaded Charles Bronson to resume his trade as the vigilante of the city streets.

On the whole, though, has the relaxation of censorship gone too far? The director Richard Brooks is one among many who believe it has. 'Some of the art was lost by some movie makers in order to deal with the specifics,' he said. It had got to the point where you had to show not just one bosom but four or five bosoms and had to move the camera in closer and closer 'until you could see the pores in that beautiful breast. Pretty soon the complaints were coming from the porno houses that they didn't have any customers; they were all going to the regular drive-ins. When you remove the restraints it doesn't mean you should remove your responsibility.'

But as the critic Pauline Kael said as long ago as 1966: 'The movies always seem to be both behind and ahead of the culture. Though the sexual revolution has scarcely found its way onto the screen and movies rarely deal with the simplest kind of heterosexual life in our time they're already treating bisexuality – like the kids who are on pot and discussing the merits of LSD before they've had their first beer.'

For this reason perhaps the sexual revolution in the cinema led to fewer – not more – opportunities for serious actresses. The emergence in the late 70s and the 1980s of women like Meryl Streep, Jessica Lange, Sally Field, Sissy Spacek and Kathleen Turner, along with the continuing success of Jane Fonda and Anne Bancroft, has done much to redress the balance. The indications are, for the moment anyway, that there is again room in the cinema for the "woman's picture", although its popularity at the box office is by no means assured and, even at its best, is negligible compared with the amount of money to be earned by science fiction (or fantasy) epics such as *Star Wars* and *ET* or the knockabout nonsense of *Rambo* and the *Rocky* series.

Besides, twenty years after the rule book was torn up the most popular ingredient in the movies is still the sex scene, usually with a large measure of full-frontal female – although not yet, or very rarely, male – nudity. Perhaps one day the films, or better still their audience, will grow up and put sex in a more proper perspective. In the meantime as Hal Wallis said in 1985: 'If Joe Breen were alive today I think he'd be a nervous wreck, seeing what goes on on the screen.'

HOLLYWOOD GOES TO WAR

Hollywood went to war with a great deal of reluctance as, indeed, did the nation itself. In 1935, for instance, when Europe in general was already growing decidedly anxious, America's foreign policy was one of isolationism, as it had been – various interests in Central America and a brief but bloody participation in the 1914–18 War apart – since the mid-nineteenth century. In that year a poll revealed that sixty-seven per cent of Americans wanted absolutely nothing to do with any foreign war in any circumstances whatsoever, while only twenty-eight per cent favoured adopting a positive stand against aggressor nations – and most of them preferred economic to military sanctions. Congress reflected and even magnified that view; as late as 1940 other polls discovered that it was even more isolationist than the populace at large. Well, wars were costly, not only in lives but in money, and America after all had only just emerged from the Great Depression. Besides, the view of Congress can hardly have been weakened by the fact that those most in favour of America joining Europe's war were the party-line Communists. True, the Nazi-Soviet Pact of 1939 had shaken them a bit, causing them to reflect that, all things considered, Hitler and his gang might not be quite such bad chaps as some people thought – in which mood they allied themselves with apparent cheerfulness with such red-necked Fascist organisations as Charles Lindbergh's America First movement. Later, when the pact had been broken the Communists realised – as, of course, they had known all along – that the Nazis were really pretty awful and so formed close attachments with various other left-wing groups, some strongly left, others merely liberal with a small "l". Later still, when the right wing was flexing its muscles and stamping on faces all over America, these alliances were universally dubbed "Communist Fronts" and caused their well-intentioned liberal (with a small "l") members no end of trouble, as we shall discover.

Hollywood's position in that prewar (or anyway pre-America's entry into the war) era was fairly clear cut. One decade, the 1930s, had ended and another, the 1940s, had begun with three of the best and certainly best-loved films of the still comparatively new sound age: *The Wizard of Oz*, *Gone With the Wind* and *Citizen Kane*. And something like forty per cent of all film grosses came from Europe, Garbo's films indeed being more successful there than they were in America. Not surprisingly, therefore, the industry – led by Will Hays and Louis Mayer – was greatly opposed to making pictures that might antagonise foreign governments, even a German foreign government, although the potential loss of revenue was not necessarily the argument they used.

President Franklin D. Roosevelt was one of the comparatively few American politicians who felt that the USA should try to influence events in Europe and he relied heavily for support on the important Jewish vote. This did not, however, greatly impress Congress, which was liberally sprinkled with anti-Semites. Nor, less predictably, did it cut much ice with the Hollywood moguls even though they were all, apart from Darryl Zanuck, Jewish. Their argument – and charity alone demands that we should listen to it and not simply assume that they were swayed by the potential loss of income from the German and Italian box office – was that antagonistic films would only make matters worse for their fellow Jews abroad. And when in 1940 news came through that several Polish exhibitors had been hanged in their own cinemas for showing Warner Brothers' 1939 production, *Confessions of a Nazi Spy*, the case for keeping a low profile was given added point. Warner Brothers, however, had declared its own war on Nazism much earlier. Quite apart from the fact that the studio was noted for making films with a strong social comment anyway, it had had a bitter experience of the Hitler regime as early as 1936 when its German representative, Joe Kaufman, was kicked to death in a backstreet of Berlin by a group of Nazi thugs. As Jack Warner noted in his autobiography: 'Like many an outnumbered Jew he was trapped in an alley. They hit him with fists and clubs and then kicked the life out of him with their boots and left him dying there.' In such circumstances Warners had little patience with the "don't make trouble" pleas of Hays and Mayer; they closed their Berlin office, pointedly refused to show the "March of Time" newsreel called *Nazi Conquest No 1* and embarked on a series of patriotic shorts featuring American history, and by extension the freedoms that America stood for, even though they knew the pictures would lose money. All this at a time when Mayer was actively keeping Jews and any portrayal of Jews off the screen, so that his films should not lose revenue in Fascist territories.

In fact, though, it was some while before Hollywood, even Warner Brothers, stopped soft-pedalling on Hitler and company. In 1934 for Universal Frank Borzage directed *Little Man, What Now?* with Margaret Sullavan and Douglass Montgomery. The theme was unemployment in Germany after the First World War but Nazism was not mentioned. Nor was it in Borzage's later (1938) picture *Three Comrades*, also starring Margaret Sullavan, and based on a novel by Erich Maria Remarque. In this case the Nazi angle was ignored in response to a front-office – the MGM front-office, naturally – directive. But perhaps front-office censorship was only anticipating Breen Office censorship, for that same year Walter Wanger produced, William Dieterle directed and John Howard Lawson (later to gain enduring notoriety as the most implacable of the "Unfriendly Ten" to face the House Un-American Activities Committee) wrote a film called *Blockade*, which started out to deal with the Spanish Civil War from an anti-Fascist angle. But thanks to the intervention of Breen and his cronies the result was total mystification. Clearly the protagonists, Henry Fonda and Madeleine Carroll, were on the right – i.e. morally and politically acceptable – side but which side was that? And who were they? And where the hell was all this going on? The Breen Office was so careful to ensure that nothing in the picture could prove objectionable or, even worse, commercially unacceptable that somehow the fact that the action was taking place in Spain almost passed unnoticed.

So in the end Warner Brothers, with *Confessions of a Nazi Spy*, a semi-documentary directed by Anatole Litvak and starring Edward G. Robinson and Paul Lukas about G-Men hunting down Nazis in the USA, were the first to stand up and be counted. But even to make the film was an act of courage. It was adapted for the screen by Milton Krims from a book by Leon G. Turrou, a former FBI agent, and to bring the story up to date both Krims and Turrou secretly infiltrated the German-American Bund in which the spy ring flourished. In this undercover role, said Krims, 'We were Heil Hitlering and everything with much gusto.' Still there must have been a certain amount of danger attached to their activities. 'Of course there was danger,' he said, grandly. 'But who thinks about danger in times like this? The Bund was a very powerful organisation especially in the Middle West, in the Milwaukee area, all through Wisconsin, wherever there were large German colonies.' The shooting of the film was a very hush hush business. 'Nobody knew what I was doing, you see. We kept that a profoundly deep secret until it was ready to go.' When it was ready to go, its plot fleshed out with newsreel shots surreptitiously taken of Bund gatherings, 'a lot of people didn't believe it to be true and yet every word of it was documented.' The Bund was understandably livid and efforts were made to stop the release of the picture by legal action, picketing and, in Milwaukee, by razing a cinema to the ground. There were even reports that death threats and menacing phone calls had been made to both Jack and Harry Warner, though Krims was inclined to discount that as studio hyperbole. He had a couple of death threats himself, he said, but he didn't think any were made to the Warners. The reaction in Germany fell short of menacing phone calls and death threats but objections to the film were raised there at high diplomatic level and Goebbels chuntered darkly about countering the adverse propaganda with a series of movies exposing American gangsters and the country's all round corruption. He did not, in fact, do so, possibly because *Confessions* was only a moderate success at the American box office, thus discouraging Warner Brothers, for the moment anyway, from further experiments in that direction. Instead, they carried on with their patriotic shorts and a series of thinly disguised recruiting films, such as *Devil Dogs of the Air*, *Here Comes the Navy* and *Rear Gunner* – the latter having been suggested by Air Force General Arnold, who had noted that recruitment among potential rear gunners was not all it might be. 'Give it some romantic interest,' he said to Jack Warner, who dutifully complied. Rear gunnery therefore being seen to be an extremely sexy occupation the air force suffered almost an embarrassment of applications.

Generally speaking, however, as the Phoney War went on in Europe, the mood in America was one of sympathy with the Allies combined with a determination to have nothing to do with the war itself. And this was underlined by the attitude of the likes of Lindbergh and Joseph Kennedy, ambassador to London and father of the future president, who were convinced that the German army was invincible and that Britain had no chance of ending up on the winning side and who, no doubt, as accomplished high-achievers had no wish to associate themselves with a bunch of

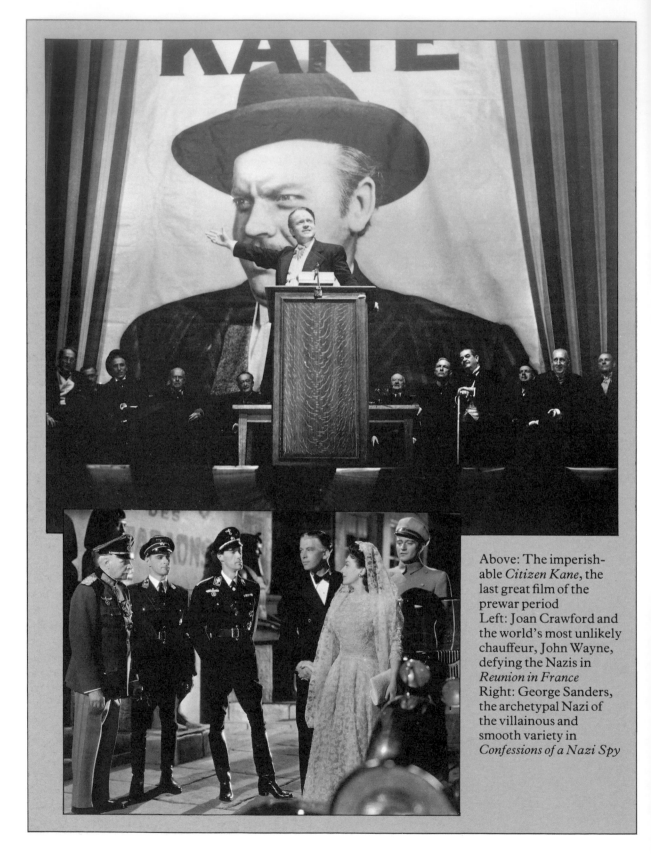

Above: The imperishable *Citizen Kane*, the last great film of the prewar period
Left: Joan Crawford and the world's most unlikely chauffeur, John Wayne, defying the Nazis in *Reunion in France*
Right: George Sanders, the archetypal Nazi of the villainous and smooth variety in *Confessions of a Nazi Spy*

losers. Dunkirk can't have helped a lot either, since the Americans have never really come to grips with the purely British notion that sometimes a glorious defeat is just as good as a victory, if not better.

Still, Warner Brothers continued to plug away at Hitlerism, though not so overtly as they did with *Confessions of a Nazi Spy*. William Dieterle's *Juarez*, released just before *Confessions*, used Mexico's struggle to throw off the despotism of Maximilian as an allegory of what was – or more properly might ideally – be going on in Europe. *Dr Ehrlich's Magic Bullet* (1940), starring Edward G. Robinson was made as a retort to Hitler's assertion that any scientific discovery made by a Jew would be worthless. The point was slightly weakened by the fact that Dr Ehrlich's discovery was a cure for syphilis and the Breen Office wouldn't allow the film actually to mention syphilis (lest, presumably, it encourage everybody to want some) but the film's heart was in the right place. In the same year *The Sea Hawk*, featuring Errol Flynn and directed by the eternally underrated Michael Curtiz, was another allegory. Ostensibly it concerned England's, and Sir Francis Drake's, repulsion of the Spanish Armada but the parallels were clear enough for anyone who cared to seek them. It was written (from a novel by Rafael Sabatini) by Howard Koch, who also co-wrote *Casablanca* for which he shared an Oscar with the brothers Julius and Philip Epstein and who deserves an honoured place among the Hollywood scriptwriters who believed that it was not possible to stress the Nazi menace too often. In *The Sea Hawk* Philip of Spain obviously stands for Hitler and the Armada for the Luftwaffe or any other German invading force. In fact Koch wanted to make the parallels even clearer at the end and broached the subject with Jack Warner himself. And with that open-handed generosity for which he was deservedly noted Warner said, certainly: if Koch would be so kind as to hand over the one and a half million dollars the picture had already cost, plus an extra million for out of pocket expenses, he could write any damned ending he pleased. Finding himself temporarily embarrassed for this trifling sum ('I had about six or seven dollars in my pocket,' he said) Koch was unable to avail himself of the kind offer. Even so the message of the film is plain enough, with Queen Elizabeth (Flora Robson) rounding things off with a speech that goes, in part: 'We have no quarrel with the people of Spain or any other country. But when the ruthless ambitions of a man threaten to engulf the world it becomes the solemn obligation of free men, *wherever they may be*, to affirm that the earth belongs . . . to all men and that freedom is the deed and title to the soil on which we exist.' The italics are not actually Koch's but he intended to nudge America, and especially the isolationists, in the ribs with a very sharp elbow indeed. And the brothers Warner had no objection because 'they were very interested,' he said, 'in doing what they could for the war effort and in supporting President Roosevelt.'

Meanwhile, though, the need for the Hays-Mayer type of appeasement had passed, if in fact it had ever existed in the first place. For Germany and Italy were beginning to ban American movies anyway and besides it had just been realised that South America offered as good a market as continental Europe. And so by 1940 other studios were beginning to make pictures that were overtly sympathetic to Britain and the fight against Fascism. Chaplin chipped in with *The Great Dictator*, a broad parody of Adenoid Hynkel, Garbitsch, Benzini Napolini and the rest, in which he felt moved so strongly as to utter his first comprehensible words (as opposed to the gobbledygook he spoke in *Modern Times*) on screen. The fact that his final plea for world peace, the summation of his own philosophy, was remarkable mostly for its naivety was neither here nor there. World War II had got to him. It had even got to MGM who came up with *Escape* (Robert Taylor rescuing his mum, Nazimova, from a Nazi concentration camp) and *The Mortal Storm* (Nazism dividing a German family). The German Embassy didn't like this one either and it cannot presumably have been best pleased by Alfred Hitchcock's *Foreign Correspondent*, in which Joel McCrea foils a bunch of spies and which ends with a clear exhortation to America to get involved with the war. And to an extent it did. In September 1940 Roosevelt bypassed Congress and, though the gesture could have cost him the presidential election, gave Britain fifty over-age destroyers. Soon afterwards the first peacetime draft in American history was introduced – the Selective Service Act – and what with Roosevelt winning the election and the Lend-Lease Bill being passed, Hollywood could now get down to bellicose business in earnest. Anti-Nazi pictures may have been a little bit dicey and not always good box office but who was going to object to staunch patriotic appeals?

Well, actually the America First movement did but happily they didn't count for much and throughout 1941 Hollywood stepped up its war effort. Tyrone Power popped up as *A Yank in the RAF*, while Robert Taylor joined *Flight Command* and Errol Flynn was the hero of *Dive Bomber*. There were even comedies with a forces background, Abbott and Costello appearing as *Buck Privates* and Bob Hope being *Caught in the Draft*. Among recruiting films – and at this stage recruitment was the main point of the exercise – by far the most important was *Sergeant York*, wherein Gary Cooper portrayed a real life World War I hero who overcame strong religious principles to join up and capture hordes of German soldiers single-handed. (Our friend Howard Koch had a hand in this one too.)

And then there was *Mrs Miniver*, whose importance as a morale-booster and winner of support for Britain is almost impossible to overstate and which is therefore virtually beyond criticism, despite its rosy and over-simplified view of British middle class (and, let's be fair, working class) grit and stiffness of upper lip. The lower orders were no doubt thinking, if not actually saying, "bless the squire and his relations and keep us in our proper stations" but when the crunch came they all pitched in together. At the end of the film the local vicar, Henry Wilcoxon, stands in his devastated church and declares, in part: 'This is not only a war of soldiers in uniform. It is a war of the people and it must be fought . . . in the heart of every man, woman and child who loves freedom.' Flora Robson in *The Sea Hawk* couldn't have put it better and Roosevelt found this sermon so moving that he had copies printed and dropped by aeroplane in occupied Europe; while of the film as a whole Winston Churchill said that it was propaganda worth 100 battleships. The eponymous heroine was the Scottish actress Greer Garson and the role came to her partly because better established Hollywood stars had turned it down on the grounds that they did not want to play somebody who had grown-up children. Miss Garson, though only thirty-three and asked to play the mother of Richard Ney (who later became her husband) took it on enthusiastically and, by way of reward, won the Oscar for best actress, which trophy she accepted with what is widely though erroneously, reputed to be the longest and most tedious speech in the entire history of Academy Awards.

Roosevelt asked MGM to get the film on general release as quickly as possible. 'And they did that,' said Miss Garson, 'so that it reached not only the metropolitan but the rural areas. And wherever *Mrs Miniver* went she had a quite extraordinary welcome. I went to little towns ... I remember a little coal mining town in West Virginia where I was warned beforehand that I might expect a good deal of isolationist sentiment and I'd better be prepared to try to offset it as best I could. But, ah, what a lesson they taught me ... They put on a parade for me that brought tears to my eyes ... they were all deeply and most emotionally involved.' The response to the picture was immediate and hugely enthusiastic on both sides of the Atlantic, even among loftier people than coal miners' wives. 'I remember the Queen Mother, God love her, said to me, "It was such a morale booster for us when we most needed it. We had no idea that we were quite so brave and were very pleased to be told that we were so heroic."' In America, Miss Garson said, 'It had an enormous effect. People were in tears, people stood up, people cheered, people clapped, embraced each other. It was extraordinary and I know because I saw the picture in many types of theatres and many types of neighbourhoods.'

But something else happened in 1941 that was far more important than anything Hollywood did, even more important than *Mrs Miniver*. On December 7 – "a date which will live in infamy," as Roosevelt put it – the Japanese made the gross error of bombing Pearl Harbor. And so, like it or not, America was at war, not to save Europe but to protect and avenge herself. One immediate result of the raid was a virulent and understandable if (as *Bad Day at Black Rock* later indicated) occasionally deplorable outbreak of anti-Japanese sentiment and in this Hollywood was not to be found wanting. It rounded up every Japanese gardener in sight and interned the lot. Take that, Tojo. War, however, brought even graver problems than the loss of their gardeners to the film community as it did to everyone else. Many of Hollywood's stars and other personnel had joined the reserve or registered for the draft straight-away, greatly to the dismay of the moguls. (Louis Mayer acting, one must assume, as selflessly as ever and no doubt in the best interests of the nation had tried to get all his stars deferred.) Among those who went off to do their bit were the "King of Hollywood" himself, Clark Gable (who volunteered immediately after the death of his wife Carole Lombard in a plane crash when she was returning from selling war bonds), James Stewart, Robert Montgomery, Mickey Rooney, Tyrone Power, John Ford, John Huston, Frank Capra and Darryl Zanuck. And Myrna Loy retired from films to do war work for the duration of hostilities. Not all the Hollywood brigade saw active service but a good many of them did and Jimmy Stewart ended up a general.

Bob Hope and Eddie Bracken, who appeared together in *Caught in the Draft* were, in fact, caught in the draft – or at least Bracken was but he was deferred for domestic and physical reasons and, like Hope and a lot of others, joined USO, touring American bases at home and overseas to entertain the troops. Bracken said: 'I went out for the Naval Welfare to entertain the soldiers in the South Pacific while Bob was doing the same in Europe. And if we were caught, if we were captured by the Germans or whoever, Bob was to be treated as a general and I was to be treated as an admiral.'

The British personnel in Hollywood reacted to the declaration of war in a characteristically British way. Douglas Fairbanks Jr recalled that he heard the news on the radio while he and his wife, along with Laurence Olivier, Vivien Leigh, David Niven and Robert Coote were cruising around near Catalina Island off the Californian coast in a yacht they had all chartered for the weekend. 'Olivier,' he said, 'went round to all the other boats in harbour and said, "You're all finished! Enjoy today because there's going to be no tomorrow." And as he looked somewhat like Ronald Colman, with a little moustache, word went round that Colman was in the yacht basin insulting all the other members of the yacht club. And they called upon Colman, who was actually on another boat sound asleep on deck, and told him that he had to go and apologise to everybody. And he said, "What for? I haven't done anything."' But, despite Colman's enjoyable embarrassment, 'We all got in a very depressed mood. Then we decided to do a lot of toasting and very shortly after that Niven decided he was going to be the first to go back and join his old regiment. He was the only one who'd been a professional soldier. And then Olivier followed as soon as he could.'

Greer Garson also tried to get back to England but MGM refused to release her, so she flew to Washington to ask the British ambassador to use his influence. 'Not that I thought I was all that important,' she said, 'but I wanted to go back. He said, "What do you think you can do?" I said, "Well, something. I won't bear arms, I'm afraid, but I can do Red Cross work or first aid or join the Air Raid wardens." He said, "Well, your value to your country would be about £2.10s. a week, whereas if you stay where you are and do the kind of pictures your studio is putting you in you're worth a great deal more," and he sent me home. I went home rather subdued and went to work again.' (Much the same thing happened to Ronald Colman. He, too, was advised to stay put and indeed he was widely regarded as Britain's unofficial ambassador to Hollywood throughout the war.)

Still, the women had an important contribution to make on the home front in America, boosting morale and raising money. 'We did what we could,' Greer Garson said. 'You'd finish a long picture and the next day you were out on a dirty old troop train, either alone with an escort or two or with a group of familiar faces. We toured a month or six weeks at a time, doing many cities in a day and finishing up with a sort of performance at night because we had an orchestra with us. We had very long, very crowded, very hectic days. Everybody would want us to come to just one more little hospital that everybody else had forgotten. So we'd go. Or there was a munitions plant that hadn't had a visit from anyone.' Joan Bennett also traversed the country by rail on what was known as the Victory Caravan – a train packed with stars which stopped almost everywhere so that its passengers could sell war bonds. 'We'd also go to army camps and set up stalls with coffee and cakes and other goodies to eat,' she said. And, too, there was the Hollywood Canteen in which she and colleagues would-talk to and dance with servicemen on leave. Jane Russell did that sort of thing as well, passing out hot dogs at the fast food counter. Furthermore, she had a whole airforce squadron named after her – "Russell's Raiders" they were called. Joan Fontaine was not so honoured but she and her husband of the time, Brian Aherne, had their own plane anyway and 'We crossed the country in it, doing what was called "Thumbs Up for Britain", raising money the whole time. I got on the sewing machine and made some terrible pyjamas for people. It was probably more lethal wearing them than the war was. Certainly they had wounds from wearing my pyjamas.'

But the film industry had an even more significant role to play than distributing ill-made and potentially dangerous pyjamas to unsuspecting servicemen. In addressing Congress, Roosevelt had outlined the six areas around which films and propaganda generally might most usefully be constructed: the war itself; the nature of the enemy; the united nations and their people; increased production; the home front; and the fighting forces. Hollywood dutifully complied despite its problems, of which the drafting of its workforce was only one. Unpleasant rumours began to abound – that there would be a dictatorship of the film industry set up in Washington, that raw stock would be rationed, that double features would be banned, that sets could cost no more than 5,000 dollars thus bringing an end to musicals and – worst of all – that salaries would have a ceiling of 25,000 dollars. None of this turned out to be true, although there was a shortage of ammunition for film purposes which meant, as *Variety* pointed out, that western heroes in particular suddenly became much better shots. Otherwise things went along pretty much as before except that there were certain restrictions on the building of sets, partly for budgetary reasons and partly through a scarcity of materials. But even this was eventually turned to advantage when the comparative skimpiness of the sets was one of the contributory factors to the introduction of *film noir*.

Indeed, there are those who claim that despite the economic strictures and the need to reduce costs that the war imposed, the 1940s were Hollywood's finest period of film making. Their arguments suggest that good sprang from adversity, that smaller budgets led to greater invention and that the new wave of writers who had been increasingly moving to Hollywood from other areas were making their presence felt more emphatically. The producer Pandro S. Berman believed that in this period the movies were less inclined to reach out, as they had done hitherto, for the biggest possible audiences, therefore arriving at the lowest common denominator, and began far more to look for approval from the critics and the Academy first and only later to hope that audiences would like the product, too.

I find all these theories debatable. If you apply them to the decade as a whole they may well be found to contain a sizeable nugget of truth. But if you look simply at the war years, it's difficult to escape the conviction that here was a wonderful opportunity lost. The films made then undoubtedly did marvels at the box office but, with a few rare exceptions, they did not noticeably advance the art of the cinema. In conversation one day Don Ameche said: 'John Ford had not seen one single picture for four or five years – I think he was out in the South Pacific. And I remember sitting with him at a golf club and he'd seen a number of pictures when he got back and he said what a total disaster for the motion picture industry those years were, because they had had the greatest opportunity ever in the history of this business to experiment and not have to worry about making money and they didn't do that, not once . . . They just made pictures as rapidly as they could to make money.'

A possible explanation for this was offered by the writer Philip Dunne: 'There was an awful lot of money and nothing to spend it on, so the nation went to the movies. One effect it had on Hollywood – and I hope this won't be taken as a snobbish remark – was that most of the better movie makers had gotten into the service one way or another; they were doing something for the war; they weren't there to make films so there was a great blossoming of second-rate talent and they became attached to very big money hits . . . I'm mentioning no names but there were some definitely second and third rate people who were involved with important projects during the war and couldn't cut the mustard afterwards.' It would take a lengthy and detailed search through the archives to identify positively all the people to whom he referred but on the whole I think the point was well made. There was a wartime hunger for entertainment and Hollywood worked strenuously, using whatever means and personnel it had to hand, to satisfy it, both in the early years (roughly until the end of 1943) when things were going badly for the Allies and later, when victory began to move into sight. In that first period the objects of the cinema were, broadly speaking, to boost morale, lionise the fighting forces and praise those working on the home front. 'The films were escapist mostly,' said Joan Fontaine. 'People could not stand any more war, any more deprivation, any more rationing and so the escape for everybody was through movies.' Yes, but there were exceptions, including *Sergeant York* (1941), co-written by Howard Koch with, among others, John Huston. The gallant sergeant, played by Gary Cooper (who won an Oscar for it), had been a First World War hero, a conscientious objector who had swallowed his scruples and gone to battle, there to win medals galore by capturing whole battalions of Germans all by himself. It looked in 1941 and looks still like a prime example of storytellers using the past to comment upon the present and the future and to warn the nation to be ready for war. Koch said: 'I think that was the intention of those who produced the picture, the studio [Warners] and the people connected with it. As far as I was concerned what I tried to do was to show that sometimes it is necessary to use violence to defend things that are important in life.' In that, he felt, the film both mirrored the overall mood of the nation and administered another sharp nudge to the isolationists.

A much greater exception to the rule that wartime pictures were not as good as they might have been given a little more boldness and imagination was one of the most splendid film of any era (and never mind such Pseuds' Corner comments as Pauline Kael's "the best bad movie ever made") – *Casablanca*, which was made in 1942. It was set at a time when America had no part in the war and was aimed very largely at the appeasers. Humphrey Bogart's line: 'What time is it in New York? I bet they're asleep in New York. I bet they're asleep all over America' has nothing to do with nostalgia for the nocturnal peace of his homeland. He is saying, "Wake up,

America,' and even though by the time the film was made America was already wide awake and getting into the thick of the action, it was a timely reminder that the nation had done the right thing after Pearl Harbor. All manner of myths and legends have sprung up about the making of *Casablanca* – that the script was written while filming was already going on (true); that two alternative endings were shot (untrue); that when Bogart nodded approval for the Free French to sing the "Marseillaise" and drown out the Germans he had no idea what he was nodding for but nodded simply because the director, Michael Curtiz, told him to (quite probably true) and that Bogart and Ingrid Bergman were both second choices, the originals having been Ronald Reagan and Ann Sheridan (quite appallingly true but at least indicating that someone up there in that Great Cutting Room in the Sky keeps a benevolent eye on the movies and is prepared occasionally to intervene and help wrest triumph from the jaws of what would certainly have been disaster if the casting people had not had second thoughts). In the same way the film has been subjected to a variety of dotty interpretations, the most amusing being that the friendship between Bogart's Rick and Claude Rains's corrupt police chief is in fact homosexual. But this, of course, is merely the work of the Gay Mafia who are always trying to make us believe that everybody is really homosexual if only we'd all admit it.

Actually, according to Howard Koch, Warners had bought the story in the first place with the idea of casting George Raft and Hedy Lamarr but this never got beyond an idea because Raft turned it down. Koch himself was brought in to work on the screenplay after the Epstein brothers had been seconded to help out elsewhere in the war effort. He had two weeks with the Epsteins while they filled him in on where the story was going, as far as they could work it out, and then ... 'I was on the last stretch for the final script and working very often on the set with the actors and the director. And I think at this stage what we were trying to do was make an entertaining picture that would say something good politically.' Two alternative endings may not actually have been shot but they were debated, he said, right up until the last moment. 'I remember Ingrid Bergman coming to me on the set, when I was working with the actors, and saying "How can I play this love scene when I don't know which man I'm going to end up with?" I made the best guess that I could, which was in line with the ending as it turned out and I think she was happy with that approach.' The alternatives were the romantic ending – Bogart going off with Bergman – or the one that was eventually chosen, the sacrifice – Bogart packing Bergman onto the plane with Paul Henreid and going off himself with Claude Rains, hence the homosexual theory. It would come as a surprise to Howard Koch to learn that there were homosexual undertones in all this. Being merely the writer he saw the conclusion only in political terms – 'anyone making a sacrifice, as Rick made one there, would be acting in a cause that was for the benefit of all human beings.'

One great advantage *Casablanca* enjoyed in being set in the period before Pearl Harbor was its lack of topicality. No matter what happened it could not be rendered out of date by events that occurred between the end of shooting and the premiere. For more standard war films the fear of becoming instantly irrelevant because of changing circumstances was very real. It was a problem that stayed around, for obvious reasons, throughout the war, although naturally it did not stop movies with more topical subject matter being made.

What kind of films were these? In his book *Guts and Glory*, Lawrence H. Suid makes a thoughtful distinction between what he calls "World War II – Fantasy" and "World War II – Reality". In the early part of the conflict Hollywood dealt mostly with the fantasy, or with the fighting man as hero rather than the fighting man as corpse. Such pictures as *Wake Island* (1942) and *Guadalcanal Diary* (1943) both set in the Pacific, both concerning US Marines trying to capture or hold on to a strategic base, both aimed at raising morale, come into the fantasy category. So, too, does *Bataan* (1943), which has a very similar story to the others, although it does introduce a harsher note in that the hero, Robert Taylor, is killed in the end. *Flying Tigers* (1942) changed the locale from the Pacific to China and the personnel from marines to airmen, led by John Wayne. And *Reunion in France* (1943) featured Joan Crawford as a Paris fashion designer helping a gallant American airman, John Wayne once more, to escape from the occupying Nazi hordes. Both of these were blatant flag wavers and helped to create Wayne's amazing reputation as the archetypal American hero even though he was never in the armed forces (rejected for health reasons) and fought all his battles on a studio's back lot.

Meanwhile, Bogart (also rejected on grounds of age and health) had followed *Casablanca* with *Sahara* (1943), which dealt with a small group of soldiers giving the Germans a very hard time during the retreat from Tobruk. It was popular in the USA but was given the raspberry in Britain, since it gave the impression that it was the Americans who were fighting in the Middle East and God knows where the British were. (Even so, it didn't arouse anything like the outrage created in 1945 by *Operation Burma*, which made it quite clear that it was Errol Flynn and a few other members of the American army who captured Burma. This notion was greeted with such indignation in the UK that the film had to be withdrawn.)

As the war went on the armed forces lent more and more facilities and co-operation to the film makers, who responded with, in particular, some excellent documentaries. Between 1942 and 1945 Frank Capra, for instance, made a series of pictures under the generic title "Why We Fight", which were intended to explain precisely that to the armed forces and were not for general consumption. Capra's *Prelude to War* was, however, shown commercially but with little success, for the public was not yet in the mood for realism. John Ford, a naval commander, added to his own legend by being injured during the filming of *Battle of Midway*. *The Hollywood Reporter* with, perhaps, a touch of hyperbole announced that he had carried on directing with 'one arm almost useless as the result of a Jap machine gun bullet'. Let us hope the wound was not quite that bad, for he and Capra had difficulties enough in making their documentaries. Sometimes they had to steal film from the army – either raw stock or captured German newsreel footage – to keep going. And both had to be constantly on the lookout for any Communist propaganda that might creep in, since a number of the writers attached to the documentary units were known to be very left wing. Notwithstanding the fact that Russia and America were allies, Communism was no more popular in the USA then than it has ever been.

Left: Errol Flynn, grimly heroic, and Fred MacMurray, a touch less confident, about to give the Hun what for in *Dive Bomber*
Below: John Ford leaning on the camera as he directs *Seas Beneath*. John Loder disappears down the hatchway. Later Ford tried to enlist John Wayne as an ordinary seaman

Greer Garson as the eponymous *Mrs Miniver*, showing the stiffest upper lips as she comforts children and working classes alike

According to the writer and director Robert Parrish, Ford was convinced in 1940 that America would go to war and so formed a US Navy Reserve Unit 'to train for combat photography or whatever might be needed . . .' Later this outfit, for which he had recruited people like Parrish and the cinematographer Greg Toland, was absorbed into the OSS 'to make films for internal OSS use, how to operate behind enemy lines and so on'. Ford, who was appointed chief of the Field Photographic Branch of the OSS with the rank of lieutenant-commander (he was later promoted to rear-admiral) made a number of notable documentaries – including one with the unambivalent title, *Sex Hygiene* – but *The Battle of Midway* was probably the most famous of them. Parrish said Ford had it in mind to make this a propaganda film but 'he wouldn't allow the word propaganda to pass his lips. When he asked me to edit this picture I said, "What is it – propaganda film?" He spat and lit his pipe, which usually took about a minute and a half, then he looked at me again and said, "How do you spell that?" So I spelt it and he said, "Don't ever let me hear you say that word as long as you're under my command. Ever. Is that understood? There's no such thing as a propaganda film. I want the mothers of America to see that their sons are fighting a war in the Pacific."' Nevertheless, despite his obscure objection to the word it *was* a propaganda film and a very effective one, the propaganda being in no way lessened by his own wound for which he received the Purple Heart. Or by the crafty way in which he manipulated the rule that said an equal amount of screen time should be given to each of the armed forces.

When Parrish was editing the film, Ford came to him and said: 'You're five feet off on the Marine Corps.' Then he took a roll of 35 mm film from his pocket and said: 'Cut this in.' It was a close-up of the President's son, Major James Roosevelt, standing to attention. Parrish said to him: 'Well, the picture's finished and if you cut in just this one roll of film, the music will stop for five and a half seconds.' Ford said: 'That's good. That'll give 'em time to think. Just cut it in.'

The picture was then shown to the President and Mrs Roosevelt at the White House. 'The President,' said Parrish, 'was a man who liked to talk – what kind of gun that was, what kind of an aeroplane was this and so on. But when it got to the close-up of Major James Roosevelt there was no sound from him or Mrs Roosevelt or anybody for two and a half minutes until the film finished. Mrs Roosevelt was wiping away a tear and the president said, "I want every mother in America to see this picture."' Which was merely an echo of Ford's own ambition.

From those war years under Ford's command, Parrish had a vivid recollection of the day John Wayne visited their office in Washington. Ford said: 'Hey, Bob, look who's come to see us – it's the Duke,' and greeted his visitor warmly. A few moments later in the course of idle chit-chat he glared at Parrish and said: 'What the hell are you sitting there for? Don't you have work to do?' Never slow to take a hint, Parrish returned to his cutting-room where he was joined after a while by Wayne, who was on the verge of tears. Ford, it appeared, had announced his intention of having the great movie star drafted into the navy as an ordinary seaman. Now to do him justice Wayne had tried to get into the war but his family commitments and a badly damaged shoulder had kept him out. Besides, he certainly didn't want to go in as an enlisted

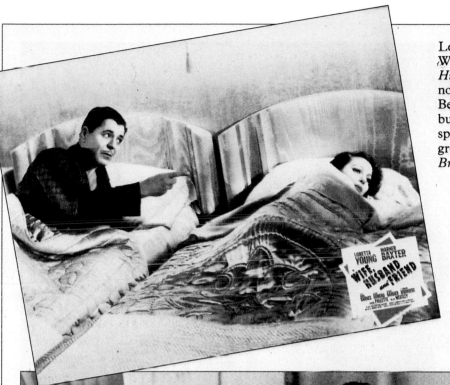

Left: Loretta Young and Warner Baxter in *Wife, Husband and Friend* – to say nothing of separate beds Below: Katharine Hepburn, Cary Grant and a spotty friend in one of the great comedies of the 1930s, *Bringing up Baby*

Above: Jane Russell, who memorably introduced the mammary to the western
Right: Jane Mansfield, even more memorably mammaried

Next page: Marilyn Monroe (with Jack Lemmon and Tony Curtis in *Some Like It Hot*) could show nothing and still be sexy. But by the time of *Blow Up* (inset) in 1966, the bra – and every other garment above the waist – was, as Vanessa Redgrave indicates, obsolete

"There goes our only evidence. Asta, how could you!"

William POWELL Myrna LOY in AFTER THE THIN MAN

Left: At the time of *After the Thin Man* (William Powell, Myrna Loy and shaggy accomplice Astor, 1936) the Censor ruled, OK. But there was still room for suggestive dialogue

Below: In *Last Tango in Paris* (Brando and Maria Schneider) in 1972 nobody bothered with suggestive dialogue. Everything was pretty well explicit

Left: With censorship more or less abandoned, came sex accompanied by violence in, for example, *Death Wish*

James Cagney does his bit for wartime recruitment as one of the *Captains of the Clouds*
Inset, left: Chaplin's contribution to the war effort – *The Great Dictator*, with himself as Adenoid Hynkel and Jack Oakie as Benzini Napolini
Right: Scarlet O'Hara takes a break, doubtless unaware that Smoking Cigarettes Can Seriously Damage Your Health

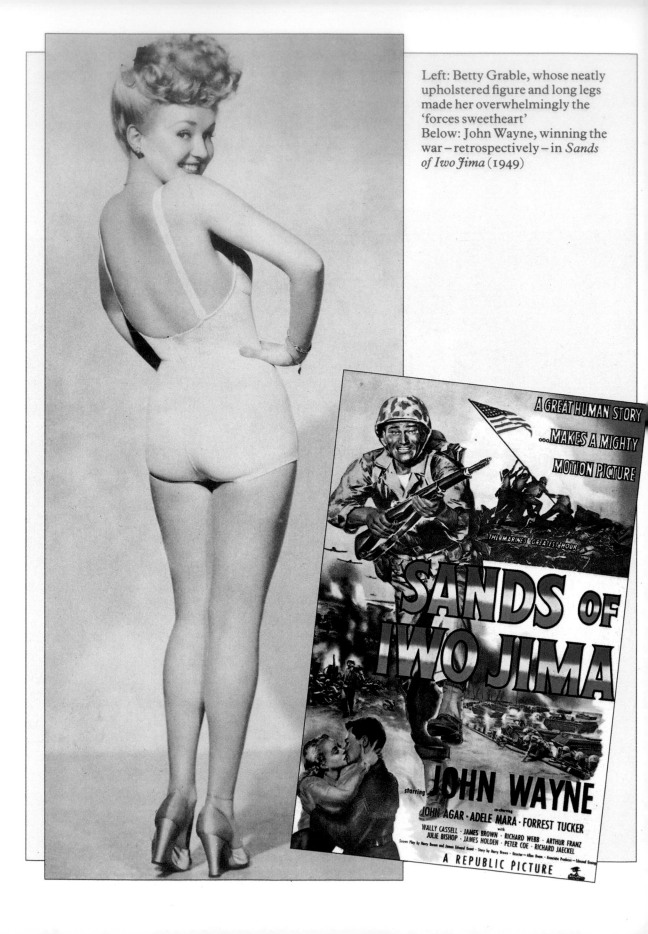

Left: Betty Grable, whose neatly upholstered figure and long legs made her overwhelmingly the 'forces sweetheart'
Below: John Wayne, winning the war – retrospectively – in *Sands of Iwo Jima* (1949)

man, not at his age – he was in his mid to late 30s – running around square-bashing with a lot of kids. He was, Parrish said, quite distraught at the prospect and kept mumbling: 'I can't do this, Bob. I gotta talk to somebody . . .' Perhaps he did manage to talk to somebody in authority because he never was drafted. Or, just as likely, it's on the cards that Ford never intended to carry out his threat; merely making it was the kind of malicious joke he was much given to playing on people.

While Ford, Capra and the like were shooting military documentaries, the Office of War Information recruited other members of the film community – writers like Philip Dunne, producers like John Houseman – to turn out more political propaganda. Dunne said: 'We made a series called "The American Scene" which showed how democracy worked to solve its problems. We were competing with the Soviet propaganda which was going to come on after the war. We knew this, we knew the competition was there.' So, for example, they made pictures which portrayed America as a melting pot wherein Serbs, Croats and all manner of other people of foreign extraction could work and live together and become Americans. Other films, featuring the likes of Toscanini, were made to be shown by the invading Allied forces in Italy and France. One, directed by Jean Renoir, was intended to 'say to the French, Here's what we're telling our troops about you. Then we could flatter them outrageously, because they needed flattering now they'd had the whey beaten out of them for four years . . . And then we made news reviews which told the story of what had happened during the time these peoples had been blacked out.'

Many of the wartime documentaries – William Wyler's *Memphis Belle*, for instance, or John Huston's *Report from the Aleutians* – were good films in their own right. Others, especially Capra's *The Negro Soldier* now look painfully dated, Capra's because its honourable attempt to stress the contribution made to the war effort by black troops cannot disguise the fact that said troops were segregated and even then had to serve under white officers. And at least one of the "Hollywood Colonels" as they were known – Darryl Zanuck – came in for a certain amount of derision because among the most notable figures in his picture, *At the Front*, was Zanuck himself, making several appearances in which pluckily and aggressively he was seen waving a Tommy gun, much to the anxiety, I imagine, of the troops on his own side. (Many years later, while he was filming *The Longest Day*, I came across Zanuck reliving these moments of heroism among the smoke and special battle effects on the beaches on the Île de Ré. On that occasion, fortunately, he was brandishing nothing more lethal than a cigar as long as a rifle barrel.)

However, while the Colonels were employing their skills to further the Allied cause, the Germans were sneakily using Hollywood's own product as anti-American propaganda. With some deft editing Joseph Goebbels rearranged the Dead End Kids' films to present an image of the USA which would hardly have been recognised by prewar filmgoers. One of the Dead End Kids, Huntz Hall, said: 'He used the pictures to show the degradation of what was happening to American youth, the message being "We have to capture this country because look what's happening to their children" . . . He took out all the good and they just saw the squalor and the dirty tenements . . . the kids living out of ashcans and swimming off the docks and the filth and the dirt in the water. He used all that. But I was proud he used it because he got beat.'

Well, indeed he did get beat but that was much later. In the meantime, back in America, the cinema-going public, ignorant of Goebbels' dirty tricks, needed its ration of escapism and so one of the side effects of the war was the revival of the musical. As a genre, of course, it had never entirely gone away but at the same time it had never entirely recaptured the popularity it enjoyed in the earliest years of talking pictures. At that time musicals proved so instantly successful that the market was flooded with them to such an extent that quite early in the 1930s the public had become surfeited. The problem was not only too many musicals but too many poor musicals, although the occasional outstanding specimen would crop up to keep interest alive – Warner Brothers' *42nd Street*, for instance whose brash toughness set a new trend. (Warner Brothers were, in fact, the market leaders in musicals in the early 1930s.) And it was the dance director of *42nd Street*, the uniquely gifted Busby Berkeley, who did most during the middle and later years of the decade to ensure that neither Hollywood nor the public could ignore the musical extravaganza for too long. Later, at RKO, Fred Astaire and Ginger Rogers did their share and more to keep the ball rolling while, as the thirties wore on, MGM, whose musical efforts had not been too notable earlier, came on strongly with their Jeanette MacDonald and Nelson Eddy operettas, Eleanor Powell spectaculars and, of course, the magical *The Wizard of Oz*. So, yes, the musical had always been around although, of late, it had not been nearly as ubiquitous as it became in the war years when something like forty per cent of the films made were musicals. By no means all of them were good but, looking back now, many of them have a certain amount of sociological and historical interest. Into that category come such flagwavers and morale boosters as *This is the Army*, with songs by Irving Berlin, and *Stagedoor Canteen* and *Hollywood Canteen*, both of which record multitudes of stars doing their bit for the war effort (Joan Crawford dancing with a GI, Bette Davis jitterbugging, Errol Flynn singing a comic song). *Star Spangled Rhythm* was much the same; it did have some apology for a story line but basically it showed every star on the Paramount lot mucking about in a good-natured way and featured Paulette Goddard, Dorothy Lamour and Veronica Lake in a number entitled "A Sweater, a Sarong and a Peekaboo Bang". It was made in 1942 and presumably pre-dated the request by the authorities to Miss Lake to cut off her peekaboo bang, on the reasonable grounds that factory girls who copied it were being dragged painfully into the machinery on the assembly line.

These, however, were "wartime" musicals in the sense that they recognised that a war was on and the troops needed certain home comforts, even if they amounted to nothing much more than the ecstasy of dancing with Joan Crawford and the like. But there was another, even more escapist, kind of musical such as *Meet Me in St Louis* which ignored global hostilities altogether, being set at the time of the World Fair in 1903. Then, too, there were such curiosities as *Rhapsody in Blue* and *Night and Day* which purported – with a great deal of what one might charitably call poetic licence – to tell the true stories of, respectively, George Gershwin and Cole Porter. In between those and the *Stagedoor Canteen* kind of movie was the sort of hybrid represented by

Yankee Doodle Dandy. This combines the biopic element with nostalgia for the good old days and a fair bit of rousing jingoism, since it's the life story of George M. Cohan, than whom nobody ever waved the Stars and Stripes with greater vigour or enthusiasm. The film ends soon after America's entry into the war.

By far the biggest musical star of the time – and in many ways the biggest star of the war years – was Betty Grable. Between 1941 and 1945 she combined being overwhelmingly the forces' favourite pin-up girl with starring in more than a dozen musical confections which were so successful that in 1943 she was America's top box office attraction. She described herself as "strictly an enlisted man's girl" but I don't think her brand of blonde, snub-nosed, well-scrubbed good looks appealed to the carnal element in the enlisted man. Rather, I suspect, did he look upon her as the ideal sweetheart, the girl back home whom he might marry when the fighting was done. With her neatly upholstered figure and long, pretty legs Grable was, in appearance, a forerunner of Marilyn Monroe, but in fact her appeal was much closer to that of Doris Day – for like Day and unlike Monroe she seemed to wear an invisible but nevertheless impregnable chastity belt of virginity and like Day but unlike Monroe she lacked sexuality. Betty Hutton, who began her career in musicals during the war, was another who came across like the girl next door, though bouncier and more tomboyish than Grable; while a more exotic touch was lent by Carmen Miranda, the "Brazilian bombshell" who went down big with the South American audiences but whose chances of making much of an impact on the libido of the average man were greatly impaired by the grotesque costumes that Hollywood inflicted on her. It is, after all, rather difficult to nurture erotic feelings towards a woman who seems constantly to be wearing the raw materials for a gigantic fruit salad on top of her head.

Escapism apart the home front, as opposed to war zone, movies concentrated mainly on boosting the morale of those who by reason of sex, age, physical disability or deferred occupation were left behind to keep things ticking over in the USA. The bulk of the audience here was obviously women but these were more independent, more confident women than they had been in the prewar years. A great majority of them were working, having taken over the jobs recently vacated by their menfolk and those newly created by the war effort, and as such they were the breadwinners and the decision makers in their households. This significant fact was not immediately grasped by Hollywood which was inclined to turn out films like *Rosie the Riveter* and *Swing-Shift Maisie* to underline the satisfaction and fun a girl could derive from heavy factory work. But then as the realisation dawned that not only did women now have money of their own but that there were far more of them than of men sitting in the cinemas, the "woman's picture" started to appear. *Tender Comrades* is a case in point: three female welders (paramount among them Ginger Rogers) set up home together while their husbands are away at the front. They rally round each other, keep their chins up and the home fires burning and comfort each other in times of bereavement, such as when Miss Rogers' husband, Robert Ryan, is killed in action. It's a weepie and might have been easily forgotten as such had not Miss Rogers' eagle-eyed mother spotted the tell-tale sign of Communist propaganda in the script.

Well, it was written by Dalton Trumbo, later blacklisted after investigation by the House Un-American Activities Committee, and Mrs Lela Rogers, who could obviously sniff out a Communist at a hundred paces, upwind, in the dark and with a clothes peg on her nose, seized triumphantly on one dastardly line in the screenplay that said, in effect, "share and share alike; that's the meaning of democracy." Oh yeah, muttered Mrs Rogers. Sez who? And she pointed this line out when testifying before HUAC as a very friendly witness. Still, all those horrors were yet to come.

Since You Went Away, a David Selznick production and the longest and most expensive film to come out of Hollywood since his own *Gone With the Wind*, was a far more lavish variation on the theme of plucky women defending the hearth while their hubbies were away at the war. It starred Claudette Colbert, Joseph Cotten, Jennifer Jones, Shirley Temple, Agnes Moorehead and a vast number of others. And like most of the "women's pictures" it stressed the womanly virtues of self-sacrifice, loyalty, devotion and quiet pluck. Nearly all these films boiled down to romantic fiction, underlining the all-embracing power of love, inducing laughter and tears and providing the kind of ending that would cause the women in the audience to sob quite painfully with happiness. It was almost as if they were saying to these women – these independent women, remember – that while charging around and being their own person was all very well in wartime, the day was coming when the chaps would be back and demanding a return to the status quo they had known before they left, i.e., a well-ordered world in which men went out to work and women stayed at home in the kitchen. In later films this message would be put across much more harshly. Even films that were not overtly to do with the war – *Now Voyager*, for instance, with Bette Davis and Paul Henreid, or *Random Harvest* with Greer Garson and Ronald Colman dished up the female loyalty and self-sacrifice angle with a fairly heavy hand.

Back in the war zone, however, the movies were taking a pretty close look at the enemy and didn't like what they saw at all. Germans, for example, were invariably brutal if they were in the Gestapo and often brutal and usually a touch cretinous if they were in the Wehrmacht. 'Heil Hitler!' says a German soldier to Fred MacMurray in *Above Suspicion*. 'Nuts to you, dope,' says MacMurray, revealing a rare turn of wit. 'I give you our German greeting, American,' says the soldier, to which MacMurray who is obviously on top form, snaps back: 'And I give you ours, dope.' This is too much for the poor German, who can't hope to match this crackling stuff, and we leave him mumbling to his companions: 'Was heisst das "dope"?' On the other hand, talking of cretinous reminds me that in the same film Joan Crawford sits down at the piano and says to Basil Rathbone, 'You remember this, Count. You were at Oxford,' and proceeds to play the Eton Boating Song.

Gestapo-type brutality cropped up in Edward Dmytryk's *Hitler's Children* wherein Nazis flog Bonita Granville. Another kind of German, possibly the worst kind, being both brutal and suave, was personified by George Sanders in *Confessions of a Nazi Spy*, *Manhunt* and *They Came to Blow up America*. English actors were often cast as Germans, probably because they had such funny accents, although occasionally a German would get to play a German, notably Erich von Stroheim who wore a memorably cultured scowl as Rommel in Billy Wilder's *Five Graves to Cairo*.

But if Germans could be either brutal or cretinous or villainous and smooth, there were no variations at all in the Japanese as depicted in the war films. The Japanese were just absolutely foul and there was an end to it. As Charles Higham and Joel Greenberg point out in their book, *Hollywood in the Forties*, the Japs were portrayed as 'repulsive, sadistic, libidinous little monkeys, grinningly bespectacled and sporting king-size choppers'. Come again – king-size what? Ah. Yes. One assumes that Messrs Higham and Greenberg are referring to the Japanese teeth since the merest mention of the size of any other part of their anatomy would certainly have been banned by the Breen Office.

Inevitably, comedy featured largely in Hollywood's war effort since the need to keep people as cheerful as possible was even greater than it had been in the height, or depths, of the Depression. There were some very good comedies, too – Capra's *Arsenic and Old Lace*, *The Man who Came to Dinner*, the earlier and best of the Bing Crosby-Bob Hope "Road" films and, on a more sophisticated level, Katharine Hepburn and Spencer Tracy in *Woman of the Year* among them. For the most part the comedy films did not have a war setting, though there were exceptions – Abbott and Costello in *Buck Privates*, Hope in *Caught in the Draft*, for example. Better than either of those, however, was George Stevens' *The More the Merrier* which starred the delicious Jean Arthur (along with Joel McCrea and Charles Coburn) in a romantic and funny tale about the housing shortage in wartime Washington. And best of all was Lubitsch's magnificently funny *To Be Or Not To Be*, a towering monument to hilarious bad taste, set in Nazi-occupied Poland. Jack Benny played a ham actor-manager (and Carole Lombard his wife and co-star) offering productions of Shakespeare that were only slightly more pleasurable than having a couple of Gestapo officers billeted in your home. Around this situation were woven plots and sub-plots involving resistance fighters, Miss Lombard's infidelities and an impersonation of Hitler. It was not, however, any of this that caused outrage but the dialogue, which included a Nazi officer saying, with a satisfied smirk, 'So they call me Concentration Camp Erhardt?' and, as a criticism of Mr Benny's Hamlet, 'Believe me, what he did to Shakespeare we are now doing to Poland.' Well, no doubt in 1942 this was a bit strong and the film was roundly condemned. Even today some of the lines have the power to shock but the overall impression that comes across now is of a brilliantly crafted comedy, written incidentally by Edwin Justus Mayer from a story by Lubitsch. What the reaction of the time proved, however, was that while audiences were prepared to laugh at some aspects of the war they did not want the comedy to touch on anything serious.

In the early 1940s Lubitsch and Capra were joined as the leading satirists of and commentators upon the American scene by Preston Sturges. His career, at least the significant part of it, was brief and meteoric but it could be argued that between 1940 and 1944 he became (albeit unintentionally) the cinema's first *auteur*. Some years were to pass before anyone realised there was such a thing as an *auteur* and then, naturally, it was the French critics who put the concept into words. The thought behind it, quite simply, is that the only true author of a film is the director, that his vision overrides all else. But to be an *auteur* you must do rather more than just direct

Above: *Star Spangled Rhythm* – illustrating, no doubt, all the fun and glamour of the wartime production line
Left: Eddie Bracken, here taking a call in *Hail the Conquering Hero*, was credited with the capture of two Japanese snipers
Right: Claudette Colbert, Jennifer Jones and Shirley Temple keep the home fires burning and display feminine pluck and loyalty in *Since You Went Away*

and Sturges most certainly did. He also wrote his own screenplays and later, though not always successfully, produced them as well. Others before him, of course, had had a hand in the scripts they directed – Welles, with *Citizen Kane*, is a prime example – but invariably they were no more than co-authors. The most common situation was for a director to be handed a completed screenplay (sometimes even with the camera angles specified) and told to get on with it. He might have some control over script alterations and choice of cast but not usually a great deal. Quite often he did not even have the right to the first or, as it was sometimes known, the "director's" cut. With *The Great McGinty*, which he persuaded Paramount to let him direct in 1940 by the irresistible expedient of giving them the screenplay for nothing, Sturges changed all that. The script – about a hobo, Brian Donleavy, who with the help of the corrupt political machine becomes state governor, then ruins his career by falling in love and going straight – won the Oscar, the film was a financial success and Sturges followed it with *Christmas in July*, which he also produced. Between 1940 and 1944 he wrote and directed eight pictures, all of them notable for a wit and flair that were remarkable at the time and are hardly to be found anywhere today. Among them were *The Lady Eve* with Barbara Stanwyck as a cardsharper and Henry Fonda as an apparent bumpkin who outsmarts her, *Sullivan's Travels*, a wicked satire of Hollywood's devout determination to put money before art or social conscience, *The Miracle of Morgan's Creek*, a parody of the Virgin Birth that somehow, amazingly, escaped the vigilance of the Breen Office and *Hail the Conquering Hero*, about a non-combatant who is mistaken for a returning hero in his home town. Eddie Bracken starred in both *Morgan's Creek*, which also derived fun from the GI's perennial nightmare – the girls back home having a riotous time while their sweethearts were away – and *Conquering Hero*.

The Breen Office, he said, objected to *Morgan's Creek* because in the original script the leading lady, Betty Hutton, got drunk, got pregnant but didn't get married – all three concepts being anathema to the censors. Sturges cleverly sorted this out with a little cosmetic surgery: the girl did not get drunk but was accidentally knocked out instead; she certainly became pregnant but only after going through a marriage ceremony which, being in a concussed state, she had quite forgotten about the next day. The Breen Office, no doubt, had moral objections to a woman becoming pregnant on her wedding night – unseemly haste, I expect, in their opinion – but even they could hardly forbid it.

Both films, Bracken said, were extremely popular with the troops. In a vote taken in eight theatres of military operations, he added, 'I came out over Bob Hope and Danny Kaye as the best comedian of World War II and the reasons for that were *The Miracle of Morgan's Creek* and *Conquering Hero*. The soldiers loved them; I could do no wrong.' Indeed he was even credited with the capture of two Japanese snipers who had crept up with murderous intent on an American base where *Morgan's Creek* was being shown in the open air. The snipers laughed so heartily at what was happening on the screen that they fell out of their tree. Or so it is said.

Of Sturges, Bracken said: 'He once said to me, and it's one of my favourite lines, "My mother brought me up to be a genius and she was one of the most successful women I've ever known." He believed it, too – and I believe it. He *was* a genius. And that was what they [Hollywood] thought of him: they loved him, respected him and he was a genius but he began making bad movies.' The bad movies came later, after 1944, when Sturges made the mistake of joining Howard Hughes at RKO, possibly because there he was promised even greater autonomy than he had enjoyed before. Certainly he wrote, directed and produced on a regular basis but never again approached the heights he had attained in that first glorious period. 'He did a couple of pictures like *The Beautiful Blonde from Bashful Bend* and they didn't do too well,' said Bracken. 'So they [Hollywood again] ignored him because he wasn't making it any more. As far as they were concerned he was through, so they were through with him. It's a very terrible situation for any man to have to go through, especially someone with the ego that Preston Sturges had.' After *Beautiful Blonde* (1949) Sturges went six years without directing a film until he made *The Diary of Major Thompson*, a French production in 1955. From then on there was nothing more until he died, aged sixty-one, in 1959. His problem was perhaps not so much that his talent had dried up though it might have done; such things happen – but that his ego and arrogance made him a difficult man to work with. And in Hollywood difficult people – as Orson Welles could doubtless have testified – are only tolerated while they are successful. . . . Nevertheless, the very least that could be said of Sturges was that he paved the way for other prominent *auteurs* such as Billy Wilder, John Huston and Joe Mankiewicz (who, in the early 1950s, won the Oscars for best writer *and* best director two years running, the films being *A Letter to Three Wives* and *All About Eve*).

Along with the first *auteur* and perhaps more significantly – the *auteur* theory having fallen into disrepute of late since, except in very rare cases, a film is the work of a committee – the war also introduced the *film noir*, which we'll discuss further in the next chapter. For the moment, suffice it to say that in this context the word *noir* means not so much black as dark. Like many another innovation the *film noir* came about by accident or through necessity serving as the mother of invention. The darkness of such movies was noticeable in two ways: first, the lighting was dim and the action often took place at night against backgrounds that suggested dingy realism; and, secondly, the content too was dark.

The genre is generally thought to have come into existence around 1944 and 1945 although, once you have established that there is such a thing, it is easy with hindsight to go further back and, as we shall see, pin the label on such pictures as *The Maltese Falcon* and *Casablanca*. There is, therefore, no acknowledged father of the *film noir*, rather are there several recognised founders, among them Edward Dmytryk, whose *Murder My Sweet* (adapted from Raymond Chandler's *Farewell My Lovely*) and *Cornered* can now be considered prime examples. When he made them, Dmytryk said, he had no idea that he was helping to create a genre. 'You know why I did that kind of lighting we used? Because it was quicker and cheaper. *Murder My Sweet* I made for 40,000 dollars; that meant I had to have a very short schedule – twenty days.' In twenty days there was no time to spare for elaborate lighting set ups. 'So what do you do? You do what we call "broad brush lighting". You light the person, you throw a shadow across the back wall and you're lit. I've worked with cameramen, particularly in the old days who, my God, if they liked a painting on the wall with a light over it would give it its own three-point lighting. If there was a little ornamental eagle on top of a piece of furniture, they would light that. It took sometimes days to light a set. Well, we couldn't do that – we had to do it fast, so we could spend our time with the actors and on the scene itself. So we got that kind of low key, or high key whatever you want to call it, contrasty lighting. The French, who don't accept anything until they've pigeon-holed it, had to call it *film noir* because they couldn't understand it.' Neither, at first, could a lot of people in Hollywood, especially at MGM where the house policy was to prettify everybody by flooding them with light. 'They could only work with beautiful people there. I mean, even nasty people had to be beautiful ... I remember I was greeted on the street one day by a director I knew, who was one of the top directors at MGM, and he was complimenting me on *Murder My Sweet* and saying, "Jesus, it's a very good picture." But he said, "I don't know, why did you make it so dark?" He wanted everything light. You know? And that was his chief criticism – of the very thing that made it eventually.'

But if economy accounts for the look of *film noir* it does not account for the darkness of the content. By 1944, the year when such movies first began to appear in considerable numbers, the war was clearly turning the Allies' way. And what these films began to reflect (and would continue to reflect over the next couple of years) was not the joy of peace but the problems peace might bring with it. How would the GIs be assimilated back into society? And what kind of society would they return to? The protagonist of the *film noir* – a private eye usually or, when the war was over, a veteran often acting like a private eye – found himself in a world of doubt and confusion in which nobody could be trusted, not even the girl he had left behind.

One of the most significant aspects of the *film noir* was its treatment of women, who were frequently depicted as femmes fatales (either evil in themselves or signalling, by their very presence, danger to the hero) or as victims. They were not victims in the tawdry sense in which they became so in the 1970s when quite often an actress's sole reason for being in a film was to be raped, brutalised, lasciviously murdered or, at best, generally terrorised. Nevertheless, the *film noir* was remarkable for the number of pictures in which women were either murdered or nearly murdered – Ingrid Bergman in *Notorious*, as also in *Gaslight*, Dorothy McGuire in *The Spiral Staircase*, Teresa Wright in *Shadow of a Doubt* and many others. In *Possessed* Joan Crawford commits murder and in almost all her films Lizabeth Scott was bound to cause serious, if not terminal, trouble for one man or another. And this reflected another aspect of peacetime, or near-peacetime, America – the problem of what to do with women now the men were coming back. They were not easily to be rounded up and sent back to the home, there to remain ideally (from a masculine point of view) barefoot, pregnant and in the kitchen. In a poll conducted just before the end of the war eighty per cent of working women said they wanted to carry on working. But though American industry was able to turn itself round very smoothly from full-time war production to an equally full-time production of consumer goods, there were still not enough jobs for everyone – not once the troops came home. Thus with the battle of the sexes now likely to be waged not only in the bedroom but also in the workplace, women were a threat. And to a large extent their treatment in *films noirs* was a reflection of this fear. Greer Garson believed that women were honoured and given prominence in films during the war because 'in wartime there is a great love of family values, family virtues and the family really centres on the wife and mother. So mature women were very much in vogue then; they were loved and appreciated.' But at the same time, as Joan Fontaine pointed out, the war 'rather masculinised women. We had women working on aeroplanes and riveting and all that kind of thing and I think they lost some of their fragility and their helplessness.' And what that led to, said the writer and director Richard Brooks, was what he called a 'sophistication' taking place, a realisation that 'a woman could be the bad guy the same as a feller could. She didn't have to be in lace and crinoline behind a white picket fence because she'd also been in a war, she also knew what a dollar was, she also knew what effect money had on a marriage, love and the lack of it and you weren't going to be able to tell the girls, "Well, you'll have babies. Stay home and have babies."' All these things contributed to the fact that as peace came closer, finally arrived and established itself fewer roles were written for independent, competent women and more for fresh young girls who, being fresh and young, could be portrayed as biddable and malleable and less likely to give their men folks a hard time.

Elsewhere, however, and on a less complex level Hollywood, in the mid-1940s, was looking at other aspects of the war and the problems of peace. What is widely regarded as one of the finest combat films of all is *The Story of GI Joe*, which appeared in 1945. It falls into Lawrence H. Suid's "World War II – Reality" category, being based on the work of a war correspondent, Ernie Pyle, who had watched the fighting from what amounted to a ringside seat. Furthermore, although the picture starred Robert Mitchum as an army officer and Burgess Meredith as Pyle himself, the cast also included 150 combat veterans, mostly as extras but often with speaking roles. According to the director, William Wellman, all those soldiers returned to battle after the filming was over and were killed. But Wellman was much given to exaggeration. Whether or not the aftermath was as tragic as he maintained, *The Story of GI Joe* was described by *Punch* as "one of the best films of the war" and by the American critic James Agee as "a tragic and eternal work of art". Darryl Zanuck's *The Purple Heart* also touched on the realities of war. It told the fictional story of eight American airmen, led by Dana Andrews and Richard Conte, who were shot down over Tokyo and then tortured and executed by the Japanese. Zanuck made it in 1944 but because the fact of Japanese torture of prisoners was not officially admitted until late that year he had to wait until the war was over before he could release it. The director of *The Purple Heart* was Lewis Milestone who also made another notable war film, *A Walk in the Sun*, which included Huntz Hall in the cast. It's the story of what happens to an army platoon one morning in 1943 during the Salerno landings and Hall believed that like *GI Joe* and *The Purple Heart* it could not possibly have been made much earlier because the grimness would have been unacceptable to the public. But as the 40s ended and the 50s began war movies increasingly dealt with reality as well as fantasy, combining battlefield heroics with a franker acceptance of the fact that people actually got killed in wartime. That was when John Wayne really emerged as the saviour of America and the American way of life.

What was curious though was the scarcity of films that were prepared to look seriously at the considerable social problems of the returning veteran. His existence was acknowledged in pictures such as *The Blue Dahlia* and *Dead Reckoning* but these were thrillers. Delmer Daves' *Pride of the Marines*, with John Garfield as a marine blinded in combat and understandably bitter about it until he pulled himself together and sought a niche for himself in society, made a somewhat overwrought attempt to come to grips with the real problem. But surprisingly few other movies did, with the outstanding exception of *The Best Years of our Lives*.

The title was, to a large degree, ironic: the three returning warriors had left the best years of their lives on the battlefield and had come back to a civilian life with which they could not cope. The bank manager/sergeant, Fredric March, sought comfort in alcohol; the soda jerk/airforce officer, Dana Andrews, found his wife, Virginia Mayo, making what looked like a full-time profession out of infidelity; and the mechanic/sailor, Harold Russell, had lost both his hands and saw no future for himself whatsoever. The splendour of the film, freely adapted by Robert Sherwood from a poetic novel by MacKinlay Kantor and directed by William Wyler, lies in its dramatic sweep and the way in which it somehow touches on all the anxieties of a nation which, though the most powerful in the world, was unable to determine quite what its international role was to be. It was immediately and deservedly successful, both critically and financially, and in 1946 it took seven Academy Awards, including one for Harold Russell, a genuinely handicapped war veteran whose first and last movie this was. Perhaps, in retrospect, it was the very excellence of *Best Years* that frightened other film makers away from the idea of trying to emulate it with their own treatment of similar subject matters. Whatever the reason it stands alone as the outstanding picture about the fears and anxieties facing the soldier back from the war. Indeed it was not until the 1950s that anything else came along to bear any kind of comparison with it. In 1950 Fred Zinnemann directed *The Men* and a year later *Teresa*, the first starring Marlon Brando as a quadriplegic veteran, the second dealing with the adjustments that had to be made on all sides when a young soldier returned home to America with an Italian war bride (Pier Angeli). Neither film, Zinnemann said, was too successful, although *Teresa* probably did better initially than *The Men*. 'When we released *The Men*,' Zinnemann said, 'the war had started in Korea and nobody wanted to see the picture because people had their fathers and sons going off to Korea. The film didn't catch on, although it had a very good actor, Marlon Brando. It was his first film but that didn't help. I think the film had much more success years later.'

There is little doubt then that, John Ford's complaint to Don Ameche notwith-standing, Hollywood did produce some exceptional films during and just after the war (whether it produced enough of them is another matter) and there is equally little doubt that the war itself made a difference to the style and the content of the movies, if not necessarily to the quality. Joan Fontaine, for example, felt that pictures became

Left: Dana Andrews, defiant, and Richard Loo, demonstrating the size of those Japanese choppers, in *The Purple Heart*
Below: Dana Andrews, Fredric March and Harold Russell in *The Best Years of our Lives* which, more successfully than any other film, examined the effects of war on the home-coming troops

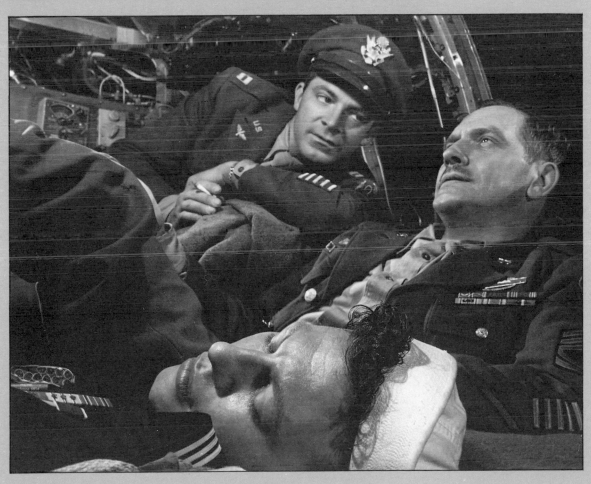

more realistic and less romantic from the middle forties onwards. And Richard Brooks attributed that and even the introduction of *film noir* not to some executive at a studio saying, "We need a new kind of movie," but to the fact that the people who were making the films had been at war themselves. 'When you've been to war and seen something that's real and your base of reference is not just another movie, then you begin to tell a personal story ... Our pictures began to deal with an individual who broke down during the war and was just trying to get through that one day. The stories became much more real and therefore probably darker.'

In a sense the films he was talking about concerned the "little man" but, paradoxically, he also believed that the war killed off the film about the little man. 'In a way that's what began to affect Capra's work. Most of his pictures are about the little man who climbs out of the crowd and makes good. But during the war Americans began to flock to the big cities to work in the factories for the war effort and get more money. They didn't want to be the little man anymore – they didn't like the little man, he bored them. They wanted to be the big man. So there was a split away from the little man kind of pictures to those about the successful man. Clark Gable ran a whole advertising agency (*The Hucksters*, 1947). That became exciting so they began to look for business and areas where the hero could function in a glamorous way. This was before the Jet Set but it was the same idea more or less. You could win the big prize.' It's an interesting theory and certainly Capra's postwar films, apart from *It's a Wonderful Life*, were less impressive than his earlier work but that is not necessarily because the American public had turned its back on the little man; it probably has as much to do with the fact that Capra's approach, always a touch sentimental, was simply not tough enough to suit the tastes of the postwar world.

What, though, had Hollywood achieved during the wartime years? Well, it had revived the musical, given great opportunities to actresses, introduced the *auteur* and the *film noir* and it had made a lot of money. As Richard Brooks said: 'After all, the bottom line in Hollywood still is now, was at the end of World War II and was before that to be profitable.' Which, as Don Ameche suggested, is the answer to John Ford's complaint about the lack of experiment. Why experiment when the public is perfectly happy with what it already knows? Well, of course, there is a reason to experiment – to further the state of the art. But artists don't run studios; businessmen do. Still, let us not be too harsh. However much one may bemoan the wasted opportunities, the war years can be neatly, if loosely, bracketed by two outstanding, indeed great, films: at the beginning, 1941, by *Citizen Kane* and at the end, 1946, by *The Best Years of our Lives*.

HOLLYWOOD AND CRIME

Crime in America, like almost everything else in that astonishing country, tends to be bigger and more spectacular than it is anywhere else. Britain may have had Jack the Ripper but the USA had Murder Incorporated; Italy gave birth to the Mafia but the leaders in Sicily enjoyed nothing like the celebrity, and indeed power, of the likes of Lucky Luciano and Vito Genovese; and only America could boast of a bootlegger like Al Capone. Throw in noted killers such as Legs Diamond, legendary bank robbers like John Dillinger and psychopaths on the scale of Bonnie and Clyde and not only have you merely begun to scratch the surface but a picture emerges of a nation that takes a quiet pride in the very enormity of its criminal classes.

It was, of course, the Volstead Act – Prohibition – which created the necessary money base for organised crime on the scale that the United States has enjoyed (if enjoyed is the word) for the last sixty years but, surprisingly perhaps for a country that prides itself on individual enterprise, there were signs long before that that criminal activities were likely to be arranged on a company basis. The pre-Prohibition gangs all tended to have an ethnic origin: the Black Hand, for instance, which was the first noted Italian crime organisation in America and was a forerunner of the Mafia. The connection is made clear in Francis Coppola's *Godfather II*, wherein the Black Hand figures prominently in the early part of Don Vito Corleone's life. Gangs such as these gained their early income and influence from prostitution, having first asked themselves – like any well-run business organisation – what the public needed most. And since the public, or that part of it in which the Black Hand interested itself, consisted of Italian immigrants coming on ahead to the Promised Land to establish themselves before sending for their families, what it needed most was sex and preferably sex with a girl who could offer a little conversation in a language known to the customer. Since there was a limit to the number of girls, especially Italian girls, who would voluntarily offer such services even in exchange for money, the Black Hand took to recruiting unwitting and newly arrived female immigrants, either by trickery or by force. By 1913 this practice was common enough in the "new" American communities to be the subject of the first US-made exploitation movie, *Traffic in Souls*, though the traffickers' interest was concentrated rather more in bodies. Indeed the activities of the white slave gangs had caused concern even earlier and in an attempt to put a stop to them the White Slave Traffic Act, better known as The Mann Act, came into law in 1910.

Merely organising prostitution, however, swiftly palled as the sole occupation for an ambitious criminal and the gangs expanded into narcotics, monopolising newspaper circulation and illicit gambling before venturing even more boldly into strike-breaking and manipulating labour by gaining control of the unions. Later all these enterprises became, and have remained, very popular with the Mafia.

But in 1920 came the Volstead Act, a ludicrous piece of legislation which, when you think about it, was almost guaranteed to turn an independent-minded citizen into a drinker even if hitherto he had been more or less teetotal. Tell such a person that he must not, on pain of law, indulge in what to most people is a harmless social pastime and he will almost certainly insist upon his right to do it. And since henceforth the manufacture, sale or consumption of alcohol was to be strictly forbidden, the rise of the bootlegger became inevitable. With booze denied the demand for it became practically insatiable – but who was to provide it? Why, who else but the criminal gangs, which already had efficient business organisations and large amounts of undeclared capital searching around for investment? What's more, in quenching the nation's thirst they were not looked upon by the public as criminals at all; rather they were regarded as social benefactors. Even the brutal Al Capone, who murdered his way to the top of Chicago's gangland and whose nefarious enterprises were bringing him an untaxed income of more than 100 million dollars a year in the late 1920s, was a popular celebrity in his home town. Nor did that make him unique for in a poll conducted in Chicago in 1931 only movie stars came ahead of gangsters as the best-known personalities in America. That being so the crime pictures in which celebrated actors impersonated only slightly less celebrated gangsters (even if the identities of the latter were changed) were bound to be popular.

To be fair, however, not all the criminals and bootleggers (if indeed there is a distinction to be drawn) were Italian. Arnold Rothstein, known as the "King of the Gamblers" and the man who actually managed to fix the World Baseball Series in 1919, was Jewish and so was Meyer Lansky, whose advice in the 1930s helped Lucky Luciano to organise the Mafia into the corporate shape it still retains today. And in Chicago Capone's competitors included Dion O'Bannion, who was of Irish descent, and Hymie Weiss, another Jew who, apart from anything else, was notable for devising a new method of disposing of unwanted rivals. The victim was manoeuvred into the front passenger seat of a car and, while chatting lightly to the driver about the weather or the high price of pumpernickel or whatever, was shot in the back of the head by an assassin placed behind him. Mr Weiss, who found this practice infallible in helping to discourage competition, referred to it as "taking someone for a ride", a phrase seized upon with alacrity by grateful Hollywood scriptwriters. I mention this simply because I do feel that credit should be given where it is due.

Of all the bootleggers, however, Capone is the one whose exploits have gone down most indelibly into American folklore and been immortalised most often in the movies. The murder, on Capone's orders, of Hymie Weiss, who was shot to death outside the Holy Name Cathedral in Chicago (some of the bullet holes can still be seen in the building today) was reflected in the gunning down of James Cagney ("He used to be a big shot") on the steps of a church in Raoul Walsh's classic *The Roaring Twenties* (1939); the St Valentine's Day Massacre of 1929, which persuaded George "Bugs" Moran, the man for whom it had been thoughtfully arranged but who by chance escaped it, that his best interests probably lay in leaving Chicago, was commemorated in a film of that name by Roger Corman in 1967; and an incident in which Capone, suspecting two of his gang of treachery, invited them to a dinner ostensibly in their honour and then – no doubt with a merry cry of "Surprise, surprise" – beat them both to death with a baseball bat, was featured in Nick Ray's *Party Girl* in 1958 and clearly inspired the "Lovers of Italian Opera" scene in Billy Wilder's delightful 1959 comedy *Some Like It Hot*, in which a man with a gun leaps out of a cake with the intention of shooting George Raft.

In view of all this it may seem surprising that Capone was a popular anti-hero but it becomes less so when you also know that he was a generous and visible supporter of charity, that he established soup kitchens to feed Chicago's unemployed and that he was most solicitous that "civilians", i.e. innocent and presumably honest bystanders should not be involved in gangland violence. In fact, when Hymie Weiss led a cavalcade of cars down the main street of Cicero, a small town just outside Chicago, to riddle Capone's headquarters with bullets and a woman minding her own business in a car nearby was hit in the eye by a ricochet, it was Capone who insisted on providing and paying for the best medical attention she could get. Whether he did this as a reproof to Weiss who, morally speaking, should have footed the bill himself, is not known but his action certainly earned him a great deal of public esteem.

By the time Prohibition came to an end with the repeal of the Volstead Act in 1932 Capone was already in jail for income tax evasion and America was in the grip of the Depression. And it was now that the hard work the bootleggers had put in over the last ten years or so began to reap its reward. Big business, legitimate business, was desperately in need of cash but with banks failing every day it was extremely hard to come by. The only people with an enormous surfeit of the stuff were the organised gangs who, like Capone, had carelessly omitted to notify the Inland Revenue Service of their astronomical incomes but who, unlike Capone, had managed to get away with it. So now the Mafia, inspired by Lucky Luciano who had instituted the "family" system with himself as primus inter pares, was able to buy its way into all manner of previously honest enterprises and so launder its cash, thus establishing the stranglehold which it still keeps on large sections of the American business community.

Now little of this had much to do with Hollywood, although the Mafia was to establish itself there, too. The gangster-turned-actor played by Richard Gere in Coppola's *The Cotton Club* has at least basic similarities with George Raft, who enjoyed what are euphemistically called "Mob" connections all his life. But with crime prevalent and not entirely unpopular in the nation at large it was understandable that, with the coming of sound, crime movies should provide a staple diet in the cinemas. Not that such pictures were completely unknown in the silent days. In 1913, for example, D. W. Griffith made *Musketeers of Pig Alley*, which was admittedly about street toughs rather than gangsters but which incidentally touched on the white slave trade. It also hinted at a connection between crime and men in high places, with a shot of an expensively tailored arm passing money to one of the crooks, although this was invariably censored, probably by other men with expensively tailored arms who felt it was striking a little close to home. The first real gangster film, however, was *Underworld* in 1927, directed by Josef von Sternberg and written by Ben Hecht, who had already ingested Herman Mankiewicz's advice about the obligatory virginity of heroes and the briefer but much more enjoyable life open to villains. The star of *Underworld* – the first gangster star indeed – was George Bancroft, who also played a similar role in von Sternberg's similar picture, *Dragnet*, in 1928. This was written by Jules Furthman (in collaboration with his brother Charles), who was later to achieve greater things with *To Have and Have Not* and *The Big Sleep* – the Howard Hawks version, not the dreadful and much later Michael Winner remake. Bancroft, already forty-five when he made *Underworld*, lasted well into the sound era but was rapidly overtaken by newer, younger actors as the epitome of the gangster.

The coming of sound was the making of the crime movie, the screech of tyres on wet streets and the rat-tat-tat of Thompson machine guns ("typewriters" as they were affectionately known to those who wielded them) adding another and irresistible dimension to the action and the hard-boiled dialogue. It's not insignificant that the first all-talking picture, Warner Brothers' *Lights of New York* in 1928 was a gangster film – and incidentally was the first to talk of taking someone for a ride though it regrettably omitted to mention Hymie Weiss's invaluable contribution to this piece of business. Around this time there was even talk of Capone himself starring in a film, the proceeds to go to charity, but by 1931 when he was in prison and Legs Diamond was dead, the more noted underworld figures decided to keep a somewhat lower profile and Hollywood turned to less obvious areas of malefaction for their crime stories. The police, being hardly less corrupt than the bootleggers they served, were one obvious source and, starting with *Alibi* in 1929, there began a brief cycle of films in which the third degree and other instances of police brutality were heavily featured. This kind of picture, however, was soon discouraged and was superseded by a series of vigilante movies, notably MGM's *Secret Six* which, in 1931, starred Wallace Beery and featured Clark Gable and Jean Harlow in the supporting cast. *Beast of the City* (Walter Huston, Jean Harlow) a year later did its best to rehabilitate the cops, being the story of a police captain determined to nail a racketeer by any means he could. The original story was by W. R. Burnett who, throughout the 1930s, was to be one of the most significant authors of crime movies in Hollywood.

Such films, however, were more or less incidental to the mainstream of gangster pictures, heralded in 1930 by Darryl F. Zanuck – then head of production at Warners – who announced that henceforth the studio would be making films "right off the front page". It was a shrewd piece of timing, for this was an era of cynicism and despair brought about by the financial crash of October 1929, and there was a widespread view that the gangster, particularly in his persona as bootlegger, was the man who had got it right and discovered how to beat the system. When furthermore he was personified by such charismatic figures as Edward G. Robinson (*Little Caesar*), James Cagney (*The Public Enemy*) and Paul Muni (*Scarface*) he was elevated into something of a hero, a tough, self-sufficient character who was not to be dragged down by the dismal effects of the Depression, or to be pushed around by anybody. He knew what he wanted and, with a philosophy later to be adopted by Rocky, he would "go for it". The immigrant communities responded to the gangster even more than the rest of the populace for he himself was an immigrant – or often bore an immigrant name – and one who, moreover, had found his own short cut to the American Dream at a time when opportunity was theoretically promised to every newcomer but in practice was denied to all but the native born.

The appeal of gangster films, however, went much deeper than that for at their best they represent the flip-side, or a perversion, of the American success ethic. For instance, in books like *Strive and Succeed* or *Struggling Upwards*, Horatio Alger exhorted underprivileged youth to take their first step towards ultimate success and wealth by becoming newsboys. Well, the criminal classes often followed his advice – with the subtle difference that instead of simply standing on a corner selling newspapers, they formed a kind of protection racket for newsboys. On the whole this proved to be far more lucrative and far less uncomfortable than hanging around in the rain trying to flog papers to passers-by who probably didn't want them. And in the movies, too, the organisation of the Mafia, the Mob or the Syndicate – whichever you choose to call it – was like legitimate big business seen in a distorting mirror: mergers were formed, takeovers were executed, rivals were liquidated and bosses were removed from office in a violent parody of what went on in Wall Street. As President Herbert Hoover said: "The business of America is business," and nobody ever followed that precept more avidly than those involved in organised crime. At the same time the gangster movie can also be seen as a deeply ironic commentary on the American Dream, since it reflects a worship of materialism and a desire for success at any price. Certainly *Little Caesar*, *The Public Enemy* and *Scarface*, the first two made by Warners, the third by Howard Hughes and each following on the others' heels between 1930 and 1932, are all obsessed with the outward trappings of success – silk shirts, sharp suits and expensive women and, in the case of *Scarface*, the wooing of the boss's girlfriend reflecting the upward social mobility that is every red-blooded American's birthright.

Before *Little Caesar*, Lewis Milestone had made *The Racket*, an attempted exposé of political corruption, and Darryl Zanuck had come up with *Doorway to Hell*, in which Lew Ayres played a gangster trying to reform but driven back to crime despite himself. *Little Caesar*, however, was something entirely new – the story of a ruthless, pitiless crook who never showed remorse or attempted to atone for his misdeeds and yet remained horribly attractive to the end (when, of course, he died because crime could not be seen to pay). The film was generally thought to have been inspired by the career of Al Capone but Hal Wallis said that in fact the main character was based on one of Capone's Chicago predecessors, Johnny Torrio, who after the rest of the boys had made an attempt on his life shrewdly came to the conclusion that he had perhaps outstayed his welcome, retired from gang bossdom in Chicago and went on to enjoy a much-respected career as elder statesman-cum-adviser to the Mafia in New York.

'Mother of Mercy,' says Edward G., dying riddled with bullets in the gutter, 'is this the end of Rico?', thus providing the cinema with another of its immortal lines. But earlier he had delivered a much more important speech in which he said: 'Be somebody – know that a bunch of guys will do anything you tell 'em. Have your own way or nothin'.' This philosophy of power for its own sake was to be repeated in all the classic gangster films, up to and including *The Godfather*. But the character of Rico remains unusual. Even Marlon Brando in *The Godfather* had some slight redeeming qualities, if nothing more admirable than a love of family. But for Rico there was nothing good to be said at all. Zanuck, pointing out this fact, predicted confidently that the film would "go over big" on account of it. And he was right.

The Cagney character in *The Public Enemy* was not quite so unremittingly evil. For a start some attempt was made to explain him by sketching in an underprivileged childhood, although his elder brother sharing the same background was unswervingly straight throughout. Cagney's credo, however, was very like that of Robinson: that if you haven't got a racket, you're a mug.

But quite apart from its important place in the development of the urban American crime movie, *The Public Enemy* is significant for emphasising the essential misogyny of these pictures in which women are generally represented as stereotypes – hard-bitten gang molls, victims or insufferably sweet madonnas trying to lure the hero/villain back to the path of righteousness. In *The Public Enemy* Mae Clarke was the archetypal victim, the girl into whose face Cagney thrust half a grapefruit. Whether he actually performed this dastardly deed or merely pretended to do so for the benefit of the cameras is open to doubt and much depends on whether you believe the testimony of Miss Clarke or that of the film's co-writer, John Bright.

Miss Clarke said she hated that particular scene but . . . 'It was the job. It was the day's work. I was an actor and I was asked to do something.' Why did she hate it? 'Well, I had an instinctive dislike of being that insulted.' Fair enough but then she said that Cagney did not actually hit her with the grapefruit. 'He picked it up here and, let's see, the camera was there, that's right, and when his hand picked it up and came over to my face, it went right past my face. The camera said it hit my face but it didn't. Honey, it's a sin for one actor to hurt another. It isn't done. You work it out, like in a fight scene you pull the punch . . .'

John Bright's version of the events is dramatically different – not that it really matters, I suppose, but this is one of the classic scenes of the cinema and for that reason worth examining, if only out of idle curiosity. He said first that the inspiration for the action came from the loveable and, as we have already discovered, inventive Hymie Weiss who actually did commit assault with a grapefruit on a lady friend. And what happened in the film, he said, was this . . .

'It was the last scene in the picture and Mae Clarke arrived at the studio with a cold, so she asked Jimmy if he would fake it. And Cagney agreed, like the gentleman he was. But his deal with her was overheard by Bill Wellman, the director, who took him aside and said, 'Look, kid, this will be the most important scene in the picture and you can't fake it. You gotta give it your everything.' And so the expression of surprise on Mae's face was genuine. She felt betrayed. And Cagney gave an added fillip of his own: he twisted the grapefruit, thereby increasing the pain in her nose and, the moment the director said "Cut", she jumped to her feet in a rage and – I don't know whether Clarke told you this or not – she denounced the studio and all of its employees, very blasphemously, and stormed off the set. And we spent the time intervening before the development of the film praying to God that it would turn out because no retakes were possible.'

Well, no, Miss Clarke didn't tell me all that. Indeed, she strongly denied any blasphemy. As to which version of events is correct, I feel it's hardly for me to say although I must confess that Mr Bright's story, being the more graphic, has the greater appeal. As John Ford so wisely remarked, if the legend is more interesting than the truth, print the legend. Here you have truth and legend side by side, though which is which you must decide for yourselves.

The character played by Cagney was not, however, based particularly on Hymie Weiss, rather was it a composite of many gangsters of the time including Capone, whom John Bright had met and whom he found to be a 'a thug, a very strong personality indistinguishable from other thugs, except by a superior sense of larceny and violence'. But, of course, Cagney and the writers also brought something of their own to the picture. John Bright said that it 'allocated responsibility to poverty. I think it was the first film that gave a chronological explanation of how gangsters are made, beginning with a broken window and a stolen purse and a mugging, done by kids. Now all of this is commonplace today but it was new then. It allocated responsibility to poverty, poverty being the villain of the piece.'

As for Cagney, he was not originally cast as the lead, Tom Powers, but as his best friend. John Bright claimed that he was responsible for the switch in casting that had Cagney and Edward Woods exchanging roles, which did a lot for Cagney but nothing much for Edward Woods, who was hardly ever heard of again.

The film itself, incidentally, was not entirely shot the way Bright and his writing partner, Kubec Glasmon, had envisaged it. 'We wrote it with greater honesty. In our version the brother capitulated to crime, in vengeance for the death of Cagney. Censorship dictated the compromise in the present version.'

Bright said that he had difficulty in persuading Darryl Zanuck to alter the casting because 'Zanuck was very pigheaded about his casting and had to be handled delicately.' But he spoke from a certain attitude of prejudice since his relations with Zanuck were never exactly easy. 'Well, I tried to throw him out of a window, for example, due to the fact that he called me a stool pigeon when what I was doing was simply discussing his casting with someone who was working at the studio on another picture.' If he had carried out his threat, he added, it wouldn't have won him a standing ovation at the studio because 'it was only a second-storey window'. Of Zanuck generally he said that 'apart from larceny' he was 'brilliant. He had a brilliant feel for films. He was personally a tinpot Mussolini and an egomaniac but professionally he was the one producer who respected writers.'

What, though, of Cagney and the astonishing impact he made in *The Public Enemy* and so many subsequent films? Mae Clarke said that he 'never did anything without thought' even down to the expression in his eyes or whether he was going to

Left: George Bancroft, the first gangster star of the movies – though little remembered now – in *Underworld*
Right: Paul Muni trying to attract Ann Dvorak's attention in Hawks' *Scarface* and Al Pacino (far right), also attention-seeking, in de Palma's much bloodier remake

Above: 'Mother of Mercy, is this the end of Rico?' No, not yet. In this scene from *Little Caesar* Rico – Edward G. Robinson – is very much on top
Left: Mae Clarke, James Cagney and *The Public Enemy*. The question is did he really hit her with that grapefruit?

Bogart and Cagney in Raoul Walsh's *The Roaring Twenties*, the film that encapsulated all the themes of the gangster movie

balance his weight on his left foot or his right. More succinctly, perhaps, the contemporary director Martin Ritt summed up the actor's appeal when he said: 'Heroic hoods were always a part of American folklore, like the westerns. And Cagney was probably the most attractive hoodlum in the history of mankind. I can't think of anybody more attractive.'

Ritt's reference to westerns, however oblique, is interesting when we move on to a consideration of *Scarface*, the third in that early trio of highly influential crime movies, for Peter Bogdanovich, another modern director and almost fanatical student of the cinema, described it as 'a western, set in the city. In a way it takes the American mythology of the west and moves it into a modern image in which, of course, everything is faster with more people getting killed by machine guns and there are cars not horses.'

Scarface, produced in 1932 by Howard Hughes, was directed by Howard Hawks and starred Paul Muni as a thinly disguised Al Capone, complete with scar and that love of opera which was a curious characteristic of Italian-American gangsters, however ill-educated. The screenplay was written by Ben Hecht in collaboration with W. R. Burnett under the watchful eye of Hawks, who claimed later that it had been his idea to add a touch of the Borgias by introducing the incest motif between Camonte (Muni) and his half-sister played by Ann Dvorak. Oddly enough, the film was conceived by Hecht and Hawks as a tragi-comedy but since it contained fifteen killings – a piffling amount when compared with the mayhem in Brian de Palma's remake fifty years later – the story had to be made harder to satisfy the censors. So a new ending was shot in which Scarface was seen to pay for his sins and, to Muni's disappointment, the character of Camonte was made far less sympathetic throughout. Even so he remains an attractive figure, possibly because Hecht was said to have been visited by two of Capone's henchmen anxious to ensure that their revered leader was not portrayed in an unflattering light. And Hawks once claimed that he had actually shown some of the rushes to Capone, who graciously expressed himself satisfied.

Both tales are probably apocryphal but the fact that they gained any currency at all serves to indicate the social power and status of the gangster in that era. And the glamour that attached to him, and specifically to Paul Muni in the film, is proof against time. Martin Scorsese, probably the most talented of all modern American directors, remembered watching a 16 mm version of the film with a friend and being deeply impressed by the scene in which Muni, seeing tommy-guns in action for the first time, acquires one for himself and starts shooting with it. 'We looked at each other and we said, "We *love* these guys! These guys are terrific!" It's that strange thing, you know – we didn't like people killing people but the way they're presented in the film is extremely glamorous. I believe that's why they had to put in the little section where there was a real Italian-American saying, "These people are giving us a bad name." They had to temper it because it did attract a lot of young people.'

True – but then so did the gangster himself. That he could achieve such prominence and be perceived, both in life and – despite the efforts of the censors – in films, as a hero, or anyway a romantic anti-hero, was a reflection of the age itself, an age of Depression, disillusionment and cynicism. 1931, for instance, was a disastrous year for musicals, not only because there were too many of them and most of those were inferior but more importantly because the public in a time of universal hardship did not want simple escapism. Capitalism had, temporarily at least, been seen to have failed and the popular movies of the time were those that commented upon the fact. For example, in Spencer Tracy's second picture, *Quick Millions* (1931) there's a line that runs: 'That's what every racketeer dreams of, boys – a legitimate racket' and another, putting things even more explicitly, maintains that 'the more you steal, the more respectable you become'. In the same year, *Blonde Crazy*, a gangster comedy starring James Cagney, featured a stockbroker who was a bigger con-man than the crooks and in it Cagney more or less summed up the popular view of the epoch by referring to it as the "age of chiselry". In this context it's worth remembering that when the musical began to make its comeback in 1933, under the inspiration of Busby Berkeley, it did so with storylines that had a Depression background, most notably of course in *42nd Street* and *Gold Diggers of 1933*.

For a while everything seemed to be viewed with cynicism – even love: in 1932 William Wellman made a film for Warner Brothers called *Love is a Racket*. And more obvious targets such as the law (*Night Court*, the story of a corrupt judge), the press (*Five Star Final* and *The Front Page*) and, of course, politics (*The Dark Horse* and *The Phantom President*) were treated with equal, if not greater, scepticism. Corruption was seen to be rife wherever you looked and though many of those and similar films were presented as comedies the message was nonetheless strong for that.

Inevitably, however, there was a backlash. The American Establishment was primarily rural and Protestant and hostile to the movies, which it regarded as foreign in origin, urban, lowbrow and working class. It was also predominantly Isolationist and opposed to immigration and tended to blame the failure of Prohibition not on the utter absurdity of the Volstead Act but on the foreign city dweller/immigrant bootlegger who had so ingeniously perverted the law. Interest groups within the Establishment began to express increasing concern at the way the cinema – in their view – was undermining traditional American values and they, led by the Catholic League of Decency, exerted pressure for more and stricter censorship. So when the new Production Code was introduced in 1934, it did not by any means interest itself only in sex in the movies: the gangster film, too, came under close scrutiny.

Furthermore, the public view of gangsters changed after the repeal of Prohibition. As bootleggers they had been seen more or less as social workers but as simple criminals involved in organised vice, the numbers racket, loan sharking and the like they were much less sympathetic. Then, too, the St Valentine's Day Massacre had appalled the nation and the Lindbergh kidnapping of 1932 had produced a public outcry against gangsters and racketeers whose work it was at first and erroneously supposed to be. Even the generous offers of Al Capone and other involuntary guests of the state in various prisons to track down the real culprits – in return, of course, for some trifling reward, such as their own immediate release – did nothing to allay suspicion. And, inevitably, the studios damaged the cause of the gangster movie, as they had done earlier with musicals, by producing a surfeit of them. So declining interest among the audiences combined with a tightening of the Code (which, for example, banned any film on Dillinger as being against the public interest) and the movie moguls' desire for respectability and acceptance to rob the gangster picture of its popularity.

· Even more important, however, was the election in 1932 of President Franklin D. Roosevelt and the introduction of the New Deal. The capitalist creed of every man for himself fell from favour; now was the time for all to pull together and rescue America from its economic mess. In films the individual was still popular but it was no longer the individual fighting his way out of the slums with a gun in his hand whom the audiences wanted to know about but the little man, courageously taking on corruption or the insensitivity of government or big business single-handedly. This was the optimistic era of Frank Capra and Mr Deeds going to town or Mr Smith to Washington. And the hard-bitten, tough-talking, nail-chewing and rust-spitting gangster was replaced by the less dangerous, more amusing Runyonesque crook or mobster – Damon Runyon himself providing the stories for such early examples as Capra's *Lady for a Day* (1933) and, the following year, *Little Miss Marker*, starring Shirley Temple. Even the hard-nosed crime fiction of Dashiel Hammett was lightened and adapted to fit the prevailing mood in 1934 with the first appearance of the very successful "Thin Man" series, featuring William Powell and Myrna Loy. Another decade was to pass before the harsher, darker crime picture in which the hero was almost as immoral and cynical as the villain would really find its place again.

Meanwhile, the public still wanted films about criminality but if the crook could no longer be the central figure who would fill the role? Hardly the police because, as Prohibition had revealed, they were just about as corrupt as the mobsters. So the FBI man was elected – the perfect hero for the time, being on the side of law and order, armed and like his boss, J. Edgar Hoover, incorruptible and probably celibate, though the movies didn't make too much of that. What's more, he also had an aptly tough-sounding soubriquet – the "G-man". For this he had to thank Machine-Gun Kelly, a pathetically wimpish villain egged on to a life of crime primarily by his wife who, when cornered, surrendered himself with the memorable line: 'Don't shoot, G-man', meaning "Government man".

The beauty of the G-man was that he could be just as ruthless and murderous as any mobster without incurring the wrath of the censors because, after all, he was committing mayhem on behalf of society, as Warner Brothers and James Cagney discovered in 1935 with *G Men*, which was hailed by no means disapprovingly by the *New York Times* as 'the headiest dose of gunplay that Hollywood has unleashed in recent months'. Interestingly, it was also an early example, later to be followed assiduously by the likes of *Rambo*, of Hollywood rewriting history, for one scene in the film is based on the siege of Dillinger at the Bohemia Lodge. In real life this turned out to be a comprehensive cock-up by the FBI but in the movie the G-men proved triumphant, although of course Dillinger wasn't actually mentioned by name.

Around this time, too, as the movies became less of a blue-collar entertainment and began to appeal more widely to the educated classes, the perception of the gangster took another subtle shift. A character in *The Petrified Forest* says of Duke Mantee (alias Humphrey Bogart): 'He ain't a gangster, he's a real old-time desperado. Gangsters is foreign – he's an American.' Another significant quote comes from Mantee himself: 'I spent most of my time since I grew up in jail. The rest of the time I felt as if I were dead.'

This sort of remark was the keynote for a new genre of crime movie such as *Dead End* (William Wyler, 1937) and *Angels With Dirty Faces* (Michael Curtiz, 1938) which investigated the social background that formed the gangster or desperado and also laid emphasis on reform or redemption. But in his post bootlegger-benefactor phase and with the New Deal looking shaky as the Depression took another bite, the gangster was the scapegoat and had to be seen to die in the cause of social reform and the public good, which is subtly different from dying simply because crime didn't pay. All these characteristics were particularly evident in *Angels With Dirty Faces* in which Cagney deters his admirers, the Dead End Kids, from a life of crime by apparently going kicking and screaming for mercy to the electric chair. Of course, we – the audience – know he was only pretending to kick and scream but this had less to do with Warner Brothers not wishing to slur the good name of gangsters than with the fact that a star of Cagney's magnitude could not be seen by the public to die a coward.

Huntz Hall, leader with Leo Gorcey of the Dead End Kids (later, in a gentler reincarnation, to become the Bowery Boys) said that "Dead End", originally a stage play, was an accurate reflection of the area of New York City in which he himself had grown up. 'All around us was squalor. Kids were getting rickets. And the picture showed the kids starving, showed what was happening and it showed the first generation gap, it showed that kids fourteen and fifteen years old could talk and shouldn't be treated like babies. They were growing up to be gangsters, every kid wanted to be tough, like the guy who was the head of the block.' *Angels With Dirty Faces* he thought was equally accurate. The kids regarded gangsters as heroes and they knew that, in the 1920s especially, people used to go to nightclubs not to see the stars but to see the gangsters, the Capones, the Dutch Schultzes, the Legs Diamonds – 'the *stars* used to go to see the gangsters.'

Angels With Dirty Faces, however, nearly ruined the Dead End Kids' career because a New York city councillor complained that 'We were a detriment to the children of America. He tried to get us censored by the United States Congress and put us out of pictures because we were a bad element.' Their studio, Warner Brothers, galloped to the rescue by putting them in a watered down sequel, *Angels Wash Their Faces*, in which they appeared with Ronald Reagan, who was obviously Mr Clean even in 1939. (Huntz Hall said: 'Reagan did two pictures with us, you know – you're laughing; so am I – but he got the greatest job in the world.')

In the mid-thirties, too, there was a series of darker films, such as *Fury* (Fritz Lang, 1936) in which Spencer Tracy played an innocent man mistaken for a murderer and very nearly lynched, and *Let Us Live* (John Braham, 1937), wherein the equally innocent Henry Fonda is wrongly convicted of murder. Both were based on true incidents and like Lang's fictional *You Only Live Once*, about a petty crook –

Fonda again – being framed for a killing, they were stark pictures which pointed to society as the true culprit and, in their look and spirit, predated the *film noir*.

But probably the most famous and successful of the crime movies of the late thirties was Raoul Walsh's *The Roaring Twenties* (1939) which charted the rise and fall of a gangster (Cagney) from the post World War One unemployment that drove him into crime, to the Prohibition era that nurtured him and the Crash that wiped him out to his eventual redemption and death on the church steps, not forgetting the immortal epitaph bestowed upon him by his girlfriend: 'He used to be a big shot.' What with that and his ridding society of his customary, evil adversary Humphrey Bogart, the film just about encapsulated all the themes of the gangster movie in that decade. (It was, incidentally, Bogart's thirty-fourth picture and later he said: 'In my first thirty-four films I was shot in twelve, electrocuted or hanged in eight and was a jailbird in nine. I played more scenes writhing around on the floor than I did standing up.') There was also a touch of wistful, wishful thinking in Cagney's line to Bogart: 'It's a new kind of set-up. You and I don't belong.'

Mind you, I suppose much depends on what you read into those words. The end of the old-style bootlegger/gangster? Probably. The end of the organised crime gangster? Certainly not, although organised crime – the Mafia – was hardly treated of in the movies at that time, possibly because Hoover was still denying its existence since there was quicker glory and publicity to be derived from hunting down smaller-time crooks like Dillinger, Machine-Gun Kelly and Baby Face Nelson than trying to crack open the Mafia.

Two years after *The Roaring Twenties*, Walsh looked with similar romantic nostalgia on the lone desperado – whose time he also seemed to believe was over – in *High Sierra*, in which Bogart played Roy Earle, sprung from jail to pull off one last big heist for his former boss. In all manner of ways Earle is the criminal *malgré lui*, a Robin Hood figure or, more likely, a throwback to the old West, especially in his decision to shoot it out to the death in the wide open spaces of the High Sierras rather than in dingy city streets. (Indeed, eight years later Walsh virtually remade the film – taken, by the way, from yet another novel by W. R. Burnett – as a western, *Colorado Territory*.)

Bogart owed the role of Roy Earle to George Raft, who declined it on the grounds that he did not wish to die at the end, and in the same year he played Sam Spade in *The Maltese Falcon* (the third filmed version of the story), also thanks to Raft who passed on this occasion because he did not want to work with a first-time director, John Huston. (Raft must have been one of the worst judges of a role in Hollywood.)

The Maltese Falcon, a far more authentic adaptation of Hammett's work than the "Thin Man" series, was notable not only for being an excellent film but for being recognised as an early and outstanding example of *film noir*. The label, designed by French critics after the Second World War when they were able to look back and see what Hollywood had been doing since 1940, was applied to those movies which, typically, portray the darker side of crime and corruption and whose heroes, as well as villains, tend to be deeply imbued with cynicism. In addition, those heroes are usually disillusioned loners, more secure with the past than they are with the uncertain and possibly menacing future. In these films nothing (in the case of *The Maltese Falcon* the blackbird itself) is quite what it seems and the people, particularly the women (Mary Astor in *The Maltese Falcon*) are equally ambivalent. And Bogart as Sam Spade gave the first of a series of performances which lend him some right to be regarded as the composite *film noir* hero. As Spade he developed the sardonic, suspicious, untrusting character whom he was to portray again in a slightly different guise in such pictures as *Casablanca*, *To Have and Have Not* and *Key Largo*: an amoral, unshockable type who expected little of life or his fellow man but who, at heart, was on the side of the angels.

The first big year for *film noir* was 1944, the year of Billy Wilder's *Double Indemnity*, Otto Preminger's *Laura*, Robert Siodmak's *Phantom Lady* and Fritz Lang's *The Woman in the Window* among others. As Peter Bogdanovich said: 'I don't know why that genre happened. There was a kind of a dark period that the forties took us through and after the war it got even worse. Then it really got black in the fifties.' But when you consider that the peak years of *film noir* coincided with the end of the Second World War and the years of the House Un-American Activities Committee and all the fears and anxiety that attended them, the prevalence of such films is probably not surprising. In any event, the genre was to thrive for a full decade, although not always in its purest form since elements of it would be borrowed for other kinds of crime movie. The true *noir* hero was a loner, but in 1948, for example, Jules Dassin directed *The Naked City*, which had the look and feel of *film noir* though its protagonists were not loners but the New York police force, tracking down a killer. The film was, in fact, a dark *policier*, a hybrid form also used by Robert Siodmak, one of the key *film noir* directors, in *Cry of the City*, again in 1948.

(Mind you, *film noir* doesn't seem to have made an impact on everybody. In 1946 Glenn Ford co-starred with Rita Hayworth in *Gilda*, a supreme example of the genre directed by Charles Vidor. But when I said to him: 'There seemed to be a darker tone to the films that were made immediately after the war. Did you notice that at all?', he said: 'No, because after *Gilda* I made a comedy – I made two comedies.' So much for *film noir*. Or so much for actors perhaps?)

But, as Edward Dmytryk (director of *Murder My Sweet* and *Cornered*) pointed out, in the mid-1940s the *film noir* offered writers and directors a rare opportunity to explore social problems in the cinema. Except in what was to all intents and purposes a crime movie, he said, 'It was very difficult to get into poor areas. Everything was supposed to be lovely and shiny and the secretary lived in a 1,000-dollars-a-day apartment and that sort of thing. But if we had a detective who had to search for a criminal, well, of course criminals lived in the poor sections – everyone knew that. So the detective could go into the ghettoes, into the poor areas and we could photograph them and show that part of life.'

The writer and director Abraham Polonsky was disinclined to attribute the rise of *film noir* to any particular postwar social conditions, arguing that it was a part of German expressionism which Hollywood had simply adopted. And it is certainly

If you think the contents of the coffee cup could be significant, well, maybe you're right. Ingrid Bergman in Hitchcock's *film noir*, *Notorious*

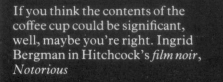

Inset: Barbara Stanwyck, Tom Powers and Fred MacMurray in *Double Indemnity*, a classic example of *film noir*. Nobody should be trusted – least of all a wife

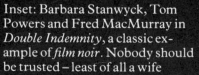

Right: Orson Welles in the influential *Touch of Evil*, possibly the best B movie ever made

true that many of the best-known *film noir* directors – Siodmak, Preminger, Lang for instance – came from the German or Austrian industry. But he did agree with Dmytryk that it was a genre that lent itself, better than any other, to the making of liberal or political comment. 'In thrillers and crime films you get an air of terror, horror, suspense by the use of darkness, of single-source lighting and by the vision of the underworld city, the underlife that's led and so on. It's a style. But also it gives you a great deal of freedom. In a crime picture you have political freedom to say whatever you please because you are dealing in an area where the intellectual content is absorbed into what people think is a dark, criminal type of picture anyhow and so there's an acceptance of it. If you did it with a nice, friendly group of Americans sitting at home people might be upset but in a crime picture it's acceptable.'

A prime example of the thinly-disguised political film was Polonsky's *Force of Evil* (1948), which he both wrote and directed and which starred John Garfield. In it, while ostensibly dealing with the numbers racket, he clearly linked organised crime figures with apparently legitimate lawyers, thereby creating an implicit comparison between the methods of the gangsters and those of big business. He said: 'I didn't invent that. That's inherent in almost all American literature; it's inherent in all American crime movies. Whenever the crime is not one of passion, it's a crime of making money out of other people.' Those making the money could be criminal gangs or big business, there being very little difference between them. 'It's not an unhappy comparison,' he said, although he felt that regarding crime and business as being two sides of the same coin was going a little far. 'The idea is to show that in America crime is part of the system.'

Underlining that point, he said that in *Force of Evil* 'you don't meet a single respectable person, including the police. In a philosophical way and looking at the whole picture you might very well say that there's a road and there's crime on one side and law on the other. But you can never tell which side which is on.' It's an attitude which is either cynical or realistic, depending on your point of view.

Before making *Force of Evil* Polonsky had examined the seediness and corruption of the fight game in *Body and Soul* (also starring Garfield), which he had written for Robert Rossen. The essentially political comment that "crime is part of the system" is implicit in both films and although the only pressure applied to Polonsky by the studio on either picture was an exhortation, which he agreed to, to make the ending of *Force of Evil* a little more optimistic (to please the censors) it is no coincidence that later both he and Rossen would be blacklisted and that Garfield's career would be effectively ruined when they all came under investigation by HUAC.

Meanwhile, the rural gangster picture re-emerged in 1945 with *Dillinger*, a low-budget effort backed by the King brothers, themselves ex-bootleggers, and the urban gangster cropped up once more in Henry Hathaway's *Kiss of Death*, in which Richard Widmark made a startling screen debut as a giggling, psychotic killer, whose style was later aped by the real Mafioso, Joey Gallo. Movies like *Dillinger* earned the strong disapproval of the Production Code which, in 1947, issued an edict forbidding the depiction by name of known criminals in films. In the short term this meant, for instance, that when Joseph H. Lewis directed *The Undercover Man* in 1949 he was not allowed to refer to the central heavy, a gang leader indicted by the US Treasury for tax evasion, as Al Capone, though Capone he was clearly meant to be. Lewis said: 'We got around that by calling him the "Big Feller" and the gentleman who played the part – we never saw him, of course, only his back – wore a white hat which was the trademark of Capone.' In the long term the effect was that the next picture to deal with a real criminal would not appear until ten years later when Don Siegel directed *Baby Face Nelson*.

As for the Mafia, its existence was still hardly more than hinted at in films, perhaps because J. Edgar Hoover continued to deny that there was any such thing, insisting that organised crime began and ended with Murder Inc. Indeed, it wasn't until 1957 and the more or less accidental arrest of twenty delegates to a Mob summit meeting at Appalachin, Ohio, that he would even recognise "la Cosa Nostra" and then he was only prepared to admit that it was a new and entirely independent crime syndicate which had nothing at all to do with anything called the Mafia. But perhaps, too, the studios own hands were not entirely clean. Harry Cohn is widely believed to have borrowed heavily from the Mob to keep Columbia afloat during the Depression years and who knows whether other studios may not have done the same thing? Polonsky said: 'There's always talk around town that this company or that company has Mob money or something like that. Who knows if it's true or not? But if they can be in Wall Street, if they can own a Wall Street brokerage company and if they can own banks in America why can't they be in Hollywood?' Still, he doubted that possible Mob involvement would have much bearing on Hollywood's reluctance to deal with the Mafia on screen. The only thing that would make Hollywood reluctant to tackle a subject, he thought, was a fear that the film wouldn't make money.

But if the extent of the Mafia's connection with the studios is debatable, the fact of its connection is not. For example, Bugsy Siegel – a close associate since young manhood of Luciano, Meyer Lansky and Frank Costello – was highly active in the Hollywood community for many years and was involved in sundry nefarious schemes with Jean Harlow's stepfather, Marino Bello. Siegel had been sent to the west coast by Mob leaders in the mid-1930s to help the local crime boss, Jack Dragna, to develop his rackets and in this capacity had introduced syndicate-controlled gambling into Los Angeles and had smuggled heroin from Mexico into California before moving on to open the Flamingo Hotel and casino in Las Vegas.

Unfortunately, he owed the Mafia money and when, in 1947, Lucky Luciano decided it was time he paid up, Siegel did not have the funds. It was at this time and in these circumstances that Richard Brooks remembered meeting him in the office of Hollywood producer Mark Hellinger (*The Killers, Brute Force, Naked City*), a well-known associate of mobsters since his newspaper days in New York.

'We used to gather in Mark's office at the end of the day, all the writers – Albert Maltz who was writing *Naked City* and me, I was writing *Brute Force* – and we'd drop in for a drink about 5.30 before everybody went home and Mark would have all kinds of characters around there, drinking with you. And one night he introduced this guy, saying "This is Ben" and the guy had a drink and finally got up and left and Mark said, "Do you know who that is? Bugsy Siegel. He doesn't like to be called Bugsy, he likes to be called Ben. He was here to borrow a million dollars. What the hell, I haven't got a million dollars. If I had a million dollars I'd have spent it. I tried to raise it for him – he's been here four hours; I called everybody, I couldn't raise anything. I couldn't even raise it for myself, let alone for him. Now, he *needs* the money, he says if he doesn't get the money in a coupla weeks he's not gonna be around." Well, he didn't get the money and in less than a couple weeks he wasn't around.' Indeed, he was not: on 20 June 1947 on the instructions of Luciano and Meyer Lansky – no doubt issued with the deepest regret, for after all Bugsy was a friend – he was shot three times in the head in the garden of his girlfriend's home in Beverly Hills and the same night associates of Meyer Lansky took over the Flamingo Hotel.

Now this story may not prove a lot but it does indicate that the denizens of Hollywood were not unfamiliar with the stalwarts of organised crime and for that reason may have been reluctant to depict them in the movies and possibly incur their displeasure. One of the first pictures to deal with the reality of that aspect of the underworld was *The Enforcer* which, in 1950, was based on the prosecution of Louis "Lepke" Buchalter, the head of Murder Incorporated. But then public interest in organised crime was not particularly strong at the time and even the Kefauver Committee, which in 1950 was looking into the matter, had very little impact since much more attention was given to the rival activities of HUAC and other Commie-hunters such as the Senators Joe McCarthy and Richard Nixon.

During the fifties and well into the sixties, crime was largely relegated to the B or exploitation movie, where there was a heavy emphasis on violence (especially against women) and brutality. The rogue cop or vigilante began to figure prominently as in Fritz Lang's *The Big Heat* in which a police detective goes undercover to track down the killers of his wife. Another example of *film noir* this one, although perhaps nobody pointed this out to Glenn Ford who starred in it. In the films of this era the general attitude to the vigilante figure was one of cautious sympathy, combining a realisation of the fact that he had been sorely provoked with a token disapproval of his stepping outside the law. In this they anticipated the later *Dirty Harry* and *Death Wish* series.

On the whole, however, crime movies fell from popularity for a period of very nearly twenty years. Apart from *Key Largo* (1948), *Detective Story* (1951), *On the Waterfront* (1954) and *Pete Kelly's Blues* (1955) there were no gangster films in the top twenty at the box office between 1939 (*Angels With Dirty Faces*) and *The Detective* in 1968 (although *Bonnie and Clyde* in 1967 figures in some but not all the lists). And during this period such pictures as did deal with organised crime fell into the B category for the most part, though there were exceptions such as John Boorman's *Point Blank* in 1967. That and pictures like Phil Karlson's *The Phenix City Story* and *The Brothers Rico*, Don Siegel's *The Line-Up* and his remake of *The Killers* and Sam Fuller's *Underworld USA* showed an awareness of the reality and scale of organised crime and its corrupting effect on American city life.

Walter Mirisch who, in the mid-fifties, ran the production unit which made, among other films *The Phenix City Story*, a tale of mob corruption in an Alabama town, believed that such pictures were relegated to the B or exploitation category because their storylines were taken – on the old Warner Brothers' principle – from the headlines. 'When you sought to make that kind of movie, if you did it on a low budget you could do it quickly; you could get it out and you could take advantage of the subject matter by getting it into the theatres much more quickly than anybody else.' He felt, too, that there was more to many such films than a simple, acquisitive desire to milk the headlines. 'There were social problems, of course, during those times, great problems of adjustment and I think a good deal of that was reflected in those films.'

The times he was speaking of were the Eisenhower years of 1952 to 1960 when, beneath the apparently placid surface of American society, great changes were going on. For one thing the teenager had been created, had adopted James Dean as its spokesman and was beginning to ask questions of its elders and betters and making the demands for greater recognition and personal freedom which were to lead to the youth cult of the 1960s. And what perhaps touched a responsive nerve in the young people who were the main clientele for such productions as Don Siegel's *Baby Face Nelson* and Roger Corman's *Machine-Gun Kelly* was that they dealt with the loner, the outsider. The fact that the subjects of these and similar films were rural desperadoes was, Corman thought, of secondary consideration 'I think the major factor was that it was one person who had the gang, one man who was the anti-Establishment anti-hero. I think that concept has been with us for a long time. Audiences have always identified with the man who is outside, who says "I can do this myself."' Neither Nelson nor Machine-Gun Kelly, of course, were contemporary criminals; they had thrived – if thrive is the word – in the 1930s.

Corman said: 'With regard to that, I think that probably in the 50s and 60s there was a looking back with a little bit of nostalgia to a slightly more rural, possibly more innocent time. Very often the lower budget films will reflect the undercurrents of society rather more than other, more expensive, pictures. It may be that the lower budget film makers are closer to that segment of society; it may be that they have a little more freedom and they're a little bit looser in their approach and sometimes a little more honest.' Not that he had approached the story of Machine-Gun Kelly with lofty sociological ideals. What had appealed to him about the man was the fact that he was a coward, despite being number one on the FBI's Ten Most Wanted list. 'When he was captured, he and his gang were in a mountain hideout and he was surrounded by the FBI who called on him to lay down his guns and come out with his hands up. He did. And when the leader of the FBI put the handcuffs on him he said, "Kelly, you're supposed to be the most dangerous man in the United States. We never thought you would give up – why did you do it?" And Kelly said, "I knew you'd kill me if I didn't." A totally logical answer but I built the film from that statement.'

But if the insertion of social comment into low budget crime movies had been more or less accidental to begin with, it began later to become deliberate. When Bud Boetticher made *The Rise and Fall of Legs Diamond* in 1960, he used the death of his main character, played by Ray Danton, to denote the end of the independent hoodlum of the 1920s and the ascendency of the Mafia. He also attempted to explain the nature of organised crime and felt that this had not been done during the first, 1930s cycle of gangster pictures because there was no need to. 'If you had people like Cagney in a film, why bother with the syndicate? Cagney's the star and he's going to get killed at the end of the picture and you were involved with him, an individual. But Ray Danton wasn't a star and nobody cared about him, so I could go into the syndicate thing and discuss what was really happening.' Francis Ford Coppola did much the same thing, only on a far bigger scale, in the eighties with *The Cotton Club*, which ends with the imminent repeal of Prohibition and the rise of Lucky Luciano.

But in the 1960s the film that drew the most enthusiastic response from again mainly young audiences was the hugely influential *Bonnie and Clyde*, starring Warren Beatty and Faye Dunaway. The explanations for its enormous success – not anticipated by Warner Brothers, who were initially reluctant to give it wide distribution – are many and varied. On the first and most obvious level both stars were young and extremely good-looking. As Martin Scorsese said: 'Don't forget the tag-line in the advertisements: They're young, they're in love and they kill people . . . We loved them, we *loved* them. We thought they were terrific and they wore the greatest clothes and, oh, they were wonderful.'

The very style of the film, then, was one of its main attractions along with its iconoclasm and rebelliousness. But more than that the film reflected a very significant change that had come over American society in the 1930s. Arthur Penn, the director of *Bonnie and Clyde*, once said: 'When Ford made the V8, which was sufficiently powerful to out-run the local police automobiles, gangs began to spring up. And that was literally the genesis of the Bonnie and Clyde gang . . . They literally spent their lives in the confines of the car . . . in American mythology the automobile replaced the horse. This was the transformation of the western into the gangster.'

So Bonnie and Clyde in life as in the film became folk heroes, much like the James gang or the Younger brothers in the old west; their exploits were followed and admired by millions and they took their place in American folklore as bad guys who could be just as fascinating and glamorous as the good guys.

The original script was written by David Newman and Robert Benton who, being much influenced by the French New Wave, wanted François Truffaut or Jean-Luc Godard to direct. In the event the job was taken over by Penn, no doubt fortunately since he would clearly have had a deeper understanding of the very Americanness of the subject than either of the Frenchmen. And Robert Towne was called in to polish the screenplay. One of the alterations he made, for reasons of dramatic simplicity, was to change Clyde from a homosexual to an impotent heterosexual.

In analysing the film's impact Towne felt that one point to bear in mind was that in earlier productions where the desperado had been presented as attractive he was invariably a wronged and misunderstood man who had to rob to stay alive. 'Then came the 50s and Eisenhower and a kind of spirit of reformation with a figure like James Dean in *Rebel Without a Cause* in which he was less of a rebel than he was a reformer . . . he was the fellow who was going to go to the police and tell the truth. I mean, if you look back, no Bible-thumping Protestant could be more of a reformer than James Dean was . . . he was the last thing from a rebel. Then came *Bonnie and Clyde* and I think it represented a sharp break from the 30s and the economic burdens that caused people to turn to crime and from the reformer spirit that felt that something could still be worked out within the system.

'By the mid-60s and Vietnam, I think there was a feeling that nothing was going to change the system and it was the first movie that made no apologies for the fact that the system was just going to have to go.' In the film Clyde shot up a house on which the mortgage had been foreclosed and persuaded the evicted farmer to fire bullets into it as well. Towne said: 'I think that was kind of emblematic of the fact that the film was saying, "Everybody goes when the whistle blows. It's no good – the whole structure is rotten and no amount of reformation or thinking we can work within the structure will change it."' The film also includes a strong and very definite rejection of family and Towne discovered that this, too, struck a chord within the young. Bonnie has a line in which she complains that she has nobody, no family and Clyde says: 'I'm your family.' Towne recalled that a number of young people to whom he had talked about the picture had told him that this had meant a great deal to them, that they too had felt that family feeling was to be discovered only among their own contemporaries.

'The film came along at a very timely moment and reflected something that was happening then . . . It took advantage of a change in the Production Code as well, it allowed us to suggest certain kinds of sexual behaviour that had not been suggested specifically on film before.' But would the effect have been the same if the picture had dealt not with Bonnie and Clyde but with urban gangsters or the Mob? He thought not. 'It created a kind of youthful family without authority figures. Bonnie Parker and Clyde Barrow were perpetual adolescents so the moviegoing audience, who were also adolescents, could go into the theatre and fantasise in a way that they could not have done if it had been a film about Al Capone or *The Godfather*. I mean, these were kids who relied on each other and had no home and no place to go and ran and ran until they died.'

And beyond even that. . . . 'This was an American gangster movie dealing with somebody who looks like Errol Flynn, being impotent and screwing around and shooting people and being thoroughly attractive. It was outrageous.' And so it was and it launched a whole wave of films – *Butch Cassidy and the Sundance Kid* and *Easy Rider* two years later are excellent examples – in which American values and society are seen from the outlaw's point of view and are therefore rejected.

In 1967, the same year as *Bonnie and Clyde*, Roger Corman directed *The St Valentine's Day Massacre* which, though not influenced by Arthur Penn's film, was perhaps equally in tune with the mood of the time. Corman said: 'To a certain extent I was trying to make a comment on capitalism. I was trying to draw a parallel with corporations and capitalist America. Capone built an organisation; Bugs Moran built a somewhat lesser organisation so you could say that here was the American Dream turned this way, whereas the president of General Motors would embody the dream turned that way.' Two years later he made *Bloody Mama*, based on the exploits of the ferocious 1930s gang leader Ma Barker and her four sons. And here perhaps Corman was influenced by *Bonnie and Clyde* because he said: 'We took a little more freedom with the facts and played a little bit more with the psychological factors within the gang. We tried to talk a little about America and about the family situation, the tensions and strengths within a family.' As Penn and Towne did with *Bonnie and Clyde* he attempted to inject humour into the story. 'I was trying to find one line that would sum up Ma Barker's attitude towards the banks and what she was doing. She was a very religious woman and the line the writer and I finally came up with was when somebody asked her why she robbed banks and she said, "Because that's where God put the money." '

He was, he said, influenced by current events. 'I was trying to make certain statements within my films about the society around us and use history as a springboard for those statements.'

A few years later and again influenced by *Bonnie and Clyde*, John Milius made *Dillinger* for American International Pictures, the outfit which spawned Corman and himself as well as a host of other equally significant film makers. Milius was offered Capone, Pretty Boy Floyd or Dillinger as the subject of his first film as a director and ... 'I said, well, Dillinger. He was the king of criminals. He never killed anyone, you know, he was not a mad dog. He was a real character, I guess a Robin Hood-like figure. He never gave to the poor, believe me, but he did symbolise a daring during the Depression. He was an American folk hero and I wanted to do the story unapologetically. I didn't want him to be a real good guy who got a bad rap from the banks and was trying to save his farm and that kind of stuff. I wanted him to be a criminal but still in the spirit of Jesse James.' Never before this period, not even in the Cagney/Robinson gangster movies of the 1930s, had the criminal been presented as such a romantic figure. Samuel Z. Arkoff, the head of AIP and thus the man behind such films as *Machine-Gun Kelly*, *Bloody Mama* and *Dillinger*, said: 'They were sympathetic heroes in a way. It was the era of the bucolic gangster as opposed to the Mafia gangsters as we see them today. They were hero figures really, particularly when people were getting tossed out of their homes and their farms and the homeless went to California. They were heroes, folk heroes, and the gangsters of today are just not hero figures.'

The appeal of the delinquent hick, the cornball criminal, was, however, limited and soon the cinema began to turn its attentions back to the urban racketeer, a theme explored in 1973 by Martin Scorsese in *Mean Streets*. As in *Little Caesar* and *Scarface* the focus was on the immigrant, the new American. Scorsese himself was brought up in Little Italy, the very heart of the Italian-American community in New York, and for most of the people there, he said, a life of crime was the only option available. 'Look at the jobs they had when they came over, look at the conditions they lived in. I just wanted to make a very accurate picture of what it was like, growing up that way. The idea is, how one chooses to lead one's life. I mean, it's a change of values – the idea of taking the American Dream, that wonderful idea that everybody can get rich quick and then finding that if they can't do it by legal means they can do it by illegal means ... it's a disruption of values. You find a lot of guys who live that way. Their idea of making money – maybe a million or two – is to steal it, to beat somebody up for it, to cheat somebody out of it. It's much sweeter, much better than earning it.'

None of which was new, of course. The same philosophy was to be found in the early Cagney/Robinson films, just as one of the underlying themes of *Bonnie and Clyde* as articulated by Carlos Clarens in his book *Crime Movies* – better to live fast, die young and leave good-looking images in the collective mind – had been expounded in 1949 in Nicholas Ray's *Knock on Any Door*. In this John Derek, an accused killer defended by Humphrey Bogart, summed up his attitude to life as follows: 'Live fast, die young and leave a good-looking corpse.' But in the 1970s, with the relaxation of censorship and the abrogation of the command that crime must not be seen to pay, films could explore the criminal mind and environment in much greater depth and with at least the appearance of greater realism than ever before.

The classic examples here were Francis Ford Coppola's *The Godfather* and its sequel *The Godfather II*, both made between 1972 and 1974. The first film, based on Mario Puzo's bestseller about the Mafia, originated at Paramount Studios, whose then head of production was Robert Evans. Until that time Coppola's record was hardly inspiring. True, he had won an Academy Award for his script of *Patton* but the four films he had directed, among them *Finian's Rainbow* and *The Rain People*, had – according to Evans – failed between them to make enough money to pay the advertising for one of them.

Therefore Evans chose Coppola to direct *The Godfather* simply because he was of Italian origin. The argument was that there had never been a really successful Mafia movie and Evans asked himself why. The reason he came up with was that Mafia movies had usually been made by Jews. A few years earlier at Paramount he had been responsible for *The Brotherhood* but. . . . 'It was directed by Martin Ritt and starred Kirk Douglas, Susan Strasberg and Luther Adler. And this was typical of every Mafia film ever made. There's a difference between a Sicilian and a Jew and Francis was the only Italian director working in Hollywood and that's why I hired him. I wanted the flavour of the Sicilian quality that he could bring out.' Both in theory and in practice Evans's idea was faultless but even so the film was not made without pain to both of them. 'I fired him four times,' Evans said, 'during and after the shooting.' Mind you, he fired a lot of other people, too – notably an editor and an assistant director who had told him, wrongly in his opinion, that what Coppola had shot was uncuttable.

Speaking in the viewing theatre at his home in Beverly Hills, Evans said: 'I edited the film right here in this room and it was brilliant. I got on the plane to New York on Sunday night, fired the editor, fired the assistant director, fired six other people and put my arms around Francis and said, "Your work is extraordinary."' Well, that's the way Hollywood behaves – it's all raw emotion and naked hearts flapping on sleeves. Still . . . if Coppola's work was extraordinary why had he been fired (and taken back) in the first two weeks and then fired again (and taken back) on three subsequent occasions? 'Oh, we had big trouble on the final cut. The picture was supposed to open for Christmas and in September it was unreleasable. I said,

"Francis, if you fix this picture it will do over 50 million dollars business." He said, "I'll fix it and you can buy me a car when it hits 50 million dollars." The day the picture hit 50 million he bought a 43,000 dollar Mercedes and sent me the bill and I had to pay for it.'

When Coppola cut the picture it ran to two hours and six minutes and Evans was hugely dissatisfied with it. (I believe that was the fourth time the director was fired.) But Evans took it away and – most unusually – actually added fifteen minutes to the running time. 'Francis was scared. He's a wonderful shooter of film but he runs scared and he was afraid to embellish the characters and the richness of it all. It looked like *The Untouchables* when he was finished with it.' (The latter comment referring to an old TV series was, needless to say, intended as an insult.) Whose idea was it, though, to cast Marlon Brando as the Godfather – Don Vito Corleone? 'It was Francis's idea and I backed him. Brando came into my office with blond hair down to here with a rubber band round it and he said he'd read the book and wanted to play the part. He *needed* the part. We tested him – and it was a wonderful thing to test him because if anyone said to me after that, "I won't test", I said, "If Marlon Brando can test, you can test."'

Such moments of agreement between Coppola and Evans were, however, rare. During the editing, Evans said, he had a very bad back and . . . 'I was carried on a stretcher from dubbing room to dubbing room and we had terrible fights. There was one night when we were out on the tennis court here arguing and I said, "You do it my way, Francis, or go back to San Francisco," and he went and took a walk and when he came back – I think he was gone for twenty minutes – he looked at me and said, "Okay, I'll do it your way – but I'll remember it." I said, "I hope you do" – and he did . . . Instead of opening at Christmas we opened in March and the film made more money in six months than *Gone With the Wind* did in thirty-seven years.'

There were many other fights. Coppola wanted Al Pacino to play Michael Corleone and Evans didn't; Evans wanted James Caan for Sonny and Coppola didn't. That one, though, ended fairly amicably with a compromise – each kept the actor of his choice and, looking at the film, each was right, in the sense that both Pacino and Caan were excellent. Despite all these arguments and squabbles the finished film has an epic, luxurious look that belies the fact that, according to Evans, it cost only 6 million dollars to make. 'Nobody earned more than 35,000 dollars in the entire picture, that's why it was made for the price it was. If you had to re-create it today it would cost 40 million, maybe 50.' In fact, Coppola got more than 35,000 dollars – he got 150,000 plus "points", a percentage of the profits; and Brando, on top of his 35,000, was given points as well. Evans said: 'I bought Brando's percentage for 100,000 dollars and he went crazy afterwards because if he had kept it, it would have meant 8 million dollars for him . . .' Coppola's percentage, which he wisely retained, earned him 8 million dollars, too, while Paramount which owned eighty-six per cent of the film 'made more from *The Godfather* than Universal made from *Jaws* or 20th Century-Fox from *Star Wars* . . .'

During the making of *The Godfather*, Coppola said he wanted to use the Mafia as 'a metaphor for America. Both have roots in Europe; basically both feel they are benevolent institutions; both have their hands stained with blood from what it is necessary to do to protect their power and interests; both are totally capitalistic phenomena and basically have a profit motive. Of course, it's a romantic conception of the Mafia.' Evans who, for various reasons concerned not only with the two *Godfather* films but also with *The Cotton Club* later, is not necessarily Coppola's most ardent admirer, dismissed that as 'artistic bullshit ... a cop out because he was making a commercial movie'. Less stringent critics, however, might be inclined to say that what Coppola had claimed he wanted to do was precisely what he did. In *The Godfather* (and then in *The Godfather II*) the Mafia are seen more than in any other film as the dark side of the American Dream, an immoral, amoral, glamorous and ruthlessly successful group of people whose dreams and aspirations are precisely the same as those of big business. And this is expressed most strongly in a scene that takes place late in the film in the Corleone garden between Brando and Pacino. It's the moment when, effectively, Brando is handing over control of the "family" and its interests to his son and expresses regret that things had turned out the way they had because, ideally, he would have liked Michael to be "legit", to become Senator Corleone or even President Corleone. Robert Towne was called in specifically to write that scene and he said: 'It certainly is consistent with Coppola's expressed view of the Mafia as a kind of cartoon of American life.' Towne, anyway, was of the opinion that America itself was 'as hypocritical as the Mafia and probably less efficient'. And he believed that one of the strongest attractions of the film – ironically, in view of the fact that he also worked on *Bonnie and Clyde* – was its emphasis on the family as a bastion. 'I think that had an enormous appeal for a country in which the family unit as such was going straight to hell.'

The theme of the Mafia as a distorted reflection of American capitalism was taken a step further by Coppola in *The Godfather II*, which is less an examination of organised crime than a study of the corruption of power. By flashing back to the comparatively simple hopes and ambitions of Don Vito as a young man (Robert de Niro) and contrasting that with the enormity of the organisation that Michael controlled and the appalling lengths (including, among other things, fratricide) to which he felt himself driven to keep it together, the film presented a highly cynical view of American corporate life. The Corleone family, after all, was now legitimate, almost respectable indeed – in which case God help us all.

As a matter of interest the two *Godfather* films won eight Academy Awards and eight other nominations between them and the first of them took close to 200 million dollars at the box office. Robert Evans, whose only close association with the sequel was to help in the editing, said that 'it never reached the heights of *Godfather I* because *Godfather I* was ascending, everyone was going up. But *Godfather II* was moralising, everything was down and people were sad. "One" was an audience film and the other may have been a great picture but it didn't have the audience appeal.' The second film, according to Evans, cost 14 million dollars and Coppola's fee was 2 million. Evans's summary of the two pictures is probably accurate but I think posterity may well conclude that the second of them is the greater work.

Yet neither of them was as influential as *Bonnie and Clyde* or, even earlier,

Orson Welles' *Touch of Evil* had been. Welles made his film, in which he co-starred with Charlton Heston, in 1958. Heston said that it was he who, learning that Welles was to play the heavy, suggested to the studio that he might as well direct it, too. 'And they seemed to regard this with the same amazement they would have exhibited had I suggested my mother direct the film.' Such a reaction is not surprising when you recall that Welles was constantly in trouble with the Hollywood bosses. 'Much as I admired Orson and his talents,' Heston said, 'I think he was to a certain extent the author of his own troubles with studios. Crews loved him – they would do anything for him – so did actors, so did writers. But the people you need really to charm are the people who give you the money to make the film. And Orson seemed to fail to understand that, or to be so outraged that it was a reality that he would not respond to it. He behaved terribly with studio heads.' Nor were things any different on *Touch of Evil*, which was produced by Albert Zugsmith for Universal-International. According to those who worked on it "the editing took for ever", the head office decided an extra scene was needed and Welles refused to shoot it and then disappeared. Zugsmith was told that 'the man has gone haywire, he's drinking, he's down at that whorehouse in Tijuana and he won't talk to us.' Eventually somebody else shot the additional scene and other people attended to the final cut. Zugsmith said that the Welles aficionados and purists were outraged – "somebody *dared* to tamper with his work and that kind of stuff, you know" – but in his opinion, not altogether surprisingly perhaps, the alterations made little difference and in fairness Heston is inclined to agree. Besides, Heston did not think it was that great a film. 'The definition I like best was supplied by an English critic twenty years ago. He said: It's the best B-movie ever made – and that's about right. It's an extraordinary film.'

What made it extraordinary, in the words of Peter Bogdanovich, was that it was 'the ultimate *film noir*. It had that marvellous grey look that started with *Citizen Kane* and it was kind of like the man who made *Citizen Kane* had now made the ultimate thriller. It really was very influential for a lot of people making pictures. I don't think the public cared about it but picture makers liked it.' It was not, though, just the style that attracted them; there was the content, too – 'the modern cop versus the old-fashioned cop', as Bogdanovich put it. He believed that the Welles character – 'a cop who had been completely corrupted and yet was right' – had not really been seen in the cinema before. He was right in the sense that he was determined to bring the criminal to book but corrupt in the way he went about doing it. Bogdanovich said: 'That's what *Dirty Harry* is about; the whole *Dirty Harry* syndrome is about how a cop can enforce the law when the law is very easy on the criminal.'

It was, in fact, the *Dirty Harry* syndrome that dominated the crime movie for the rest of the 1970s and into the eighties, whether the protagonist was a cop who moved outside the law to administer justice or, as in the *Death Wish* films, a civilian vigilante. John Milius, who worked as a writer on the original and on *Magnum Force*, the second of the three Dirty Harry Callahan films that starred Clint Eastwood, felt that the strength of the pictures lay in the fact that the protagonist was totally self-reliant. Furthermore, in the original film when Inspector Callahan moves outside the law to track down and kill the utterly heinous villain of the piece he becomes less a policeman than a citizen acting on his own. 'Ultimately that's where everything lies,' Milius said. 'The solution to problems eventually lies with the citizen, doesn't it?' Well, up to a point, Lord Copper... Milius also said: 'I certainly don't think we should have more cops with wider powers on the street. I'm very alarmed at the idea of the police; I don't particularly like the police. I'm a great advocate of the Second Amendment ... ' The Second Amendment is the one that gives Americans the right to bear arms, or to put it Milius's way, 'the Second Amendment is so that if the police become too oppressive, you can shoot them.'

I really don't think we should take this outrageous statement too seriously. Milius has often been accused of being a Fascist but in fact he's more of an anarchic right-winger with a deep suspicion of liberal thought and tendencies, who reserves the right to change his stance whenever it suits him. Thus in *Dirty Harry* Callahan was to all intents and purposes a vigilante but in *Magnum Force* and in his capacity as an upright policeman he was obliged to track down a vigilante who was killing pimps and gangsters in cold blood. That, Milius said, was not meant as an apology for the first film but to 'show the other side of the coin'.

Coincidentally with the *Dirty Harry* trilogy came the first of Michael Winner's *Death Wish* films, starring Charles Bronson. Here the main character is a true vigilante, a businessman who hunts and kills muggers in revenge for the murder of his wife. Milius, changing stance again after *Magnum Force*, thoroughly approved of *Death Wish*. 'I thought it was wonderful, I mean, I'm all for that guy. I think there should be a lot of loose vigilantes in our society, running around shooting dope dealers and muggers every night...'

In the same year (1976) as *Death Wish* there came Martin Scorsese's *Taxi Driver* in which Robert de Niro played an unhinged cabbie, a Vietnam veteran, who was driven to acting the vigilante because of the vice, violence and squalor he saw all around him in New York. Scorsese, however, said the intention of the film was anti-vigilante. 'The whole key to the picture is that there's a difference between having a feeling and acting it out ... Acting it out is not the way to go ... It wasn't meant to have a reaction where the audience would say, Yeah, let's go out and kill. The idea was, if at all possible, to create an incredible, violent catharsis for the audience so they'd find themselves saying, "Yes, do it – kill" and then afterwards thinking, "My God, it's almost like being at a strange therapy session." '

The three main vigilante films – *Dirty Harry*, *Death Wish*, *Taxi Driver* – inevitably attracted scores of inferior imitators and all three were criticised either for their violence or their apparently Fascist undertones, or both. But what tended to be overlooked at the time and is now becoming more apparent is that each of those front-runners reflected, consciously or not, a concern about the state of American society; each in fact suggested anxiety about the way in which that society appeared to be breaking down. Scorsese said: 'I had those feelings, too. I think most urban society is breaking down; the cities are getting old, things are not working, the bridges need repairing, the Subway needs repairing, the plumbing needs repairing, the water pipes in the streets are breaking ... Who's going to take care of it? What's going to happen? A complete decay of a city is constant.'

But that, of course, is only the surface concern. There were, too, the psychological problems that afflicted America in the 70s. Commenting on the fact that the de Niro character in *Taxi Driver* is a Vietnam veteran, Scorsese said: 'I think that's important; it was extremely crucial in the sense that he had life and death around him every second when he was in South-East Asia and so his awareness becomes more heightened when he comes back – an image in the street at night reflected in the dirty water in the gutter becomes more threatening.'

Abraham Polonsky who, in the late 60s had co-written *Madigan*, directed by Don Siegel and starring Richard Widmark, which dealt with a Brooklyn cop risking his own life to bring in a dangerous criminal, said that after every war – not just the one in Vietnam – men came home who 'knew how to do terrible things and . . . you get them angry, they know what to do'. It was, therefore, a natural tendency in films to 'take one such character and to say, "The nature of society is such or a situation is such that he has a right to want to do this thing," and now you have the heroic criminal . . . In a crazy picture, with crazy people doing things it's just a question of how do you catch the son of a bitch; whereas in a real crime picture it's what happens to the strange man who has these contrasting feelings and is driven to do something because he has been hurt . . .' In the main vigilante films we had a combination of the crazy criminal (all those who were being hunted down) and the heroic (Eastwood, Bronson, de Niro) – except that the latter were not strictly identified as criminals, simply as people bending the law in order to dispense justice more efficiently. 'We [i.e. America] were looking for Dirty Harry,' John Milius said. 'We wanted the sheriff to walk down the street and solve our problems.'

Yes, but why at that particular time? He said: 'At the end of the 60s there really was a feeling that things were running amok and, of course, it all came to a head with Watergate, didn't it? When the President was running amok, that really shook people to their foundations. But what shook people to their foundations more than anything about that time, the Watergate time, was that they realised that these public officials were willing to sell out their ideals. And that's what's important – the ideals. These people were willing to sell out for 30,000 dollars and that was really horrifying because ultimately we like to have enemies who are much larger than ourselves.' And perhaps that's why the thriller based on the "conspiracy theory" was also much in evidence in the mid-seventies with films like *The Parallax View* which ascribed John Kennedy's assassination to big business interests and *Three Days of the Condor*, which had the CIA double-crossing and killing everyone who got in its way. Milius seemed to feel that such pictures were popular because, in a curious way, the public was almost consoled by the thought that it faced enemies of incredible power against whom it could do nothing. In his, more ironic, opinion, however, the truth was rather different. 'People like to think that the Arabs and the Russians and everybody – you know, the very wealthy of the world – are conspiring how to rule us all. They're not: they're conspiring how to get the next 50 grand.'

One film that, in a way, encapsulated that thought was *Chinatown*, directed by Roman Polanski, produced by Robert Evans and written by Robert Towne. Evans said that Towne was so involved with that story that at a time when 'he had a dollar

Right: Robert de Niro and Jodie Foster, vigilante and child hooker in distress in Martin Scorsese's brilliant *Taxi Driver*
Below: Brando and Pacino, father and son in *The Godfather*, an everyday story of an Italian-American family . . .

fifty in his pocket on a good night I offered him 175 thousand dollars to write the script of *The Great Gatsby* and he turned it down. He said "I'm writing something about a detective and it's called *Chinatown*," and I said, "I don't know what the hell you're talking about, Bob, but it sounds interesting," and I paid him 25 thousand dollars rather than the 175 thousand he'd have got for writing *Gatsby*. . .'

Chinatown is a story inspired by fact of conspiracy in that it concerns a group of very wealthy Los Angeles citizens (headed by John Huston) who gained control of the city's water supply, thus becoming even richer and more powerful, and who were prepared to kill to protect their position. Towne said that his interest was aroused because 'that's the kind of crime that gets rewarded really' – in other words the crime against society in general, rather than against individuals. *Chinatown*, which was set in 1937 and featured Jack Nicholson as a private eye who is the obverse of Philip Marlowe, since he does divorce work as a matter of routine and is by no means honourable or moral, is an excellent example of *film noir* in colour. It's a black and bleak film that features incest between John Huston and his screen daughter, Faye Dunaway, an element that Towne introduced to point up the fact that horrible though this crime was it was not, in the long run, as horrible as the greater crime which Huston and his associates were committing against the community.

A couple of pieces of incidental intelligence about *Chinatown* . . . Polanski said that Miss Dunaway, not Huston, should be killed at the end of the film; Towne argued vociferously that it should be the other way around. Polanski, backed by Evans, won. Evans said: 'Bob still contends to this day that if Huston had been killed and not Dunaway the picture would have done double the business because it would have had an "up" ending . . .' He is, however, unpenitent. 'I'm glad it had a down ending. It's remembered – and that's the greatest wealth in the world, to be remembered.' The second point is an interesting indication of how Hollywood works. According to Evans, the first choice for the female lead was Jane Fonda but . . . 'Jane didn't want to do it. The next choice was Faye Dunaway. Now Faye Dunaway's agent said that for her last picture she got half a million dollars. I offered her 50 thousand. I said, "It will save her career." He said, "Are you crazy? I can't make that offer to Faye. Arthur Penn is willing to pay her 250 thousand." I said, "Well, Jane Fonda is going to sign in forty-eight hours," which was a lie. The agent calls back and says, "You're terrible. She'll do it for 50. I can't believe it. Is it a deal?" I says, "Yeah, Jane Fonda didn't want to do it anyway," and the agent says, "Well, Arthur Penn didn't really want Faye . . ." So Faye did the picture for 50,000 and it turned her career around: on her next film she made half a million.'

In the 1980s the conspiracy thriller died away; the vigilante film struggled on with increasingly inferior *Death Wish* sequels; and violence persisted, often violence against women (as in Brian de Palma's *Dressed to Kill*) but more usually violence of a general nature (as in de Palma's remake of *Scarface*, which features Al Pacino as a dope-dealing Cuban immigrant in Florida). The film itself is coarse, over the top and disappointing but is not without sociological interest. According to the original version the Italian-Americans of the twenties and early thirties made their fortunes by peddling booze; now, according to the sequel, the progress of science and the drug trade has opened even greater opportunities to the new Hispanic Americans of the eighties. The dark side of the American Dream is as powerful as ever – a concept that is also explored in Michael Cimino's *Year of the Dragon*, in which again the dope trade is the means to wealth although here the protagonists are Chinese-Americans. In both those modern films violence is depicted on a scale that would have been quite unthinkable when Hawks was making the original *Scarface*.

De Palma's *Scarface* was set in modern times but in fact it was a throwback to the early gangster pictures as, more obviously, were Sergio Leone's *Once Upon a Time in America* and Francis Coppola's *The Cotton Club*. Leone's film was set in Prohibition times and was similar in concept to *The Godfather*, except that here the mobsters were not Italian but Jewish – "Kosher Nostra", as many people were quick to point out. It's a long, sprawling, grossly flawed but hugely entertaining epic; and much the same might be said of *The Cotton Club*, with the addendum that here the flaws are even more visible. The film was originally conceived by Robert Evans as "*The Godfather* with music" but for various complicated and financial reasons he lost creative control to Coppola who, according to Evans, extracted revenge, as promised, for having to cut *The Godfather* the way Evans wanted it. 'Possibly the single most destructive incident of my career was turning the reins [of *The Cotton Club*] over to Francis,' was the way Evans put it.

His idea had been to show the end of an era – the Prohibition era – with Anglo-Saxons, Italians, Jews, Irish and blacks all in the same criminal melting pot and by setting all this around the Cotton Club, the famous jazz night spot in Harlem, to illustrate the story with the music of the time. 'I can't think of a film that I had a bigger dream of than *The Cotton Club*,' he said. 'I wanted to show blacks and whites living together, fighting together, hating each other, loving each other . . . I ended up not even going to the opening. The picture that I had in mind is on the cutting-room floor . . . I was supposed to direct the film, by the way; I'd raised all the money for myself to direct it and something happened in my personal life that meant I couldn't do it . . . I'm not taking away from Francis's talent but I had a dream and my dream became a nightmare. I spent six years on that one picture and in the end I was lucky to get my house back, which I'd mortgaged for the film. I ended up lucky to be alive – I don't mean alive financially, I mean *alive* because of the pressures that were put on me . . .'

Well, that, too, is the way Hollywood works: the number of cinematic dreams that have turned for one reason or another into nightmares is incalculable. Besides, financially *The Cotton Club* was something of a nightmare for everyone concerned. Individual sequences and performances in it were remarkably good but on the whole the public did not take to the film. Generally speaking, Evans said, the public isn't really interested in gangster movies anyway. 'There are not many gangster pictures which are successful. The kids who go to the movies don't want to see the things that people in Hollywood or London want to make, because the people who are making the films are too old to know what the people who are going to the movies want to see.' But that, of course, is a far wider problem that affects all kinds of films, not just gangster movies.

By and large, though, as the 1980s draw to a close violence and films about violent crime are – so long, presumably, as they don't deal with gangsters – still prime ingredients at the box office.

Arthur Penn excused, or perhaps explained that, when he said with reference particularly to the popularity of *Bonnie and Clyde*: 'We have a violent society. It's not Greece, it's not Athens, it's not the Renaissance – it's the American society and I would have to personify it by saying that it is a violent one. So why not make films about it?'

The outrageous John Milius, who once subdued a party of Arab revellers who were roistering across the lake from where he lives by firing rifle shots into the water, put it perhaps even more strongly. Violence, he said, was central to the American character. 'We came to a violent country. We seized it violently. Even our type of "laissez-faire" free enterprise is kind of violent, if you think about it – you know, let's go out and seize the market. Violence is essential to a wilful people and we are a wilful people.'

In *Chinatown* a cop asks Jack Nicholson what happened to his nose. Nicholson replies: 'Your wife closed her legs'

HOLLYWOOD AND POLITICS

During a hearing of the House of Representatives Committee on Un-American Activities (HUAC for short) in 1951, the following exchanges took place:

Mr Valdi (committee chairman) You are here to give us information which will enable us to do the work that was assigned to us by the House of Representatives, which was duly imposed upon us to investigate reports regarding subversive activities in the United States.

Lionel Stander (actor and witness) Well, I am more than willing to co-operate . . .

Valdi Now just a moment . . .

Stander . . . because I know of some subversive activities in the entertainment industry and elsewhere in the country.

Valdi Mr Stander, the committee is interested . . .

Stander If you are interested, I can tell you some right now.

Valdi Primarily any subversive knowledge you have . . .

Stander I have knowledge of some subversive action . . .

Valdi . . . in the overthrow of the government . . .

Stander I don't know about the overthrow of the government. This committee has been investigating fifteen years so far and hasn't even found one act of violence.

Valdi That is entirely . . .

Stander I know of some subversion and I can help the committee if it is really interested.

Valdi Mr Stander . . .

Stander I know of a group of fanatics who are desperately trying to undermine the constitution of the United States by depriving artists and others of life, liberty and the pursuit of happiness without due process of law. If you're interested in that I would like to tell you about it. I can tell names and I can cite instances and I am one of the first victims of it. And if you are interested in that and also a group of ex-Fascists and America-Firsters and anti-Semites, people who hate everybody including Negroes, minority groups and most likely themselves . . .

Valdi Now, Mr Stander, let me . . .

Stander . . . and these people are engaged in a conspiracy outside all the legal processes to undermine the very fundamental American concepts upon which our entire system of democracy exists.

And having thus summed up the House Un-American Activities Committee to his own entire satisfaction Lionel Stander found himself, like so many others, included on a quite unofficial blacklist which meant that he was unable to work in American films for more than twelve years. Well, it didn't worry him too much because he had been put on a blacklist all by himself years before and had grown used to being persona non grata around the Hollywood studios.

But how did Hollywood – how did America – get itself into a state in which actors, writers, directors and others were deprived of the opportunity to work and had their careers ruined because they were, or had been, or were thought to have been members of the Communist Party or sympathisers with Communist aims?

Ostensibly, the activities of HUAC from 1947 onwards were a by-product of the Cold War but the genesis of the Red scare could be found much earlier and in Hollywood could be traced back, roughly speaking, to the formation of the Screen Writers' Guild (SWG) in April 1933, under the presidency of John Howard Lawson, a self-confessed Marxist and an active member of the Communist Party. Quite possibly Lawson saw the SWG as a potentially useful political weapon but the bulk of the membership regarded it simply as a form of self-protection. According to the writer and director Philip Dunne, whose credits in one capacity or another include *The Count of Monte Cristo, The Last of the Mohicans, Pinky, The Robe* and *Ten North Frederick*: 'I think the big issue was control of screen credits more than anything else. The credits were then allocated by the studios and, of course, they went to studio favourites – they went to nephews, sons-in-law. Nepotism was rampant. So that was the most important of all the issues.'

Understandably, the formation of the guild was not exactly greeted by the studios with friendly smiles and congratulatory pats on the back. Irving Thalberg is reputed to have dismissed all the now unionised writers as "a bunch of Reds" and Darryl Zanuck predicted gloomily – and, as it turned out, quite incorrectly – that 'They will be able to control the screen destinies of the stories they work on. I can imagine nothing that would kill this business any quicker.' In the *Los Angeles Examiner*, William Randolph Hearst described a proposal by Lawson to amalgamate the SWG with the Authors' League, the Dramatists' Guild, the Newspaper Guild and the Radio Writers' Guild as "a device of Communist radicals". Prompted by much the same suspicion the studios struck back by offering all the writers on their payrolls long-term contracts, by asking them to sign mimeographed letters of resignation from the SWG and by inviting them to join a rival, overtly right-wing organisation called the Screen Playwrights Inc. This was inspired by Thalberg and Louis Mayer and had the backing of the Hollywood establishment.

Philip Dunne said: 'They tried to fire everybody who was a member of the guild, or intimidate us one way or another. For instance, at my studio my friend Darryl Zanuck was the boss and he played hard ball in any game he played. He had two writers sitting in a bungalow with resignations from the guild in duplicate – one copy to the guild, one copy to his office. I think only a handful of us declined to sign these things. Most writers were easily intimidated. We had a large, sleeping membership which had officially resigned but was actively calling us up every day, saying, "I'm still with you." But they didn't dare come out in the open. It was pretty sad.'

Consequently it was some years before the SWG finally achieved official recognition but even so the organisation continued to be viewed with such suspicion that when HUAC began its main activities in 1947, witnesses were asked not only 'Are you now or have you ever been a member of the Communist Party?' but 'Are you a member of the Screen Writers' Guild?' as if in the minds of all right-thinking people the two things were pretty much the same.

It should not, however, be thought that the studios' hostility to the SWG and, in July 1933, to the formation of the Screen Actors' Guild (SAG) reflected an attitude of doggedly blinkered reaction on the part of the hierarchy. Many of the bosses – notably the Warner brothers – were aware that social reform was necessary and desirable and were not reluctant to say so in the films they backed. For example, at Warners in 1932 Mervyn Le Roy directed and Paul Muni starred in *I am a Fugitive from a Chain Gang*, which was based on the experiences of a genuine fugitive, Robert F Burns, who was still on the run when he advised on the making of the film and which led to a change in the laws in some of the southern states. The following year and for the same studio William Wellman directed *Wild Boys of the Road*, which argued that the social deprivations brought about by the Depression were leading youngsters into a life of itineracy and petty crime and showed them being harassed by bullying and repressive cops. The film was not a box office success but at least it was made. And even while the studios were battling against the dangerous "liberals" of the SWG – the guild was not really given recognition until it threatened to strike in May 1941 – they continued to make films of pretty radical content. Between 1934 and 1935, for instance, Warners produced *Massacre* (ill-treatment of Indians by corrupt and greedy administrators), *Bordertown* (ill-treatment of Mexicans) and *Black Fury*, which dealt with exploitation of labour and the need for effective unions. Even MGM, in 1936, allowed Joseph L. Mankiewicz to produce and Fritz Lang to direct *Fury*, the story of a lynch mob in a small American town, which subject was tackled again by Warners in 1937 with *They Won't Forget*. This apparent ambivalence – trades unions were perfectly acceptable for coal miners in *Black Fury* but fiercely to be opposed for screen writers – is perhaps explained by the fact that social issues were all very well when confined to the cinema and making money but not to be tolerated when they threatened to impinge on the power of the studios.

So while the poverty of the kids in *Wild Boys of the Road* was deeply to be deplored, it was another matter altogether when poverty in California was introduced into real politics by the decision of the author, Upton Sinclair, to run for governor. Sinclair's slogan was, in fact, "End Poverty in California", with which in mind he proposed high taxes on studio profits and on those in the upper income brackets. The studios reacted as one studio to work for the victory of the Republican candidate and incumbent Governor Frank E. Merriam over Sinclair who was, depending on how you looked at it, either a Democrat or "a most dangerous Bolshevik beast".

To Sam Marx, story editor, producer and studio executive at MGM from the early 1930s onwards, Sinclair had 'a marvellous, idealistic notion' but . . . 'I do think the studios ganged up on him. I know for a fact that they sent out newsreels which were edited so that if a good-looking, well-to-do man on the street said, "I'm for Upton Sinclair," he ended in the trash can. The bums and the tramps who were interviewed in the railway sidings, if they said they were for the governor, they were thrown out. The film was edited very carefully so that the well-to-do all came out for Sinclair's rival and the poor and the dirty were only used if they were for Sinclair.' But the anti-Sinclair campaign, with studio help, went further than the doctoring of newsreels. The writer, John Bright, worked in the Sinclair campaign headquarters and reckoned that at least thirty-five propaganda films were turned out by the opposition to destroy his candidature. 'They were short films and programme fillers and they were presented to us as entertainment. They were pure propaganda of the most blatant and primitive sort. They were so absurd they were laughable. For example, they showed that the election of Sinclair would result in derelicts in power and other absurdities so outrageous you have no idea.' The man behind them, he said, was Irving Thalberg.

Meanwhile, the two Los Angeles papers, the *Times* and the *Examiner*, printed pictures of down and outs arriving on freight trains to cash in on the End Poverty campaign. What everyone absent-mindedly omitted to mention, however, was that the photograph in the *Examiner* was posed for by costumed extras hired for the purpose from Central Casting. The film establishment's attitude – expressed, so it is said, by Irving Thalberg in answer to a reproof from Fredric March – was that "nothing is unfair in politics". Many of their employees, especially those in the SWG, reacted against this by forming the California Authors' League for Sinclair but it did no good. The Republican candidate won overwhelmingly, thus no doubt reinforcing Louis Mayer's belief in the veracity of his own remark to the MGM staff: 'What does Sinclair know? He's just a writer.'

So what with the screen writers forming a union and Upton Sinclair trying to end poverty and raise taxes it was clear to the hierarchy that some kind of frightful Bolshevik plot was afoot in Hollywood. And even if the studios didn't really believe that, they pretended to because they – in common with other right-wing conservative elements in America – habitually attached the label of Communism or Bolshevism to anything that smacked of liberal thought in the hope that some of the mud would stick to Franklin D. Roosevelt's New Deal, this being extremely unpopular among those to whom it might cost money. Thus, in 1934 the American Legion began drawing up lists of allegedly subversive organisations and individuals – among them Eleanor Roosevelt and Chiang Kai-Shek.

Well, that may be laughable but, on the other hand, there is no doubt that quite a number of the SWG members were also members of the Communist Party. Edward Dymtryk, who was one of their number, said he joined the CP because 'they were the only ones in town who seemed to be doing anything'. Budd Schulberg's reasons stemmed from a feeling that 'Fascism was coming, the old world was dying, a new world would be born' and coupled with that, he said, was 'some sense of guilt about being in Hollywood, living that prosperous life, knowing that millions of people were suffering in America, unemployment was horrendous and the whole world was sort of hurting'. But what sort of Communists were they in the SWG? Philip Dunne, an executive of the guild and never at any time a Communist sympathiser, said: 'They worked hard and licked the stamps. They were the people who were most likely to do the donkey work, run the errands, man the telephones and so on.' But at the same time they were 'sweating democracy at every pore. They supported FDR, who detested them.' And Ring Lardner, who was both a Communist and an officer in the SWG, said: 'In those years just before the war the activity of the Communists in the Hollywood section was very little different from the left-wing liberals generally.'

And what the left-wing liberals generally were doing was joining the Popular Front, a generic term for a number of political organisations whose concern was to combat the growing threat of Fascism and Nazism. There were, for example, the Anti-Nazi League, the Motion Picture Artists' Committee to aid Republican Spain and the Motion Picture Democratic Committee. Active on all these committees were men who would later be blacklisted and in some cases imprisoned after being called before HUAC. But, as Philip Dunne pointed out, the members also included 'everybody of any real stature – tons of good people: Freddie March, Jim Cagney, Humphrey Bogart, Melvyn Douglas among the actors; directors like William Wyler; many writers, of course ... I think the Communists had a great deal to do with forming the organisations but they did it purely on an anti-Nazi basis. At this point the Russians were terrified of Hitler, with reason. And they were desperately trying to win friends and influence people and the way they tried to do it was to form alliances with liberals and democratic groups in other countries. That was the Popular Front. But it's important to remember that none of the objectives were Communist objectives: they were anti-fascist objectives. And they themselves endorsed democracy, even capitalism, to the point that during the war the Communists in America took a no-strike pledge.'

Against that another, and sharply contrasting, view of the Popular Front was put forward by Roy Brewer, the former leader of IATSE (International Alliance of Theatrical Stage Employees) the technicians' union, and a dedicated anti-Communist. In his opinion there was unquestionably a Communist conspiracy to take over Hollywood in the 1930s and 40s. 'As a matter of fact our union was a particular target of the Communists because they wanted to take control of the Hollywood unions. The base of our union was nation-wide and they couldn't reach all of our people, so what they hoped to do was to cut off the Hollywood unions from our international union and there were a great number of efforts on their part and very effective ones.'

To what end, though? Were they trying to smuggle Communist messages into Hollywood films? Brewer thought they were. 'And,' he said, 'there's no question that they succeeded to a point.' One example of a picture in which, at least in IATSE's opinion, the message came through loud and clear was *Blockade* which, in 1938, dealt with the Spanish Civil War. It looks remarkably bland stuff now, especially as neither the Loyalists nor the Republicans nor Franco could be mentioned by name. Nevertheless, as rewritten by John Howard Lawson from Clifford Odets' original script, the film showed which side it was on. And at the very end Marco (Henry Fonda) says: 'It's not war. War is between soldiers. This is murder. We've got to stop it. Stop the murder of innocent people. The world can stop it. Where's the conscience of the world?' Conservative elements in the USA grasped the message at once. Roman Catholics picketed the Radio City Music Hall in New York where the film was showing; the Knights of Columbus lobbied the Hays Office; priests told their congregations to stay away; Fox West Coast Theatres refused to show the movie as a first run. And IATSE announced that 'projectionists will not be responsible for the handling of propaganda films by its members'.

Roy Brewer listed other, later, films in which he detected the Communist message. 'One of their main objectives,' he said, 'was to destroy the religious feelings of the country. You look at almost any picture that the Communists did and some place you will find some area where a priest or a minister was discredited. It runs through them, particularly with Dalton Trumbo. Take *The Sandpiper* or *Hawaii* . . . the whole thing was written so that you lose your confidence in the people who spoke for the church. And that's still going on – if you don't believe it, look at *Monsignor*, which was written by Abe Polonsky, who was an admitted Communist.' True, he was; and so was Trumbo. And both were blacklisted during the HUAC era.

Brewer also thought that *Pal Joey*, a play by John O'Hara that was later adapted for the screen, showed signs of Communist influence. 'It was the first Broadway show where the hero was a bum. You know? They made a hero out of a bum. They began to change our values of people. I believe firmly that the trend that they started – the glorifying of the right of the individual to do what he wants no matter what happens and that sort of thing – those are the type of long-range things they had in mind and I think it's been a growing thing, I really do.' Well, these are certainly points of view, though I cannot offhand think of any critics, for example, who picked up the Communist propaganda in the works he mentioned. *The Sandpiper*, after all, ends with the clergyman (Richard Burton) rediscovering his simple faith after being tempted by the fleshpots and though a certain amount of corruption is evident in the priests in *Hawaii* and *Monsignor* the church itself is never assailed.

Still, Brewer's views on the Popular Front in the 1930s cannot be ignored because they were widely shared. In his belief the Front was far more than the simple grouping of liberal organisations. It was, he said, 'a way to infiltrate and destroy a democracy . . . It was actually on 5 March 1935 that the party line changed and the old revolutionary format of the Communist structure, where you were not permitted to say anything good about the United States, changed overnight and they began being patriotic, infiltrating patriotic organisations. And it's been very successful in my judgment.'

The fact of the infiltration can hardly be denied but the effectiveness is very much open to dispute. In the end perhaps it comes down to a question of semantics. Abraham Polonsky said the Communist Party tried to influence the work of its Hollywood members 'only in one sense. It felt they should deal with social problems.' But, of course, films dealing with social problems have always existed in Hollywood and, as Philip Dunne said, some of them were "extraordinarily liberal". He cited as examples *The Grapes of Wrath* and *How Green Was My Valley* (for which he wrote the script), both of them being in praise of the common man and opposed to capitalist greed. But neither he nor any of the other liberal or Communist writers to whom I spoke believed that it was possible to introduce a revolutionary or even hard left-wing message into a movie, if only because finally the contents of a picture were dictated by its prospects at the box office. 'Messages,' as Sam Goldwyn said, 'are for Western Union.' Besides, with the exception of the Warner brothers in the 1930s, the studio bosses were hard-nosed Republicans who certainly had no interest in replacing American democracy with Bolshevism. But obviously much depends on your interpretation of individual films. What might be liberal to Philip Dunne or Abraham Polonsky could easily be Communist to Roy Brewer.

In any event whatever hope the Communists might have had of subverting Hollywood through the Popular Front vanished in August 1939, with the signing of the Nazi-Soviet Non-Aggression Pact. The result of this was to destroy the Front itself. The Communists naturally followed the party line but the broader-based liberals wished to have nothing to do with either side in the agreement. Many people indeed felt strongly enough to resign even from such organisations as the Anti-Nazi League and the Motion Picture Democratic Committee but in some cases they were already too late, for within a few years they were to be hauled before HUAC to answer the gloriously Orwellian charge of being "premature anti-Fascists". Their defection in face of the pact did, however, lead to one splendid irony – the Communist Party finding itself snuggled up in the same bed with Charles Lindbergh's rabidly right-wing America First League, which on the whole seemed to feel that the Nazis were pretty good chaps.

But in fact there was already a very good reason for those of more moderate views to dissociate themselves from the Communists even before the German-Russian agreement. In 1938 the Dies Committee (later to be transmuted into HUAC) had been created by an alliance of Republicans and Southern Democrats, united in their hostility to the New Deal, whose broad objectives of tackling poverty and social reform and attempting to give everybody an even break were anathema to them. The committee took its name from its chairman, Congressman Martin Dies of Texas, and was dedicated to exposing Communist conspiracies. In August of 1938 Dies made a coast-to-coast radio broadcast in which he claimed that members of the Anti-Nazi League were, at best, Communist dupes and he had before him, he said, a list of nearly forty film personalities (he didn't name any of them but they included Paul Muni and Joan Crawford) who were on record as contributors to Communist causes, whatever that might mean and in the Dies definition it could mean almost anything. Hollywood, he told the Press, was "a hotbed of Communism" and in the summer of 1939 his committee began its hearings at the Hollywood Roosevelt Hotel, an apt enough location bearing in mind that to Dies and his merry men the words Hollywood and Roosevelt were virtually synonymous with Communism. He had before him, he said, another list – kindly provided by a former CP member named John L. Leech – in which forty-two movie people were named as Reds. This list was leaked to the press and one day the likes of Humphrey Bogart, Franchot Tone and Lionel Stander found themselves identified as Communists. More than that, Bogart along with Fredric March, James Cagney and Philip Dunne were grouped together as the four most dangerous Communists in all Hollywood.

Philip Dunne was particularly indignant because he was by then involved in a furious row with the Communists over the Nazi-Soviet pact and so he insisted on appearing before the committee – 'I had no reservations about answering questions' – and tracked it down to San Francisco, whither it had gone after doing its work in Hollywood. 'We all went to Dies – Bogart, Freddie March, Jim Cagney and I – and said, "What do you want to know?" I had articles I had written, evidence of the positions I'd taken and I put them all on record. Afterwards there were newsreels in which Dies and I were shaking hands and he was saying what a fine American I was ... Perhaps that saved me a lot of trouble later on when the witchhunt started because they had it there in their records – their own founder calling me a fine American. It was ludicrous.' Ludicrous but not funny. For Fredric March, Dunne said, it was particularly serious: 'He was damn near drummed out of the business.'

In the end, though, everyone who had been named was cleared, except Lionel Stander, who ended up being fired. Even then he did not think the Dies Committee was responsible. 'I didn't appear before them until 1940,' he said, 'and incidentally they gave me a clean bill of health. I swore I wasn't a member of the Communist Party and had never been and that was it ... They professed to investigate un-American activities but what they actually did was to attack anyone and everyone who supported Roosevelt's New Deal.' But if he was cleared, how did he come to find himself on a personal blacklist that was even more unofficial than the ultra-unofficial (and indeed officially denied) blacklist that came into operation in 1947? He attributed it to a speech he had made, well before the Dies Committee hearing, at a meeting of the Screen Actors' Guild.

The background to his speech was this: IATSE, the International Association of Theatrical and Stage Employees, was universally recognised by the studios and was therefore the union with most muscle in Hollywood. Unfortunately (and I stress that this was before the time of Roy Brewer) it was controlled by the Mafia through its president, George E. Browne and his Hollywood representative, Willie Bioff, pronounced "buy off", which is what he and Browne were good at. In return for kickbacks from the studio executives they would ensure that their own union made only minimal demands. Louis Mayer and various other moguls reckoned that they saved about 15 million dollars by buying off Bioff and his good friend Browne.

Now at the SAG meeting, Stander said, 'I got up and read their criminal records and exposed their connections with Capone.' (The specific link with Capone is a little hazy, since by that time he had been in prison for some years. Still, the link with the Mafia generally was well-established.) 'A week later,' Stander said, 'Westbrook Pegler, a right-wing columnist syndicated throughout the United States, published their records. The government moved in and took action but it took two years.' Nevertheless, in 1941 Bioff and Browne, along with Joseph Schenck, chairman of the board of 20th Century-Fox and brother of Nicholas Schenck of MGM, were sent to gaol on charges relating to tax irregularities and union payoffs. (Joseph Schenck is as famous for this as he is for his later role as patron and lover of Marilyn Monroe.) The way Stander put it was that 'the producers had been paying these monsters under the table for labour peace for many years.' When he raised the matter at the SAG meeting, he said, 'Nobody opposed my reading the records but they opposed my recommendation, which was that we should not have anything to do with these gangsters. Unfortunately, they voted me down.' The direct result of his public-spirited action was that ... 'I was immediately put on the blacklist. I had the dubious distinction of being the first person politically blacklisted in Hollywood, because the monsters who controlled the union at that time went to the head of my studio, Harry Cohn, and at the next meeting of the Motion Picture Producers' Association he said that he wouldn't renew my contract and that any studio that signed me would be subject to a 1,000 dollar fine. My agent told me, "Don't worry, kid, it'll blow over," but unfortunately it didn't blow over: it took about fifteen years.' More than that, actually, bearing in mind that he was blacklisted again in 1951. But from 1939 onwards ... 'I worked for independent studios, who weren't affiliated with the Motion Picture Producers' Association.'

In a sense, I suppose, he was blacklisted by the Mob rather than by anybody else, an indication that the Mafia was able to lean quite heavily on the studios. Stander said: 'They had tremendous power in Hollywood. Poor Joe Schenck was the fall guy – the other producers were as guilty as he was but he took the rap, he went to jail.'

In June 1941 Germany invaded Russia, making something of a nonsense of the non-aggression pact, and at about the same time the American isolationists made their last stand. A pair of senators, Burton Wheeler and Gerald Nye (of the America First committee) introduced a resolution calling for Senate investigation of motion picture propaganda designed to bring about American participation in the war – 'The most vicious propaganda that has ever been unloosed upon a civilised people', so it was said with more indignation than grammar. Mind you, this propaganda included such films as *Confessions of a Nazi Spy*, *Sergeant York*, the *March of Time* newsreels and *The Great Dictator*, all of which some people might find rather less vicious than, say, the anti-Semitic films produced by the Nazis. This, however, was not a point of view that would have cut much ice with Senator Nye who revealed the sinister fact that the men responsible for these frightful American films had been born overseas and had brought with them 'their inborn hatreds and prejudices ... quite foreign to America and her best interests'. With that kind of sensitivity it probably came as quite a surprise to him that his committee was not exactly welcomed with deafening cheers by the studio heads, the producers or the SWG, many of whom happened to be of foreign extraction. Industry figures such as Darryl Zanuck and Harry Warner, however, did in fact testify before the Senate Sub-committee and did so to such effect that the hearings fizzled out. As the writer and former newspaperman Milton Krims said: 'Mr Nye happened to have Mr Warner on the stand and Nye was berating him for creating these horrible films that were going to destroy the world and Warner handed him a telegram – from Nye himself! – which congratulated him on making a picture as patriotic as *The Confessions of a Nazi Spy*. I think many of these people were idiots, myself.'

America's entry into the war on 11 December 1941, not only rendered the Wheeler-Nye Committee both obsolete and ridiculous but also brought a temporary halt to the Communist witch-hunting. Indeed, it was now more than acceptable to make pro-Russian films, such as *North Star* (written by Lillian Hellman and directed by Lewis Milestone), which told of a Russian village defending itself against the Nazis; or *Days of Glory* (more Russian peasants fighting Nazis), which introduced Gregory Peck to the screen.

And then there was *Mission to Moscow*, directed by Michael Curtiz for Warner Brothers and adapted by Howard Koch from a book by Joseph E. Davies, the US ambassador to Russia. The background to that film was that Koch, who had just worked on six pictures in a row and was tired and needed a holiday, was called in by Jack and Harry Warner, who came as close as was seemly for moguls to imploring him to write the script. They had had lunch with the President, FDR himself, and he had handed them Davies' book saying, 'You want to help the war effort, do this picture because we need it to understand our ally better.' Jack Warner in particular was a man who was impressed by presidents, or any kind of politician come to that. In his office he had two sets of signed photographs – one of leading Republicans and one of leading Democrats and these would be displayed or concealed depending upon who was about to pay him a visit. By and large, though, he was a Democrat and an FDR man and so he was prepared to allow Koch all manner of concessions, including going home to the east coast to work, so long as he wrote the script.

Having thus been made an offer he could hardly refuse, Koch agreed to the task and produced a workmanlike piece of wartime propaganda, which showed the Russians as warm-hearted and likeable allies and rather skated over the prewar Stalin purges. Jack Warner was very pleased. 'I have a letter from him,' Koch said, 'complimenting me on the script. He changed his mind a little bit, later...' A splendid piece of understatement this, as we shall discover.

One way or another, however, the war years created a climate that was hospitable to left wing and liberal causes and, if anything, it was right-wing activity which alarmed people most of all. Partly to combat this the Hollywood Democratic Committee merged in January 1945 with another broadly based liberal organisation to become the Hollywood Independent Citizens Committee of the Arts and Sciences, the acronym for which cumbersome mouthful was the barely more manageable HICCASP.

It described itself as a "national, non-partisan political organisation of cultural workers that will markedly influence the peace". Non-political is stretching it a bit for its aims certainly appeared to be anti-right wing, including support for the founding of the United Nations, the peaceful use of atomic energy and opposition to the stationing of troops in Indo-China. Besides, its chairman was a Communist (and ex-violinist) named George Pepper.

Roy Brewer looked upon this outfit darkly and described it to me as: 'The most successful Communist front that ever existed. There were a lot of people in there that didn't believe that: they thought they were running it but they were being manipulated.' Among the membership were the soon to be blacklisted (or jailed) Edward Dmytryk, John Howard Lawson and Robert Rossen who, I imagine, could be listed as manipulators. Others, like a certain Ronald Reagan, would hardly come into that category, so I suppose you would have to put them down as Communist dupes.

The point in question, however, is that in 1945 HICCASP was perfectly acceptable and so were such films as *Cornered*, with Dick Powell tracking Nazis to South America and directed by Edward Dmytryk. In essence it was a picture which expressed strong liberal disapproval of social wrongs as, over the next few years, did others like *Crossfire* (1947; Dmytryk again; produced by Adrian Scott and attacking anti-Semitism), *Gentleman's Agreement* (1947; directed by Eli Kazan and also exposing anti-Semitism), *All the King's Men* (1949; written and directed by Robert Rossen and dealing with political corruption in a southern town), *Home of the Brave* (1949; written by Carl Foreman and about racism in the army) and *Pinky* (1949; co-written by Philip Dunne, directed by Elia Kazan and a story of racial bigotry in the American south). Is it a coincidence that every writer, director and producer in that list fell foul to some degree or another of HUAC? I rather doubt it because, although the fact was not too evident – certainly in 1945 – social conscience was going out of fashion. For the keen observer, however, and particularly for those with the invaluable aid of hindsight, the warning signs were there. In 1944 at the home of the screen-writer James K. McGuiness the Motion Picture Alliance for the Preservation of American Ideals (MPA) was formed. Its officers and members included the likes of Walt Disney, Gary Cooper, John Wayne, Adolphe Menjou, Ward Bond, the columnist Hedda Hopper and Roy Brewer – a group of people who would have regarded Attila the Hun as a dangerous pinkoe. Immediately, in a statement published in *Variety*, the MPA pledged itself to fight the "Communists, radicals and crackpots" who, in its view, were dominating the movie industry. Soon after that it wrote to the Southern Democratic Senator Robert Reynolds describing the 'flagrant manner in which the motion picture industrialists of Hollywood have been coddling Communists' who were disseminating un-American ideas and beliefs. The following month (April 1944) as if on cue HUAC investigators had another tentative sniff at Hollywood, though little was immediately to come of it.

Roy Brewer was not a founder-member of the MPA; he joined later bringing the strength of IATSE with him but he said it was formed largely to counteract the Screen Writers' Guild which 'was to all intents and purposes under Communist control until after the hearings of 1947 ... I would think the mentor [of MPA] was Jim McGuiness, who was the head of writers at Metro-Goldwyn-Mayer ... The big power was the people at Metro.' What gave Brewer his clout as an anti-Communist fighter was a jurisdictional dispute between IATSE and the Conference of Studio Unions (CSU) which started in 1945, petered out for a while, then flared up again in the summer of 1946. The CSU had been created in 1941 by the craft and technical unions which were not affiliated to IATSE; it was a more radical and politically aggressive outfit than the senior union and the clash between the two was over which would represent the set decorators. The studios recognised the IATSE men and the CSU went on strike. The Screen Actors' Guild led by Ronald Reagan (no longer presumably a Communist dupe, the scales having no doubt fallen from his eyes), George Murphy and Robert Montgomery voted to cross the CSU picket lines and so did the SWG.

The leader of the CSU was one Herbert K. Sorrel, whom Roy Brewer accused of being a Communist. According to Brewer the whole of the union was Communist influenced and the studios were aware of it. 'Louis B. Mayer knew he was hiring Communist drivers but he didn't think it was important . . . The producers just wanted to make money, that was the bottom line. They made money with the Communists, so they used them . . . When the issue took place the producers had to choose between the economic power of IATSE, which manned the theatres where the box office dollar came in, and the Communists who made trouble for them in Hollywood. That was their choice and if it had not been for the economic pressure I'm certain they would have gone along and the Communists would have taken over . . . because they called illegal strikes and they organised everybody.' It was then a political as much as a labour dispute and, in the view of Philip Dunne, it propelled Ronald Reagan into national politics. 'That was the rock on which he founded his career. The theory was that the painters, the set decorators and the secretaries were going to take over Hollywood – that was the expression – and he played that fairly well up and down the country on radio, at meetings, dinners, fund raisers, saying how he had headed off this Communist takeover plot. Which was, of course, sheer, absolute eyewash – it never existed.'

The strike lasted initially for eight months and there were violent scenes outside Warner Brothers who employed thugs, tear gas, the fire department and the studio's private police to break the picket lines. The same kind of violence was repeated in July 1946 – this time outside MGM as well as Warners – when the strike started again. Eventually, said Philip Dunne, 'It was savagely broken by the goon squads and the Warner Brothers police. The writers rather tenderly sat it out, called it a lock-out. The actors went through the picket lines and that led to Reagan's fantasies about packing a pistol when he went through the lines. He was afraid they would throw acid in his face, you know – that sort of thing which he played up to fairly well over the years. Extraordinary behaviour.'

One of those involved in the strike-breaking was Chuck Roberson, later to become a stunt man in westerns and John Wayne's double, but at that time working as a Culver City policeman at Warners. 'Quite a few people got hurt pretty bad,' he said. 'We lived in a basement there. I don't know how many cops they had but quite a few and we all ate and slept right there, round the clock. I didn't know how many days even . . . But it was a bad strike, probably as bad as they've ever had. And they [the CSU] didn't want anybody crossing that line and we was out there, wrestling with them . . . Today we couldn't have got away with the rougher stuff as we did then . . . I didn't like to work the strike at all. You know? I don't like to push people around. All they were doing was screaming, "Don't pass, don't cross the line and work". On the other hand, if a guy wants to work, I kinda hate to see somebody try to keep him from working . . .'

So in an atmosphere of violence, recriminations and accusations of Communism, the strike was eventually settled with IATSE emerging stronger than ever and Roy Brewer established as a doughty fighter against the Communists and all their works, in which capacity he was soon to play a significant role in the aftermath of the HUAC hearings.

Before the union dispute was settled in March 1946, and at Fulton, Missouri, Winston Churchill had delivered his celebrated speech, which was to introduce a new phrase into the language . . . 'From Stettin in the Baltic to Trieste in the Adriatic, an Iron Curtain has descended across the continent . . .' America generally decided that this was precisely what it would have said, if only it had thought of it first. But the nation was even more impressed by a later passage in which, speaking of the Russians, Churchill said: 'There is nothing for which they have less respect than weakness . . .' The Iron Curtain was down, the Cold War was on and the USA was not about to appear weak, either militarily or in any other way. Henceforth radicalism was out, the forces of reaction took over and significantly Russia, the ally, was now Russia, the enemy. In the autumn the Republicans and the right-wing Southern Democrats made sweeping gains in the national elections and for the first time for more than a decade dominated Congress. President Harry S. Truman described it as "the worst Congress in history" but as a liberal Democrat, I suppose he would.

There probably never was a good time to be a Communist in America but this was the worst and it was especially bad in Hollywood, for in June 1946, Congressman John L. Rankin, of Mississippi, had announced HUAC's intention of investigating 'one of the most dangerous plots ever instigated for the overthrow of the government'. And this foul plot emanated not from traitors in Washington or revolutionaries in the armed forces but from the make-believe world of Hollywood. In January 1947 HUAC's new chairman, J. Parnell Thomas of New Jersey, announced the committee's plans for the coming year. Among its targets was the East German born Gerhart Eisler, an alleged Communist master spy, and by association, his brother Hanns, a composer. The investigation of Hanns Eisler was significant for two reasons: first, he had composed music for such films as *Hangmen Also Die* and *Woman on the Beach* and, secondly, when he had applied for an entry visa in 1939 he had been helped by Eleanor Roosevelt. Thus it was possible at the same time to smear both Hollywood and Roosevelt and that was important because one of the strongest themes behind the accusations levelled by HUAC was "the un-Americanism" of the New Deal and those who approved of its liberal objectives. What Parnell Thomas was about to do was to try to prove that the Roosevelt administration had compelled Hollywood to produce pro-Russian films – notably *Mission to Moscow* and *Song of Russia* – and was therefore communistic. (*Song of Russia*, incidentally, was made in 1944 and starred Robert Taylor as an American musician caught in Russia at the beginning of hostilities and admiring the citizens' war effort. It is, frankly, an awful film, which thoroughly deserved to be condemned, though not necessarily by politicians. By movie lovers, yes; by HUAC, no. And it's worth remembering that *Newsweek* said of it: 'MGM performs the neatest trick of the week by leaning over backwards in Russia's favour without once swaying from right to left.')

In March, Eric Johnston, president of the Motion Picture Association of America, was informed by HUAC representatives that every Communist employed in Hollywood should be dismissed, since they were obviously dedicated to the overthrow of the American government and would use films to achieve their end. Johnston replied that no Communist had ever been able to influence a script and 'there is nothing which will enable us to discharge a person in Hollywood because he is a Communist'. If he was hoping thereby to deter the committee and enlist the support of the studio moguls he was disappointed, for a month later Jack Warner broke ranks with his colleagues and called for "an all-out fight on commies". Thus encouraged, Parnell Thomas held a series of closed hearings at the Biltmore Hotel to take the evidence of "friendly witnesses", among them good old Jack, Louis Mayer, Robert Taylor and Adolphe Menjou. Apparently these sessions yielded a disappointing lack of information and subversive names, so Thomas asked Hoover and the FBI for a little help and this was forthcoming in the form of memoranda which were passed to the committee 'with the understanding that under no circumstances will the source of this material ever be disclosed'. With this assistance the HUAC investigators beavered away and informed the studio heads that 'the committee means business'. And so it did. On 21 September HUAC issued subpoenas to forty-three Hollywood people summoning them to appear at committee hearings in Washington in October.

The Congressional hearings began on 20 October 1947. They lasted for ten days, were broadcast on the radio and opened with testimony from "friendly witnesses", those prepared to co-operate. First among these was Jack Warner, who assured the committee that 'there is not a Warner Brothers' picture that can fairly be judged to be hostile to our country or Communistic in tone or purpose.' What, he was asked, did he think about this proposal for a blacklist? Jack was against it; didn't think it would be legal; didn't agree with men banding together to stop another man working. 'I would not be a party to it,' he affirmed, stoutly. What about Communists, though: had he spotted any of them in Hollywood? Well, yes, he had actually: he had spotted twelve, among them Dalton Trumbo (MGM's highest paid writer), Ring Lardner Jr, John Howard Lawson, Robert Rossen, Emmett Lavery (a bit of a boo-boo, this, because Lavery was president of the SWG and had been most co-operative to HUAC) and Howard Koch. Howard Koch? The man he had implored to write *Mission to Moscow* which, as he had already assured the committee had not an ounce of pro-Communist sentiment in it? What had Howard Koch done?

'Well,' said Howard Koch, 'Jack Warner said they had to watch me because I was slipping Communist propaganda into their films.' Forty years later he could laugh at that. But why would Warner have said such a thing? 'Not because of anything against me,' said Koch, 'but because he was under fire from the committee. He was in a vulnerable position. Here he was, the head of the studio, and he and Harry Warner were in the forefront of having made a number of progressive films, including *Mission to Moscow*. And they were scared.' Whatever his motives, Jack Warner's testimony was to put a considerable blight on Howard Koch's career.

Meanwhile, waiting in the wings were nineteen "unfriendly witnesses", those who were not expected to co-operate. But their turn was not yet. For after the friendly ones came a group of "concerned patriotic citizens", including Robert Taylor, Gary Cooper, Adolphe Menjou (an almost fanatical Red-hunter) and Ronald Reagan. They didn't publicly name anybody but by lending their support to the hearings they did a lot of good for HUAC's publicity.

At that stage public opinion, especially in Hollywood, was opposed to the hearings. Eric Johnston told the nineteen unfriendly witnesses that he and his colleagues were embarrassed that Jack Warner "made a stupid ass of himself". Many of the newspapers were disapproving, too, and in an editorial the *New York Times* said: 'We do not believe the committee is conducting a fair investigation. We think the course upon which it is embarked threatens to lead to greater dangers than those with which it is presently concerned.' But perhaps the most concrete opposition came from the Committee for the First Amendment, which had been formed in September at a meeting in Hollywood by Philip Dunne, John Huston, William Wyler and the actor, Alexander Knox. The First Amendment to the American Constitution states that: 'Congress shall make no law abridging the freedom of speech' and it was this which the CFA felt the nineteen unfriendly witnesses should invoke in their own defence. The reasons for the creation of the CFA, said Philip Dunne, were twofold: first, to oppose censorship of films, which had been called for by the ultra right-wing William Randolph Hearst and, second, to prevent the introduction of a blacklist.

'Nineteen people had been subpoenaed,' he said. 'We were against that. But what was much more important to us was the way "friendly witnesses" were spewing names under Congressional immunity ... For instance Adolphe Menjou, an actor who specialised in playing gentlemen, was enough of a gentleman to give the committee the name of a director at whose house he had dined and accused the director of saying that capitalism was doomed, which got the poor man blacklisted.' With the support of people like Evelyn Keyes, Edward G. Robinson, Humphrey Bogart, Lauren Bacall, Danny Kaye, John Garfield and Gregory Peck, the CFA took out advertisements ('signed,' said Dunne, 'by practically every star in Hollywood') in the trade papers and bought radio time for broadcasts not only by stars but also by US senators and the likes of Thomas Mann – all to protest against HUAC.

Finally, twenty five or so CFA supporters chartered a plane and flew to Washington, Huston and Dunne being the spokesmen for the group. Eric Johnston, who had openly criticised HUAC both in letters to the committee and in advertisements in the *Washington Post* and the *New York Times* and had declared that: 'As long as I live I will never be a party to anything as un-American as a blacklist', was about to give evidence. And the CFA felt that its presence, represented by the likes of Huston, Bacall, Garland and many others, coinciding with Johnston's anticipated defence of the industry would help to discredit the committee and prevent further HUAC interference. As it turned out, however, the wily politician Parnell Thomas was way ahead of them ...

But what was the atmosphere like in Washington at that time, as the unfriendly nineteen waited to be questioned? Howard Koch, who was one of their number, said: 'It was very frightening. All our phones were tapped. We had to meet on streets to have talks that wouldn't be relayed by wire to the committee. There was a general feeling, I think, that we were in an alien land, that we weren't in our own country, because this wasn't the way we thought of America – quite the opposite. Here we were like refugees in our own country.' When they did talk in their rooms, he said, they had to 'wave bits of metal and so on' to negate the bugging equipment. And when Huston and Dunne visited the nineteen in their hotel to discuss tactics . . . 'We went to see them at midnight, clandestinely, because it would have been bad publicity, not so much for us as for our actors.'

Dunne was at pains to point out that the CFA was not a support group for the unfriendly witnesses, although its sympathies were with them. Its main concern was with what it saw as the undemocratic nature of HUAC. And so at that midnight meeting, he said, he presented them with a statement 'that I implored them to make'. In answer to the question: 'Are you now or have you ever been a member of the Communist Party?', he wanted them to reply: 'I must respectfully decline to answer that question on the grounds that the information is privileged under the First Amendment of the Constitution.' Just that and no more. But they ignored his advice. 'Their tactic,' he said, 'was to say that they were trying to answer the question in their own words and it resulted in a shouting match. Because their own words were an attack on the committee, which was foolish. When you're in the lion's den, don't make the lion any madder than he is – to begin with, use a chair, in this case the First Amendment. I think they were extremely foolish and had very bad legal advice.'

The first shouting match took place on the Monday morning after the weekend of clandestine meetings and Parnell Thomas outwitted the CFA by calling not Eric Johnston but John Howard Lawson, the most undeniably and unashamedly Communist of all the unfriendly nineteen. Lawson asked to be allowed to read a prepared statement, as all the friendly witnesses had done; Thomas refused. Lawson then proceeded to describe the friendly witnesses as 'a parade of stool pigeons, neurotics, publicity-seeking clowns, Gestapo agents, paid informers and a few ignorant and frightened Hollywood artists'. Parnell kept using the gavel, Lawson kept refusing to say whether or not he had been a member of the CP and in the end he was forcibly removed from the stand. Evelyn Keyes who, as the wife at that time of John Huston, attended the hearing said: 'The most I remember were those lights everywhere and that gavel going. Every time Lawson would open his mouth this gavel would come and it was right beside a microphone. I get chilled even to this day. It was the most frightening thing because it was like really shutting off the freedom of speech.'

Not everybody shared Philip Dunne's dismay at the attitude of the unfriendly witnesses, all of whom – or all of those who were called – followed Lawson's example, generally speaking, in refusing to answer the basic question. The one who came closest to accepting Dunne's advice was the producer Adrian Scott, who took the First Amendment, not that it helped him much. When asked what he thought of the conduct of the unfriendly ones, Howard Koch said: 'My attitude was one of admiration. They were my friends. I was not a member of the Communist Party. Some of them were and some of them weren't but that wasn't the question. The question was: were we going to suppress free thought in order to have no dissension from policies that would lead to the Cold War? That's the bottom line.' And Abraham Polonsky, whose turn to face HUAC would come four years later, said:

Lauren Bacall in *To Have and Have Not*, combining war, crime and a lesson in whistling for Humphrey Bogart

G MEN

JAMES
CAGNEY
ANN DVORAK

Margaret **LINDSAY**
Robert **ARMSTRONG**
Directed by William Keighley
A FIRST NATIONAL PICTURE

A
**WARNER
BROS.
PICTURE**

CASABLANCA

Left: Clint Eastwood striding confidently through the mayhem of his own making in *Dirty Harry* Below: A nice family picture this one – Brando with his sons Freddie (John Cazale), Michael (Al Pacino) and Sonny (James Caan) in *The Godfather* Previous page, top: Cagney in *G Men* could behave as violently as any gangster and still have the law on his side. Bottom: Bogart, Bergman and *Casablanca* – 'Here's looking at you, kid'

Above: De Niro (as
Noodles) with girlfriend
(Darlene Fluegel) in
Sergio Leone's flawed
but powerful *Once Upon
a Time in America*
Left: That same Noodles
– with gang – on the New
York streets in the 1920s

Above: *The Grapes of Wrath*, a prime example of the kind of social-consciousness movie Hollywood could make, without political interference in the 1930s
Left: Edward G. Robinson, a notable victim of HUAC until he apologised for being what he never had been – a political dupe

Above: Christopher Walken and Robert de Niro serving – or about to serve – God and country proudly in *The Deerhunter*, which was more anti-war than anti-American

Left: A scene from *Apocalypse Now*, Coppola's nightmare vision of the Vietnam War

Right: Diane Keaton with Warren Beatty in *Reds*, the story of an American Communist that predated the "Rambo" era

Left: Vicious Russian soldiers about to execute innocent Americans in *Red Dawn*, whose virulent anti-Communism paved the way for *Rambo*
Below: And here we are back in the Cold War with Chuck Norris saving America from the Communist hordes in *Invasion USA*

'They were all different characters but their attitude was to combat the committee on the question of the First Amendment. Now, of course, you can do that in a very distinguished, quiet way. You can say, "I refuse to answer here but if you wait until I get outside I'll tell you" – and then nothing happens. They wanted to get rid of the committee and so they took the attitude that they were going to fight it. I don't think there's any prize for good behaviour in politics, only for success.'

Well, yes, but success did not attend John Howard Lawson and his cohorts. Altogether ten of the nineteen unfriendly witnesses were called before Parnell Thomas unexpectedly cancelled the rest of the hearings. And all those who had given evidence, the "Hollywood Ten" as they came to be known, were cited for contempt of Congress. They were: John Howard Lawson, Ring Lardner Jr, Sam Ornitz, Dalton Trumbo, Herbert Biberman, Alvah Bessie, Albert Maltz, Lester Cole, Adrian Scott and Edward Dmytryk. Scott was a producer, Biberman and Dmytryk were directors, the rest were writers. Writers, it was felt, had been particularly singled out because as the men who invented the stories, the situations and the dialogue they were clearly in the best position to destroy the United States by inserting Communist propaganda into the films.

The reason for the abrupt cancellation of the rest of the hearings has never been made quite clear; it is possible that the adverse criticism HUAC was getting in the press and the hostility towards it in Hollywood may have had some influence. In any event, the sessions ended on the Thursday of the second week and were not resumed for another four years. At the time when Lawson and company were taking the stand support for HUAC in Hollywood, according to Philip Dunne, existed only in a small minority, the right-wingers. 'Ronald Reagan possibly,' he said, 'although he made a good statement against it on the stand. But as things transpired he was slipping names to the FBI, so who knows how he felt.' There is, however, no doubt how Roy Brewer felt: he welcomed the announcement of the hearings. 'I'd been a voice crying in the wilderness. But I didn't get very much help, personally, from the first hearings. They were anti-labour as well as anti-Communist and they did not give me much recognition or give me much of a chance to tell my story ' Indeed, in reply to a newspaperman asking why Brewer was not being given more attention, a member of HUAC said he 'wasn't gonna give the damn unions any chance to get off the hook'. Brewer was disappointed with this response. 'But,' he said, 'I ultimately proved that I saw them [the Communists] as a great danger and I finally proved that I was fighting them on all fronts and then I began to get more support.'

But as support for Roy Brewer increased after the 1947 hearings, support for the Hollywood Ten declined rapidly. The studio heads, said Philip Dunne, 'ran like rabbits – ran for cover. Willie Wyler and I, after the hearings, went around and visited every one of them personally – except Jack Warner, who was hopeless. He was one of the friendly witnesses, out of fright I'm sure; he really crawled. But we went to all the others and said, Whatever you do, don't give in. The minute you fire one man the lid is off; they'll get you to fire everybody. We knew that people who were not Communists at all would then be affected and they were. But finally, when the pressure came on them this Motion Picture Producers' Association, like a tower of jelly, collapsed at the first touch. Swoosh – it was all gone. And that, of course, left everybody hung out to dry; we'd lost. They were the people who did the hiring – what could we do?'

One of the problems, from the studios' point of view, was that they already had enough trouble without antagonising HUAC. Anti-trust suits were going through the courts to divorce the studios from their cinema chains, thus depriving them of the main outlet for the pictures; Olivia de Havilland had sued Warner Brothers and broken the suspension clause; the sale of television sets was increasing; foreign markets were protecting their own products by introducing quota systems for American films; and cinema attendances were beginning to fall. The last thing the moguls, and more especially the money men in New York, wanted was to provoke powerful, patriotic organisations like the American Legion and risk a boycott of their movies. As far as the money men were concerned there was much to be said for placating HUAC and casting the Hollywood Ten adrift. And so, on 24 November – less than a month after the hearings ended – on the same day as the House of Representatives voted overwhelmingly to approve HUAC's contempt citations, the studio heads and their executives met at the Waldorf Astoria Hotel in Manhattan to decide what they were going to do. And what they did was to appoint Louis Mayer, Joseph Schenck, Walter Wanger, Dore Schary and an attorney, Mendel Silberburg, to draft a statement – the Waldorf Statement – pledging total solidarity with Parnell Thomas and his committee.

It began: 'Members of the Association of Motion Picture Producers deplore the action of the ten Hollywood men who have been cited for contempt. We do not desire to prejudge their legal rights but their actions have been a disservice to their employers and have impaired their usefulness to the industry. We will forthwith discharge or suspend without compensation those in our employ and we will not re-employ any of the ten until such time as he is acquitted or has purged himself of contempt and declares under oath that he is not a Communist. . . .'

And there was more. The association was not content with getting rid of the ten. "Alleged subversive and disloyal elements in Hollywood" were also to be weeded out. 'We will not knowingly employ a Communist or a member of any party or group which advocates the overthrow of the government of the United States by force or by illegal or unconstitutional methods . . .' Nor was the association to be dissuaded from this policy 'by hysteria or intimidation from any source', though it was 'frank to recognise that such a policy involves dangers and risks. There is the danger of hurting innocent people'. But, boldly facing these risks and dangers, the studio bosses would 'invite the Hollywood talent guilds to work with us to eliminate any subversives, to protect the innocent and to safeguard free speech and a free screen wherever threatened'. And so the principle of the blacklist was formulated, although the existence of any such thing would be strenuously denied.

To Philip Dunne, the Waldorf Statement was 'a complete surrender to what I like to call the un-Americans, the people who included HUAC itself, their supporters within the industry, the Motion Picture Alliance for the Preservation of American Ideals – how's that for a title? I don't know what ideals they were interested in preserving but certainly not the Bill of Rights – and the American Legion and the other organisations that arranged the blacklist.'

One of the first to suffer because of the Waldorf Statement was the writer, Ring Lardner Jr. He said: 'I was the only person [among the Ten] under contract to 20th Century-Fox and Darryl Zanuck said he wasn't going to fire me unless specifically ordered to do so by his board of directors. And they obliged within a couple of days . . .' In fact, all of the ten who were under contract were fired immediately but so were scores of others who had not been cited for contempt of Congress. Howard Koch, who had been subpoenaed but had not been called to testify, went to some trouble to inform those whom it might concern that he was not a subversive of any kind. He took an advertisement in the Hollywood trade papers to declare that he was not and never had been a Communist but reserved the right not to say that to HUAC because it was none of their business. (It's worth repeating, I think, that at that time it was not illegal to belong to the Communist Party anyway.) He exhorted the Hollywood community to remain firm. Well, it did – but not in the way he had hoped: it remained firm in its decision to get rid of anyone it even suspected of Communist sympathies, including Howard Koch. Nobody ever told him he was on a blacklist but . . . 'The telephone stopped ringing. That's all. I knew what that meant.'

But what exactly had he, and scores of others like him, done? They hadn't even been accused of anything, after all. Well, no matter. They were all found guilty, in the wonderful phrase of the time, of "premature anti-Fascism."

'In other words,' said Edward Dmytryk, 'if, before we entered the war, you were against the Fascists you were suspect, because you had to be a left-winger. During the war, of course, it was fine because we were fighting the Fascists. What a ridiculous, childish kind of standard that is. A lot of very innocent people were hurt by this. I'm not thinking about the Hollywood Ten – we knew what we were getting into and we did it with our eyes wide open. But there were a lot of people who had maybe signed a letter or something, protesting against Franco's treatment of some-one or other, or had donated ten dollars for the Republican relief fund in Spain. And they were in serious trouble and couldn't work for a long time.' It was a question, then, of guilt by association.

As a result of the 1947 and 1951 HUAC hearings men like Dmytryk and Adrian Scott, Howard Koch, Carl Foreman and Joseph Losey had to seek work in Britain; Lionel Stander went to Italy; John Bright to Mexico; Ring Lardner wrote a film in Switzerland. Those who remained in America – the writers at least – could find employment of a kind but there were drawbacks.

Lardner said: 'People who were either sympathetic or just looking for a bargain hired us to do anonymous jobs at considerably less than our normal salaries. I did some work for individuals like Franchot Tone and Burgess Meredith, who had their own company. They hired me to do a script and I remember meeting Franchot Tone in a bank in Beverly Hills where he withdrew money and paid me in cash.' Much money? 'Not much money, no.'

(Two classic examples of blacklisted writers working under pseudonyms. . . . In 1956, the Oscar for "best motion picture story" went to the writers of a film called

The Brave One. The script was adapted "from an original story by Robert Rich". But when, at the Oscar ceremony, Robert Rich was asked to step up and receive his award, nobody appeared – because Robert Rich was, in fact, Dalton Trumbo, persona non grata. The following year *The Bridge on the River Kwai* won seven Academy Awards, among them the prize for best screenplay. It was given to Pierre Boule, the Frenchman from whose book the film had been adapted and who had taken the screen credit as writer, despite the fact that he didn't speak English. It was not until 1985 that the Academy officially recognised the truth of the matter: that the script was actually written by Carl Foreman and Michael Wilson, both of whom were on the blacklist when the film was made.)

After the Waldorf Statement the only outfit offering anything like open support for the Hollywood Ten was the Committee for the First Amendment and that rapidly fell apart – 'through fear and misrepresentation, I think,' said Philip Dunne. A "Freedom from Fear" committee had been set up to raise money for the Ten in their legal battles with HUAC. It was nothing to do with the CFA, though several CFA members made donations. But the fact that it existed was regarded with suspicion in Hollywood and . . . 'This was a handy excuse for the people who were frightened to run out. And among those, I'm sorry to say, was Bogart.' Bogart, Danny Kaye, Edward G. Robinson and others were the big names in the CFA; they had signed anti-HUAC petitions and had made the trip to Washington. Dunne said: 'They had stuck their necks out and so they were the targets. I don't blame them for pulling out. Well, I do blame them now. Lauren Bacall and Bogart both said they pulled out of the CFA because we'd changed our approach. But we hadn't.' Bogart, indeed, was persuaded to send out a mimeographed letter asserting that he was an American and, as such, naturally not a Communist or Communist sympathiser and that, on the contrary, he detested Communism just as any decent American did. It was a pretty cringe-making document but these were bad times and there was a lot of fear around.

For two and a half years after the 1947 hearings, the Hollywood Ten fought the contempt citations through the courts but in April 1950, the Supreme Court denied them a hearing for an appeal and the "unfriendly witnesses" went to gaol – eight of them for a year and the others for six months. They had gone to the courts to challenge HUAC's right to behave as it had done. But, Ring Lardner said: 'While our case was in the courts the leaders of the Communist Party [in the USA] were arrested under the Smith Act and were convicted by the time our case came up before the Supreme Court.' Lardner and Lester Cole were each sentenced to a year at Danbury prison in Connecticut where one of their fellow inmates was none other than J. Parnell Thomas, who had been convicted of padding his Congressional payroll and diverting government money into his own pocket. 'It was entertaining to see him there,' Lardner said. 'I never really had any contact with him much in prison except that because I worked in the parole office and he was up for parole he was very alarmed that I might somehow sabotage him.'

The alternative to prison would have been to make an act of contrition before Congress, to purge their contempt. But it would not have been enough simply to say sorry: they would have been expected to show their good faith by naming other possible Communists, even though this was entirely unnecessary. The committee already knew who were Communists, fellow travellers or "premature anti-Fascists". Howard Koch said: 'It had done very big research on all of us who had been part of progressive organisations. They were very up on this – they knew who were members and who were not. They asked the questions but they knew the answers. And I would say they had certain people who were informing.' Chief among those informers was the FBI. 'It turned out,' said Philip Dunne, 'that under the leadership of their thoroughly corrupt chief, J. Edgar Hoover, they were funnelling information to HUAC. I didn't know this until a few years ago when I sent for my own file [his FBI file] under the Freedom of Information Act.' What he discovered from this, he said, was that any accusation against him was passed on, unchecked, to the committee. 'Anybody in off the street could say, "Philip Dunne is a Communist." Didn't matter who. And this raw stuff was being handed over to the committee. Now they had enough sense not to use it but there it was. I was really shocked by that. It brings up another point, too, you know. It came out last year [1985] that Ronald Reagan had been informing the FBI in this period. Which raises a very interesting question: what on earth was happening in the Screen Actors' Guild that could come under the heading of espionage or sabotage? So what could he have been giving the FBI except possibly the names of people he *suspected* of being Communists? And, being Ronnie, there were lots of people he suspected of being Communists. And then what happened was that they [the names] went to the FBI and were passed on to HUAC. HUAC was passing them on to all those extra-legal organisations that were organising the blacklist. So what Reagan, in all innocence, might have offered the FBI as his suspicions could have resulted in some of his fellow actors being deprived of work.'

Beyond all that, in raising a flat stone to reveal apparently rabid Communism in Hollywood, HUAC had also released other, slimier creatures such as anti-Semitism. One of the committee's members, Congressman John Rankin, brought up the matter of a CFA petition and its signatories in the House of Representatives . . . 'One of the names is June Havoc. We found out that her real name is June Hovic. Another name was Danny Kaye . . . his real name was Daniel David Kaminsky. Another is Eddie Cantor, whose real name is Edward Isskowitz. There is one who calls himself Edward Robinson. His real name is Emmanuel Goldenberg. There is another who calls himself Melvyn Douglas, whose real name is Melvyn Hesselberg . . .' To Rankin and many like him Jew and Communist were synonymous.

In this kind of political climate Eric Johnston, president of the MPA and erstwhile staunch supporter of the freedom of speech, told the Screen Writers' Guild in 1948: 'We'll have no more *Grapes of Wrath*. We'll have no more *Tobacco Roads*. We'll have no more films that show the seamy side of American life. We'll have no more pictures that deal with labour strikes. We'll have no more pictures that show the banker as villain.' And for some while, nor did they. Instead, urged on by Californian Senator Richard M. Nixon, Hollywood began turning out a series of anti-Communist movies. Howard Hughes more or less set the ball rolling with *I Married a Communist* (otherwise known as *The Woman on Pier 13*) in 1949. A certain irony here since it is most likely that Hughes, as the owner of TWA, paid for the plane that took the CFA delegation to Washington. Other films with Communist heavies rapidly followed: in *The Whiphand*, the Reds tested bacteriological weapons in the USA; in *I Was a Communist for the FBI* – made with FBI assistance – a steelworker becomes an undercover agent to trap commies; in *Walk East on Beacon* (based on a book by J. Edgar Hoover) the FBI – who again helped in the production – exposes Communist spies in America; in *Big Jim McClain*, big John Wayne sniffed out yet more reds and the film was dedicated to HUAC "undaunted by the vicious campaign of slander launched against them"; in *My Son John*, a Catholic family discovers to its horror that its eldest son is a Communist; in *Blood Alley*, John Wayne surges to the rescue again by helping innocent Chinese to escape Communist clutches. And so on. In 1948, Milton Krims who had written the anti-Fascist *Confessions of a Nazi Spy*, demonstrated his total impartiality by also writing the anti-Communist *The Iron Curtain*. People had to adapt to the times.

This is not to say, however, that Hollywood was implacably unforgiving. In March 1949, Roy Brewer was instrumental in forming the Motion Picture Industry Council (MPIC), an amalgamation of unions, guilds and producers whose purpose was to expose Communists in the film business, bring them to the attention of the studios and publicise their purging of contempt and general rehabilitation, so that the industry could be seen to be keeping its house in order. Between 1949 and 1951 the presidents of the MPIC included Brewer, Dore Schary (who replaced Louis Mayer as head of MGM), Ronald Reagan and Cecil B. de Mille. It was possible, as several people were to discover, to get off the blacklist with the help of this organisation. And it was necessary to have some influential aid because the FBI was openly Red-hunting too and by 1950 was keeping a baleful eye on such assorted characters as the United States Attorney-General Tom Clark, Adlai Stevenson, Harry Belafonte and Helen Keller, as well as tapping the phones of Fredric March and Edward G. Robinson.

From all this it was perhaps a logical step to re-open the HUAC hearings and indeed they began again in March 1951 and continued intermittently until 1954. But now it was no longer a matter of vague charges about Communist propaganda that might have filtered into the films for which the witnesses were responsible; now names had to be named. And it was at this time that Lionel Stander made his appearance at his own request – or rather at his own demand – since, to his great indignation, he had been accused of being a Communist by an actor called Marc Lawrence. Stander's name had already appeared on various unofficial blacklists circulated by certain zealously patriotic publications and this fact, coupled with his probably ill-advised condemnation of HUAC as an un-American conspiracy, served to put him firmly on the roster of the unemployables. So he earned a living for a while as a Wall Street stockbroker and then went to Italy and later to Britain.

Abraham Polonsky, who had been the head of a Communist cell at Paramount Studios – the other members being Sterling Hayden and a couple of scene shifters – also made his appearance before HUAC in 1951. He got there because he appeared to have been named by practically everybody. 'I don't remember who named me.... eight, nine, ten people, I don't remember how many.' Why had they done this?

'Because I was a member of the Communist Party and they were stool pigeons. What other reason do you need?' He received his subpoena outside 20th Century-Fox where he was working at the time and said to the man who served him with it: 'Why didn't you come to my house?' And the man said, 'Well, we didn't want to embarrass your family or anything.'

It was around the time of the 1951 hearings that witnesses who had been summoned and wished to get themselves off the hook started naming people who were already known to be Communists. Budd Schulberg did this on the grounds, he said, that 'Frankly I thought those people had already become so identified with the party that I didn't feel as if I was fingering the criminals.' Polonsky didn't think much of that argument and said of Schulberg and others who followed the same course: 'It was the reason they gave themselves for doing it. The committee had all the names to begin with. The Los Angeles police department and the FBI knew every single member of the Communist Party ... So it was like in the Inquisition, if you named a name publicly you then broke off your relationship, such as it had been in the past, with the Communist Party and became an honourable member of society again. The problem you had to face was a question of moral honour rather than giving information, because the information was already possessed. They never got any information out of all those hearings that was of any significance whatsoever.'

Sometimes those who were about to name names that had already been named even asked those they planned to name if they minded. 'Those kind of people,' Polonsky said, 'still being friends in their own minds with the people they were about to name, thought it would be more polite to ask someone if he would like to be Jesus Christ, because they were about to nail a few people to the cross and if he had already been named it wasn't really another nail after all, it was the same old nail.' Polonsky didn't take too kindly to this approach. 'I'd usually kick them out of the house,' he said.

Edward Dmytryk, who had served six months in prison as a result of the 1947 hearings, was another who named names when he volunteered to testify again in 1951. He testified, he said, because 'I wanted to do it. Most people didn't understand that. I wanted to get rid of the onus, that's all.' He had been a member of the Communist Party and 'the thing that most people don't realise is that it wasn't enough to say "I'm no longer a member". You had to do something to prove it, otherwise you were always tarred with that brush ... We had all lied during the hearings; we had all pretended that none of us was a Communist and every single one of us was ... And the only way to get out from that was to say, "Look, I'm not only not a Communist now but I just don't believe in Communist ideology any more at all; I think it's a corrupt ideology ..."'

But what of the people he named? 'I named nobody that hadn't been named or that they didn't know. It was an easy way out, of course ... but the point is that I think we all felt that it wasn't anything because all these people had publicly been named as Communists by somebody or other before. I named no new people at all, so it was nothing, you know.'

One man, however, who named names of those who were already identified as

Communists and regretted it until his death was Sterling Hayden. He had been, in his own words, 'a romantic Communist – the only person to buy a schooner and join the Communist Party in the same week'. He was not a member for very long but nevertheless in 1951 ... 'I was working on some damn western somewhere and came out for lunch and somebody handed me a subpoena to appear before the committee in Washington, D.C. Well, I was frankly scared...' Hayden had already asked his lawyer what he should do in such an eventuality and the lawyer had written to Hoover for advice. The answer was for Hayden to contact the Los Angeles office of the FBI – which he did – and tell them everything he knew and having done that, not to worry. Yet the subpoena arrived anyway.

'And right there I got into a period of personal hell,' he said, only a few weeks before he died in 1986. 'Right up until almost the last minute I knew what I was doing was wrong for me, as a human being, and yet I felt myself being almost inexorably drawn into it, perhaps because of personal weakness ... I was in psycho-analysis and I met with the analyst one night and began to go over the pros and cons. And finally it became clear that the only thing for me to do really, since I didn't feel like going to jail, was to go along and be a rat. And it was then I got lost in a sort of personal hell, in that I thought, "I don't know why I'm doing this; I mean, I'm going to regret it all my life." The only conceivable excuse – it's not an excuse; there is no excuse but it's a good reason perhaps – is that I was trying to get custody of my four children at the time. It was pointed out to me by the same lawyer that if I defied the committee I could damn well forget any hope of getting my children ...'

So he went, as he said, "to be a rat" – to list, on the instructions of the FBI, dates and names even though he knew that he was not really on the witness stand to provide information. 'They already knew everything.' He was there, he felt, to be made an example of in 'the national press or the international press or whatever'. And recalling the occasion, he said: 'Oh Christ, yes, it was a rough day; it was a very rough day.' He named all the names he could think of – 'Abe Polonsky whom I knew a bit personally and whom I admired enormously' – and a man, not in the movie business, who had 'been a friend of mine, beginning way back in childhood almost ... He'd exposed me to the world of Upton Sinclair and Jack London and the whole wonderful thing of the radical dream. And he was fired the next morning, ten o'clock sharp, because his name came out, given by Hayden ...'

The right wing in Hollywood greeted him as a hero. He had cables of congratulation from William Holden and Ronald Reagan and the chairman of Paramount called him into his office to say, 'Sterling, we're all very proud of you.' The headlines in the newspapers, he said, 'were about "Hayden does this to Party, Hayden does that..." And from that time on I just sort of stumbled along ... There's a very strange twist here, that when a man performs an act of personal betrayal of his friends he's regarded as a 100 per cent all-American patriot ... But I thought then, as I'm thinking now, that I guess it's the only thing I've ever done in my life for which I'm ashamed. It's that simple: the only thing.'

The testifying and the giving of names was described by Philip Dunne as "a degradation ceremony" that the witnesses were obliged to go through in order to emerge purified. Those who agreed to it – Edward G. Robinson among them – were deemed to have been rehabilitated and could resume their careers. Some of them, Dmytryk probably the outstanding example, owed their re-establishment in society to a large extent to Roy Brewer and the Motion Picture Industry Council, which carried through its promise to help the penitent and the unjustly accused to get off the blacklist. (Although Brewer denied that there was such a thing. 'In the true sense there was no blacklist but there was discriminatory hiring.')

Dmytryk had already made up his mind to make a complete break with the Communists – for ideological reasons – before he approached the MPIC and, said Brewer, 'we reached out a hand to help'. Mostly the rehabilitation of Dmytryk was a public relations exercise, organised by the MPIC. Brewer said: 'I said, "No way should we let him take the brunt of this." He did what we asked him to do. We asked him, if he was really sincere, to tell his story to the public and he did in a *Saturday Evening Post* article, which really stung the Communists. He told how he'd been approached by John Howard Lawson to change certain things in his picture. (The picture was *Cornered*, a revenge thriller about Dick Powell seeking a Nazi who had killed his wife, which Dmytryk directed and Adrian Scott produced in 1945. The basic theme was anti-Fascist.) And he [Dmytryk] told him he wouldn't do it and so Lawson told him, "Well, you're a Party member, you're under discipline and if you don't want to foul Party discipline you've got to resign," and he did. So I said that it was our place to defend him.'

After his testimony Dmytryk came off the blacklist – or perhaps Roy Brewer would say he benefited from positive discriminatory hiring. But there was also something, equally pernicious, called "the grey list". One of the most virulently anti-Communist publications of the time was *Red Channels*, published by the American Business Consultants. It listed all known and suspected Communists and acted as adviser to potential employers who were in doubt. Thus if a studio was uncertain whether an actor, writer, director or whatever was safe to be taken on the payroll it would ask *Red Channels* for advice. And *Red Channels* would either clear or condemn the man in question or – and this is where the grey list came into effect – would say: 'Well, we're not sure so it's best not to touch him.' One who suffered badly from this was the director Vincent Sherman who from 1948 to 1951 was unemployed in Hollywood because he was tainted with premature anti-Fascism.

'There was very little you could do,' he said. 'In fact, it was more difficult to fight being on a grey list than a blacklist. You're fighting shadows when you're on a grey list, you see – you're fighting rumours, you're not fighting anything concrete.' In the three years when Hollywood refused to touch him only one man, an executive at Allied Artists who had been asked to sign Sherman for a film in England, told him why he was shunned. 'My agent took me in to see the head of the studio and he said, "I can't hire you. Even though I have a request from London to hire you I can't because you're on a list. I hate the damn situation but that's it, that's the truth. And if you tell anyone what I told you, I'll deny it." ' Eventually Sherman was only able to extricate himself by going, on his agent's advice, to see Congressman Donald Jackson of California and HUAC. 'I talked to Jackson and he said, "Well, we don't

Left: Lionel Stander giving evidence to – or rather haranguing – the House Un-American Activities Committee
Below: The Hollywood Ten with their lawyers

Left: Marlene Dietrich among the pickets during the CSU strike which helped the rise to power of Roy Brewer (above), head of IATSE

Above: Stalin and Churchill sharing a match in *Mission to Moscow*. Howard Koch wrote it by presidential decree but he was blacklisted nevertheless

Above right: Gregory Peck made his screen debut in *Days of Glory* (1944) when the Russians were still America's brave allies. But when Robert Ryan appeared in *The Woman on Pier 13* aka *I Married a Communist*, in 1949 (right), the only good Red was a dead Red

Far right: Sterling Hayden, who named names for HUAC and regretted it for the rest of his life

want to see an innocent man hurt. Are you willing to talk to one of our investigators?"
I said, Okay and I did and that was the beginning of the clearance, although it still
lingered for a while. But this man said, "If anyone says you can't work because of
such and such an incident, ask them to call me," and little by little the whole thing
was cleared. Jackson was basically responsible and Harry Cohn was second.' What
the normally much-maligned Cohn had done was to call Sherman in to do some
reshooting on a film that had gone wrong. He was then warned that Sherman was a
premature anti-Fascist and therefore dangerous to know. 'He called in his vice-
president and said, "For God's sake, I know this guy. He's been a registered
Democrat ever since he was old enough to vote. Where the hell do they get off, saying
he's a Communist?" So Cohn stood up against the blacklist. He stood up much better
than Warner did.'

But even with the help of a member of HUAC and Harry Cohn it took time to
clear his name. When in 1951 Sherman made his comeback film at MGM – *Lone
Star*, a western starring Clark Gable – Wayne Griffin, the producer, summoned him
one morning. 'He said, "I have some bad news for you. An actor that Clark knows
very well called him and said: This man Vincent Sherman is a well-known Red.
Gable was very upset but he likes you. So I spoke to Eddie Mannix (one of the top
studio executives) and asked if you'd be willing to sign a loyalty oath." I said, Yes –
no problem. So I went up to talk to Mannix who said, "Vince, I don't like this whole
business but we have to do something about it. Would you mind signing the loyalty
oath?" And I said, "Not at all" and I signed it and went to work on the picture and
never heard anything more about it.'

(Two points: some time later Sherman was given a dossier that listed all his
allegedly subversive activities, including the anti-Fascist organisations to which he
had subscribed. He said, 'I would say about forty per cent of it was accurate.'
Secondly, while he was grey listed he made a film in Britain called *The Hasty Heart*.
The stars were Richard Todd and, with a nice irony, Ronald Reagan.)

In the new round of HUAC hearings under the chairmanship of Congressman
John S. Wood, of Georgia, between 1951 and 1954 the "unfriendly witnesses"
invoked the Fifth Amendment ('Nor shall any person be compelled to bear witness
against himself') rather than the First. The result was much the same: pleading the
Fifth was tantamount to being a Red and therefore meant blacklisting. But there was
also the "Augmented Fifth", whereby witnesses declared they were neither
Communists nor sympathetic to the Communist Party but refused to say whether
they had been either in the past and also refused to name names. The director Robert
Rossen took the Augmented Fifth and was blacklisted, though later he testified again
and named fifty-four people. Then, too, there was the "Fully Diminished Fifth",
which meant talking fully about oneself but refusing to mention anyone else and
naturally this also led to blacklisting as Lillian Hellman discovered. In May 1952
according to the Los Angeles *Daily News*, Roy Brewer declared that none of the
witnesses who "hid behind the Fifth Amendment" had subsequently been offered
work. Not surprisingly therefore most of the witnesses decided it was better to be
friendly and from these spewed forth a multitude of names. The writer Martin

Berkeley, for instance, named 155 people which must surely have prompted HUAC to wonder darkly whether he knew anyone except Communists. Of the more celebrated witnesses Edward Dmytryk delivered 26 names, the actor Lee J. Cobb 20, Budd Schulberg 15, Elia Kazan 11 and Sterling Hayden 7. Not all of these were necessarily volunteered by the people under examination; quite often if they couldn't actually think of any names to mention they were kindly provided with some by HUAC itself.

Occasionally, however, even the naming of Reds and fellow travellers was not enough to get the witness off the hook. Larry Parks, who had become a star overnight in *The Jolson Story* in 1946, completely blew it when he testified in March 1951. He spoke frankly enough of his own past membership of the Communist Party but said: 'I would prefer . . . not to mention other people's names . . . This is not the American way; to force a man to do this is not American justice.' HUAC, unfortunately, was not about to enter into a discussion of the finer points of American justice. 'We will ask your co-operation . . . in helping us to ascertain those who are or have been members of the Communist Party,' it told Parks, pointedly, rejecting his plea: 'Don't present me with the choice of either being in contempt of this committee and going to jail or forcing me to really crawl through the mud to be an informer.' Eventually he gave in and named twelve people but obviously he had not done it willingly enough and so his career was wrecked anyway. He appeared in supporting roles in only three more films before he died in 1975.

John Garfield – like Edward G. Robinson – was another who took up HUAC's invitation to help clear those who had been wrongly accused and, again like Robinson, had difficulty in straightening matters out since he had never been a Communist and therefore had nobody to name. Abraham Polonsky believed in any case that Garfield had been picked on almost arbitrarily. 'They had a choice of three stars, that is to say that three stars were associated with going to the Russian Embassy and things like that. Garfield was the only one who didn't have a studio connection; he was an independent so they picked him and let the guys in the studio off.' He declined to name the other two but added: 'I think I should say about Garfield that a lot of people condemned him because he attacked the Soviet Union and said he never was a Communist – he was a 100 per cent American and thought the committee was doing great work. But he couldn't remember a single Communist name or any Communist he'd met in his life. So he had what I called "a street boy's honour"; he says, You want me to say that, I'll say it because I don't care what I say about myself but don't ask me to give anybody's names because I'm not a fink. After he was dead everybody said, "Oh, he was just about to name names before he died," but, of course, they can't prove that, can they?' Well, indeed they can't. After appearing before the committee twice and with his case still unresolved, Garfield died in 1952, ostensibly of a heart attack although there are people who still believe that it was the blacklisting which had kept him out of work for a year that really killed him.

The blacklist and the grey list flourished on throughout the 1950s, supported by such publications as *Red Channels*, *Counterattack*, *Confidential Notebook* and the American Legion's *Firing Line*, all of which listed known or suspected "subversives", their names culled from back issues of *The Daily Worker*, the letter-heading of long defunct Popular Front organisations or the HUAC and FBI files. Apart from the government agencies, the American Legion with its vast funds and three million membership was the most powerful of the anti-Communist outfits because, by arranging a boycott, it could destroy a film's box office chances. So in March 1952 the Producers' Association and the Legion's national commander, Donald Wilson, devised a mutually acceptable method whereby suspected subversives could clear themselves by letter. The named employee would be invited to write to his studio answering the charges against him and explaining why he had joined such and such a listed organisation and at whose invitation, naming those whom he in turn had encouraged to join and giving the reasons he had resigned from it and when. Then Roy Brewer and the MPIC, or some other clearing agency, would study the letter and declare its contents satisfactory or otherwise. But even that was not always enough. The MPIC and the Legion were not the only organisations to be placated – there was also the Wage Earners' Committee.

This was formed by a waiter, a telephone linesman, a small restaurant owner and a retired salesman. It published a magazine called *The National Wage Earner*, wherein it listed ninety-two films which 'employ commies and fellow travellers and contain subversive subject matter designed to defame America throughout the world'. Among these was *Death of a Salesman*, which the Wage Earners' Committee picketed declaring that it was "written by a Communist" (Arthur Miller). For good measure it picketed all of MGM's films as well in the belief that the studio's head of production, Dore Schary, was also a Communist since he had belonged to the Anti-Nazi League in 1936.

That the studios paid attention to such rabid and often cranky outfits was due to the fact that they could not afford to withstand the economic pressure that picketing and boycotting could exert. Therefore they played along with the black and the grey lists and for a decade made virtually no films that dealt with controversial subjects such as social or political stories. As *Variety* put it rather neatly on 22 April 1953: "H'WOOD NIX ON MESSAGE PIX". Even the Korean War was largely avoided as a cinematic theme, being dealt with in only a handful of movies in the time (1950–3) when it was being waged. The message, such as it was, of all of those was probably best summed up in *Bridges at Toki Ri* with these words: 'Militarily this war is a tragedy. But if we pull out they'd take Japan, Indo-China, the Philippines. Where would you have us take our stand? At the Mississippi?' That speech was delivered by Fredric March, who had long been regarded in some circles as a fellow traveller to say the least, and no doubt did much to rehabilitate him.

In 1954 Senator Joseph McCarthy, head of the Senate Permanent Sub-Committee on Investigations, America's witch-hunter general and a man whose name has gone into the language in the form of the pejorative noun "McCarthyism", over-reached himself in his accusations and was formally censured by the Senate. By then there was already a growing feeling within America that McCarthy and his associates had gone beyond what was reasonable in their zeal to stamp out Communism. Almost overnight McCarthy himself lost much of his credibility and most of his power; he pretty well vanished into obscurity and died soon afterwards, mourned I imagine by very few people. Well, John Wayne who once told me that in his opinion 'Senator McCarthy was one of the finest Americans who ever lived,' mourned him and I daresay that Ward Bond, who was even further to the right than Wayne, did, too. McCarthy himself had not taken part in the investigation of Hollywood's Communists but he was the driving force behind America's entire Red-hunting operations and with his decline hunt-the-commie began to fall out of favour as a national sport. Even HUAC gave up its hearings. But the black and the grey lists were still in force.

This was the time of "the front", a time when blacklisted writers, unable to sell their work under their own names, would by arrangement put somebody else's name on it and that person would claim it as his own when selling it to a film or TV company. Abe Polonsky, who used various fronts in his film and television work during this period, said: 'Some did it for money but most of the people offered themselves because they were opposed to what was going on. Some people took ten per cent or something like that but that was rare; most did it because they wanted to do it and then we destroyed their lives, of course, because their relatives would call up and say, "My God, we saw your show on television. It was absolutely beautiful. You must be making a fortune nowadays, can you lend me five thousand dollars...?"' Using a front was safer than using a nom de plume because if somebody grew suspicious about the true origins of a script a real person could at least be produced to state that it was all his own work; but it was no better-paid because, after all, no studio would pay as much to a hitherto unheard-of writer as it would to, say, Abraham Polonsky, assuming Abraham Polonsky were persona grata again.

Of the films that Polonsky wrote with the aid of a front only one has been identified and that was *Odds Against Tomorrow*, a crime thriller with racist (or more accurately anti-racist) undertones which starred Robert Ryan and Harry Belafonte and was directed in 1959 by Robert Wise. The script was originally attributed to a friend of Belafonte's, a black author named John O. Killens. But then Nelson Gidding, a bona fide screen writer, was given joint credit. 'He got associated with the picture,' Polonsky said, 'so that it would have a Hollywood aura about it because nobody was going to believe that this novelist no one even knew about had written a picture.' It was Wise who, in his autobiography, revealed the true identity of the scriptwriter. Polonsky would not do so and still refuses to disclose which other films he wrote under somebody else's name. 'Those people whose names we used have a right to their privacy and since they don't reveal it, why should we? But let me tell you something – you can't believe everything I say because we [the blacklisted writers] took it as a general rule that all pictures attributed to us we claimed we wrote. And we even claimed those we never wrote because there's no reason why we shouldn't add a little confusion to what others created.'

In 1959 then there was still a blacklist but slowly it was beginning to weaken for in that year one Nathan E. Douglas was nominated for the best screenplay Oscar along with Harold Jacob Smith for their work on *The Defiant Ones*. Just before the ceremony Nathan E. Douglas revealed that he was, actually, the blacklisted Fedrick

Young (Harold Jacob Smith, presumably, was just Harold Jacob Smith). Nevertheless he won the Academy Award and three days later Dalton Trumbo announced that he was in fact the mysterious Robert Rich, who had failed to claim his Oscar a few years earlier. The Academy immediately rescinded its rule that it would not accept nominations for "Fifth Amendment witnesses".

Perhaps it was this that led the way to Frank Sinatra openly declaring the following year that he had hired the blacklisted Albert Maltz to write the script for *The Execution of Private Slovik*. The Hearst Press attacked him, so did the American Legion and disc jockeys were exhorted not to play his records. Sinatra therefore capitulated to "the majority opinion of the American public", fired the unhappy Maltz and sold the rights to the film. Others, however, were bolder than he. First – and still in 1960 – Otto Preminger gave a screen credit to Dalton Trumbo on *Exodus* and Kirk Douglas gave him another on *Spartacus*, while the exiled Jules Dassin, another blacklistee, was publicly congratulated by Hollywood celebrities when he turned up as guest of honour at the Screen Directors' Guild showing of his film *Never on Sunday*.

For others, though, getting off the blacklist took longer. In 1960 Ring Lardner was still uncredited for his work on *A Breath of Scandal* and it was not until 1962 that Otto Preminger hired him – and announced that he was doing so – to write the script for *The Genius*. When the American Legion predictably made a protest Preminger replied: 'I feel that I am serving the public by doing openly what other producers have done secretly for many years while giving hypocritical lip service to an illegal blacklist.' As it happened *The Genius* was never made. Lardner said: 'It wasn't till three years later that I first got a screen credit again, so I was really seventeen years between credits.' (The film on which he was at last credited was *The Cincinnati Kid* in 1965.) But even when the American Legion was making a fuss about his association with *The Genius*, he said, 'It had already been demonstrated by *Exodus* and *Spartacus* that there were no boycotts and no pickets outside the theatres. So the blacklist broke down gradually over a few years for most of us. It never did break down for a lot of people who were either not very well established in Hollywood when it started or a few who were considered particularly dangerous and have never been hired since.'

Lionel Stander also came off the list in 1965, thanks to the British director Tony Richardson. 'Tony put me in the film *The Loved One* and he was notified by the studio that he couldn't use me. He said, "Why? Put it in writing," but naturally they couldn't put it in writing because it was an illegal blacklist and he broke the blacklist for me.' Haskell Wexler, the co-producer and cinematographer on that film, recalled that there was a little more to it than that. 'When it came out in Hollywood that he [Stander] was going to be hired tremendous pressures came on to MGM and we were told not to hire Lionel Stander. Then Tony threw a temper tantrum – at least that's what they called it, a temper tantrum – and he insisted that it was vital to the picture to have Lionel Stander and his screams stepped up and we backed him up and Lionel Stander appeared in the film and did a good job.'

Abraham Polonsky's acceptance back into society occurred a little later when the producer Jennings Lang approached him to write the pilot for a TV series. 'I didn't want to do it because who wanted to work for television at that time when he could work for movies? But he said he would put my name on it and so I agreed to do it. And then when Jennings Lang submitted my name to NBC who had to approve of the writer, the director and the leading actor and they suggested he get another writer, he told them to go screw. I think they were the very words he used. So they said Okay and that was the end of the blacklist.' And when was that exactly? 'I think it was '65 or '66. I mean it was for ever; it seemed it went on for ever – '64, '65, '66 I'm not sure of the year but I know I'd become very old by then.'

There was one other Hollywood witch hunt that took place, briefly, in 1950 and although strictly speaking it had no connection with HUAC it is indicative of the prevailing mood in the movie colony at the time. In the autumn of that year Cecil B. de Mille spearheaded a resolution calling for the introduction of a compulsory loyalty oath to be signed by all members of the Screen Directors' Guild. He chose to do this in the absence of the Guild's president, Joe Mankiewicz, who was on his way back by sea from Europe. De Mille's motives were perfectly clear: he was fervently anti-Communist and had even formed the Cecil B. de Mille Foundation for Political Freedom, which graciously gave its members the freedom to agree with Cecil B. de Mille on all political matters. In a signed but open ballot his resolution was passed and the first Mankiewicz knew about it was when he disembarked at New York and reporters asked him what was all this about a loyalty oath.

To a large extent de Mille's action was a personal move against Mankiewicz, whom he suspected of being a dangerous leftie. Mankiewicz said: 'One of the things that drove them [de Mille and his aides] mad was the fact that I'd never belonged to any of the so-called anti-Nazi, pro-Communist, leftist, rightist or whatever movements in Hollywood. I didn't even join the Anti-Nazi League – I could hate Hitler all by myself, I didn't need a League.' So an investigation of Mankiewicz's political past turned up nothing even vaguely detrimental to him but still de Mille remained suspicious. 'At that time he was at his absolute pinnacle,' Mankiewicz said. 'As I once put it he, more than any other director, had his finger up the pulse of the movie-going public . . . and he had all the rewards you could have for that sort of thing. They even got the Academy to give him an honorary award for bringing people to the box office and he was a very ambitious man – very ambitious. One of Hollywood's patriots, Adolphe Menjou, slept with a loaded pistol under his pillow because he knew the Communists were going to attack Beverly Hills. This is true – Adolphe really believed that. And that was the feeling out there. My own belief – and I'm quite convinced of this – is that de Mille wanted eventually to be the Commissar of Loyalty or the Gauleiter of Loyalty throughout the entire entertainment business in America. He already had IATSE [Roy Brewer's union] in his pocket; he knew he could put the Directors' Guild in favour of the loyalty oath and once the directors were in favour the writers would have to follow. And then the Actors' Guild. And then he would move east and take over Equity . . .'

Well, it's a fanciful notion but, accurate or not, it serves to point up the antipathy between de Mille and Mankiewicz, who found the idea of a compulsory loyalty oath perfectly abhorrent. 'I just thought that signing a loyalty oath was an absurd thing to do. It's like making me go to church and pray to prove my belief in God. If I were a member of the Communist Party the first thing I would do would be to sign the bloody loyalty oath, that's for sure. It would mean I'd infiltrated or whatever the hell they do.' But his objections went beyond that. Each month the Directors' Guild had to send the studios a list of members in good standing, that is those who had paid their dues. Now, however, the list would also include – if de Mille had his way – those who had signed the loyalty oath; anyone who had not signed it would not be in good standing and therefore, in Mankiewicz's view, in agreeing to the resolution the directors had agreed to a blacklist. He pointed this out to John Ford, who said: 'I hate blacklists.' With this encouragement Mankiewicz called a membership meeting to discuss the matter further but before that took place he was invited to a smaller gathering in de Mille's office where de Mille asked him to perform an act of contrition. 'He actually used that phrase – an act of contrition. Since Torquemada I don't think anybody's used that phrase; I wouldn't use it in a screenplay. I said, "Well, you can take your act of contrition and shove it. I'm not going to be contrite. This is silly." ' The next day Mankiewicz sent out notice of a meeting of senior Guild members to be held at the Beverly Hills Hotel on Sunday, 22 October.

Mankiewicz's advisers on tactics were John Huston and Elia Kazan, who helped him draft the speech he was to present. 'But as we came to the door of the meeting hall, Kazan drew me aside and said, "I'm not going in with you." I said, "Why not, Gadge? I need you. You're a jungle fighter. You'll get 'em up off the floor scream-ing." He says, "De Mille's waiting for me to come in there; he's gonna use me to kill you." I thought I was going mad – this was a very bad melodrama being played around this loyalty oath thing. But Gadge said, "Look, kid, he knows I'm going to Washington to testify before HUAC" and he gave me a hug and walked away. And de Mille WAS looking for him when we got in there.'

Of the meeting itself Mankiewicz said: 'I have never seen, nor has there ever been, a meeting of creative men and one woman, Ida Lupino, in which so much emotion spilled over to reveal the tension that was in the world at that time, the anti-Communist hysteria that was in the country. There was Rouben Mamoulian getting up and saying, "Mr de Mille, you were born an American; I chose to become an American. I'm a better American than you, Mr de Mille." And Fritz Lang getting up and saying, "For the first time since I am here I realise I speak with an accent and you have made me afraid, Mr de Mille." And there was de Mille hearing himself booed by the entire Directors' Guild as he said, "Let me read the names on the affidavit supporting Mr Mankiewicz – Fred Zinnemann, Villy Vyler, Billy Vilder . . ." and the sort of anti-Semitic reading of these names prompted the booing and for the first time you saw a look of bewilderment in this old man's eyes . . . You know, it was an incredible thing. And Willie Wyler said, "I am sick and tired of being called a Communist . . . The next person who calls me a Communist, no matter how famous he is, how old he is, I am going to kick the shit out of him." '

For Mankiewicz, however, the most important person at the meeting was John Ford. 'My eyes never left him. He was sitting on the floor in the middle of the meeting with the corner of his handkerchief in his mouth and his pipe and his sneakers and his dark glasses and his cap and he just sat there listening till about 2.15 in the morning ... and I kept my eyes on him knowing that no matter what impassioned speech had been made on either side, the way John Ford went that meeting was going to go because this was the claim he had on all of us, as a director.'

As chairman of the meeting Mankiewicz called on one speaker after another but still Ford sat silent. 'And then up went his hand and I said, "Jack, it's your turn ...."' There was a stenographer at the meeting recording all the speeches and so when Ford stood up he delivered himself of the famous line, 'My name's John Ford, I make westerns,' not because he suspected there might be some present who didn't know him from a gatecrasher but to identify himself to the stenographer. And having cleared up any lingering doubts as to his name and occupation he turned to de Mille and said: 'Cecil, you and I go back a long way, 19-what-16, was it? We went through all sorts of hell together. I tell you, nobody makes movies that please people the way you do and for that I respect you ...'

Mankiewicz said, recalling the moment: 'As he said that my stomach turned over and I thought, Where in Paris can I go to live? Or can I get some place in Chelsea ... But then Ford said, "But I don't like you, C.B., and I don't like a damn thing you stand for ...."' Mankiewicz's stomach stopped doing backflips at once as Ford went on: 'Joe has been vilified here and he deserves an apology and I think you should give it to him.' The motion was passed more or less by acclaim. Mankiewicz said: 'The next morning I *was* the Guild and I had to face one very important decision: don't sign the oath or, look, sign it if you want to. If you don't sign you're not going to be blacklisted. Well, I chose the second course because I didn't want the Guild torn apart by what was going to be a continuing fight for the next five years in the United States of America. I've been attacked for sending that letter, advising them to sign, but I think I was right. Just sign the bloody thing and forget about it. That's all. The Supreme Court said the whole thing was nonsense anyway, so that was it.' What had been achieved by this whole episode? Nothing very much – except a point of principle. But from it all came the reassurance that hysteria was not rife everywhere and that the ideals of American democracy were still strong in Hollywood, despite HUAC and all the friendly witnesses.

But, to return to the wider issues, what had HUAC itself achieved and, just as importantly, what had it hoped to achieve? Abraham Polonsky believed that the investigation of Hollywood was essentially a public relations exercise. By concentrating on a few famous people and condemning them as subversives, Congress and the entire US government attracted public attention to what it perceived as the Communist menace threatening the country. 'Hollywood was the advertising place,' Polonsky said, 'but the real dirty work was done in the [trade] unions.' By "dirty work" he meant HUAC's dirty work because it encouraged the populace to be on the alert for anything that might remotely smack of left-wing thinking. 'They [HUAC] helped to destroy what was left of the progressive radical and liberal movement in the unions, the major unions of the United States ... With the exception of a few unions, all leadership changed as the more radical leaders lost their jobs and that was all due to the Cold War, anti-Communism and stuff like that ... The objective was to strengthen the United States' position in the Cold War, therefore you wouldn't want any major American unions led by radicals who might attack the government for its foreign policies.' The crux of the matter, in his view, was that 'America has no real religion but it has an obsession'; that obsession was anti-Communism but, ironically, he believed that anti-Communism as an obsession was more likely to destroy democracy than Communism itself.

The view of HUAC as a cautionary, rather than a punitive, body was supported by Lionel Stander, who said: 'The purpose of any investigating committee in Congress is to propose legislation. In the many years that this committee was in existence it never proposed one piece of legislation. What it actually did was illegal because the blacklist is illegal. It enabled the industry to blacklist people that the committee didn't like.'

Apart from depriving many people – some, but by no means all, undoubtedly Communists – and alerting the nation to the dangers, real or imaginary, of a Communist takeover it has been argued that HUAC actually achieved nothing. Its investigations and the hours of listening to testimony did not, according to Philip Dunne, unearth anything that was not already known. He said: 'One of the curious things that isn't generally understood is that all through this period the Los Angeles police department had a mole in the Hollywood Communist Party who was in charge of the membership rolls. So they knew exactly who the Communists were.'

In any case and from this distance it's difficult to imagine that anyone ever seriously believed that some kind of Bolshevik revolution would be started in the fleshpots of Beverly Hills or that its insidious message would be disseminated through the medium of popular motion pictures. As Lionel Stander said: 'The industry is engaged in only one thing – that is the production of pictures to make a profit. The power of the industry is based on two big banking groups and you'd have to really be insane to think that they are engaged in the production of Communist propaganda.' Well, perhaps America was collectively insane at that period. Certainly it seemed to abandon the very principles on which the nation was founded, for HUAC's policy of overriding the First and Fifth Amendments to the Constitution appears to have been far more anti-American than it was anti-Communist. If the execution of Admiral Byng was, as Voltaire said, "pour encourager les autres", then perhaps we have to assume that the implacable persecution of a number of wretched cocktail bar Communists in Hollywood was "pour décourager les autres". Whether it actually worked is, I would imagine, impossible to judge. Roy Brewer thought it did but then, no doubt, he would. 'It certainly prevented them taking over the business,' he said. 'I think they would have taken it over because they were really very strong. They controlled producers and money and stars and they made stars and they broke stars. They were very powerful. Anyone who thinks they weren't is not realistic and the average person was scared to death of them.' He was convinced that HUAC had truly cleaned Communism out – 'for the time being. It's infiltrating back in the younger generation, though. They're still there working. They've given up the unions – well, I won't say they've given up but they are very, very astute; they no longer try to get control of the unions, you see. That was where they made their big mistake – when they tried to take control and oust the regular leaders. The unions mobilised against them and they were the force that really defeated them – not only us but the Teamsters and many of the others.'

Well, it's a point of view, though it's hard to think of any Hollywood Communist who could have been said to control producers, money and stars. Nobody with anything like that kind of power seems to have appeared before HUAC. After all, the vast majority of the suspected or admitted Communists who were banned and blacklisted were writers and directors, who were controlled by the producers, who were controlled by the studios, who were controlled by the banks. And I doubt if anyone truly believed that the bankers of America were involved in a Communist plot to overthrow the government.

So in the end it is possible to argue that HUAC did far more harm than good. Because some people testified and others refused – and it's not difficult to understand either point of view – friendships were broken and never repaired. Philip Dunne was at a dinner party in 1986 when a guest, who had been blacklisted, got up and walked out because another guest, who had named names, had come in. Abe Polonsky talked of "stool pigeons", people to whom he had once been very close – 'people who had borrowed money from me, for instance; I mean as close as that' – to whom he had never spoken again. 'But that's because it was too embarrassing to talk to them – it wasn't so much because of hatred.'

Yet there was hatred and bitterness and they still exist, along with suspicion. Evelyn Keyes sees Hollywood as 'a less free and less open society than it was before HUAC'. Martin Ritt, who was blacklisted as a TV director in the early 50s, said: 'There is a residue of bitterness still today. I find it mostly among the wives because they were punished in a way that was very difficult for them to deal with.' (The wives, though entirely blameless whether their husbands were or not, were generally ostracised.) Ritt said: 'I find it quite hard to be bitter, although I'm still angry. I was very lucky. I emerged out of all that, so in all truth the bitterness subsided to some degree but I'm glad to say the anger has never subsided. But some people have never recovered, either from the bitterness on the left or the shame on the right.' (Martin Ritt – who later went on to make *The Front*, in which Woody Allen played a bookmaker who lent his name to blacklisted writers – was taken off the blacklist himself in 1957 to direct *Edge of the City* or, as it was known in Britain, *A Man is Ten Feet Tall*, for MGM. Because he had been on the blacklist he was paid 10,000 dollars for what turned out to be a year and a half's work. 'That's the going rate for a coffee getter,' he said. 'But I was happy to take it.')

As Edward Dmytryk saw it the damage that was done to and within Hollywood during the HUAC years was great and lasting. 'It polarised Hollywood and it's still polarised today. There were many places where I couldn't work even when I was still in the industry and for two reasons: Jack Warner said, "Over my dead body" because I had been a Communist; other liberals said, "Over my dead body" because I was now a renegade ex-Communist.' Howard Koch tended to agree. 'It put fear into people. I have to be careful – "Am I saying the right thing?" and so on. We didn't used to think in those terms; we thought, this is something we do to entertain people and also to make them think about things that matter . . . Now the question is, can we get something done that's not going to step on someone's foot . . . Writers and producers began to feel that we didn't want to get into trouble again.'

Glenn Ford was another who felt that Hollywood had never really recovered. 'It's hard to get anybody to come out and say what's really on their mind about certain political positions taken by the government. They're very reluctant because they don't want to be labelled Communists, so they've got to be careful. There's still a lot of people who remember those Red-baiting days.'

Bitterness still exists in John Bright, who went into self-imposed exile in Mexico for ten years rather than testify and when he returned he was forgotten and his career was virtually over. 'You're only as good as your last picture and when somebody asks what you've done lately and you haven't had your name on a film in ten years . . .' Yet in truth there were others who claimed they had not suffered too much on account of the blacklist. Ring Lardner indeed said that today having been one of the Hollywood Ten was 'almost a badge of honour on the whole. The rare times I go out in Los Angeles to meet younger people in the movie business, they seem to take it as an honour, so there are really no repercussions left over. I even got a letter from the President the other day, thanking me for having supported him in the 1984 election, which I didn't do, and saying that I was one of a special group of people that he was writing to.' Of course, the fact that the special group were those to whom President Reagan was granting the enormous privilege of being allowed to contribute money to the Republican cause in the 1986 Congressional elections took a little of the gloss off the letter but I'm sure Ring Lardner was deeply moved nevertheless.

However, although the blacklist was no longer effective by the mid-1960s, the aftermath of the McCarthy/HUAC investigations lingered on. Controversial subjects were still for the most part avoided in Hollywood films – certainly controversial political subjects – and even the Vietnam War, the most pressing political problem of the decade, was dealt with directly only in one major film, *The Green Berets*, in 1968. But even then the star and co-director John Wayne, and his son and producer, Michael, did not see the picture as a political statement but as a story of good versus bad. As the Duke put it: 'Simple themes save us from the nuances.' Even so the film was condemned by the *New York Times* as a "caricature of patriotism". The audiences liked it, though – enough to place it tenth in the top box office list for 1968, thus indicating that right-wing attitudes were still popular in the American cinema.

This, however, was soon to change and so was Hollywood itself. Towards the end of the 60s the anti-war movement in the USA became ever more vocal and, paradoxically, aggressive. Demonstrations, often violent, took place at the Pentagon in 1967, the Chicago Democratic Convention in 1968 and at universities all over America. For a while this led to a spate of films which, broadly speaking, took the side of youth against the Establishment. *Easy Rider*, the 1969 cult movie made by Peter Fonda and Dennis Hopper about a pair of drug-using, drop-out motorcyclists is probably the prime example but there were many others, among them – and all in 1970 – *Getting Straight* (political comedy set in a college, with Elliott Gould and

Left: John Wayne directing himself and everyone else in *The Green Berets*, his gung-ho endorsement of the Vietnam War
Below: Even boxing got involved with politics when Sylvester Stallone took on the Russkies in *Rocky IV*

Candice Bergen); *The Strawberry Statement* (rebel students occupying college building); *The Revolutionary* (Jon Voight as timeless but sympathetic revolutionary); and *RPM* (meaning "revolutions per minute" and starring Anthony Quinn as a professor spreading liberal ideas in college). With the exception of *Easy Rider* all these were quite dire.

But then, too, there was *Medium Cool*, written, directed and photographed by Haskell Wexler in 1968. The film he made included footage of the riots at the Democratic convention in that year. The protagonist was a TV news cameraman, awakened from his apathy by those very riots. Wexler said: 'I was interested in the effects of television news on all of us; I was interested in the anti-war movement and I was interested in making a film about a person whose profession led him into conflict with accepted ideas.' Unfortunately, that was not the film Paramount was expecting. Paramount was expecting a film about a boy who discovered wild animals living in Manhattan. No doubt this is the sort of trifling misunderstanding that can arise at any time between director and studio but Paramount was not pleased with what it saw. Indeed, the studio was so upset that it discovered all kinds of reasons why it should not release the film at all and Wexler was obliged to go to the Supreme Court to make it do so. He said: 'They then put the film out, reluctantly, with an X rating, keeping young people from going to see it and not spending any money on publicity. They complied with their contractual relationship with me but effectively squashed the film.' The reason, he was convinced, was that the studio was uneasy about the political content, which was undeniably liberal in tone.

If, however, the war itself was absent from the screen during the Vietnam years it was still dealt with, allegorically, in such pictures as *Little Big Man* and *Soldier Blue*, both in 1970, which drastically revised the traditional view of the history of the west by showing the Indians as victims of racism and imperialism. In *Ulzana's Raid*, directed by Robert Aldrich in 1972, both whites and redskins dealt in violent cruelty and savagery. The message here was delivered by the cynical scout Burt Lancaster: 'What bothers you, Lieutenant, is you don't like to think of white men behaving like Indians. Kind of confuses the issue, don't it?' Around the same time films like *Patton* (1969) and *MASH* (1970) took a similarly unheroic view of America's part in World War II and Korea.

It was a time when, briefly, radical opinion was permissible in the movies. In 1975 Bert Schneider, the son of the chairman of Columbia Pictures, produced a documentary called *Hearts and Minds*, a bitter indictment of America's activity in Vietnam. Columbia refused to touch it but it won the Oscar for best documentary and Schneider, accepting the award, read out a "message of goodwill" from the provisional Vietnamese government. The forces of reaction, in the shape of Frank Sinatra, stepped in before the ceremony ended to divorce the Academy from Schneider, his actions and his opinions. But by giving the film the award the Academy voters had shown at least a certain sympathy with Schneider's views.

A year earlier Jane Fonda had not been half so indulgently received when with Haskell Wexler she made her own documentary in Vietnam, *Introduction to the Enemy*. It was made, Wexler said, in the belief that America had been able to wage the war so long only because it had managed to depersonalise the Vietnamese. 'So this film was to show the face of the enemy.' It was violently criticised because 'anyone who was against the war in Vietnam was someone suspect and someone who was less than American.' On the way back from Vietnam, before the film was even finished, Wexler said he was followed about by the CIA at Orly airport in Paris and then questioned for the best part of a day by Customs and Immigration when he returned to America. But as he was to discover, there were worse things to come.

For Miss Fonda, however, there was some kind of official forgiveness in 1978 when she and her co-star Jon Voight both won Oscars for *Coming Home*, the story (written by the formerly blacklisted Waldo Salt) of a paraplegic Vietnam veteran and his love for someone else's wife. It was a pretty slushy tale, not nearly as powerful as *The Deerhunter*, starring Robert de Niro and directed by Michael Cimino which dealt with the tortures inflicted on American prisoners in Vietnam and which won the Academy Award for best picture that year. Better and more harrowing than either of them, though, was Francis Ford Coppola's *Apocalypse Now* which came out in 1979 and concerned itself with the horrors of Vietnam in particular and by extension warfare in general.

There was little heroism in any of those films except *The Deerhunter*, nor was there in the overtly political pictures which made their comeback in the seventies. What these reflected was a deep cynicism about the American political system – hardly surprising perhaps since this was the decade of Watergate and Nixon's disgrace. Two such films were directed by Alan J. Pakula – *The Parallax View*, which showed a successful conspiracy by big business to assassinate the President, and *All the President's Men*, the story of the unravelling of the Watergate affair by two *Washington Post* journalists. Pakula described the first of these pictures as "the death of the American hero" and the second as "the rebirth of the American hero". The newly resurrected American hero was to remain with us from then on but, as time went by, in a very different form.

On the whole the seventies represented the decade in which the liberals struck back or, at least, came out of hiding. Once more "the system" was being questioned in films as it had not been since the end of the 1930s. But this is not to say that the Establishment was entirely happy or quiescent. It, too, could strike back as Haskell Wexler discovered first when he was mysteriously removed – in his view by the intervention of the FBI, though he cannot prove it – from his job as cinematographer on *One Flew Over the Cuckoo's Nest* and later when he made a cinéma vérité documentary about a group called the Weathermen. 'These were a sort of residue of the old students' left-wing movements. They were in hiding and they had allegedly and, I think, actually engaged in certain violent acts that didn't result in the killing of anybody. But in my opinion it's safe to say they *were* violent acts – bombs and so on.' Contact was made with this group and the filming was arranged, a cloak and dagger business involving phone calls from certain booths, appointments at certain times in certain parks, hiding on the floor in the back of cars – even a man with a beard turned up. Wexler said it wasn't a very good documentary and I think he agreed to make it mainly out of curiosity. But when it was finished he and the other film makers involved were subpoenaed by the FBI and ordered to turn over all the tapes and film.

'We refused to do it,' Wexler said. 'We felt it was our First Amendment right not to turn over what essentially were our journalistic notes. So we told them that when we had finished the film they were welcome to see it but we wouldn't turn anything over . . . Then the FBI took a very strong stand and we were on our way to jail until the Hollywood community came to our defence in force. I mean many, many, many names, people who were not generally considered part of any left-wing groups in Hollywood, signed petitions asking that we should not be subpoenaed . . . and the FBI withdrew the subpoenas and we were exonerated.'

The sting in the tail to all that came a few years later when Wexler asked, as he was entitled to, for a copy of his personal FBI file and found a page on which were printed: Name – Haskell Wexler; Nationality – Jewish . . . The FBI, he said, still takes a close interest in Hollywood film makers 'because they recognise the tremendous force, the tremendous power to influence other people'. But if it's watching now, in the late 1980s – and somehow I feel sure it is – it must feel happier about what it sees, for the era of liberal expression appears to have passed and a new, fierce patriotism whose political message, crudely expressed, is far to the right of centre has taken its place.

Perhaps the first indication of this gung-ho, red-blooded Americanism came with John Milius' *Red Dawn* and it came unexpectedly, since the film followed within a year or two of *Reds*, in which Warren Beatty played John Reed as a heroic, idealistic American Communist (albeit back in 1917) and *Missing* and *Under Fire*, both of which were critical indictments of contemporary US involvement with repressive right-wing movements in South America.

Red Dawn was something of a revelation, not artistically because it was a simplistic, comic book sort of story which predicated that the Russians and the Cubans had, for some reason which escaped most onlookers, chosen to invade a small town somewhere in middle America. The invaders were shown to be heartless killers of women and children but wholly inefficient warriors, since they were harried and harassed and more or less decimated by a handful of high school kids who took to the hills and waged guerrilla warfare on them. The effect of the film was astonishing: audiences throughout the United States flocked to it and screamed their approval and it was openly and publicly admired by President Reagan and General Alexander Haig, who described it as 'an important, realistic and provocative lesson on the need to maintain our military strength'. John Milius declared himself happy with these endorsements. 'I think the Russians needed to hear that,' he said. 'They'd just shot down an airliner full of women and children and, you know, people don't seem to remember that.' So it was a political statement he was making? 'Yeah. It was "don't tread on me".'

To be fair he also claimed that *Red Dawn* was an anti-war movie because nobody was seen to win in the end but it was hardly perceived that way by the mass of the audience. And the films that followed it, no doubt inspired by its financial success, could not remotely be described as anti-war. They reached their apotheosis or, depending on the way you look at it, their nadir in *Rambo: First Blood Part II* in which the American hero, as personified by Sylvester Stallone, returned as a one-man killing machine, slaughtering Russians and Vietnamese alike and, as it were, rewriting history to give the Vietnam War a happy ending from the American point of view. A kind of poor man's Rambo was provided by Chuck Norris in *Missing in Action* and *Invasion USA*. In the first he, like Stallone, rescued American prisoners of war in Vietnam single-handedly and in the second saved America from a Russo-Cuban invasion, again single-handedly. In both he killed positive hordes of people.

As a diversion from this warlike stuff, Stallone cropped up in his pugilistic guise in *Rocky IV* to demolish a Russian heavyweight and sneer at the Communist way of life. So, in a sense, the wheel has turned full circle and the Russians are identified, if anything even more clearly than they were in the films of the fifties, as the enemy. In all these contemporary films they were depicted as brutal and rather stupid – no match for one determined and well-armed American. At a time when the leaders of Russia and the United States are at least paying lip service to the idea of getting together to do something about the arms race and bring about international peace, the making of crude propaganda pictures of this kind would hardly seem to further anybody's cause.

It could be said that they mirror the current mood of America – a country that has decided the time has come to stop apologising for the Vietnam War, beating its breast and crying "Mea culpa" and instead to stand up straight and pat itself on the back. Certainly the attitude within the United States during the 1984 Olympic Games in Los Angeles seemed to be "we are the greatest". John Milius, however, had a different interpretation. *Rambo*, *Rocky IV* and the Chuck Norris films, he thought, reflected 'a feeling of the American people that they're sick of being pushed around by the Soviet Union. I think people are sick of thirty years of tension and they're telling it to their own leaders, too. They're saying, "Do something about it, one way or the other" . . . These films are really a boost in a way to a country that has a sagging morale as far as its ability, its military potency goes . . . I mean, Rambo is almost like a religious figure, who can do no wrong. He slays the enemy that the rest of us can't slay . . .'

On the wider question of whether Hollywood films were really able to convey political points of view, either left or right, he said: 'They help. They help the tone of the country. Throughout the 60s and 70s there was certainly a leftist tone that came out of Hollywood and it reached almost ridiculous proportions. Now that seems to have turned around and I hope it'll be a little more even-handed. I'm not in favour of the right either, believe me; I do not like my country's foreign policy. You can pick holes in it all day long and I certainly don't want to get involved in a war in Central America, another Vietnam. But at the same time I want the Russians to know that they cannot run rabid all around the world either. And I think Reagan has done a good job with them in that category.'

Abraham Polonsky, on the other hand, declared that no political films were currently being made in Hollywood, no films that had a political philosophy. Not even *Rambo*? 'That's different,' he said. 'That's only political in the easy sense of the word. The United States makes lots of films like that from time to time, all countries do. I mean, Rambo went to Vietnam and won the war which we lost and made everybody happy. That's not a big important thing.' The true significance of *Rambo*, he thought, was that 'it happens to be one of the few movies the President of the United States can understand'.

Would it be easy, though, to make a political film in Hollywood today, one with a political philosophy? The consensus of opinion seemed to be that as ever – except during the madness of the HUAC years – everything would depend on its box-office prospects. The bankers, after all, are still in charge. But, I said to Martin Ritt, if you want to make a political film would it generally speaking be easier to make one that was in favour of the status quo?

'Yes,' he said. 'Unequivocally, yes.'

Well, that's no great revelation: the status quo has an abiding appeal among all Establishments at all times. But the political status quo in the United States at the moment is considerably further to the right than it was in all but the last two years of the 1947–54 HUAC period, so perhaps it's not entirely coincidental that the vast majority of films coming out of Hollywood today are either staunchly conservative (where they have any political point of view at all) or totally anodyne, escapist box office fodder for the young and/or unthinking. Economic forces may well have much to do with that but it is also possible that something of the atmosphere of those years of the witch hunts, which stirred up fear and suspicion and turned long-time friends into lifelong enemies, still prevails. When I asked around among the people I interviewed to discover whether they thought anything like HUAC could happen again, the overall impression was that yes, they thought it could. Not HUAC itself but the spirit of HUAC – something much subtler, less overt; no public hearings but assiduous working behind the scenes. Maybe something like that – the sorting out of "undesirables" whether political or otherwise – is going on now; maybe it goes on in every industry.

But in fact the McCarthy/HUAC era only came about through the historical accident of the two antagonists, America and Russia, sharing a common enemy – Nazi Germany – that worried them both. Unless and until such an eventuality occurs again and Russia is once more seen to be the lesser of two evils, anyone – no matter how devout a Communist – who even tried to infiltrate pro-Soviet propaganda into a Hollywood film would have to be practically certifiable. Apart from anything else the money men wouldn't allow it because it doesn't work at the box office. Quite certainly there are still Communists in America but I should be very surprised if any of them are trying to make a living and spread propaganda as scriptwriters in Hollywood.

THE B MOVIE

The director George Sherman was looking around one day for an actor to play a small supporting role in the film he had just embarked upon. Other directors making other films at other studios would, naturally, have consulted the casting office; Sherman, working at Republic Studios, consulted the wardrobe department.

'Right,' said the wardrobe department when the problem had been outlined. 'I got a size 40 suit and a $7\frac{1}{2}$ hat and that's all I got, okay? So don't go bringing me some seven-foot guy, because I can't go out and rent the clothes.' And in that sort of way, said Sherman, the minor casting at Republic was always done by the wardrobe people. 'We'd bring an actor in and we'd look at him and the first thing we'd ask is "How tall are you?" We'd say, "What's your hat size?" And the guy would look at us ...' Sherman assumed an expression of some bemusement to show how the guy would look at them and it's not difficult to understand the guy's point of view. To lose a part in a film because you are too old or too young, too fair or too dark is one thing: to lose it because the studio didn't have a hat to fit you is a little hard to take.

But then Republic was a studio that made B pictures and in B pictures you didn't spend money. You improvised. If you only had a small horse you found a small rider for it; if you only had two left boots you hired an actor with two left feet. All right, so maybe he wasn't Gable – but could Gable wear two left boots? 'We used what was available to us,' Sherman said, 'and that was really the beauty of the business.'

Besides, parsimony was rather appropriate because the B picture was a child of the Depression. Between 1930 and 1933 cinema attendances fell from around ninety million a week to sixty million. Work and money were increasingly hard to find and the customary fare of a single feature film supported by cartoons and shorts was beginning to lose its appeal. So the double-bill was introduced offering not one feature but two to three hours of entertainment instead of a mere two hours or so and all at the same price. The Depression audiences reckoned this was a bargain and the fact that the second movie was a low-budget quickie, featuring the only actors in town who could get into the clothes, was neither here nor there. Never mind the quality, feel the width.

'A B picture,' said Nick Grinde, a director speaking with the authority of one who rarely made anything but B pictures, 'isn't a big picture that just didn't grow up: it's exactly what it started out to be. It's the 22 dollar suit of the clothing business; it's the hamburger of the butchers' shops; it's a seat in the bleachers – and there's a big market for all of them.' As early as 1932 the cinemas and therefore the industry as a whole had begun to realise just how sizeable that market was; in 1935 the two big chains, RKO and Loew's, adopted the double-bill in all their principal theatres; by the following year eighty-five per cent of American cinemas had followed suit and to fill the increased demand for product the major studios had set up their own B units, run by men with expertise in turning out films quickly and cheaply. At Paramount there was Sol C. Siegel; at Warners Brian Foy, director of *Lights of New York* but henceforth to be known as "the keeper of the Bs"; Lucien Hubbard and Michael Fessier jointly controlled matters at MGM; Irving Briskin was at Columbia and at Fox there were Ben Stoloff and Sol Wurtzel of whom it was said, I expect with affection, "from bad to Wurtzel".

The studios, in fact, were not unhappy with this new development because it helped to pay the overheads. The B pictures, according to Vincent Sherman who worked for a time for Brian Foy at Warners, were called "the bread and butter pictures". He said: 'Let's say, for instance, at Warners you'd got maybe twenty or thirty writers under contract, maybe eight or ten directors, eight or ten producers and a stable of stars and lesser players. Well, that means you had to be turning out material. It was like a factory making shirts or shoes or suits of clothing. If people aren't producing and are lying idle, then you're losing money because you've got a weekly payroll to meet. And so the B pictures kept the studios going. Brian used to make, oh, I think he made thirty or forty films a year – B pictures only. I think sometimes he used to make fifty and sixty pictures. So every week he would throw something into production, sometimes with three or four days' notice.'

But in addition to sparing the moguls the anguish and the deep ache in the wallet that came from seeing highly paid employees loafing about, waiting for something to turn up, the B movies served another purpose: they provided a training ground for new talent. In the early 30s William Wyler made low-grade comedies at Universal and at the same time George Stevens was directing such epics as *The Cohens and the Kellys In Trouble*. Edward Dmytryk served a long apprenticeship in B pictures, directing films like *Confessions of Boston Blackie* for Columbia and *Captive Wild Woman* for Universal. Fred Zinnemann had a spell in the B unit at MGM and Mark Robson and Robert Wise learned their trade under Val Lewton at RKO.

'When you were down the scale as a novice director,' Zinnemann said, 'you would be told what you'd got to do. They'd say, "Here's the script. You start in four weeks. Susan Klutz is going to play the lead . . ." You didn't really have much leeway. People would say, "How's your picture?" and you'd say, "About 10,000 feet." There wasn't much respect for the B movie.'

Not much artistic respect, perhaps, but a lot of appreciation in the accounts department. Edward Dmytryk said: 'We knew that if we made a Boris Karloff picture for, let's say, 100,000 dollars it had to make money. Because there were enough Karloff fans in the world to make money on a 100,000 dollar picture. If it went to 120,000, we didn't make money . . . A "Boston Blackie" picture could make so much money, no more, no less. But almost every studio could pay its expenses with the Bs. They took their chances with the As but the Bs paid – they kept people working, they kept crews working so that studios were able to do something they can't do today, keep people on salary throughout the year.'

It was not, however, only famous directors who cut their teeth on low budget quickies – many of the stars did, too. Lana Turner, Judy Garland and Donna Reed all got some of their earlier breaks playing opposite the diminutive Mickey Rooney in the "Andy Hardy" series; Ava Gardner was in a number of B pictures before receiving promotion to the first division in 1946 after appearing with Burt Lancaster in *The Killers*; and Elizabeth Taylor first came to public attention when she co-starred with a dog in *Lassie Come Home*. Glenn Ford reckoned he had appeared in 222 films – most of them now consigned to oblivion, being the kind of pictures you forget even while you're watching them – on account of his training in the B unit at Columbia. 'It would turn out a film every five days and you had to work awfully hard. The hours were usually from six in the morning until ten, eleven at night and you had to learn your craft . . . You were never allowed over two takes. If it wasn't good on the first or second take, they'd print it anyway, so it got you to the point where you could go onto the set of any studio on any film and, boy!, were you ready.' If he could wish young actors anything at all nowadays, he said, he would wish them a B unit where they could learn.

So the B unit was a training ground and it paid the overheads. But it could also be used by the shrewder moguls as a kind of cinematic Siberia for recalcitrant actors and a conveyor belt for the recycling of old stars. In 1939, having incurred Warner Brothers' wrath, Humphrey Bogart was sentenced to play a moronic thug in something called *King of the Underworld*, which some reference books do not even mention at all, possibly out of a sense of tact or human decency. Meanwhile, people like Richard Arlen, Warner Baxter and Richard Dix, all of whom had been big stars in their time ended their days lending a bit of nostalgic clout to daft second features, a salutary reminder of the eternal truth of the maxim: be nice to people on the way up because you never know when you might need them on the way down. Not, I'm sure, that the Arlens, Baxters and Dixes minded too much for after all working in a B picture is better than not working at all, an attitude adopted by Kay Francis when Warners was trying to force her to break her contract. The honourable motive behind the studio's action was that Miss Francis was no longer quite as big a star as she had once been but she was still under contract and still costing them 5,000 dollars a week and the parting with every cent of it was as a knife stuck into the collective heart of the brothers Warner. It was Jack, ever the action man of the family, who came up with the bright idea.

'He thought: I'll give her to Brian Foy. She won't want to make a picture with Foy, so she'll walk out on her contract,' said Vincent Sherman. 'But Kay said later, she said, "As long as they pay me my salary, I'll sweep the stages if they give me a broom." So Foy called me one day and said, "I'm going to do a picture with Francis. We're gonna remake *Dr Socrates*", which had been made originally with Paul Muni. I said, "Well, which part is Francis gonna play?" He said, "She's gonna play the Paul Muni part . . ." and she did. We made the picture.' And what was that picture called? Why, *King of the Underworld*, featuring a certain H. Bogart as a moronic thug. 'Nothing I'm proud of,' said Sherman, 'but we made it in sixteen, seventeen, eighteen days – something like that.'

Now hitherto we have been discussing the luxury end of the B picture trade – astronomical budgets of 100,000 dollars or so and leisurely shooting schedules of up to eighteen days. But these idyllic conditions were only to be found in the B units of the major studios. In lesser places, like Republic, time and money were much tighter.

George Sherman started at Republic as an assistant director on 125 dollars a week. But he was ambitious, a young man eager to get on. He wanted to be a director, so they made him one – at 100 dollars a week. 'I took a 25 dollar cut to become a director,' he said. 'I had 25 dollar options every six months. It was amazing. Every time, a week before the option was due – and it was their option, not mine – the general manager, a guy by the name of Manny Goldstein, would call me into the office. He had a stern face and he'd say to me, "Who do you think you are – Frank Capra?" And I'd say, "Why?" and he'd say, "You've got a 25 dollar raise coming up and you're not worth it." And I never did get that bloody raise . . .' An exaggeration. When he left the studio he was earning 250 dollars a week but that was a good many years later.

Republic was owned by Herbert Yates, a former tobacco sales executive who had moved into the film business to make Fatty Arbuckle movies in 1910. Then he set up a processing laboratory and as Sherman said "parleyed that" through consolidations and mergers into Republic Picture Corporation, of which he became president and chairman of the board. As time went by Yates grew ambitious for greater things. Sherman said: 'He hired John Ford and gave him carte blanche and he aspired to make the place a major studio. But one of the troubles with Republic was that there was a stigma attached to the name. We were making cheap melodramas. We tried to do them as well as we could with the money and the schedules but if you came from Republic Studios it was difficult to get a job anywhere else. We specialised in B films and everybody turned their backs on you, even though working at the studio was a delight and a joy. It was great while I was there.'

A delight and a joy perhaps but never easy. The budgets were between 50,000 and 60,000 dollars, the shooting schedules five or six days per film. 'If it rained one day you had to pick up that day on the next picture. Consequently we shot films back to back.' On western series like "The Three Mesquiteers", which starred John Wayne, life could be even harder; sometimes the budgets were as little as 45,000 dollars. 'At that time actors like Wayne were getting 1,000, 1,200 bucks a film. I remember Gene Autry complaining bitterly because Wayne was getting 1,250 and Autry was only getting 1,000 dollars to make a picture.'

In such working conditions it was vital to stay within the limits imposed by the studio. The unforgivable crime was to go over budget or over schedule. There was no time for fine editing. 'I cut the film in the camera,' Sherman said. 'In other words, I knew exactly how much footage I needed; I knew how long the scene should run and when I felt there was enough I said, "Cut". We spent hardly any time in the editing room. When I'd finished a film I would look at it with the studio executives and they'd cut fifteen, twenty feet and ship it.' Most pictures, especially westerns, were filmed outdoors, because it was cheaper, and usually at the same place – a location called Garden of the Gods – because it was close at hand. Since the same locations and very often much the same script material were used from one film to another, considerable ingenuity was required – shooting from different angles and in different light – to avoid evoking a powerful sense of déjà vu in the audiences. This was rendered more difficult because Republic never used stock material. 'We never had a stock library,' Sherman said, 'because they couldn't afford to buy the material. You buy for five or ten dollars a foot but we could shoot it cheaper than that.'

In the end, though, he thought the best technique for staying within the limitations was by 'just being goddamn fast on your feet. Just know what the hell you're doing; be prepared; never stop to go to the water cooler and have a drink of water; never stop to talk; never stop to have a cup of coffee . . .' And this was a delight and a joy? Yes, it was, he said, because Republic was very much a family studio. 'Everything had to be done in a helluva hurry. Nobody made much money. We worked Saturdays until midnight and on Sundays I used to look for locations for the following show. It really wasn't necessary because we generally shot them in the same area but we always went looking for another way to shoot a scene. It was a very family, very happy place.'

There were, however, complications, especially when Herbert Yates fell in love with a former Czechoslovak skating champion named Vera Hruba Ralston and determined to make her a movie star, with the assistance of George Sherman. 'I was in the unfortunate position of having to direct two pictures with her,' Sherman said, 'and then he wanted me to continue. But I knew it would be destructive to my career if I stayed with Vera. She was a very nice girl, a good ice skater but she'd had no training as an actress – she had a blinding ambition to be one, combined with a lack of ability.' The two films he made with her were *The Lady and the Monster*, a science fiction effort, and *Storm Over Lisbon*, a weary imitation of *Casablanca*, both of which co-starred Erich von Stroheim. The public didn't like those much, any more than it liked Miss Ralston's twenty-four other films but Yates persisted in his attempt to make her a star because 'that was a love affair. He was married and he had a family in New York or wherever but he was madly in love with her – an old man in love with a young girl. And, you know, love wins over all . . .'

Well, indeed it does – or, in this case, it almost did. Yates' infatuation with Miss Ralston made him a laughing stock in Hollywood and came close to destroying the studio. But he did marry her eventually, in 1952 when he was seventy-two and she was thirty-one. Before then, however, his obsession had caused most of his top executives – and George Sherman – to leave the studio. 'He was a very domineering man and insisted on having everything his way. When I made those two pictures with Vera he had his office moved to the set so he could control her. In other words, I had no function as a director as far as she was concerned. She came on the set already prepared by Yates.' Seeing no future in this, especially as Yates wanted him to continue working with Miss Ralston, he asked for and was granted a release from his contract, which still had three or four years to run.

Yates, though, was game to the last. Even though he had been deserted by his trusty staff he continued to try hoisting Republic up the studio hierarchy and in the mid-1940s, a time when production costs were rising by sixty per cent, he devised an ingenious scheme to enhance his studio's image. He organised Republic's production into four categories. First, there were "Jubilee" pictures, almost exclusively westerns such as *Night Riders of Montana* and *Dakota Kid*, that were shot in seven days and on 50,000 dollar budgets.

Then, one step up the scale, came the "Anniversary" pictures – *Old Amarillo* and *Havana Rose*, for instance – which had two-week schedules and cost between 175,000 and 200,000 dollars. Loftier still were the "Deluxe" movies – *The Black Hills* or *Fighting US Coast Guard*, comparatively lavish efforts at 500,000 dollars apiece and taking twenty-two days to shoot. And finally, top of the market, came the "Premiere" films, genuine main features such as John Ford's *Rio Grande* and *The Quiet Man*, Allan Dwan's *Sands of Iwo Jima* and Orson Welles' *Macbeth*. Vera Hruba Ralston, meanwhile, was still plugging away at the B pictures and failing signally to become a star to anyone but Yates.

Unfortunately the attempt to shove the studio up market came too late. For reasons which we shall look into later the B picture was already on the way out. Nevertheless Yates kept Republic in business until he resigned in July 1959, soon after which the premises were sold to CBS television. One way or another a similar sort of fate befell all the studios specialising in B films: Monogram, Grand National and the like. In the 1940s and 1950s particularly they merged, emerged, remerged, re-emerged and changed their names frequently in an increasingly desperate bid to keep going. Monogram merged with Allied Artists; from the ashes of Grand National rose an ailing Phoenix with an identity crisis, being called at one time or another Progressive Pictures, Producers' Distributing Corporation, Sigmund Neufeld Production and finally Producers Releasing Corporation. But that, too, vanished in 1947 when it was absorbed into Eagle-Lion, a distribution company owned by J. Arthur Rank. In the end all the B studios had to die because their market was gone along with the glorious days of the 30s when, as another noted B movie director Joseph H. Lewis recalled, it was possible to make an episode in a western series for as little as 12,000 dollars. No, not just possible – obligatory.

Lewis, director of such classics as *Singing Outlaw*, *Invisible Ghost* and *The Mad Doctor of Market Street*, remembered with nostalgia the first film he ever made. 'It was a six-day western, shot back to back with another western. I finished one today and tomorrow I started the other. Well, I couldn't possibly conceive of preparing two pictures at once so I thought, Joey, just do the first one and let the second come warmly and naturally and it worked very nicely.' Were they very different in context though, the two films? 'Heck no, they were all the same, those westerns.'

He had no regrets about making such pictures – it was a way of going to school in the business, growing up, paying your dues. And it taught him discipline, because when the studio said, 'Look, we got to take six days over this film; we get just so much for it and not a dime more, so if you go one hour over we've lost the profit,' he knew they meant it. 'I've seen the time, in the middle of a scene, when they'd pull the switch and all the lights would go out. "That's a wrap, gentlemen", that's how strict they were.'

For him, as for George Sherman, improvisation was a necessity and he rose to the challenge triumphantly enough to earn the honourable soubriquet of "Waggonwheel Joe". 'In those days, when I was shooting those six-day westerns, we had no actors. We'd use a cowboy who brought his own horse and would speak the lines and he was disgraceful. I thought, What the devil can I do about this? Well, we had a sort of stock company of waggon wheels – spokes this wide and that wide, you know, unusual wheels and I'd put one in front of the camera and shoot through the spokes and before you could analyse the scene it was over. You knew, artistically, it was very nice ... They accused me of making picture postcards and finally they gave me the name of "Waggonwheel Joe" but I had to do that because I had no actors.'

At Monogram it was very much the same, according to Walter Mirisch. He joined the company around 1947 as a graduate of the Harvard Business School and was promptly made producer of a film called *Fall Guy*, another effort that is decently ignored by a good many reference books. 'Generally speaking,' he said, 'Monogram did series pictures. After my first film I decided that if I was going to remain with a company like that I would have to find myself a series. So I got the idea to do a junior Tarzan type picture which was called *Bomba: the Jungle Boy*. It starred a young man named Johnny Sheffield, who'd played Johnny Weissmuller's son in the Tarzan series and that became the basis for the early years of my career. We made two of those films a year and I think eventually twelve of them were made.' The "Bomba" series, along with the Bowery Boys and Charlie Chan pictures, helped to keep Monogram afloat until, in 1953, it gave up the struggle and became Allied Artists. The studio had begun as Monogram in 1930 and in the early years made a brave bid for the quality market with screen adaptations of *Oliver Twist*, *Black Beauty* and *The Moonstone*. But, like other B studios, Monogram had great difficulty in persuading well-known actors to work there. Of course, they did sign Cagney – but, alas, not James Cagney, only his obscure brother William, who made a number of undistinguished thrillers before turning producer and making films of his own, which were equally undistinguished. In the 1930s Monogram had been Republic's main rival in the field of low budget westerns, serials and action pictures but it was usually outgunned, although in this case it was a matter of comparing a small pea-shooter with a larger pea-shooter. Whereas Republic's cowboy stars included the then unknown John Wayne, Gene Autry and Roy Rogers, Monogram's were the even less known Bill Cody, Tim McCoy and Tex Ritter, who were rather lower down the scale of B movie stars, as was Bob Steele, whom both studios employed at one time or another. Still, the studio aroused enough affection in cinéastes for Jean-Luc Godard to dedicate his first film, *Breathless*, to Monogram.

Walter Mirisch, of course, went on to form the Mirisch Company Inc with his two brothers, Marvin and Harold, to become president of the Academy of Motion Picture Arts and Sciences, to win the Irving Thalberg Memorial Award during the Oscar ceremony of 1978 and generally to become a most respected elder statesman of the movie colony. But it was Monogram that he used in the early years as a stepping stone to these higher things.

In his time there, he said, the budgets were around 80-90,000 dollars and the profit margins were 'very slight'. It was he who, in the early 1950s, tried to upgrade the studio's product, just as Yates was doing, or attempting to do, at Republic. 'A great many rather good so-called "nervous B films" came out of that period, films I'm still quite proud of – *The Invasion of the Body Snatchers*, for example; *The Phenix City Story*; *Riot in Cell Block 11*, films of that nature, exploitation films, I suppose, based on current social problems.' But before this attempt to inject a little depth, or if not depth then a touch of quality, into the product Monogram had been 'I suppose more of a factory. You were very limited in your expectations. You didn't dare go very far over budget or schedule and there wasn't any of the excitement or the romance of the big films.'

Nevertheless, B films could be pretty lucrative. When Huntz Hall, Leo Gorcey and the Dead End Kids had been transformed, partly because of copyright problems connected with the name, into the Bowery Boys and had been turned from a gang of street toughs into a gang of lovable clowns they made a lot of money for Monogram. Huntz Hall said: 'They used to put big MGM pictures into little towns in the west and the Bowery Boys would get top billing above them.' Hall refused to recognise a difference in quality between an A and a B picture, preferring loftily to quote Federico Fellini's dictum that greatness came from B pictures because they had to be inventive. If you accept this and apply it to your own work it must take much of the sting out of the knowledge that, slice it where you like, yours is still a B picture.

'Some of the greatest were B pictures,' said Hall, stoutly, and he claimed he was happier at Monogram than at bigger studios. 'I went in and did my job in six or eight days and goodbye, I'll see you in three months. I was unhappy when I was under contract: I couldn't do anything elsewhere. But when I did the Bowery Boys films I made four a year and between times I could do anything I wanted. I could do a play between times. I made a lot of money. We each had a third of the picture, we got up-front money – 10,000 dollars a film each – and our percentages and we were free. I was making a quarter of a million dollars a year. What did I care if they wanted to hire me at MGM? I didn't care.' Nor did he care that for much of his career he had been associated in the public mind with just one character, that of Satch in the Bowery Boys. To most people, he said, Satch was a buffoon but to him ... 'He was a Walter Mitty. He lived in a dream world. He wasn't a buffoon, he was the guy that got everybody into a situation and he got 'em out of it, so you had to be a good, good actor.' Certainly you had to have a good memory. 'You worked twelve hours a day and you did ten pages. At MGM you might do three pages in four days. Monogram was the training ground for some of the greatest people today who are producers, who are directors, who worked that studio because it was the learning ground. It was the greatest training in the world. We never believed in cutting. We'd say, If we can get it in one take, keep it that way, don't break it up, don't cut into a close-up because it's better in medium shot.'

When he started at Monogram, he said, the budgets were 36,000 dollars. 'We used short ends. You know what short ends are? If you have a thousand feet of film in a camera and there's 100 feet left at the end of the day, Monogram would buy that 100 feet and use it. So instead of paying three cents a foot, they'd pay a penny a foot. You had a scene that ran 50 feet, they'd use a short end.' Sometimes they seemed to use scripts like short ends, too. 'We used to take scripts and rewrite them and put different names in them. It was the same story but with different names and different locations. I mean, like the Bowery Boys were sixty per cent improvisation. Actors were free.'

Invention, innovation, improvisation – these, he thought as others did, were the hallmarks of the B picture and, he added, defiantly, 'I've seen more great B pictures than great A pictures', a claim which I should have thought would be hard to substantiate and perhaps he thought so, too, because he didn't try.

Meanwhile, back at the luxury end of the business – the B units of the major studios – life was always a little easier. Budgets of up to 250,000 dollars were permissible and, unlike Monogram and Republic, the likes of MGM and Warner Brothers had vast libraries of stock footage as well as standing sets that could be used and reused. When, in 1941, Vincent Sherman was making an anti-Nazi film called *Underground* he used most of the sets from *Confessions of a Nazi Spy*. The apartment house in *Cat People* was actually the mansion built for Orson Welles' *The Magnificent Ambersons*. Action sequences from Wesley Ruggles' 1931 production of *Cimarron* cropped up time and again in succeeding westerns. And, of course, the plots were constantly regurgitated. In 1932 Howard Hawks made *Tiger Shark* for Warners; in 1936 the same story reappeared as *Bengal Tiger*, only now instead of two men, one girl and a shark there were two men, one girl and a tiger. When a film was finished at Warners, apparently, the script was placed at the bottom of a huge pile. New writers would be instructed by Brian Foy to take one from the top and rework it.

Sometimes original scripts were written, though. Vincent Sherman who, in the late 30s was a writer at Warners, said: 'I did a film once with Kay Francis. It was called *My Bill*, not a very good picture. Johnny Farrow directed it. He called me on a Thursday and said, "I gotta have a script Monday morning". And, believe it or not, I worked Thursday night, Friday, Friday night, Saturday, Sunday – Monday morning I gave him a script and I think next Thursday we started shooting.'

But most of the films from Brian Foy's unit were, as Sherman said, 'quick remakes of A pictures, with a little twist, a little change of background and character. The first film I ever worked on was a Bogart picture called *Crime School*, a B picture with the Dead End Kids. I'd only been in the studio three or four months when Foy said, "We're gonna do this *Crime School*. Use half of *The Mayor of Hell* (an old Cagney picture) and half of *San Quentin* (that had been made with Annie Sheridan and Pat O'Brien) and put the two together." Some of it didn't make any sense so I had to fix things to get it right but it was very successful. That little film, *Crime School*, cost 186,000 dollars to make and grossed over two million dollars.'

Needless to say, though, movies cobbled together in this haphazard fashion and then shot on the run were often packed with glorious howlers. Ralph Bellamy remembered with a great deal of quiet joy a Pat O'Brien picture in which in one scene the set consisted of three rooms – the entry hall, the dining-room and the kitchen. 'The walls had been taken out so the camera could follow a person from the front door into the kitchen. The person was Pat O'Brien. He came in the front door, went through the entrance hall, put a cigar in his mouth and came through the kitchen door smoking a cigarette.'

Left: The B movie as
training ground for
talent: doleful Mickey
Rooney with his *Andy
Hardy* co-stars Judy
Garland, Ann Ruther-
ford and Lana Turner
Above: Even Elizabeth
Taylor – E.T. herself –
did her stint in B pix,
lending support to Lassie

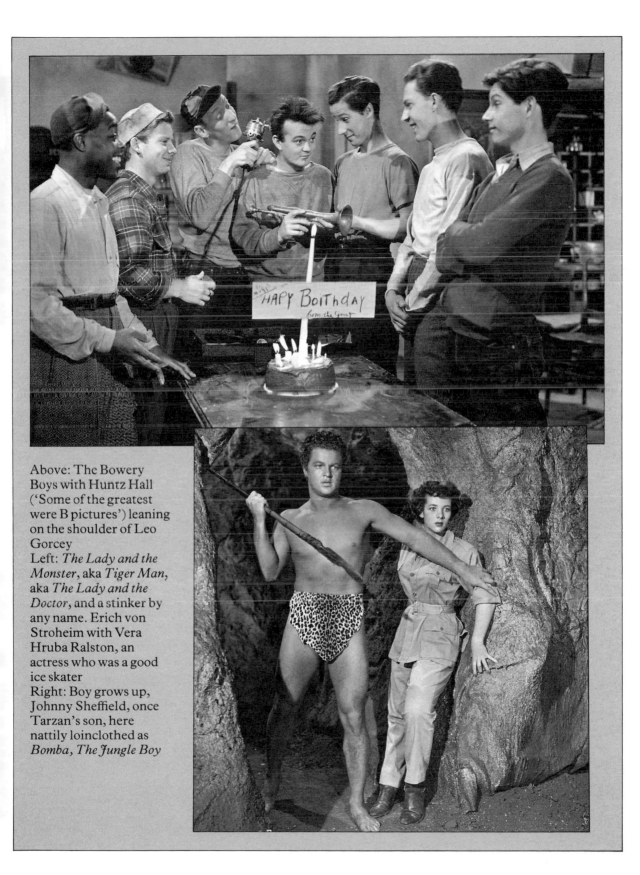

Above: The Bowery Boys with Huntz Hall ('Some of the greatest were B pictures') leaning on the shoulder of Leo Gorcey

Left: *The Lady and the Monster*, aka *Tiger Man*, aka *The Lady and the Doctor*, and a stinker by any name. Erich von Stroheim with Vera Hruba Ralston, an actress who was a good ice skater

Right: Boy grows up, Johnny Sheffield, once Tarzan's son, here nattily loinclothed as *Bomba, The Jungle Boy*

Bellamy made B pictures himself, shooting anything up to twenty pages a day sometimes. 'You worked six days a week and sometimes seven, until Sunday noon when the leading lady fainted or something. Harry Cohn told me once that any picture that cost less than 150,000 dollars would make money. In those days the big pictures, the A pictures, cost between five and 800,000.' Like many others he spent much of his career moving fairly smoothly between A pictures, such as *The Awful Truth* and *His Girl Friday*, and Bs, including the Ellery Queen series. Mae Clarke was another whose career alternated between the two, a fact which she explained philosophically: 'It's better to keep working, no matter what. There are no small parts – just small actors.'

At Republic and the other independent studios, said Joseph H. Lewis, they turned out B pictures "like sausages"; so they did at the majors but at least there it was possible to graduate to bigger and better things, although it was never easy. When he was head of the script department at MGM, Sam Marx submitted a story he had written himself as a vehicle for Clark Gable. The studio liked the script well enough, but not for Gable. They thought it would be more suitable for, well, Arlington Brew. Arlington who? Marx rushed into Louis Mayer's office. 'Mr Mayer,' he said, 'I did this kind of just for you and just for the studio. I wish you'd put Gable in it. I think it's good enough for him.' No use. Mayer delivered a lecture about how Gable was already established and Arlington Brew wasn't although, said Mayer, mark his words this Brew was a potential million dollar star for MGM. So Marx's projected A film for Gable became a B film for Arlington Brew. The picture was called *Society Doctor* and Arlington Brew was called Robert Taylor, under which more fortunate name he did indeed become a million dollar star.

Sometimes B movies could transcend their lowly origins and develop a prestige or even cult following of their own. Much of the early work of Don Siegel (*Invasion of the Body Snatchers*, for instance) comes into that category, though such pictures were often what Walter Mirisch called "nervous Bs" to begin with, which is to say that they were conceived as at least very superior Bs. Joseph H. Lewis' *My Name is Julia Ross* helped to make him an idol of the French – and later other – critics. The reputation of Sam Fuller, described by the critic Andrew Sarris as "an authentic American primitive", rests almost entirely on a string of B movies. Joseph L. Mankiewicz, however, was said by Sam Marx to have been promoted to producer of A's because he made such a mess of his first and only B film. It was made in 1936, was called *The Three Godfathers* and must never be confused with the film of the same name directed a decade or so later by John Ford. Marx said: 'It was terrible. When we came out of the preview I remember Joe had an angelic grin on his face, walking up to Louis B. Mayer and the other executives and saying, "Well, fellers, I guess this proves I can't make a B picture." So they gave him *Fury* to produce...'

Such good fortune, alas, never attended Edward G. Ulmer, who is considered by many to have raised the B picture almost to an art form in itself. He was a Viennese who worked in Germany as an assistant to F. W. Murnau and from 1933 onwards directed a lengthy series of films in Hollywood. He was burdened throughout his career with minuscule budgets and dubious scripts but with unique style and flair lent all his productions a distinction they would not otherwise have deserved. His chef d'oeuvre, I suppose, is *The Black Cat*, made in 1934 and starring Boris Karloff and Bela Lugosi, which is now generally recognised as a masterpiece of the horror genre. Ulmer was once asked to make a film with Shirley Temple but declined on the grounds that he did not wish to be chewed up by the Hollywood machine. He worked a great deal for the Producers Releasing Corporation because 'it was a nice family feeling, not too much interference . . . When I would say "I want to make *Bluebeard*", that's what we made.' He chose artistic freedom rather than money and came to be known as "the Frank Capra of PRC". (Incidentally, Ulmer's two leading players in *The Black Cat* – Karloff and Lugosi – are good examples of actors who became international stars while working almost exclusively in B pictures.)

But if Ulmer and a few other independent directors saw B movies as a way of exploring the artistic possibilities of the medium, the major studios did not. To them a B remained primarily what it had been designed to be in the first place – a programme filler. Whether the Bs were good or bad there was always a market for them because the studios owned theatre chains as well. And even when they were dealing with independent cinema owners they could always off-load the minor product by exerting a little muscle. If, said Joseph H. Lewis, a man with some fifty cinemas wanted the latest Greer Garson or Clark Gable picture MGM would say: 'Fine, but you've got to take twenty-four of these B films as well.' The man might well protest, saying: 'What the hell am I going to do with twenty-four B movies?' To which MGM would reply: 'We don't know but that's the only way you're going to get the Gable picture.'

This happy state of affairs – happy for the majors anyway – came to an end around 1953 when the Anti-Trust Laws finally divorced the exhibition and distribution ends of the business from the production end. Coincidentally cinema attendances were once again in decline, sliding rapidly from the postwar peak of 100 million admissions a week to the 40 million they would reach in 1957. But now, unlike in the 1930s, cinema audiences didn't want more – they wanted better. Television had taken over the role of producing what amounted to B pictures. If you could see an indifferent western or crime series on TV for nothing, why go out to the cinema and pay for much the same sort of thing? And at the same time the teenager was invented, a creature hitherto unknown to mankind. Previously there had been children and adults, with a brief period of awkward and impecunious adolescence in between. Nobody made movies for adolescents. What for? They had no money and anyway they were here today and gone tomorrow. But teenagers were a different matter. They emerged fully developed at thirteen, lined their pockets by baby-sitting and the like and were still around six years later. They were a new economic power in the land – in America especially – and they wanted their own films; they didn't want to see movies about children or grown-up people, they wanted to see movies about themselves.

So to satisfy this need and to fill the production gap left by the majors, who were now getting rid of their contract players and technicians and were making fewer films every year, there arose the exploitation picture. In many ways it was indistinguishable from the B picture, being made at very low cost and in a great hurry. But unlike the B picture it was custom-built for a specific audience – the very young audience that was now providing the cinemas with most of their business while its parents increasingly stayed at home to watch TV.

The exploitation movie might therefore be seen as a movie that exploited the young, although no maker of exploitation pictures would agree with such a definition. Rather, said Walter Mirisch, it's a film 'which takes advantage of the public's interest in the subject matter – a prison break, for example, that gets a lot of headlines or some sensational or lurid scandal'. Suddenly then the movies had turned full circle with stories "plucked from tomorrow's headlines", which is what Warner Brothers had boasted in the early 30s.

Old-time B picture makers such as William Castle and Sam Katzman, whose greatest coup had been to recycle Johnny Weissmuller into Jungle Jim when he grew too old and paunchy to play Tarzan, leapt enthusiastically on to this bandwagon. So did comparative newcomers like Albert Zugsmith, who made his first film, *Look Into the Future*, for 98,998 dollars and 75 cents and still came in 50 cents under budget and went on to turn Mamie van Doren into a wiggling menace to the morals of American youth in *High School Confidential*. ('Zuggy was my No 1 fan,' said Miss van Doren. 'He was very aware of sex.')

But one of the first and most abidingly successful of the exploitation movie makers was Samuel Z. Arkoff, an Iowa lawyer who with his partner James H. Nicholson, a cinema manager from the west coast, founded American International Pictures (AIP). Their simple policy was to take a sensational title – *I Was a Teenage Werewolf*, for example, *The Amazing Colossal Man*, *Hot Rod Girl* – and then, having ascertained from their potential customers the cinema owners that there might be a demand for such a thing, build a film around it.

'And the Devil whoops, as he whooped of old: "It's clever but is it Art?"' Well, no, it wasn't art but the exploitation men were never in the art business. To Arkoff the cinema was, and always had been, "Barnum and Bailey time". The trick was to define your audience and aim directly at it: young males for action pictures, young males and females for teenage pictures. And it worked. Parent Teachers Associations and other concerned bodies might, and did, complain that children were being corrupted and being led into sex and violence. But in fact – and herein lay much of the cunning of the exploitation picture – the advertising was invariably far more lurid than the content of the film.

The exploitation movies were not shown as B pictures; they were shown often in a double bill, purporting to be two main features. If successful enough the first time round they would be pulled out again a little later, dusted off and sent out in support of another, newer exploitation picture. Usually they were quite as shabbily made as any B picture had ever been but they didn't sell on the strength of their style or production values, they sold on their titles, the topicality of their subject matter and their appeal to youth. And they left the majors floundering in their wake. You could say the majors have learned better now or, alternatively, you could say they have stooped down to the level of their exploitation rivals. But in the early days they

Above: AIP's *I Was a Teenage Werewolf* – an exploitation movie, not a B pic. But what's the difference?

Above right: Perhaps the greatest of the B picture stars, Bela Lugosi and Boris Karloff, in perhaps the greatest of the B pictures, Edgar Ulmer's *The Black Cat*

Right: *Invasion of the Body Snatchers*, a "nervous" B movie when it was first made in 1956

Below right: Upgraded to an A – but hardly improved – when remade with Donald Sutherland in 1978

would not stoop, not them, to pandering to kids with a taste for the sensational, the gruesome or the suggestive, which was tough luck on the majors for they were rapidly losing what was left of their audience to exploitation movie makers who were supple and flexible enough to stoop lower than might have been thought humanly possible. Horror, violence, hot-rod girls, wasp women, nasty things from outer space – if there was a buck to be made from it, they made a movie about it.

In the late 1950s Russ Meyer, the son of a policeman and a nurse who rather greedily went through six husbands, made something of a breakthrough when his film *The Immortal Mr Teas* became the first soft-core porno movie to return a huge profit – an investment of some 24,000 dollars bringing in more than a million. What did you do in the war, Daddy? Well, son . . . An historic event, however, comparable to *Playboy*'s achievement in being the first mass circulation magazine to show a woman's pubic hair. Not very much later the majors, of course, were copying Mr Meyer, too. Indeed, after he had made a 6 million dollar profit on a 76,000 dollar investment with a typically crude, sexploitative picture called *Vixen* in 1968, Meyer himself was signed by 20th Century-Fox to produce two feeble efforts on the sex and violence theme called *Beyond the Valley of the Dolls* and *The Seven Minutes*. The moguls of old – the Mayers, the Warners, the Zanucks and the Cohns – would doubtless have wept to see how low their successors had sunk. In their day B picture makers came in through the tradesmen's entrance, not through the front door with a red carpet to save wear and tear on their footwear.

B picture? Whoops, sorry. The doyen and most revered of all exploitation movie makers, Roger Corman, reacts with 'anger and sadness' to hearing his work referred to as B pictures. 'My films,' he said, 'were always designed to be the top half of a bill . . . or just stand on their own as a single feature.'

At one time, he said, they were called "exploitation films". Well, most people call them that still but Corman did not like the term. 'When the major studios began to do a similar type of film, they couldn't really call them exploitation . . . More recently they've been called "high concept films". I like the words "high concept" very much.' He defined such films as those whose concept alone was enough to bring people into the cinema without benefit of large budget or star names in the cast. Corman was the first and most distinguished graduate of AIP, to say nothing of being also a graduate of Leland Stanford and Oxford Universities. An extremely intelligent man with a dry sense of humour, a sharp eye for an exploitable subject – as well as for potential talent in others – and a keen sense of where the money is. More than any other exploitation movie maker (let us have no truck with "high concept") he has developed a powerful, even adoring, cult following particularly in France and Britain – not for such epics as *Attack of the Crab Monsters* (which erroneously sounds like a film about some frightful sexually transmitted disease) but for his idiosyncratic and sometimes tongue-in-cheek treatment of Edgar Allan Poe classics like *The Masque of the Red Death* and *The Tomb of Ligeia*, both of which starred another internationally celebrated B movie star, Vincent Price.

Corman began with AIP in the mid-1950s, working with budgets of about 30,000 dollars. But then he always worked cheap and fast. 'I did one film really more as a joke to see if I could do it – *The Little Shop of Horrors* which was shot in two days and a night. After I did *Little Shop* a good friend of mine, Bob Towne, said to me, "Roger, it's not a track meet; it's not how fast you go", so I never worked that fast again.' Nevertheless he continued to work pretty quickly and in an extremely individual way. For instance, his film *The Terror* in 1963 came about because (a) he had just finished making *The Raven* and thought he could squeeze more mileage out of the sets and (b) because it was raining one Sunday and he couldn't play tennis, so he thought he would dream up a film instead. 'I made an arrangement with Boris Karloff to come and shoot a few days on the sets and with my friend Jack Nicholson to play the lead. I only had time to write that portion of the script that fitted Boris' words, so we shot those few days, then I wrote the rest of the film.' Corman himself directed the bulk of the picture but Francis Ford Coppola and then Monte Hellman did some more, until each was offered a better assignment elsewhere. 'Then finally on the last day of shooting Jack Nicholson said, "Look, everybody in town has shot part of this picture, let me shoot the final sections." So he did and we cut it all together and the film didn't make a great deal of sense. Each director had modified it slightly and I looked at it and I said, This doesn't really hold together. But by that time I was doing another Edgar Allen Poe film . . . So I got Jack and Dick Miller, who was playing a small role, and at the close of shooting one day on whatever the Edgar Allan Poe film was I held the crew over and paid them a little additional money and brought Jack and Dick in and Jack grabbed Dick and threw him against the wall of this set and said, "All right, I've been lied to ever since I came to this castle. I don't understand what's happening. Tell me what's going on," at which point Dick told the plot of the story and we tied the whole thing together.' So exploitation films – and movie lore – are made.

In his early days with AIP Corman was turning out, virtually back to back, typical exploitation pictures shot on ten day schedules. 'They would send them out two at a time as double bills – two horror films, two gangster films, two science fiction films. When they wanted me to do two more black and white horror films I got a little tired and convinced them to switch to colour and shoot one film at a time and shoot it in three weeks . . . I felt I was in the big time with that.' Thus began his Edgar Allan Poe series, starting with *The Fall of the House of Usher* and continuing as straightforward horror pictures until he grew bored and began to inject humour where none had been intended. This proved particularly irksome to Robert Towne, who had written the script for *The Tomb of Ligeia* and had meant it to be taken seriously.

'I said, "Roger, whatever you do, don't get Vincent Price for this movie because I'm writing about a necrophiliac and Vincent is liable to give away the gag very early on." So I wistfully said, "How about Maximilian Schell?" Well, Roger called me one day from London and said, "We're going with *The Tomb of Ligeia*. We've got Vincent but it's all right, we've got Marlene Dietrich's make-up man." I don't know what he meant by that – I don't think any of us did but that was his reasoning.'

Towne was one of an impressive number of now famous film makers discovered, or at least nurtured, by AIP and in particular Corman in the 60s and 70s. Another was Peter Fonda who in *The Wild Angels* in 1966 became AIP's most important star.

(Jack Nicholson either wrote or appeared in many AIP pictures but did not become a star until much later.) Fonda landed the lead role more or less by default. George Chakiris was to have played it, with Fonda and Bruce Dern in support, but after one day of practice on a Harley-Davidson motorbike Chakiris said, 'There's no way I'm going to ride that thing. You'll have to get a double,' Corman said, 'There's no way I'm going to use a double,' and so exit Chakiris – 'in a friendly way,' Corman said – and everybody else moved up one, Fonda thus being promoted to star of the film. It was Fonda who insisted that the name of his character should be changed from Jack Black to Heavenly Blues, heavenly blues as he explained to Corman being flowers whose seeds, when ground to a powder, mixed with water and drunk would induce a psychedelic experience. *The Wild Angels* was an enormous success; according to Fonda it 'made more money for AIP than everything else they ever did combined'. Furthermore, it made Peter Fonda the idol of the young generation – a picture of him astride his Harley-Davidson became a bestseller – and introduced a cycle of "biker" movies, whose popularity Corman thought stemmed from the fact that there was 'a whole philosophy around the Hell's Angels. It was very much an anti-Establishment time and the Hell's Angels were the epitome of an anti-Establishment culture.' (The majors tried to copy the biker movies just as they had also tried to copy AIP's teenage beach party pictures but, as usual, they got the formula wrong.)

Fonda followed *The Wild Angels* with *The Trip*, also directed by Corman and written by Jack Nicholson. As the title suggests it was about an acid trip and to that extent it broke new ground as, in it, did Fonda himself by becoming 'the first man in a non X-rated picture to appear bare-arse naked. I wasn't embarrassed about it at all. In one shot, where I'm in the pool, they had to cut a piece of the film out because in the water things get out of proportion, if you know what I mean. Roger had to make a slight jump cut. I said, "Leave it in. No one will know what it is – they'll think it's a big snake following me about."'

The Trip enhanced Fonda's reputation as the cinematic spokesman of the anti-Establishment generation and his next film, *Easy Rider* – probably the most successful exploitation picture ever made – established it beyond doubt. It was his own project, which he co-wrote with Terry Southern and Dennis Hopper, who also directed, and he decided to make it out of perversity. At a film expo in Toronto in 1967 he heard Jack Valenti extolling the virtues of the forthcoming *Dr Dolittle* which, he insisted, was the kind of family film the industry should be making. 'He said we had to stop making these films about motorcycles, drugs and sex and he was looking right at me because I was making the motorcycles, drugs and sex films . . . so I went back to my hotel room and I said, Okay, that's it – I've got to go and make a movie about motorcycles, sex and drugs and I wrote the story [of *Easy Rider*] that night.'

The original intention was to make it for AIP with Corman as executive producer but 'Sam [Arkoff] wanted to take the film away from Dennis if he ran three days behind schedule and I said that was too difficult', so they took the project to Columbia. That was bad news for AIP, for the story of two drug-dealing drop-outs riding motorbikes across America grossed 60 million dollars world wide and made Peter Fonda more money than his father, Henry Fonda, made in his entire career.

Meanwhile, Corman himself decided to leave AIP and set up his own company in 1970. From then on he concentrated mostly on producing and incidentally encouraging a new generation of film makers, although that was not really his intention. 'They were people who were friends or acquaintances of mine who I thought were good. I was doing two things: I was giving them an opportunity to make their first film and I was getting a film made for less money than if I were to hire an established director . . . Jack Nicholson wrote an article once in which he said, as near as I can remember, "Roger hired us all when nobody else would hire us and for that *we* will be eternally grateful. He underpaid us and for that *he* will be eternally grateful . . ." But in my own defence I must say that I was paying the guild minimums so everyone was getting reasonable union rates.'

Among those he helped, either at AIP or later, were such of his assistants as Menahem Golan (now, along with Yoram Globus, the head of the Cannon Group) and Francis Ford Coppola, whose first film as director – a pretty frightful, very low budget horror pic called *Dementia 13* – was made swiftly in Ireland in 1963 with Corman as producer.

Peter Bogdanovich worked, uncredited, on *The Wild Angels* in 1966 as assistant director and assistant scriptwriter and the following year Corman gave him the chance to direct a thriller called *Targets* with Boris Karloff. Bogdanovich said: 'The point was Karloff owed Roger two days' work and Roger said to me, "How would you like to make a film on your own?" Obviously, I said I would and he said, "Well Karloff owes me these two days so why don't you go and shoot some footage with him and then you can shoot with some other actors for ten days and take forty minutes of Karloff footage from this other picture we did and put it all together and we'll have a new 80-minute Karloff picture."' And that's how *Targets* was made, although in the end Bogdanovich used only about three minutes of the earlier Karloff film, *The Terror*.

Corman financed the film himself for 125,000 dollars – of which Karloff received 22,000 and Bogdanovich 3,000 – and released it through Paramount. The only rule he imposed, Bogdanovich said, was that the cost must be kept down. He seems, on the whole, to have been rather good about giving people a job and letting them get on with it. Once he bought a Russian science fiction film about some men going to Venus and found difficulty in getting distribution because there were no women in the cast, so he asked Bogdanovich to do something about that. Bogdanovich wrote some scenes with women and Corman said: 'Shoot it. No dialogue. You can't have sound. Put in some sound later.' Bogdanovich agreed, persuading himself that people probably didn't speak a lot on Venus anyway and . . . 'We went down to the beach and shot with Mamie van Doren and six other blondes. I decided everyone on Venus was blonde.' Once again, that's how exploitation pictures are made.

Of Corman himself, Bogdanovich said: 'I think Roger's a very important figure in the movies. He's had tremendous impact. Just look at the number of people to whom he's given a start . . . He taught us all a way of making pictures at a certain price and working quickly, with economy and preparation.'

Robert Towne, like Jack Nicholson, met Corman when they were all attending the same acting class in the late 50s. 'Roger knew that I wanted to write. He said, "I hear you wanna write; write a script for me." That was it.' The first script he wrote was for *The Last Woman on Earth* in 1960. 'The schedule would be about five or six days. At least it was quick, that's about all I can tell you. He'd shoot films back to back, side by side. His motto was "roll 'em, show 'em" – if nobody fell down, that was a print. Now, Roger was better than that, more concerned about quality than that but I always suspected that he never had a firm conviction that one take was really going to be that much better than another.'

Martin Scorsese was another who was given his first break by Corman. He had studied film at New York University and, over a period of three years, had made a very cheap picture called *Who's that Knocking at My Door?* Corman saw it, liked it and asked him to direct *Boxcar Bertha*, a sort of poor man's *Bonnie and Clyde* made in 1972. Corman himself was the producer and, said Scorsese, had a very clear idea of how he wanted the movie made. 'He gave us a set of rules in a way, exploitation rules. The violence was built into the script but the nudity had to be observed carefully. This was his rule: every fifteen pages of the script there should be a touch of nudity, just to keep the audience's interest up, right? Just maybe a little off-the-shoulder, a little leg, not complete nudity but something to keep the interest going. And we went in there and inserted that . . . But the main thing Roger did was to channel my energy and show me, literally, how to make a picture in the most economic way and once he saw that I was totally prepared he said, "Fine, that's it. You just continue" . . . Only once did he have to come on the set and scowl – for the crew, not for me. He said, "I'm gonna scowl – it's not for you," and he walked around, scowling, and the crew was looking on and they shaped up immediately.'

Corman could have been, indeed was going to be, the producer of Scorsese's next film, the one on which he built his reputation, but there was a snag. The picture was *Mean Streets* and it stemmed specifically from Scorsese's own experience and observation, being about two young Italian-American wise guys – Robert de Niro and Harvey Keitel – hustling in New York's Little Italy. But . . . 'Roger's brother, Gene, had made a film in Harlem, a black film, and they were making a lot of money with it. So Roger came to me and said, "Marty, if you could swing a little and kinda conceive *Mean Streets* as black we might be able to do it in New York, non-union, shoot it very fast." And I wanted to make it so badly, I didn't say, "Oh, no, no, forget it. It's outrageous!" I said, "Let me think about it." So I actually went back and thought about it for another hour and then I said, "I can't. I cannot do it. How can I? I just can't make it black – it's about Italian-Americans, it's impossible."'

Go non-union, shoot it fast, make it black – or brown, or yellow, or Regency-striped if there was money in it. That was the way of the exploitation movie maker, although to be fair the major studios had not behaved all that differently in their heyday.

Another notable graduate of the AIP school of cinema – though he never worked with Corman – was the writer/director John Milius. In 1968 the company gave him his first writing assignment on *The Devil's Eight*, which owed its inspiration and much of its plot to *The Dirty Dozen*, a big success of the previous year. Five years later they offered him a film to direct. 'They were doing these gangster movies and they were doing black monster movies – you know, *Blackenstein*, *Blackula*, *Blackzilla*, everything . . . They said, "Well, you can have your choice of that or you can do *Capone* or *Pretty Boy Floyd* or *Dillinger*," and I chose *Dillinger*.'

In AIP's terms this was to be a big, prestige picture; it would cost 1,200,000 dollars and it was the most expensive film they had made at that time. Milius said: 'The thing that was great about it was that the whole place was behind me. They said, "God, we're going to go out and make a great movie. We're going to make one that will compete with the majors." Everybody was there behind you – the janitor came in and looked at the rough cut and gave his opinions . . . You felt that if you made a bad film, if you went a dollar over budget, you'd be letting down every secretary there. And that was a wonderful feeling. I've never had that feeling again in a studio. The studios antagonise you, usually. Most producers just try and steal whatever they can; they're just trying to get through the movie and keep their office and make the next deal. At AIP there was a real sense of belonging . . . a sense of being the underdog . . . They didn't take themselves seriously; they were making exploitation films; they said, "We're the little guys," and there was a wonderful feeling to the things they did . . . At AIP they had no pretensions. They were wonderful.'

In the end and despite their protestations, the exploitation companies are not so different from the old B picture studios. The very quality that kept Edgar Ulmer at PRC – the freedom to get on with the job unhindered by what Peter Fonda called "the suits", the pinstriped men from head office – was what so deeply impressed Milius, Scorsese and Bogdanovich at AIP and Roger Corman's company. Corman himself flirted briefly with the majors around the time he left AIP. Indeed, as early as 1964 he had made *The Secret Invasion*, a kind of predecessor of *The Dirty Dozen*, for United Artists. Then, in 1971 and for the same company, he directed a First World War story, *Von Richthofen and Brown*. Between times he made *The St Valentine's Day Massacre* for 20th Century-Fox. 'I was given bigger budgets,' he said, 'but less freedom. Certain decisions on casting, on the way the pictures would be edited were reserved for the studios, so I was not completely happy with my experiences there.'

By 1986 Corman had formed and sold one company of his own and had founded another. The last film he had directed was *Von Richthofen and Brown* and since then he had concentrated on producing, on being in effect a mini-studio tycoon. He even branched out into distribution, having been responsible for importing into America such European films as Fellini's *Amarcord* and Ingmar Bergman's *Cries and Whispers*. But he thought that, with his new, more stream-lined company, he might go back to directing. What kind of films, though – the familiar, low-budget, fast-schedule productions? Or would he try his hand at the now popular mega-bucks epics? 'The thought has occurred to me to work in that league,' he said. 'But I'm not certain I have the patience to sit six months on a set and shoot. Maybe my choice to stay with independent, low-budget films was partially because I knew I would have autonomy and the freedom to get it over and done with: whether it was a two-week schedule or a three-week schedule, I would walk clear at the end of it.'

Again that is not so very different from the way the contract directors worked at the major studios in the 1930s and 40s, before films grew fat and the making of them became a lengthy, laborious business in which the main object – the picture itself – was pegged down, like Gulliver in Lilliput, by deals and horse-trading and the intervention of a plethora of agents and lawyers.

In their early days the exploitation movies and their makers were objects of scorn and derision. But now it's possible to look at them a little more clearly and to perceive that their place in the history of the industry is more important than was originally thought. They filled the void left by the disappearance of the B picture but they did more than that. They may have begun by trailing along behind the ailing major studios but in the end they led the way, for all the trends in the cinema of the last twenty years – sex, violence, things from outer space – were first explored in exploitation pictures. They could therefore also be said to have launched the new generation of "Movie Brats" that dominates the industry today. For whether these people – Spielberg, Lucas, Coppola, Scorsese and the others – learned their trade in exploitation movies or film school or both, the pictures they grew up with, the pictures that influenced them, were the pictures of AIP and Roger Corman and their contemporaries.

Left: Roger Corman, master of the exploitation movie, directs Bruce Dern (centre) and Peter Fonda in *The Wild Angels*
Below: John Milius directing *Dillinger* but looking just as ready to shoot him

THE WESTERN

The era of the wild west – the settling of the land, the cowboys and cavalry versus the Indians, the establishment of law and order – lasted for approximately fifty years. In 1901 Robert Leroy Parker and Harry Longbaugh, better known as Butch Cassidy and the Sundance Kid, perpetrated their last train robbery, celebrated the success of this piece of private enterprise in New York and then, realising that their form of simple capitalism was increasingly frowned upon in their own country, set off somewhat misguidedly to seek the Promised Land in Bolivia. A few years later another legendary figure of the west, Bat Masterson, erstwhile deputy to Wyatt Earp, was appointed sports editor of the *New York Morning Telegraph*, in which capacity it is doubtful that he was ever again obliged to give somebody twenty-four hours to get out of town.

One age had ended but another, the age of the western movie, had already begun and by now it has lasted nearly four decades longer than the era it depicts. Mind you, there are those who will insist that this age, too, is dead. It was pronounced so, prematurely, in 1929 in an editorial in *Photoplay* and in 1974 the critic Pauline Kael, having examined the body and found no sign of life, repeated the diagnosis. In her case there was much greater justification but even she was a shade too eager to get on with the burial for only two years later the corpse of the western movie twitched vigorously into life again as Clint Eastwood delivered one of the abiding classics of the genre, *The Outlaw Josey Wales*. For the best part of a decade after that, however, mourning was indeed pretty much in order as the western lay moribund, a state in which it finds itself once again even today.

Well, many things account for that but what accounts for the enormous popularity it enjoyed for more than seventy years? At its simplest (and often for that matter at its best) the western is a modern Morality tale, a clear-cut struggle between good and evil in which both sides are easily identifiable, good wearing the white hat and evil the black. The western has often been guilty of rewriting history but, having done so, it made sure that there could be no doubt about the issues. In *My Darling Clementine* or *The Gunfight at the O.K. Corral* when the Earps and Doc Holliday went out to face the Clantons, the whiteness of their hats was almost blinding. Likewise when Gary Cooper stood alone on mainstreet in *High Noon* waiting for the showdown with the killers there cannot have been a single viewer in any cinema anywhere in the world whose heart was not with him. You knew where you stood with the western – the use of the past tense here was quite accidental but perhaps that in itself is indicative of the current state of the genre – and this reason alone helps to explain its appeal.

But beyond anything else it was and is, even more than the musical, America's most significant contribution to the cinema, since it sprang exclusively from the country's own roots. It was, as Peter Bogdanovich said, 'the essential American myth' and that myth had started long before the cinema came along to exploit it. It had originated in the dime novels and pulp fiction – the works of Ned Buntline and the like – that had begun to appear in the 1860s, in the paintings of Frederic Remington and Charles M. Russell and the thriving wild west shows (notably Buffalo Bill Cody's) of the Victorian era. Buntline even "killed off" Wild Bill Hickock before his time (thereby making Wild Bill even wilder than usual), having him shot to death by a couple of women gunslingers in one of his stories. In fact, Hickock died some years later – in 1876 – in Deadwood City where he was shot in the back by Jack McCall when on the point of cleaning up in a poker game with a full house of aces on eights – the famous "Dead Man's Hand" later immortalised in *The Plainsman* by Cecil B. de Mille and also by John Ford in both *Stagecoach* and *The Man Who Shot Liberty Valance*.

So by the time the cinema got in on the act the line between fact and fiction was already becoming blurred. The cinema, indeed, saw the dramatic possibilities of the west at a very early stage. In 1894 Thomas Edison showed wild west items on his kinetograph and four years later he depicted a western saloon in a vignette, *Cripple Creek Bar-room*. In 1900 the infamous Wild Bunch held up the Union Pacific Railway and within three years Edwin S. Porter had commemorated the event in *The Great Train Robbery*, which lays some claim to being the first western to tell a coherent story. One of the players in that film, Gilbert M. (Bronco Billy) Anderson promptly went into partnership with a book agent named George K. Spoor to form Essanay (the phonetic pronunciation, roughly speaking, of their initials) and between 1908 and 1915 he wrote, directed and starred in a Bronco Billy western every week, thus becoming the first credited movie actor and western star. The films cost about 800 dollars each and tended to gross somewhere in the region of 50,000 dollars.

Others were quick to see that what was on offer here provided even better profits than the California gold rush. In 1909 "Colonel" William Selig (a former magician who seems to have conjured his military title out of thin air) set up a studio in Hollywood and employed a young stunt man-cum-actor named Tom Mix to appear in his films. And from 1910 onwards D. W. Griffith regularly trouped off to California with a bunch of actors and technicians to make his own westerns. A year after that Thomas H. Ince acquired 20,000 acres of land around Hollywood, modestly called it Inceville and began making yet more westerns for the Motion Picture Company. So rapidly indeed did the western, the oater, the horse opera – call it what you will – begin to proliferate that as early as 1913 a reviewer in *The Moving Picture World* was surfeited enough to write: 'A closed season ... may safely be declared on these overworked and senseless types: the Outlaw, the Sheriff, the Queen of the Ranch, the Half-Breed, the Bandit ...' No chance. The public *loved* westerns and throughout the 1920s the genre flourished ever more prosperously, producing stars like Anderson and Mix, Ken Maynard, William S. Hart, Harry Carey, Buck

Jones, Hoot Gibson, Tim McCoy and the fastest of them all – not necessarily on the draw but certainly on foot – Rin Tin Tin.

As a movie form it had been lent dignity in 1914 with de Mille's massive six-reeler *The Squaw Man* (later remade twice when he couldn't think of anything better) and the success of this proved that the western could stretch from programme-filler to epic. Epics duly followed – Paramount's *Covered Wagon*, directed by James Cruze, was so popular that the following year, 1924, western production increased three fold to around 150 films, among them another epic, *The Iron Horse*, directed by a certain John Ford. For the rest of the silent era westerns, often shot quickly and cheaply on location, provided if not the meat then assuredly the potatoes of the cinema diet and the coming of sound proved only a temporary setback.

The cinematographer William Clothier, who later shot such films as *The Horse Soldiers*, *The Alamo* and *Cheyenne Autumn*, was working as a twenty-four-year-old camera assistant when sound came in. Prior to that, he said, westerns had been an important part of the industry. 'Western pictures made money – all of them. Regardless of what they were like people went to see them. Every week you got a new one and those pictures made money. They'd make a feature film in a studio and sometimes it made money and sometimes it lost money and that loss was a big one. But in western pictures you couldn't lose much dinner money because they didn't cost anything.'

The initial difficulty of sound was, of course, sound itself. In the very early days, said Clothier, they used discs six-feet in diameter, several of them, each pointing at an individual actor to pick up the dialogue. That created problems enough, even on an indoor stage; outdoors it was considerably worse. For a year or two the western became bogged down in a morass of silent action and static dialogue but by 1929 Raoul Walsh was able to take his microphones out into the wide open spaces and pick up the noises of gunfire, hoofbeats and even the frying of bacon in *In Old Arizona* (a film, incidentally, on which William Clothier was employed). By the time that happened, however, Maynard, Hart and to a large extent Mix had been driven out of the business, Lindbergh had flown the Atlantic and the western had been declared dead by *Variety* magazine in 1928 and by the *Photoplay* editorial of April 1929, which declared that 'Lindbergh has put the cowboy into discard as a type of national hero. The western novel and motion picture heroes have shrunk away into the brush, never to return. Within the past two years, western pictures, always surefire profit earners, have lost their popularity . . .'

Well, perhaps, but only temporarily for the history of the west had a stronger hold on the collective American imagination than *Photoplay* or *Variety* knew. Fritz Lang, who made two fairly considerable westerns in *The Return of Frank James* and *Western Union* in 1940–1, likened the legend of the west to the Niebelungen saga in Germany. Or, as Bogdanovich put it, 'It's the only mythology America has. It was really what founded the country . . . it's part of the American Dream. The guy with the white hat riding into town is almost a metaphor for the taming of America, a kind of propaganda for the American way of life – you know, get rid of the Indians, get rid of the bad men and get the American Dream going.'

Above: Clint Eastwood
as *The Outlaw Josey
Wales*, the latest – and
maybe the last – great
western. And the first
western with a coherent
story (inset), *The Great
Train Robbery* made by
Edwin S. Porter in 1903
Left: *The Squaw Man*,
which de Mille directed
in 1914 and which he
always remade when he
couldn't think of any-
thing better to do

But possibly the appeal was even more basic than that. Richard Brooks, growing up in Philadelphia in the 1920s, dreamed of having a pony – 'to be out there in the west where you could test your mettle as a person and didn't have to wait a lifetime to become President of the United States. You'd be a hero just by riding that pony and being true blue west.' It was a theme reiterated by Budd Boetticher, who made half a dozen or so excellent westerns with Randolph Scott – 'the Americans grew up with the west. When I was a kid we wore cowboy hats, we had ponies, we had our little guns . . .' Time after time the people I spoke to, people who had spent a considerable part of their professional lives making western movies, talked of the lure of the wide open spaces, of horses, of the freedom of the range. None of them so far as I could tell, except perhaps Boetticher, had actually availed themselves of such things even when they became rich and independent enough to do so but these are all magic symbols, deeply rooted in the American psyche. And more than that there is the true history of the west itself, which as William Clothier said 'is part of our heritage. My Gosh! My ancestors crossed this country. My grandmother has told me about coming from Virginia to Illinois and they were crossing a river – I don't know which river it was; they never told me – but my grandfather was riding on a horse and my grandmother was riding in a wagon, a covered wagon, with my father in her lap and the wagon broke loose from the team and floated down the river. And some of those horsemen got out into the middle of the river and caught the wagon as my grandmother and the child were floating away . . .' Well, take that, add a touch of boy-girl romance and an attack by savage Redskins and you've got the plot of a thousand westerns right there.

By the late 1920s when the obituaries of the western were already being written, such events were certainly history – but very recent history. Emmett Dalton, the last of the notorious outlaw brothers, was still alive and hearty, having played himself in the 1915 movie *Beyond the Law*. Frank James, brother of Jesse and latterly a starter at a horse race track, had survived until that year; Cole Younger, as noted an outlaw as Jesse James himself, had died in 1916 and Bat Masterson lived on until 1921. John Ford complained bitterly that Wyatt Earp, most celebrated of all the real life western heroes, was in the habit of wrecking his filming schedules on silent westerns by getting drunk with the cowboys until Earp himself died in 1929.

Western history then was still alive, still remembered by people who had lived through it, when *In Old Arizona* succeeded well enough to prompt Hollywood to forget the In Memoriam notices and carry on making western movies. As Harry Cohn was to say, albeit a little later, films 'are about cunt and horses' and although at that time the two did not meet up much in the same picture the dictum held true in 1929. In that year Gary Cooper in *The Virginian* (directed by Victor Fleming for Paramount) delivered the immortal line 'If you want to call me that, smile'. He did so in an impeccable accent which had been taught him by a bit part player from Virginia named Randolph Scott. With both Walsh's and Fleming's films proving popular a brief cycle of big, ambitious westerns ushered in the 1930s. Exhorted by President Hoover to mark the centenary of the march of the pioneers from Independence, Missouri, in 1830 Fox and Raoul Walsh made *The Big Trail*, a huge and ill-fated venture notable now only for the fact that it introduced, for the first time in a leading role, one Marion Morrison, aka John Wayne. The film flopped and so did Wayne and he returned to comparative obscurity for a number of years. King Vidor's *Billy the Kid* with Johnny Mack Brown in the title role and Wallace Beery playing Pat Garrett fared considerably better, both in America where the ending had Billy escaping to Mexico, there presumably to live happily ever after, and in Europe where, the audiences being made of sterner stuff, the climax had Garrett gunning Billy down.

In 1931 RKO produced *Cimarron*, directed by Wesley Ruggles, in many ways the most significant western of that era and perhaps the most significant western of them all, though few would argue that it's the best. What makes *Cimarron* unique is that it is the only western ever to win the Oscar for best picture. In fact only nine specimens of the genre – among them *Stagecoach*, *Shane*, *High Noon* and *Butch Cassidy and the Sundance Kid* – have even been nominated in that category. *Cimarron* was an epic story of the development of a small Oklahoma town from its beginning in the 1880s to its growth into a large industrial city. The stars were Richard Dix and Irene Dunne and the film was an instant success. Ironically, though, that very success could be seen now to have worked against the western as a main feature movie because it prompted the studio to revive its output of low budget "quickies", which it had abandoned due to the difficulties in the early days of sound of filming outdoors.

Other studios followed suit and the brief flowering of the western at the beginning of the decade ended as suddenly as it had begun; for several years it was to be found for the most part lurking humbly among the ranks of B pictures, series and serials. One reason for that may have been that despite *Cimarron*'s Academy Award, the western was still not quite respectable. William Clothier said that the stars of such films were not regarded, even in their own studios, as being as important as those who appeared in perhaps more sophisticated dramas and comedies. Then, too, there was the matter of cost. With the development of sound equipment it was now possible to shoot cheaply and quickly out of doors and besides, ever since the silent days Hollywood had had a surfeit of the kind of people who were vital to the making of westerns – cowboys, wranglers, stuntmen and the like – and these could be hired at very little expense.

Their traditional hangout was Gower Gulch, or Poverty Row, the area on Sunset Boulevard where tiny or even fly-by-night studios had been set up early in the 1920s to make low budget westerns. The actor Iron Eyes Cody, a Cherokee Indian who came to Hollywood with his father and brothers around 1925, remembered Gower Gulch well. 'There was a drug store and a bar where all these old cowboys would hang around and I've seen shooting and killing at that Gower Gulch. This was a low dive. They all hung around with their real pistols – I'm not kidding you, *real* pistols. Some of them had real shells, some didn't. There were cowboys, bronco riders, everything. And they had a hotel not too far away, a cheap hotel because this was Poverty Row, and they'd drink there and I'd try to save my father from drinking because he was an alcoholic and just like the rest of those guys – wild.'

One other factor that helped to bring about the demotion of the western was the introduction of the double-feature. Most exhibitors could not afford to rent two A pictures: what they wanted was one A, for which they paid a percentage of the box office take, and one B, which cost them a flat and more modest fee. Thus from the studios' point of view the more inexpensively the B pictures could be produced, the greater the profit and not many films could be made more inexpensively than low budget westerns.

So the 1930s became the Golden Age of the B western, churned out virtually on a conveyor belt with the story line hardly differing at all from one picture to another. 'The studios usually made the same kind of films with one star,' said Joseph H. Lewis. 'Like Johnny Mack Brown. I made a lot with him – a famous football star from Alabama. They made a series, they'd shoot one about every month or so and then make another one. They had 'em presold, you see.' At Republic, according to George Sherman, they were making 'practically one a week'. Sherman worked on the serial "The Adventures of Red Ryder" that starred Don Barry and put him for several years in the annual list of the top ten money-making western actors, and also on "The Three Mesquiteers" series, which featured John Wayne, now relegated to this kind of picture after the lack of success of *The Big Trail*. Sherman said: 'You make a picture, you take a break for a day or two and, bang, you go into another western.' What made this rate of production possible was the repertory company of extras and bit part players who "were always at the gate" waiting for a job. 'We knew who could ride and who couldn't; we knew who could fall off a horse without breaking his neck; and we had a special group of stuntmen. We had Yakima Canutt, the classic stuntman who doubled for Wayne, and we had Kenny Cooper double for Gene Autry. It was a marvellous company.'

Autry was a curious product of the B western for it was he who really introduced what purists would regard (quite properly in my view) as a most deplorable development of the genre, the singing cowboy. Other cowboy stars had sung before him – Ken Maynard, for instance – and there is some evidence that points sternly towards John Wayne as the man who introduced this appalling habit when, around 1932, he appeared in a series for Monogram as "Singin' Sandy". It's true that he didn't actually sing himself, being dubbed by Jack Kirk, and it's also true that he soon repented of his error but nevertheless a certain amount of blame must be laid firmly at his door. Still, it was Gene Autry who, with his first starring vehicle *Tumbling Tumbleweeds* in 1935, made the singing cowboy popular, so popular indeed that his films were among the top moneymakers of their time and he himself was dubbed the "King of the Cowboys".

He was, however, a mystery to George Sherman. 'He was always elegantly dressed and never soiled his beautiful western clothes and he played the guitar and sang and he fascinated me. I kept looking at him – I made two or three films with him, I guess – I kept looking at him and I couldn't fathom his success. I'd say, what the hell is this? What is this guy? It was amazing. The Singing Cowboy is probably the thing that grabbed everybody and I think he was the first on the scene with those beautiful clothes and the guitar and the clean look. In most of the westerns the guys looked grubby but he was very neat for a western actor.' He was also very smart – financially as well as sartorially, since he invested his money so shrewdly as to become a multi-

Above: *Cimarron*, not
the best, but perhaps the
most significant western
because it's the only one
with an Oscar for best
picture
Left: Gary Cooper and
Walter Huston in *The
Virginian* (1929). 'If you
want to call me that,
smile'
Right: Villainous Brian
Donlevy and Marlene
Dietrich, the golden-
hearted tart, in *Destry
Rides Again*

millionaire – and he regarded himself as a force for moral good. As he always played himself on screen, Autry the actor was indistinguishable to his essentially youthful audience from Autry the man and to lead that audience on the path of righteousness he produced "The Cowboy Code", according to whose dicta a cowboy was never unfair, always faithful and truthful, kind to children, old people and animals, clean and patriotic, respectful of women, the law and his parents, a hard worker, free from prejudice and generally eager to lend a hand. Since his screen persona by and large lived up to all these lofty ideals the amazing thing is that he didn't throttle his film career to death with his own halo; on the contrary he was so beloved that he spawned a host of singing imitators of whom the only one who truly rivalled him – and indeed eventually supplanted him as King of the Cowboys – was the equally clean-living and saintly Roy Rogers.

George Sherman worked with Rogers, too, though only on his screen test. 'He was with The Sons of the Pioneers [a western singing group, much favoured later by John Ford in his films] and I was doing a "Three Mesquiteers" and they said, Put a scene in with this guy. We never really tested anybody because that would cost money so we used them within the framework of a film and took that as a per se screen test. He sang a song and played the guitar and strolled through and they said to get close-ups because they were thinking about using him in future films. His name then was Leonard Slye.'

Like Autry, Rogers epitomised the clean-living, elegantly dressed sort of cowboy who, fifty years earlier, would certainly have been hooted off the range. So, too, did William Boyd, alias Hopalong Cassidy, whose adventures spanned a multitude of episodes in which violence was kept to a minimum and there was no visible bloodshed. But at least Boyd had the decency not to sing, in strong contrast to Roy Rogers who, in the 1940s, showed a marked tendency to turn his films into musical westerns, with production numbers replacing the action sequences.

Now while all these warbling cowboys were enjoying their heyday and the studios were turning out a plethora of B pix, serials, series and general programme-fillers, the A western was having a very thin time. In 1936 it had a brief revival, notably on account of Cecil B. de Mille's *The Plainsman*, which starred Gary Cooper as Wild Bill Hickock and Jean Arthur as Calamity Jane and compressed much of western history into one narrative. In the same year, and also for Paramount, King Vidor directed *The Texas Rangers*, while Universal produced an ambitious – and disastrous – epic called *Sutter's Gold*, based on the California gold rush of 1849. The original director was Sergei Eisenstein but he was replaced by Howard Hawks, who stayed only long enough to get rid of the leading man, the British actor Francis L. Sullivan and sign Edward Arnold in his stead, before he was ejected in his turn in favour of James Cruze. After this flurry of activity, however, the genre was relegated once more to the basement where B pictures were made and pretty well stayed there until 1939.

And that was an extraordinary year for the western. Suddenly every studio seemed to be making them and making them big. For Paramount, de Mille directed *Union Pacific*, undoubtedly the blockbuster of the year, being a sprawling saga about the building of the Union Pacific railway. Henry King made *Jesse James*, with Tyrone Power as the eponymous hero and Henry Fonda as brother Frank; at Warners Errol Flynn starred in *Dodge City* with Michael Curtiz directing; Universal produced one of the best of all western parodies with *Destry Rides Again*, featuring James Stewart and Marlene Dietrich and directed by George Marshall; back at Warners Lloyd Bacon made *The Oklahoma Kid* with James Cagney and Humphrey Bogart; elsewhere John Ford starred Claudette Colbert and Henry Fonda in *Drums Along the Mohawk* but before that – and best of all – Ford had made *Stagecoach*.

Astonishingly, this was not only Ford's first sound western, it was the first western he had made for thirteen years, his output of some forty silent pictures in that genre having come to an end in 1926 with *Three Bad Men*. In the interim he had made twenty-five talkies and won himself the Academy Award for *The Informer* in 1935 and it is no doubt an indication of how low the western had sunk that, despite his earlier track record, nobody had even thought to offer him one for so long. *Stagecoach*, however, amply made up for all the years of neglect. It plucked John Wayne from obscurity and turned him, overnight, into a star; it established Ford himself as the master in that particular field; and more than any other film, even in that bonanza year of 1939, it gave the western a respectability that it had never approached before. What Ford proved was that in the right hands this kind of picture could, quite as well as any other, combine human drama, fact and legend, grandeur and poetry. Over the next twenty-five years he was to underline that point again and again.

The success of *Stagecoach* owed something to its very literacy (the basic story was inspired by de Maupassant's *Boule de Suif*) and not a little to an element of chance. Just as it was largely luck that was to give us Bogart and Bergman instead of Reagan and Sheridan in *Casablanca* so it was good fortune, allied to Ford's stubbornness, that teamed Wayne with Claire Trevor instead of the original pairing of Gary Cooper and Marlene Dietrich. Quite possibly the film would have been just as good with the latter couple in the leading roles but it would not have had the freshness and the element of surprise that were provided by the comparatively little known Wayne and Trevor.

Yet it was not the Oscar-nominated *Stagecoach* that was to set the trend for the next run of westerns but the more prosaic *Jesse James*. That, too, was a box office success and it was followed by a number of films which similarly took a romantic and sympathetic look at the traditional bad men of the west. The notorious Dalton gang was whitewashed in *When the Daltons Rode*, as too was *Billy the Kid*, this time impersonated by Robert Taylor. The Younger brothers were driven to a life of crime by their social environment in *Bad Men of Missouri* and Jesse James himself had been so rehabilitated that in 1941 Roy Rogers played him in *Jesse James at Bay*, a film I have always refused to see for fear that I might be faced with the obscenity of Jesse bursting into song.

Meanwhile there was a concurrent vogue – thanks to *Union Pacific* – for historical or semi-historical westerns. De Mille himself made the rather boring *Northwest Mounted Police* and Errol Flynn followed *Dodge City* with *Virginia City* and *Santa Fe Trail* (both in 1940 and both directed by Michael Curtiz) before teaming up with the director Raoul Walsh the following year to play Custer in the hugely inaccurate but very enjoyable *They Died With Their Boots On*. Walsh also directed *The Dark Command*, which starred John Wayne and dealt with Quantrell's Raiders and in this same period, the early 1940s, the founding of both Arizona and Texas were celebrated, with a certain amount of poetic or anyway journalistic freedom on film. Fritz Lang told of the establishment of *Western Union*, Joel McCrea played Buffalo Bill and Walter Brennan gave a memorable performance as the dreadful Judge Roy Bean opposite Gary Cooper in *The Westerner*.

Another of those 1939 hits, *Destry Rides Again*, can also be credited with inspiring a small horde of imitators or at least other films which sent up the west. *Buck Benny Rides Again* with Jack Benny was one of these; *The Marx Brothers Go West* was another. W. C. Fields and Mae West produced a delightful parody in *My Little Chickadee*; Abbott and Costello appeared less delightfully in *Ride 'Em Cowboy* and Joe E. Brown in *Shut My Big Mouth*.

By the time many of those aforementioned films were shown America, like the rest of the world, was at war and perhaps that fact helped the western to maintain its new-found popularity. Escapism was what the cinema audiences wanted most and stories of the old west, set fifty years and more ago, provided it in much the same way as an historical drama such as *Lady Hamilton* did. The western was even used in a couple of totally undistinguished instances to help the war effort: *Cowboy Command*, made in 1943 as part of the "Range Buster" series, had Nazi agents being seen off by cowboys and featured a rousing little aria entitled "I'll get the Fuehrer sure as shooting", while *Texas to Bataan*, which appeared a year earlier, exhorted its audience to "Blast a Jap with scrap".

But at the same time as those two pieces of rubbish were being botched together there appeared one film which was to have a far-reaching effect on the later development of the western – *The Ox-Bow Incident*. On the surface it's an indictment of lynching: three men are pursued and caught by a posse and hanged for cattle rustling, hanged that is without benefit of trial. Soon after their deaths indisputable proof of their innocence is provided and the leader of the posse kills himself, not out of remorse but for fear of the disgrace and dishonour that were coming to him. The story itself is bleak but what gives the film its – for that time – pretty well unprecedented air of pessimism was that it had no hero to come to the rescue. Even the leading character, Henry Fonda, is no more than a bystander, an observer. To say that *The Ox-Bow Incident* was the first psychological western is probably stretching the point further than it will easily go but it was perhaps the first western to combine a social conscience with an attempt to psychoanalyse its characters and allow wrong to triumph. The black hats don't actually get away with it (as the suicide indicates) but the white hats do nothing to bring retribution upon them.

The film was made largely at Henry Fonda's insistence (as a child he had himself witnessed a lynching in Nebraska) and rather against the wishes of Fox and Darryl Zanuck. It was therefore not given much of a boost by the studio and was in any case too grim and off-beat to appeal to a wide audience. But although it was not a financial success it was influential in changing the treatment of western characters. Henceforth straightforward, uncomplicated men like Ringo in *Stagecoach* were to become rarer and heroes and villains with all manner of chips, angsts and psychological problems were to become the norm. Many of the films in which such characters appeared were excellent but they tended to take the western away from its historical perspective and make it less of a morality play than an allegory of modern times. The classic western themes were simple: settlers versus Indians, cattlemen versus sheepmen, ranchers versus farmers, and vengeance. In my view, when they became more complicated, when Freud and Jung were consulted by the screenwriters more often than Roget's *Thesaurus*, the genre began to die.

But in 1943 such developments lay in the future and were probably not much considered; besides another, raunchier one, far more immediate in its impact, was on its way. Howard Hughes was about to introduce blatant sex to the west. Some say that Marlene Dietrich had already done that in *Destry*, though the film's most suggestive line – 'There's gold in them thar hills' uttered as she stuffed money down her cleavage – was excised by the censors. But even Dietrich was not so aggressively sexy as mean, moody, magnificent and top-heavy Jane Russell in *The Outlaw*. As we have seen, the film was made in 1943 but not properly released until 1946 though the delay made very little difference to its impact. The world was no more ready for Miss Russell's boobs in 1946 than it would have been three years earlier. The film was a bizarre reworking of the Billy the Kid story, which somehow managed to drag in Doc Holliday and completely ripped up items eight and nine – "a cowboy is clean . . . in thought, word and deed" and "a cowboy respects womanhood . . ." – in Gene Autry's ten point cowboy code. In fact, the Russell character in the film is deemed by the men around her to be simply an object of lust and of far less general value than a horse.

Still, sex as portrayed in *The Outlaw* was a touch adolescent and appealed mostly to the breast-fixated. Sex as treated in *Duel in the Sun* (1946) was, however, rather more adult. The film was produced by David Selznick and at a cost of some 6 million dollars was said at the time to be the most expensive ever made. It was an epic tale of one family headed by ruthless cattle baron Lionel Barrymore but what earned it its renown, its box office success (after allowing for inflation it is still thought to be the most lucrative western ever made) and its soubriquet – "Lust in the Dust" – was the steamy nature of the passion, rivalry and jealousy engendered in Barrymore's two sons (Gregory Peck and Joseph Cotten) by a half-breed girl. Naturally in 1946 this character was not actually played by a half-breed but by an artificially darkened Jennifer Jones. Thus in one year first the mammary and then eroticism were introduced into the western.

Would it ever be the same again? Well, yes it would, as a matter of fact – some of the great, straightforward classics of the genre were still to come but henceforth sex would crop up more and more frequently and more and more blatantly. So, too, would the "psychological" approach. In *Pursued* (1947), directed by Raoul Walsh, Robert Mitchum played a man about to be lynched and, in flashback, trying to sort out his life, his psyche and how the hell he ever got into this mess in the first place.

From then on the thoughtful, introspective western hero would become increasingly common.

Fortunately, however, the day of the less complicated and altogether simpler hero, the decent, upright man fighting for a west fit for honest folks to live in was not yet past. Ford brought him gloriously to life, with the aid of Henry Fonda, in *My Darling Clementine*, the director's first western for seven years. Fonda played Wyatt Earp, a shy, altruistic and therefore greatly romanticised Earp to be sure but an Earp who, without being wishy-washy about it, would have earned even Gene Autry's approval.

Then, in strong contrast to Ford though still maintaining the western tradition, came Howard Hawks with *Red River* in 1947. Hawks had never made a western before but immediately showed himself to be a master in that field, thanks at least in part to Ford's own protégé, John Wayne. Wayne played that stock figure the ruthless cattle baron, seizing land where he fancied it and inspiring his men with fist and whip; Montgomery Clift was the cowboy who rebelled against his bullying tactics and with whom Wayne had a quasi father/son relationship. In many ways the film was an allegory of how the west was won and in it Hawks not only revealed a much harsher, more realistic and less poetic vision than Ford's but extracted from Wayne such a powerful performance that Ford, on seeing the picture, remarked: 'I never knew the son of a bitch could act.'

With the advent of Hawks and Ford's second return to the west there began perhaps the most fruitful period the western has ever known. Ford followed *Clementine* with *Fort Apache* and a remake of *Three Godfathers*, which he dedicated to Harry Carey Sr, an old friend and one of the stalwarts among the early western stars, before going on in 1949 to make *She Wore a Yellow Ribbon*, a lyrical tribute to the US cavalry. The star of all of these was John Wayne, though in *Fort Apache* he shared the billing with Henry Fonda as the stubborn, glory-seeking cavalry commander who leads his men to destruction against the Apaches. That film was important, too, in that it underlined Ford's philosophy of the west – that if you have a choice between the truth and the legend and the latter is more glorious you should – as he spelled out later in *The Man Who Shot Liberty Valance* – "print the legend". In *Fort Apache* the legend as recounted by newspapermen to Wayne was that far from leading his troops rashly into an ambush Fonda had died heroically fighting off a rampaging horde. And Wayne, who knew better, replied: 'Correct in every detail.'

Many years afterwards in an interview with Peter Bogdanovich Ford explained his "print the legend" theory like this: 'We've had a lot of people who were supposed to be great heroes and you know damn well they weren't. But it's good for the country to have heroes to look up to.' Such simple and, again, poetic values were, however, to be undermined by the westerns of the 1960s and 1970s but Ford clung to them doggedly through pictures like *Wagon Master* and *Rio Grande* both of which he made in 1950 before taking another break from the western.

The 1950s opened strongly then with Ford in good form and the advent of such directors as Anthony Mann, who made *Winchester '73* with James Stewart, and Delmer Daves whose *Broken Arrow* was a particularly important contribution to the

Left: Roy Rogers, the warbling King of the Cowboys and thus an offence to all western purists, posing with his wife and co-star Dale Evans

Below: *Duel in the Sun* was known, unofficially as "Lust in the Dust". The dust was there anyway; Jennifer Jones and Gregory Peck provided the lust

Above: 'Come back, Shane!' wailed Brandon de Wilde, though not in this scene because Shane (Alan Ladd) hasn't gone anywhere yet
Right: John Wayne (with Kim Darby) winning his only Oscar as the "one-eyed fat man" in *True Grit*
Below: In *The Wild Bunch* Sam Peckinpah insisted that you had to depict violence in order to condemn violence. Oh yeah?

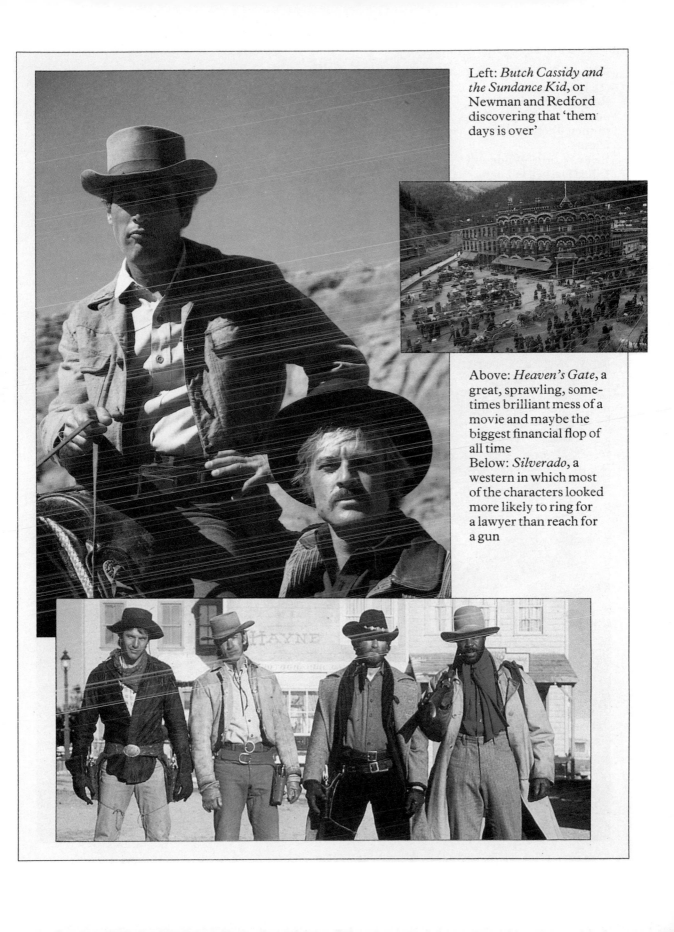

Left: *Butch Cassidy and the Sundance Kid*, or Newman and Redford discovering that 'them days is over'

Above: *Heaven's Gate*, a great, sprawling, sometimes brilliant mess of a movie and maybe the biggest financial flop of all time
Below: *Silverado*, a western in which most of the characters looked more likely to ring for a lawyer than reach for a gun

Right: *Becky Sharp*
(1935), directed by
Rouben Mamoulian and
notable mostly for being
the first Technicolor
feature
Below: Cornel Wilde and
Linda Darnell in *Forever
Amber*. Darnell was the
second choice after
Peggy Cummins had not
quite come up to scratch

CECIL B. DEMILLE'S

SAMSON
AND DELILAH

CECIL B. DeMILLE'S "SAMSON AND DELILAH" · LAMARR · MATURE · SANDERS · LANSBURY · WILCOXON · TECHNICOLOR

Above: Yes, by all means see all that – and also see, as Groucho Marx put it, that 'Samson's tits are bigger than Delilah's' Left: *Quo Vadis* (1951). As the audiences grew smaller, the spectacle grew larger. Try squeezing this lot into a TV screen

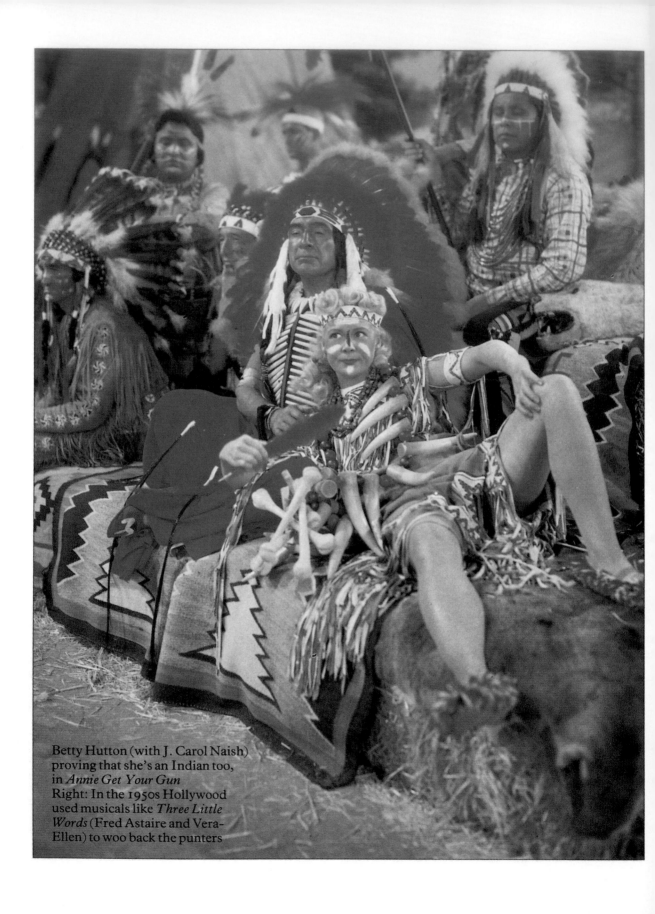

Betty Hutton (with J. Carol Naish)
proving that she's an Indian too,
in *Annie Get Your Gun*
Right: In the 1950s Hollywood
used musicals like *Three Little
Words* (Fred Astaire and Vera-
Ellen) to woo back the punters

Above: *House of Wax*, the first more or less acceptable 3D feature
Left: The Sharks and the Jets gather in *West Side Story*. Hollywood was still pinning its hopes on musicals

genre in that more emphatically than before it presented the Indians' point of view. James Stewart played an army scout seeking peace between the whites and the Apaches to which end he learned the Apache language, married an Apache woman and befriended Cochise (Jeff Chandler, who afterwards made something of a career of playing Cochise or somebody very like him). What made *Broken Arrow* different was the fact that it broke away from the hitherto orthodox view of the Indians as murderous assassins not much gifted with brains. (After all, as somebody pointed out, the marauding Redskins in *Stagecoach* would have had much more success if they had attempted to kill the horses rather than the people. To which, of course, Ford replied rather tersely that had they done so the film would have been over a damn sight quicker.) In a sense until 1950 the Indians had been the forerunners of invading aliens in science fiction movies: frightening but faceless, not really identifiable as people. *Broken Arrow* changed that view, putting forward an alternative image of them as brave, considerate humans beings with a culture of their own. This new attitude was long overdue but eventually it, too, had a part to play in weakening the appeal of the western by chipping away at its basic, uncomplicated structure. What the audience wanted in a story of cavalry or settlers versus pesky Redskins was an enemy to hate, one of implacable and ruthless cruelty beyond comprehension; it was never quite the same when we were asked to understand and sympathise with that enemy because it destroyed the concept of good versus evil. Not-entirely-good versus not-altogether-bad doesn't have the same appeal.

Undoubtedly the war had much to do with the more enlightened approach to the Indians. Richard Brooks, who directed a couple of westerns himself, said that having served with American Indians 'it was not difficult for me or someone else to say: "What's wrong with an Indian being a good guy?" I had no big jump in my reasoning to make that change.' In addition America was beginning to look at the plight of its Indians and was somewhat horrified by what it saw. As George Sherman put it: 'When people asked me why we treated the Indians so badly in motion pictures, I said, "Well, we didn't. We tried to depict them as we thought they were." But once we started to learn about the terrible tragedies that they experienced and are still experiencing it was time to do something that was right and show them in a proper light.'

In addition it's worth considering the theory that the 1950s was the decade in which the western grew up. By 1954 the B western along with the serials and the series had vanished, their function now taken over by television. In order therefore to entice people out of their homes and into the cinemas the A western felt obliged to stretch itself and to reflect modern life, morality and psychology while telling tales of the old west. Where once the hero exuded assurance he now began to exhibit doubt. Instead of simply getting up and doing what a man's gotta do he began to think about it and even wonder why he'd gotta do it at all. And all that went along with a spate of films in which, for instance, Charlton Heston played a white man raised by Indians (*The Savage*), Burt Lancaster was a sympathetic Apache in *Apache*, an Indian, Iron Eyes Cody, was – most unusually – allowed a featured role (as Crazy Horse) in *Sitting Bull* and even John Wayne got in on the "let's hear it for the Redskins" act when in

Above: *Union Pacific*, de Mille's contribution to the bumper crop of westerns in 1939
Left: John Wayne (with Claire Trevor) achieving stardom at last in *Stagecoach*, John Ford's first western talkie

Left: *The Ox-Bow Incident* starred Henry Fonda and introduced psychology into the western. Henceforth angst was to trouble the hero even more often than the Indians

Below: Gene Autry was always fastidiously dressed, played the guitar and sang. And he called himself a *cowboy?*

Columbia Pictures presents

GENE AUTRY
World's Greatest Cowboy

and

CHAMPION
World's Wonder Horse

RIM OF THE CANYON

Nan Leslie · Thurston Hall · Clem Bevans

Screen Play by John K. Butler

Directed by JOHN ENGLISH · Produced by ARMAND SCHAEFER

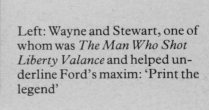

Left: Wayne and Stewart, one of whom was *The Man Who Shot Liberty Valance* and helped underline Ford's maxim: 'Print the legend'

Hondo he was required to say, memorably: 'I'm part Indian and I can smell you when I'm downwind of you. I could find you in the dark, Mrs Lowe.' It left you with the feeling that after they had parted Mrs Lowe might well have been found surreptitiously sniffing her own armpits and wondering if she was using the right kind of soap. And so it went on. This is not to say that before *Broken Arrow* Indians had never been portrayed in a sympathetic light. Indeed, the white man's persecution of them had been pointed out in *End of the Trail*, a B picture in which Tim McCoy starred for Columbia in 1932 and in which he declared that the palefaces had 'never kept a single treaty with them'. But it was from the time of *Broken Arrow* onwards that the Indian as murderous and more or less unthinking savage became the exception rather than the rule.

Meanwhile, and also in 1950, the darker side of the western was explored in Henry King's *The Gunfighter* wherein Gregory Peck played a gunfighter who wanted to get out of the business and retire but could not because wherever he went his reputation preceded him and there was always some ambitious young punk waiting to build himself a reputation by killing him. Until that film the rather samurai-like existence of the professional gunslinger had been exalted in the movies; here it brought forth, if only by implication, the sharply drawn breath of disapproval. And, too, there was another underlying message in *The Gunfighter* – one that was to be repeated often in the ensuing years – namely that "them days is over". In films emphasis began to shift from the heroic heyday of the west to the decline of the west as civilisation (or what passes for it these days) moved in and the man with the gun on his hip became an anachronism.

Even one of the great classics, *Shane* (1953), reflects that. Alan Ladd knows perfectly well that them days is over, or pretty nearly so, and wants to get out while he's ahead and settle down to humdrum domestic life. But circumstances, in the shape of evil Jack Palance, demand that he should strap on his guns one more time, do what a man's gotta do and then blow town in search of peace and quiet elsewhere. A year before that another of the very greatest westerns, *High Noon*, had contained similar elements. All Marshal Gary Cooper wants to do – as any sensible man in his position would – is go away with his gorgeous young wife, Grace Kelly, and raise a family. But he can't because the bad guys are coming and somebody has to face them. In the 1930s he would have done so with the full support, if not the actual help, of the townspeople. In 1952 he is isolated, just as Peck and Ladd were; his quaint idea of personal honour and obligation to the community is regarded as archaic even by Miss Kelly. At that time the approach by the writer Carl Foreman and the director, Fred Zinnemann, was unusual enough to upset the traditionalists. Zinnemann said: 'I think they felt threatened by the fact that the western hero was a man who was not fearless. He had enormous courage but he was not fearless. He was afraid and the traditionalists thought the western hero was a man who didn't know what fear was. I always thought that was very childish.'

Of course, it should be remembered that the film was made during the time of HUAC and America's anti-Red hysteria and the image of a man risking everything, even his life, not for gain but for something he believed in was regarded in some quarters as vaguely sinister. To some extent those who held this dark view of *High Noon* had reason on their side. Foreman said he saw the film as a reflection of America's political situation at the time, particularly as he was himself blacklisted by HUAC. 'There's the scene,' he said, 'with the man who offers to help and comes back with his gun and asks, Where are the others? Cooper says, There are no others . . . I became the Gary Cooper character.' Zinnemann, however, didn't see it that way at all and was therefore astonished when the violently patriotic John Wayne condemned the picture, saying of the scene at the end when Cooper takes off his marshal's badge and throws it on the ground that it was 'the most un-American thing I've ever seen in my whole life . . . I'll never regret having helped run Foreman out of this country.'

Possibly influenced by all these current trends Ford came back to the western in more sombre mood than before with *The Searchers* in 1956. It was the story of a search over ten years by two men, John Wayne and Jeff Hunter, for a white girl, Natalie Wood, who had been kidnapped by Comanches and used by them as a squaw. Hunter's intention is to rescue her, Wayne's to find and kill her because she had been irredeemably besmirched by her sexual contact with the savages. It's a moody, haunting film which can lay strong claim to being perhaps the best western ever made and it's notable, among many other things, for its understanding attitude towards the Indians.

Around this time, the early fifties, there was a brief vogue for western musicals, some – *Annie Get Your Gun, Seven Brides for Seven Brothers* and *Oklahoma!* – adapted from stage shows, others like *Calamity Jane* tailor-made for the movies. And, as a sort of curiosity, a few films featured women in the leading roles: Marlene Dietrich starred for Fritz Lang in *Rancho Notorious*, Joan Crawford played the lead in *Johnny Guitar* and Barbara Stanwyck was the *Cattle Queen of Montana*. Such movies never really caught on because in a matriarchal society like America the one place where a man might reasonably expect to escape from female domination was at a western; the very last thing he wanted there was a leading character wearing eyeliner and a skirt.

Much more popular were the films of Anthony Mann and Budd Boetticher, both of whom were prolific makers of westerns during that decade. Mann's pictures often starred James Stewart – *Winchester '73* and *The Man from Laramie*, for example – but this was a harder, tougher Stewart than audiences were accustomed to. In Mann's westerns he was usually some kind of saddle tramp bent on revenge and frequently nasty with it – 'a man who could kill his own brother', as the director put it. In these films, too, the violence was shown more coldly and harshly than had previously been the case, though it was never as explicit as it was to become later. Boetticher's pictures were rather different. For a start they were more modestly budgeted, virtually on the scale of B movies, and were more traditional in concept. The protagonist was usually Randolph Scott and the motif revenge, on several occasions inspired by the murder of Scott's wife. As was the case with Mann's heroes, Scott was a loner imbued with a strong personal code of honour. As Jim Kitses put it in his book *Horizons West* he knows that 'revenge is meaningless since the wife is dead; yet it is necessary because it is evidence of a way of life that the hero embodies: "Some things a man can't ride around." ' Or a man's gotta do what a man's gotta do.

Boetticher himself did not feel that his stories were particularly moral, nor were they intended to be. 'They were just stories about somebody I liked immensely who thought the same way I did and set out to do a job and believed in marriage and decency . . . In those days men pulled out chairs, they lit women's cigarettes for them – if women were allowed to smoke – and there was a chivalry and a courtesy that today people don't know about; they're not educated. This is the way I like to live and Randy was that kind of person.' The other notable point about Boetticher's westerns was the important part played by the villains.

'Before, the villain was always the villain,' he said, 'there was never a pull on the audience's sympathies between the leading man and the guy he eventually killed. But my villains were charming . . . You loved these guys because you saw in Randy's eyes and his dialogue that he admired them, too . . . If any of these gentlemen had shot Randy nobody in the audience would have cared. The association was with the villain because the villain loved Randy so much that he would have been a sheriff if he'd been born on the other side of the fence. So I think the charm of the Scott pictures was that the two men were equal. There had never been great villains in westerns before that you wanted to take home with you.' For that reason perhaps Boetticher's films did more to enhance the careers of those who played the heavies – the likes of James Coburn, Richard Boone and Lee Marvin – than for Scott who carried on where he had always been, just below the top level of stars, a solid comfortable performer who seemed to have been born in well-preserved middle-age and continued to look like that for ever.

Mann's westerns had a grandeur to them, Ford's a lyricism, Boetticher's were spare. His was the traditional west of the movies, a dangerous place where men could test themselves and each other far from civilisation, a place in which a man who didn't have "a big problem to overcome when he woke up in the morning had better invent one or he was going to get old in a hurry". In his west revenge and chivalry were all-important and women didn't have anything much to do – 'They were wives and sweethearts . . They tried to keep their men alive, which was a hell of a lot harder job than going out and shooting Indians but it wasn't romantic.'

Within a decade, however, Boetticher's approach would be out of date for generally speaking the 1950s saw the last real flowering of the old style western. The theme of the winning of the west was continued in such pictures as William Wyler's *The Big Country* and the taming of it in, for example, John Sturges' *Gunfight at the O.K. Corral* and Delmer Daves' *3.10 to Yuma*. But already more modern themes were cropping up in Nicholas Ray's *The Lusty Men*, which dealt with the lives of rodeo riders and in 1958 Arthur Penn and Paul Newman brought the Method to the west in *The Left-Handed Gun*, in which Newman portrayed Billy the Kid as a neurotic teenager from the back streets of New York. It was a downbeat but much-praised (in my opinion overpraised) film in which the psychology overshadowed the action.

Howard Hawks brought the decade to an end with a fine flourish when he made *Rio Bravo* in 1959, a film that was so successful and which he liked so much that he virtually remade it as *El Dorado* seven years later. The plot in both pictures has the lawman, John Wayne, standing up against the bad guys without the help of the townspeople, in which sense Hawks' films were very similar to *High Noon*, though their mood was much lighter. But there were a couple of significant differences: Wayne, unlike Cooper, had at least some assistance, notably a reforming drunk (Dean Martin in *Rio Bravo*, Robert Mitchum in *El Dorado*) and, more importantly, he was not refused but actually declined the aid of the local citizenry. This reflected both Hawks' political conservatism and his dislike of *High Noon*, much of which stemmed from his rejection of the idea that red-blooded American citizens would be too cowardly to rally round their sheriff. In his films the citizens were eager to rally round but Wayne declined their help because they simply were not good enough as gunfighters to go up against the men who were threatening them. His attitude, as Hawks put it, was: 'If they're really good I'll take them, if not I'll just have to take care of them.'

Not to be outdone by the upstart Hawks – his chief, though far less prolific, rival as the greatest of all western directors – John Ford was also in splendid form in 1959 with *The Horse Soldiers*, another of his romantic tributes to the US cavalry. Wayne starred again, of course, with the support of William Holden. Then, two years later, Wayne himself turned director, as well as producer and star, with *The Alamo*, which treated America's early equivalent of Dunkirk with a positively Ford-like sentimentality and romanticism, though without Ford's flair. It was an epic production totally overshadowed in public esteem by John Sturges' more modestly budgeted but far more enjoyable *The Magnificent Seven*. This was a colossal and cheeky piece of plagiarism: Akira Kurosawa's masterpiece *The Seven Samurai* transplanted in the west. There were some who chided Sturges for this act of apparent larceny, but in fact it seems perfectly reasonable since Kurosawa has admitted himself that some of his own films were merely westerns transplanted in Japan. Sturges changed the locale to Mexico and the samurai into professional gunfighters but otherwise left the basic story more or less alone. It worked as a western very nearly as well as it had worked as an eastern and made an international star of Steve McQueen. Yet here, too, the "them days is over" theme recurred: the Seven help the threatened Mexican villagers without reward, not from altruism but because, as gunfighters, they had nothing else to do; their kind was no longer in much demand.

Not that the celebrating of the west was entirely over because *How the West Was Won* did precisely that in 1962. Another epic this, a great sprawling story about four generations of a pioneering family directed not only by Ford but also by Hawks and George Marshall and featuring practically everyone from Wayne, Fonda and Stewart to Widmark, Peck and Debbie Reynolds. This apart, however, the western was now beginning to show increasing signs of disenchantment and pessimism and even Ford was affected. His *Sergeant Rutledge*, starring the black actor Woody Strode as a cavalry NCO wrongly accused of rape and murder, had a slightly cynical edge to it and *The Man Who Shot Liberty Valance* (1962) was something of a lament for better times despite the strong and reassuring presence of Wayne and the fact that the "print the legend" motif was as powerful here as it had ever been. Peter Bogdanovich believed that by this time Ford himself was 'obviously ambiguous about the western' and saw *Liberty Valance* as the bottom of a negative spiral in which the director was becoming increasingly gloomy. In conversation with Harry Carey Jr he went even further and gave the opinion that the film was, in a way, the last western because it seemed to him that Ford had come to the conclusion that the western period was now over. True, Bogdanovich did admit to me that when he put these views to the man himself Ford replied that he didn't know what the hell he was talking about. But the theme of *Liberty Valance* – the old west giving way to the new – is treated with a kind of brooding regret. And Ford's last western, *Cheyenne Autumn* in 1964, a story of the resettlement of an Indian tribe on a new reservation, lacks the master's spark, almost as if he had lost interest. Indeed, Carey, who knew him well and appeared in many of his films, thinks he did in fact become bored with the picture. 'He cut huge amounts out of the original script. I think if he had shot that original script it would have been an unforgettable film but as it turned out it wasn't well received.' Carey also thought that the air of melancholy and sadness that hung over the picture reflected the director's own mood as he approached "his twilight years". Richard Widmark, I have to add, retorted that 'Harry doesn't know what he's talking about. Ford loved that movie.' Even so, it was not one of the master's best.

But even in the 1960s there were still directors who tried to bring to life the old west as the younger Ford had done, notably Andrew McLaglen, son of Victor (who had played character roles in *Fort Apache* and *She Wore a Yellow Ribbon*). In pictures like *McLintock*, *Shenandoah*, *The Rare Breed* and *The Way West* Andrew McLaglen mixed all the trusty ingredients, the white hat against the black hat, good triumphing over evil. At the same time, however, other westerns were reflecting the more modern mood of disenchantment, concentrating heavily on the last rather than the early days of the west. Sam Peckinpah's *Ride the High Country* teamed Randolph Scott and Joel McCrea as a pair of old timers striving to make a crust in a west where progress and civilisation had passed them by. The theme of Richard Brook's *The Professionals* in 1966 was similar in that it dealt with a group of men, experts in destruction, whose time seemed over until they were brought together by a rich man to rescue his wife who had apparently been kidnapped by Mexican bandits. But the strength of the film, and its appeal to Brooks, was not so much that as the integrity displayed by the professionals when they realised that the wife had not been kidnapped but had actually run away from her appalling husband.

Marlon Brando made a couple of westerns in the 1960s – *One-Eyed Jacks* in 1961, wherein he played an ex-convict seeking revenge and looking like a man in urgent need of psychiatric help, and *The Appaloosa* (retitled no more attractively in Britain as *Southwest to Sonora*) in 1966. This one, along with such films as *Alvarez Kelly* and *Nevada Smith*, both also made in 1966, foreshadowed the far more graphic violence that was to become a feature of the western in the next decade. As a sort of antidote to all this there was also *Cat Ballou*, which won Lee Marvin an Oscar, and would probably rank as the best western send-up since *Destry Rides Again* were it not for the fact that *Support Your Local Sheriff* (1968), distinguished by a marvellous performance from James Garner, was even funnier.

So as the decade drew to a close, the western found itself being pulled in several different directions at once. Should it adopt the psychological approach or go for comedy or would sheer violence appeal more to the audience? By and large it was the latter that seemed to win the vote. By now the spaghetti western, as created by Sergio Leone, had begun to make its presence felt in the international marketplace. *A Fistful of Dollars* (1964) and its successors had converted Clint Eastwood from a likeable television performer in *Rawhide* to a major star not least because their stories were simple and violent. Hollywood's ambivalence towards the latest and conflicting trends was amply summed up by two films that appeared in 1969 – *True Grit*, which played for safety by combining a touch of comedy with a tale of a veteran lawman (John Wayne) clinging on beyond his time and facing the bad men alone and Sam Peckinpah's *The Wild Bunch*, which went bald-headedly for violence and death in slow motion. Wayne won the Oscar but it was Peckinpah's film that was to have the greater influence. It was set in 1912, when cars and electric light were becoming quite common, and William Holden's wild bunch were already an anachronism. As they face the final shoot-out in Mexico, Holden says to Ben Johnson: 'Let's go,' and Johnson replies: 'Why not?' Well, why not indeed: there was nothing else left for men such as these.

The Wild Bunch with its fatalistic heroism was an extremely fine movie, though its depiction of graphic violence – with blood gushing from bullet-riddled bodies – was much condemned at the time. Peckinpah's apologia, that it was necessary to show violence in order to condemn it, was greeted as such statements should always be, with much scepticism. But other directors seized upon it as a valid excuse to show even more of the same. Ralph Nelson did so in *Soldier Blue* in 1970, the film being unpleasantly remorseless in its portrayal of the slaughter and dismemberment of men, women and children alike as it recounted a true event – a raid by the US cavalry on an Indian tribe in Colorado in 1864.

Better in many ways than all of these, however, was *Butch Cassidy and the Sundance Kid*, the first and best of all the modern buddy movies and the film that more clearly than any other declared lyrically, movingly and excitingly that "them days is over". Henceforth there would still be occasional pictures (Andrew McLaglen's *Chisum* for one) that would hark back to the old times but by and large the movies no longer reflected the romance of the west. As the 1970s began America was growing increasingly disillusioned with its role in Vietnam and that unhappiness was reflected in the cinematic reproduction of the country's past. The movies stopped printing the legend and indeed began to tear down America's heroes, the one to suffer most from this revisionism being General Custer. In *They Died With Their Boots On* he had been a romantic, wholly admirable figure but by 1970 and *Little Big Man* he was being portrayed as an egotist and a paranoid, very nearly a psychopath, the sort of man who was unfit to run a Boy Scout troop, let alone lead the cavalry against Sitting Bull.

Little Big Man reflected a new, unsentimental attitude towards the west and also, incidentally, was the first big budget picture to cast an Indian, Chief Dan George, in a major role, though he only got it because Laurence Olivier, Paul Scofield and Richard Boone had turned it down. *A Man Called Horse* took the pro-Indian approach a considerable step further with its portrayal of life among the Sioux tribe as experienced by Lord John Morgan, played by Richard Harris. It strove earnestly enough towards authenticity to satisfy even that stern critic Iron Eyes Cody, who declared it to be his favourite western. Not that from now on the Indians were to have it all their own way, for with *Ulzana's Raid* in 1972 Robert Aldrich arrived at the conclusion that Palefaces and Redskins were equally vicious. As Burt Lancaster was called upon to say: "Ain't no one of us right."

By now the western had changed dramatically since *Stagecoach*. Even the role of that invaluable stock character, the cowboy, was being reassessed. In 1954 the critic Robert Warshow had written: 'The westerner is par excellence a man of leisure. Even when he wears the badge of a marshal or ... owns a ranch he appears to be unemployed.' But in *Will Penny* in 1967 Charlton Heston portrayed the cowboy as a man of work, an itinerant labourer, possibly illiterate and certainly not heroic. This depiction was taken even further three years later in *Monte Walsh*, starring Lee Marvin and Jack Palance. Here the cowboy was seen to be not only a man accustomed to a life of drudgery but one in a declining industry. Less glamorously than *Butch and Sundance*, the film anticipated the coming age of conformity and ranches owned not by cattle barons (like Wayne in *Red River*) but by corporations, a development pointed up even more firmly in 1972 by *The Culpepper Cattle Company*.

And so the demythification continued. The once heroic Jesse James was a neurotic killer in *The Great Northfield Minnesota Raid* (1971); Billy the Kid was similarly reclassified as a worthless punk in *Dirty Little Billy* a year later; and the west itself was viewed with a mixture of poignancy and parody in *The Life and Times of Judge Roy Bean*, directed by John Huston and written by John Milius and made in 1972. Under Huston's treatment it became a western that with wry humour seemed to be lamenting the decline of its own genre, which had never been Milius' intention. To me he said: 'I didn't like the movie at all. It was a Beverly Hills western.'

More obvious burlesque was to be found in Mel Brooks' *Blazing Saddles* in 1974. As with nearly all Brooks' work it was an uneven but very funny movie and, perhaps most significantly, it became one of the most commercially successful westerns ever made, possibly because even more than Huston's film it made fun of the western as lustily as it did the west. Robert Altman's *Buffalo Bill and the Indians* eschewed action for chat and humour and an almost clinical destruction of Buffalo Bill's legend. In the same year, 1976, Arthur Penn's *Missouri Breaks* aped the method of *Judge Roy Bean* by mocking the genre with a mixture of darkness and humour. With the exception, of course, of *Blazing Saddles* all these films were box office failures, a fact which tended to underline Pauline Kael's assertion in 1974 that the western was dead. She was, as I said earlier, a shade premature because in terms of quantity if not necessarily of quality 1976 was a good year for the western.

In addition to Penn's and Altman's films there were also *The Shootist* and *The Outlaw Josey Wales*, the latter reviving briefly the glories of the traditional western, the former celebrating its last rites. *Josey Wales*, starring and directed by Clint Eastwood, was the saga of a man avenging the murder of his wife, a story that began in the savagery and uncertainty of the post civil war era and ended optimistically in a more settled age when the west and the western hero were alive and flourishing. Reviewing the film in *Time* magazine, Richard Schickel wrote of Eastwood: 'He reminds us of a traditional American style of screen heroism – a moral man, slow to rile but wonderfully skilled when he must finally enforce his concepts of right and wrong. In those moments he links us pleasingly, satisfyingly with our movie pasts, rekindles briefly a dying glow.'

True enough but almost at the same time that glow was being doused by *The Shootist* in which John Wayne played an aged gunfighter dying of cancer and simply wanting to be left alone. It opened with a montage of sepia clips from Wayne's own westerns though not in order to celebrate the glory, the courage, the heroism and the hope of the earlier films but to point up the cynicism and pessimism with which the legend of the west was being rewritten. In the movie's most telling passage the local, small-minded sheriff says to Wayne: 'The old days are gone and you don't know it. We got water works, telephone, lights and we'll have our own streetcar electrified by next year ... Once we're rid of people like you we'll have a goddamned Garden of Eden.'

Perhaps with that film the western really did die because it seemed to be both a valedictory note on Wayne's career (it was his last picture) and on the kind of films in which he had built his reputation. On the other hand, of course, to speak of death in this context is really to go too far: western movies have been made since 1976 – in 1980, for example, Walter Hill directed *The Long Riders* in which the brothers Carradine (David, Keith and Robert) and the brothers Keach (Stacy and James) played the brothers Younger and James. In the same year there came Michael Cimino's *Heaven's Gate*, very possibly the most expensive disaster in the history of the cinema. It was a long, sprawling tale set in Wyoming in the 1890s when the cattlemen were fighting and slaughtering the immigrants and despite moments of brilliance it was so incoherent and self-indulgent that it led virtually to the demise of United Artists and seemed to drive yet another six-inch nail into the coffin of the western.

It was not surprising that after that there was another lengthy period in which the genre lay dormant until, in 1985, there came a small revival. In that year three westerns were released: *Pale Rider*, *Lust in the Dust* and *Silverado* – but none of them really worked. The best of them, *Pale Rider*, was an attempt by Eastwood to mix the basic plot of *Shane* with the religious mysticism of his own *High Plains Drifter* in 1972. *Lust in the Dust* was an affectionate but not very effective parody and *Silverado*, though not at all bad, served most of all to stress the basic problem in trying to make a western today: modern actors simply do not look convincing in that ambience. The cast included such able performers as Kevin Kline and Jeff Goldblum but they were just not believable. They looked like easterners, not westerners; they looked like the kind of men who, offered insults or violence by fellows in black hats, would instinctively reach for a lawyer rather than a gun. None of these films, not even

Eastwood's, proved popular and perhaps we must now resign ourselves to the prospect of the western lying moribund again until a new Ford or Hawks arises simultaneously with a new Wayne or Eastwood.

Is it, though, merely the lack of such people that has brought about the decline of the western? I don't think so: the causes are much deeper and more complex. But before we go into that subject it might be worthwhile to look a little more closely at the sort of people who made the western the great and glorious form of screen entertainment that it was at its very best. To begin with, as *Silverado* indicated, a special type of actor was needed.

Budd Boetticher said: 'You had to be a man to be a western star. Look at Wayne, look at Cooper, look at Randy Scott.' Well, yes, agreed but that's only a start. Modern actors would no doubt claim indignantly that they are men, too, but perhaps they are not the same kind of men as Cooper and company. Glenn Ford, a western star himself, gave a rather more precise definition: 'It takes a man who's been around horses and knows about the west. Once you get out there in the middle of the prairie and you're about a thousand feet from the camera and you have to ride across the hill and the sun's coming up, you think to yourself "Can you imagine being paid to do this?" These New York actors come out here from the stage and they get on the set and suddenly they're confronted with dust and wind and tumbleweed and the horses are rearing and snorting and they find it's not that easy.'

More than anything else perhaps that defines the kind of person who cannot be a western star. Would *Stagecoach* have been a hit if someone like Woody Allen had played Ringo? Hardly. Because, as Andrew McLaglen said, the westerner had to be a man who looked at home in the wide open spaces – a man, in the words of Harry Carey, like Wayne or Cooper who 'were outdoor guys, men's men, rugged and physically strong'. Beyond even that, though, they had to look like men who were also morally strong and reliable as well as upright, courageous and honest, men of action rather than words, for surely a great nation like America could not have been founded by any lesser breed. With such a mental image in place it's obvious that actors like Cooper, Wayne, Fonda, Stewart, Eastwood were designed by nature to star in westerns. But who is there among the modern breed of actor who could replace them? Sylvester Stallone? No, thank you, for his character is essentially urban man driven perforce and not by choice to exist in the wild.

But if a western needs precisely the right kind of actor it also needs, though perhaps not to quite the same extent, the right kind of director. John Ford was, of course, pre-eminently that kind of director. Another of his dicta laid down the basic ground rules for western film making. 'We were doing a picture in Monument Valley,' said William Clothier, 'and we had these waggons pulling cannons and the road got a little bit dusty and the wind came up and someone called for the water waggon to wet down the dust and old man Ford said, "What the hell is he doing?" I said, "Well, he's wetting it down. He don't like the dust." And Ford said, "To hell with that," and he called the guy over and said, "Look, you can't make a western without dust and horse shit."' Ford loved the west, dust and horse shit and all. So did Hawks. So did the likes of Raoul Walsh and Henry Hathaway possibly because all of them were born and brought up at a time when the stories of the west and the men who figured in them were still alive and had not yet become history.

To put it another way they and the great western stars belonged to a more innocent age when the world accepted that a man had to do what a man had to do whereas in this modern era it sometimes seems perfectly acceptable – certainly in movies – for a man to wonder how he can avoid doing what he has to do and still come out ahead. Perhaps Hollywood's mistake lay in forgetting that the western is essentially a costume drama. To be successful it has to be made by people who can think themselves back into the period, not by men who seek to interpret nineteenth-century events with twentieth-century hindsight.

Indeed, it was precisely the tendency to imbue nineteenth-century frontiersmen with the motives of modern urban man that weakened the very foundations on which the western was built. In decrying the "psychological western" Budd Boetticher said: 'Those guys in the old west had only one problem and that was the whole story. There were no psychologists' couches in those days; you didn't go to a fellow and say, "I have a problem: I'm not sleeping enough." That's absurd. The minute they tried to do this on the screen they destroyed the western.' By extension he applied the same criticism to the films that "revised" the images of the western heroes. 'The western,' he said, 'should not be an exposé.' Similarly Richard Brooks said: 'The moment you become as complicated as I did in *The Last Hunt*, which dealt with the extinction of the buffalo and the fact that nobody cared about the beast, you predicted the failure of the western. It was too psychological a story to tell as a western. Westerns should be uncomplicated.'

Mixed-up heroes, sympathetic Indians – these things don't gel with what Charlton Heston saw as the essential appeal of the western, the fact that it 'explores certain verities about the American character, about the way Americans perceive themselves. It's about survival, endurance, honesty, courage and all these things are part of the American experience.' But in a more cynical and more sophisticated age do Americans still perceive themselves like that? John Milius was inclined to think not. 'In most westerns the issue is decided with a gun and one bullet. The guy draws and he shoots and the bad guy falls. If you watch *Miami Vice* the issue is decided with many bullets. People whip out their machine guns and blaze away at each other and eventually the bad guy falls down. That says a lot about how we feel about ourselves. One time, if we had to settle the issue with violence it was a kind of clean violence. Now we don't feel we can do anything without a lot of bullets. I think people really just don't care any more about a man and a woman struggling in the desert, trying to make a home for themselves.'

So if you listen to the pessimists like Richard Brooks the western is extinct; if you take a slightly optimistic view it's lying fallow or, and this I think is a more accurate assessment, it's still with us but in a different form. 'The kids,' said Brooks, 'who pay five dollars to see a movie, their horses are motorcycles and cars.' Exactly. And are not the bike movies, from Peter Fonda's *Easy Rider* onwards, simply westerns in modern dress? Perhaps John Milius is wrong; perhaps people do still care about a man and a woman struggling to survive and perhaps what he called 'the archetypal American myth: that you could go over the next ridge and make a life for yourself' still holds true. Only now the audiences want that myth in a glossier, more up to date form. It's not over the next ridge but on the next planet that a man and a woman can make a new life for themselves these days.

As Peter Bogdanovich said: 'The mythology of the west was related to some innocence in the country, some frontier thing that's gone. For kids everything moves faster now ...' And it moves, as far as the cinema is concerned, in space. 'Let's face it,' Bogdanovich said, '*Star Wars* was really a western only they used space ships instead of horses. I think it's all been taken over by other genres; they just don't call them westerns any more.'

That's probably true, too, but it offers little consolation to the purist who still thinks back wistfully to the poetical elegiac westerns of Ford or the harder-nosed but still romantic films of Hawks. Without such men to make them it seems doubtful whether western movies in their true guise, not masquerading as something different, will ever enjoy a protracted revival. In his picture *Targets* Bogdanovich had a line which ran: "All the good movies have been made." On second thoughts he believed that maybe now it should be changed to "All the good westerns have been made." In the late 1980s this sounds like a sadly appropriate epitaph; one can only hope that it's as premature as the utterances of all those who, in the past, have looked upon the body and pronounced it dead only to see it struggle to its feet and reach for its gun.

The Wild Bunch—plenty of violence, plenty of blood and death in slow motion

NINE

THE DECLINE OF THE STUDIOS

In 1946, as any fool could see, Hollywood and the studios stood on the threshold of a golden age that was clearly going to be even more glorious, not to say lucrative, than anything that had ever existed before. That year, the first full year of peace, 90 million people – or roughly seventy-five per cent of the potential audience – went to the movies every week. It didn't matter what was showing, 90 million people saw it. To put it another way, this meant that three out of every four Americans who were old enough, mobile enough and compos mentis enough to go to the pictures went to the pictures. No doubt about it, the grip of the cinema as the cheapest, most easily available, most comprehensive form of mass entertainment in the history of the world was keener than ever. Wasn't it?

Well, no it wasn't actually and the warning signs were there, for those who cared to seek them out, even in 1946. In the first place a poll conducted the previous year had discovered that an alarming eighty-four per cent of Americans would, if obliged to make the choice, rather give up the movies than the radio. Secondly, Olivia de Havilland was in the process of having the dreaded suspension clause declared illegal; thirdly, the US Supreme Court was about to divorce the studios from the cinemas; fourthly, television was lurking around the corner, flexing its muscles; and beyond all that a remarkable number of American women had become or were working hard to become pregnant.

None of these factors could, alone, be held responsible for the weakening of the movie industry or the shattering decline in cinema attendances which by 1950 had shrunk to sixty million a week and thereafter were to carry on shrinking. (TV indeed was not to become a real threat until around 1949/1950.) But each had a significant part to play. Take Miss de Havilland, for example. In 1943 she had come to the end of her seven-year contract with Warner Brothers only to discover that, on account of past suspensions, the studio reckoned she still had another six months to serve. At first, like everyone else, she accepted that. But then, she said, 'They loaned me out for a film that had only about twenty pages of script. They were going to write the rest of the script while they were shooting. Well, it was doomed, absolutely doomed to failure. So I took another suspension and this was on extension time.' At which point enter a lawyer raising the interesting query as to whether a seven-year contract under Californian law meant seven years of work or seven calendar years. It was a matter nobody had ever seriously discussed before because the actors and other studio employees to whom it applied had been too scared to do so. Miss de Havilland, however, feeling she had very little to lose said, Let's go ahead, let's take it to court.

So she did – and she won. A seven-year contract, declared the Superior Court of California, could run for seven calendar years and not a day longer without the consent of both parties. Jack Warner, naturally, was not going to be content with that. 'So he appealed,' said Miss de Havilland, 'and we won a unanimous decision at the Appellant Court and Warners appealed again to the Supreme Court of the State of California which agreed with the former decisions. This became known as "the De Havilland Decision" and if you look it up in the law books you'll find it under D, that's where you'll find it.'

In fact the case had not been nearly such a simple or civilised business as she made it sound. As the litigation started Warners sent out injunctions to every production company they could think of enjoining them not to employ her and while the case was on nobody did offer her work. Indeed, Miss de Havilland said she didn't receive any support at all except from the Screen Actors' Guild. 'Individually most actors were kind of alarmed for me and anxious because they didn't think I could win.' An interesting sidelight to this is that when the litigation began in 1943 a great many actors were in the forces. 'They were under suspension all that time,' she said. 'When they came back they would have to begin their contracts where they'd left off, at the same salary, even though they were more valuable than they had been when they left and inflation had set in and all that sort of thing. But when I won my action it established a precedent and then Jimmy Stewart went to court to get a ruling, quoting my case, regarding the term of suspension of a player who'd been off serving his country and the judge ruled in his favour and the studios didn't challenge it.' Miss de Havilland herself did not work for three years but, as a happy ending to the story, when all the legal business had been satisfactorily resolved she starred in *To Each His Own* in 1946 – for Paramount – and she won an Oscar for best actress.

By far the most important result of the de Havilland case, however, was that it broke the studios' hold on their contract players. From now on a contract would expire when it was supposed to expire and not when the studio decided it should. Taken in isolation this in itself might not have been much more than an irritant, causing the companies to think twice about offering a highly paid player a totally unsuitable piece of work. But in the broader view it was a sign that the old order was weakening and changing, that the studios were beginning to lose both control and touch.

In 1947 cinema attendances fell and continued to fall. Why? All manner of reasons have been suggested – for instance, that the quality of the films was poor because Hollywood had misjudged or failed to recognise the audience's more sophisticated taste and carried on believing, as the war years had taught it to do, that any old picture would be good enough. That may certainly have been one reason but if so it must be the first time in recorded history that H. L. Mencken's dictum: 'Nobody ever lost money by underestimating the taste of the public' had been proved false. Some people have suggested that because American industry had turned round quickly from full-time war production to the full-time production of consumer goods the "affluent society" had sprung into being with the result that people had more time and more money to pursue other interests such as golf, travel and going to the ball game. That was possibly true in 1946 but it became less so in succeeding years as the percentage of money spent on such leisure activities declined.

Perhaps as much as anything the postwar baby boom accounted for the drop in cinema attendances. On balance making love has always been rather more popular than making war and never so much as in the immediate aftermath of a war. With the advent of peace Americans fell to making love with enormous gusto and over the next few years the resulting babies meant that the very people – the young of marriageable age – who had boosted attendances in 1946 were stuck at home, the baby-sitting industry not yet having developed. And by the time it had, in the early 1950s, television was firmly enough established to make sure that the young parents were now inclined to stay at home.

At the same time as all these trends were developing, the studios were struck a potentially crippling blow by the US Justice Department, which even before the war had been concerned about the monopolistic way in which film studios and cinemas were owned by the same people. Now it decided to do something about it. In a series of actions – United States v Paramount Inc – in a series of courts, the Justice Department asked for ownership of the cinemas to be separated from ownership of the producing and distributing companies and finally, in July 1949, a judgment was delivered in the Department's favour. It was true, as one Supreme Court judge said, that the five major studios, MGM, Warners, Fox, Paramount and RKO, owned only seventeen per cent of America's cinemas but they tended to own the best cinemas and this gave them a virtual monopoly over the vital first-run exhibition in the biggest cities. In view of the courts' decisions the studios had no alternative but to divest themselves of their control of the theatres and by 1954 all of them had done so.

What this meant, in theory, was that henceforth each film would have to be sold on its merits, although in fact block booking – the system by which a cinema was obliged to take a number of films it did not want in order to acquire the one it did – could have gone on covertly. That it didn't was because there was no longer a demand for it; indeed there was a decreasing demand for films and production was on the wane. In 1946, that isolated and magic year which did not, after all, herald the coming of another golden age, the studios' net profits had been $121 million; two years later they were down to $48 million and things had grown so bad that not only were 12,000 workers laid off but Louis Mayer cut his own salary by 25%. Among other reasons for the alarming drop in profits was a decline in overseas revenues brought about by the practice of European countries in particular of protecting their own film industries by imposing a quota on the number of Hollywood movies which could be imported.

By the end of the decade the once-rosy postwar prospects were looking decidedly bleak; the industry was in turmoil and nobody was safe, not even Mayer whose noble act of belt-tightening in dropping his basic salary by around $200,000 failed to protect his job. In 1951, when he was sixty-six, the unthinkable happened and MGM fired him. The actual cause of his dismissal was a power struggle between himself and the twenty years younger Dore Schary whom he had brought into the studio to be head of production. The differences between them grew so acrimonious that Mayer told Nick Schenck, MGM's capo di capi, that he would have to choose between him and Schary and to L.B.'s everlasting mortification Schenck chose Schary. John Huston, who was inadvertently involved in all this, believed however that Mayer was "headed for oblivion" anyway. Although the studio's 1951 profits were around $7.6 million, the same as they had been in 1950, the prognostications for 1952 were not good and indeed the profit that year fell to considerably less than $5 million, the lowest since 1935.

Huston's role in Mayer's downfall came about because he, and Schary, wanted to make *Red Badge of Courage* and Mayer was against it on the grounds – quite right, as it turned out – that the picture would be uncommercial. Huston said: 'The film took on symbolic aspects. If L.B. got his way and the movie wasn't made, why then it was his triumph and he was back in the saddle. If, however, Dore had the film made it meant that his word was over L.B.'s. The grey eminence in all this was the shadowy figure of Nick Schenck back in New York. He was referred to either as "New York" or "The General". Anyway, I heard about the bitterness that was evolving and I wanted no part of it. I went up to see L.B. and I said, "Look, L.B., I don't want to make bad blood here in the studio. There's a very easy way out of this: I just won't make the film. I'll withdraw it." L.B. said: "John Huston, do you believe in making this film?" I said: "Yes, of course." He said: "Then stand by your guns. You make it, come hell or high water. I'm against it and I tell you frankly that I'm against it but if you're for it, you fight for it." ' So Huston did and Schary did and Mayer went.

It was the end of an epoch: Mayer *was* MGM. As Greer Garson said, he had been 'the beating heart of MGM' and from her standpoint as one of the studio's contract players 'he was most unkindly shovelled out of the nest though he'd done more than anyone else in building up this great corporation. It was a rather bitter parting and those of us who really loved him felt great distress.' Nor was that distress lessened by the introduction, after Mayer's dismissal, of what she described as 'a pogrom, a policy of petty attrition against Louis B. Mayer's loyal stars'. Trivial things, she said – expenses were cut, limousines were no longer standing by to dash the actors hither and yon. A film Mayer had planned for Miss Garson – "a big, expensive picture" – was cancelled and instead she was asked by Schary to go on tour to help promote *Julius Caesar*, in which 'Deborah Kerr and I played the two little, tiny, lady parts'. If she would do that, Schary said, her cancelled picture would be restored to the schedule. 'I said, "Shake my hand on that." He shook my hand and I don't know how he could have done it because he was already planning not to put the film back on the schedule.' So she bought herself out of her contract and left, in which action she was but anticipating the dismissal that was soon to be the fate of the rest of MGM's much-vaunted, more-stars-than-there-are-in-heaven contract players.

As for the great Mayer, he became a rather sad figure and spent most of his remaining years (he died in 1957) trying to stir up rebellion against Nick Schenck among the stockholders of Loew's Inc, MGM's parent company. (It probably had nothing to do with Mayer but I daresay he was not exactly desolated when, in 1955, Schenck himself was kicked upstairs to become figurehead as chairman of the board.) For a while Mayer was consultant to Cinerama but after his ejection from MGM he was seen as a loser and in Hollywood nobody likes a loser, or rather they like to see the odd loser around because his dismal fate makes them happier about their own lives but nobody wants to hobnob with him. George Sidney, though, was an exception. He said: 'When he left or was disposed of or however you want to put it, I think he was treated badly. Any time a king is deposed you think he was treated badly. I never stopped my great friendship, my great love for Mr Mayer because I had the greatest respect for him and I still do. I remember, after he had left the studio, going to his home and it was coming up to Christmas and he said, "Come in here, boy," and I walked in and there on this long mantelpiece were just a couple of Christmas cards . . .' Well, that was predictable: what had Mayer done for anybody lately and, more to the point, what was he ever likely to be able to do again? Nobody sends Christmas cards to a loser. Although John Huston, too, confessed to a liking for the man and 'I felt it a melancholy duty to go up and see him in his isolation whenever I came back to the US.' Mayer was perhaps the greatest of the Hollywood tycoons and if he was not invulnerable then, as his contemporaries were to discover, nobody was. His dismissal can therefore be seen, if only sentimentally, as the moment when the studio system really began to break up.

On the effect of the anti-trust laws, the divorcement of studios and cinemas, opinions differ. John Houseman, who went to MGM as a producer soon after the decree was signed, said: 'That consent decree was never as drastic as anybody feared. They got around it; they formed different companies; the money was still the same.' But George Sidney, who was also at Metro at the time, disagreed. 'It hurt,' he said. 'It certainly hurt us as suppliers and we stopped being an industry.' The movies were, in fact, already becoming a sort of cottage industry and independent production was beginning to play an increasingly important part. As early as 1946 Frank Capra, William Wyler and George Stevens had formed their own company, Liberty Films, to give themselves the freedom to choose the pictures they wanted to make and, of course, to share more liberally in the profits. For complicated tax reasons Liberty ran swiftly into difficulties and was sold to Paramount but it had done enough to prove that there was a future in independent film making. It was not just the directors and producers who realised this but the stars and the agents as well. In 1950 MCA (the Music Corporation of America), perhaps the most powerful agency in Hollywood, persuaded Universal to let James Stewart star in *Winchester '73* for fifty per cent of the net profits. Points, or percentage, deals had not been unknown in the past, especially in the silent days, but this was the first time a star had been given such a large share of the cake. The film was a great box office success and earned Stewart a very large sum of money. The advantages of such an arrangement soon became obvious to other stars, especially as freelance actors – a rarity before the war – were now fairly common. Charlton Heston, for instance, arrived in Hollywood around the time Stewart was making *Winchester '73* and signed a non-exclusive contract with Hal Wallis' independent company. He believed this was only the second such contract ever given, the first having gone to Marlon Brando a year or so earlier. He said: 'Hal Wallis gave me in effect the freedom to do films for other people, to do plays, to do television – which was then anathema to the movie colony – because

In *Winchester '73* James Stewart
(here with Shelley Winters) was
the first star to dip his bread in the
rich gravy of the profits
Opposite page: Brando – 'You
want I should clear your place, too?' –
in *A Streetcar Named Desire*

he knew the studio system was ending. Within three or four years nobody was under contract.' Again, if we're looking sentimentally for one precise moment when the contract system could be seen to have reached its end, that moment arrived in 1954 when MGM released Clark Gable, "the King of Hollywood" himself, because they could no longer afford to pay him his annual salary of $520,000. In fact the studio weakened and asked him to stay on when his last film for them, *Mogambo*, began to make money but by then Gable was happy to leave for he, too, wished to dip his bread in the gravy of points deals. (Later on creative accountancy was to make any agreement based on a percentage of net profits virtually worthless and the stars, led by Brando, began to demand and be granted a percentage of the gross take. Not only the stars either: Alfred Hitchcock is reputed to have been given seventy-five per cent of the gross of *Psycho*.)

Now the significance of these developments – points deals, non-exclusive contracts – was not lost on the agents. In 1948 Burt Lancaster, then a comparative newcomer, had formed a company with his agent Harold Hecht and the producer James Hill and was thriving. The bigger agencies, MCA in particular, took this development one step further and came up with the package deal: from their own stable of clients they brought together a star, a director, a writer and perhaps a producer and offered them to the studio as a job lot. The day of the deal-maker had arrived and is with us still. The first major company to turn this to its own ends was United Artists, which had never owned a studio – a fact that had been a cause of weakness in the past but was now to become an advantage. In 1951 Charlie Chaplin and Mary Pickford relinquished their power at UA to two attorneys, Arthur Krims and Robert Benjamin, and astutely these men converted the company into a sort of clearing house for other independent productions, for even though they had no studio they did have a most efficient distribution network.

Thus in all manner of ways the power in Hollywood was transferred from the studios to the stars and, through the stars to the agents. Philip Dunne recalled that some time before Darryl Zanuck left 20th Century-Fox to become an independent producer himself, he was in Zanuck's office chatting about the future and . . . 'He said, "I'll tell you what the business is going to be like and I'm not going to be in it. The other day an agent was in here representing a star and telling me how to rewrite the script. I threw the son of a bitch out of the office but he'll be back. The agents and the stars are going to be running the business and when that happens I don't want to be here and I'd advise you not to be here either." I think he was right: that's what happened.' Some time later Dunne himself had an experience of star power. 'I was casting a film called *Ten North Frederick*, which I wrote and directed. Eventually the star was Gary Cooper but at the time we had Spencer Tracy and he was making *The Old Man and the Sea* at Warner Brothers. I was doing tests of actresses to play opposite him. We wanted an unknown but he didn't like the one we picked. So I made something like fifteen tests of young, aspiring actresses and I had to get in my car and drive out to Warners to show them to Spence and this was something that Zanuck wouldn't tolerate. An actor had nothing to do with the casting of a picture – that was done by him, Zanuck.'

But while the stars and the agents were flexing their muscles the studios had something even more menacing to worry about – television. At first, according to John Houseman, 'Hollywood took a long, long time to feel that it was in any way threatened. The myth persisted that people would still want to go out to cinemas. Some did not believe that: David Selznick was convinced from the beginning of the 50s that television was here to stay and was going to take over. He was a very shrewd man. Dore Schary, however, was always a bit of a dreamer and thought the movie business was there for ever.' Robert Wagner remembered that at Fox at about the same time, 'Most of the people said, "Don't worry about it, it's not going to happen." ' But this was simply whistling in the dark and besides was not a universally held belief. A number of people told me that for some years the very use of the word "television" was banned in Hollywood studios, as though the dreadful bogeyman would go away if ignored.

Of course, it was not obliging enough to do so, however much people strove to ignore it and by the early 1950s it was quite clearly the biggest threat Hollywood had ever faced – cinema audiences were dwindling rapidly, cinemas themselves were closing, the demand for B pictures was diminishing as the serials and series on the box took over the function of low-budget westerns and thrillers. All of which makes it even more ironic that, as Robert Wagner said, the studios could have controlled or even owned TV. 'It's always amazed me,' he said, 'that they could have bought television stations instead of hanging on in the theatres.' Indeed, George Sidney said that at one time there was a suggestion that MGM and NBC should form a joint company but 'in New York the people running the studio at that time said, "Television is nothing." ' No doubt any such merger would also have fallen foul of the anti-trust laws but it's not inconceivable that something could have been worked out. As it was Hollywood suffered horrendously for its lack of foresight and very quickly found itself seeking all manner of desperate measures to ward off the voracious advances of TV.

In this MGM was, for a while, the most successful of the studios for, to a large extent, it put its faith in musicals. The obvious advantage the cinema had over its rival was the ability to offer sheer size and spectacle – to say nothing, at that time, of colour – and the musical was the ideal vehicle for these things. The history of the film musical had been slightly bumpy hitherto: a period of great popularity with the coming of sound had led to a surfeit and a spell of public indifference that was followed by a revival, stimulated by Busby Berkeley and continued by Fred Astaire and such choreographers as Hermes Pan. Until the war musicals had mostly been made in black and white and up to the late forties were rather like light comedies with music, almost akin to operettas. But in 1948 the Freed Unit at MGM, headed by lyricist-turned-producer Arthur Freed, took the genre into a new dimension with *On the Town* in which the likes of Gene Kelly, Frank Sinatra and Ann Miller burst into song or a bit of a buck and wing as the mood took them and the musical numbers, instead of providing a punctuation point, helped to carry the action along. From then until the mid-1950s MGM musicals were among the most important products, commercially, to come out of Hollywood and from 1948 to 1952 there were invariably two or three of them in the top box office hits. The films included *Annie Get Your Gun*, *Showboat*, *Kiss Me Kate*, *An American in Paris*, *Seven Brides for Seven Brothers* and, of course, perhaps the best of them all, *Singin' in the Rain*. With the help therefore of Kelly, Astaire (in *Easter Parade* and *The Band Waggon* to mention but two of his pictures) and singers like Howard Keel MGM defied TV for several years as too, with their own less frequent musicals, did other studios. In 1956 Goldwyn's *Guys and Dolls* (with Brando, Sinatra and Jean Simmons) was the number one film at the box office, followed by Fox's *The King and I* (Yul Brynner and Deborah Kerr). MGM's *High Society* (Crosby, Kelly and Sinatra) was at number four and Columbia's *The Eddie Duchin Story* (Tyrone Power, Kim Novak) came in at number eight. But though in the next few years other musicals such as *Pal Joey*, the enormously popular *South Pacific* and *West Side Story* did well in the money charts, 1956 was the peak year for this kind of film. Even before then the comparative failure of *It's Always Fair Weather*, co-directed in 1955 by Kelly and his frequent partner Stanley Donen, had indicated that the public's appetite for musicals was not insatiable and in 1957 Kelly's *An Invitation to the Dance* was regarded by the more sour critics as heralding the very death of the screen musical. As later films showed it was not exactly that but the bonanza days were certainly over.

Meanwhile, other forms of movie spectacular were being summoned up in the struggle against TV, among them the Biblical epic which, naturally, brought the old maestro Cecil B. de Mille back into prominence. Of de Mille one of his star discoveries, Charlton Heston, said: 'He was the 600lb gorilla. He could do whatever he wanted to do and Paramount would finance whatever he wanted to make because in seventy-one films, as he was fond of saying, he had made only one failure – a picture called *Four Frightened People*, which he made in the early 30s with Claudette Colbert. De Mille, in effect, was the guarantor of Paramount's success as a studio; his films were undoubtedly the most successful ever released.' So, in these parlous times as TV grew ever more threatening the 600lb gorilla saved Paramount's bacon with *Samson and Delilah* (which starred Victor Mature and Hedy Lamarr and of which Groucho Marx said: 'I didn't like it. Samson had bigger tits than Delilah') and the lavish remake, starring Charlton Heston, of his own *The Ten Commandments*. He also, on a more contemporary theme, starred Heston in the circus film, *The Greatest Show on Earth* which, incidentally, won de Mille his only Oscar.

In the same period other studios made other spectaculars – *David and Bathsheba*, produced by Zanuck and starring Gregory Peck and Susan Hayward, *Quo Vadis*, Robert Taylor and Deborah Kerr starring for MGM, Zanuck again came up with Edmund Purdom in *The Egyptian* and so on. They all did rather well at the box office but, as with the musical, their charms began to pall and although occasional epic productions like Mike Todd's *Around the World in 80 Days* and the multi-Oscar winning *Ben Hur* were still able to pull in vast numbers of punters the species as a whole was on the decline from the middle of the 1950s onwards. In 1960 indeed the most ambitious epic of them all, *Cleopatra*, very nearly destroyed 20th Century-Fox. For all manner of reasons, including the ill-health of the Queen of the Nile herself, Elizabeth Taylor, it was subject to so many vastly expensive postponements and rearrangements of schedules and locations that it cost at a conservative estimate $45 million and finished the careers of its producer, Walter Wanger, and its original director, Rouben Mamoulian, who was replaced by Joe Mankiewicz. Two years later another expensive flop, MGM's remake of *Mutiny on the Bounty* with Brando and Trevor Howard, similarly finished the career of the director Lewis Milestone.

However, Hollywood did not put all its faith in bigger and – fingers crossed – better productions than TV could offer. It also went in for technological innovations to woo back the disappearing audience. For a start there was 3D, with which people had been experimenting for some time. The major studios had little faith in it, feeling – correctly as it turned out – that the public would rapidly get fed up with having to wear special glasses to look at a movie. But in 1952 an independent producer, Arch Oboler, made an African adventure movie called *Bwana Devil*, which sold quite well on the slogan "a lion in your lap" although, in truth, it was pretty turgid stuff. Warners at any rate were sufficiently encouraged to make a three-dimensional horror picture, *The House of Wax*, which starred Vincent Price and was rather better than *Bwana Devil*, thought still not much good. At one point, however, Jack Warner was optimistic enough to summon his executives, show them a pair of 3D spectacles and announce that within a few years everyone in the country would own such things. Of the early 3D films the best was George Sidney's *Kiss Me Kate*, inspired by *The Taming of the Shrew*, but on the whole the 3D experiment was a failure as it was when it was revived in the early 1980s, notably in the awful *Jaws 3D*.

Cinerama, which used a giant curved screen and three projectors and was introduced in 1952 with the travelogue, *This is Cinerama*, didn't fare much better. Of all the innovations around this period the one real success was Cinemascope, despite George Stevens' contemptuous assessment that it was 'only suitable for filming coffins and rattlesnakes'. Certainly it did produce a long, thin picture which, as John Houseman said, called upon creative people to 'make vermiform films, films in the shape of earth worms'. Fox introduced it in *The Robe*, a Biblical epic starring Richard Burton, in 1953 and it caught on well enough for other companies to bring out similar, rival systems such as WarnerScope, TechniScope, PanaScope, SuperScope and finally Panavision, which more or less supplanted the others.

What was greeted most enthusiastically of all, however, was a system that had been around for years but until the 1950s had been used quite sparingly – Technicolor. The first Technicolor feature, *Becky Sharp*, was directed by Rouben Mamoulian in 1935 and before the war a number of notable movies also used the process, among them of course *Gone With the Wind*, *The Wizard of Oz* and the best of all historical action movies, *The Adventures of Robin Hood*, directed by Michael Curtiz and starring Errol Flynn. But Technicolor was a costly business and during the war years it was hardly ever used. By the early 50s, though, it was seen as a vital weapon in the campaign against TV, at that time available only in black and white. The public took immediately to colour, although even as late as 1960 it was still possible for Robert Rossen to make *The Hustler* in Scope and monochrome. But when colour was introduced to TV and a new generation of viewers grew up who, both at home and in the cinema, had become unaccustomed to black and white

As audiences (and the box-office take) fell, in came the gimmicks – like 3D in which Jack Warner showed misplaced faith. The best of the 3D films was *Kiss Me Kate* (above) with Howard Keel and Kathryn Grayson. But the "flat" version was better still

images it became increasingly difficult for anyone to make a film except in Technicolor. In the mid-1980s hardly any director, save perhaps Woody Allen, has the power to insist on monochrome and the mindless demand for colour that has now, so we are told – although admittedly by those with a vested interest – become so clamorous that the public refuses to watch anything else has finally led to the obscenity of "colourisation", the process of using a computer to tint prints of classic black and white films in grubby and garish pastel shades. The first film to be so abused was Capra's *It's a Wonderful Life* and if the process catches on, as alas it seems it must, it will soon be almost impossible to watch any movie – even, though God forbid, such great works as *Citizen Kane*, *Casablanca* and *High Noon* – in the original black and white.

By the end of the 1950s Hollywood had tried just about everything to entice back its audience – musicals and epics, technological gimmicks, colour, location shooting to bring such famous but unfamiliar sights as the Eiffel Tower, Buckingham Palace, the Trevi Fountain and various mysteries of the Orient to a nation which, at that time, had not yet taken to globe-trotting on its holidays. For a while both the nation and the industry welcomed in particular the movies made in foreign parts. From 1956 and 1958 inclusive the Oscar for best film went, respectively, to *Around the World in 80 Days* (shot just about everywhere), *The Bridge on the River Kwai* (shot in Ceylon) and *Gigi* (shot in France). In 1959 it went to *Ben Hur*, which was shot in Italy but which did not, for obvious reasons, show such attractions as the Trevi Fountain.

Each of these experiments and innovations had a beneficial effect on box office takings but only briefly. So, too, did sex (the steamy rompings of Deborah Kerr and Burt Lancaster in *From Here to Eternity*) and talk about sex (*The Moon is Blue*) which also created an occasional stirring of interest among people who felt the lack of such stuff on TV. Movies made with youth in mind – especially those of James Dean – had their hours of success as well but the era when the young and its needs and interests were to dominate the cinema entirely was yet to come. The importing of foreign films, particularly the works of men like Federico Fellini, Akira Kurosawa and Ingmar Bergman, which dealt more frankly with sex, politics and social problems than Hollywood dared to do proved popular though only in limited areas, the subtitles being a deterrent to most Americans who were damned if they were going to the movies to read, for Chrissake. But possibly inspired by these more exotic offerings and realising that the day of the "family picture" was coming to an end, some directors were driven to the desperate lengths of making serious films on serious subjects in the hope that somebody out there might be paying attention. Directors like Huston, Mankiewicz and Richard Brooks brought to the screen adaptations of heavyweight books and plays ranging from *Lord Jim* and *Moby Dick* to *Julius Caesar* and *Cat on a Hot Tin Roof*. Many of these, like the Biblical epics, tended to be unnecessarily long and sprawling on a kind of "never mind the quality, feel the width" basis, as if an audience might be persuaded to buy a film at so many minutes per dollar.

But nothing worked for very long; true, from year to year cinema attendances might rise or fall but mostly they fell and the industry seemed to have lost direction.

Peter Bogdanovich said: 'My feeling is that Hollywood sort of died in 1961 and nobody noticed for about ten years. Now I could be wrong but it seems to me that the last great American movie of the old, original Hollywood, was *The Man Who Shot Liberty Valance*. The fifties, I think, were a terrible transitional period in which you had a kind of breakdown of the family unit in America and a kind of breakdown in a funny way of a lot of things in terms of sex on the screen and so on. So the fifties were the last part of the Golden Era; that was the end of it. With *Psycho* in 1960 Hitchcock killed mother in the ultimate way, which was happening slowly in the fifties anyway. That kind of put the death knell on it and then in 1961 Ford said, "Well, you know, the modern America isn't really what we hoped, is it?" And there we were. The sixties were pretty bad. There were one or two good pictures but very few.'

By the beginning of that decade in any event Hollywood had more or less surrendered to the enemy, television. It had embraced TV-trained directors and writers such as Arthur Penn, Sidney Lumet and Paddy Chayevsky; it had long since forgotten its solemn vow not to sell its backlog of old films to the box in the corner; and it had even thrown open its sound stages and studio lots to the making of television productions. TV had not needed a Trojan horse to infiltrate the capital of the movie world: it had walked in brandishing an embossed invitation and was swiftly becoming the most important industry in Hollywood.

In the film business itself the power had shifted increasingly to the stars, the agents and the deal-makers. Mayer had gone and so had Harry Cohn and Selznick and Zanuck (though he was to return to Fox in a position of some power later on). Goldwyn's influence had diminished and only Barney Balaban at Paramount and Jack Warner were still tenuously in control of their domains. The director Billy Wilder had a favourite saying: "The situation is grave but not serious"; in the Hollywood studios it was both. The alarming decline in revenue had left them all perilously weak and within a few years each of them had been gobbled up by some voracious multi-national conglomerate or had simply gone out of business. Paramount was taken over by Gulf & Western, United Artists by TransAmerica, Warners by Kinney National Service, later to be known as Warner Communications. Columbia was bought by Coca-Cola; Fox is now owned by Rupert Murdoch, whose other international interests include newspapers and TV stations; RKO was sold by Howard Hughes to the General Tyre and Rubber Company in 1955 and ceased trading the following year; MGM was absorbed by the hotel owner Kirk Kerkorian and more recently by Ted Turner and later Lorimar Productions both of whom made their fortunes in TV. Today only Universal, of all the major studios, has a parent company that is solely concerned with show business. In 1962 it was taken over by MCA which, faced by the threat of anti-trust legislation, decided to sell its agency and keep the studio. Even Universal, however, derives a large part of its income not from film and TV production but from its famous studio tour whose patrons are privileged, among other delights, to be attacked on a lake by Jaws and to learn the secret of how de Mille parted the Red Sea.

What the financiers bought were largely brand names, four-wall studios (sound stages, cutting rooms etc. for hire to independent producers), a library of old films and most importantly distribution clout and know-how. A film presented by a major studio today may carry that studio's name and logo but often it was actually made by an independent production company; all the studio has done is perhaps to finance it and to distribute it.

One result of all these changes was that a prediction made by Clifford Odets to Peter Bogdanovich in 1961 came true. 'Odets said to me, "You know, it's all falling apart as we speak, it's ending. The industry is going to fall into the hands of people who are not movie people and when it does that it's really going to be in trouble."' He was right: what's more not only are the studios owned by financiers but they are also run by people whose experience lies in deal-making, not film-making – lawyers and former agents (Lew Wasserman, the head of Universal, for example.) The only genuine film-maker now in control of a major studio is probably David Puttnam, the president of Columbia.

Perhaps, though, the present trend became inevitable as soon as the moguls began to be shoved off their perches. After Mayer was dismissed from MGM, Greer Garson said, executives came and went with bewildering speed. 'Everything was in such disarray, so disorganised. They never put a brass plate on a door with anybody's name on it – there was just a bit of cardboard with ink lettering. You really had to make very cautious enquiries, if only at the telephone switchboard, to find out who the president of the company was that week.' And that, pretty well, is how it has continued ever since.

But on the subject of the swallowing up of the studios by conglomerates, Jack Valenti said: 'The bad news is that sometimes the corporations were trying to take over a studio and run it as they would, say, a steel company, which of course you can't do. The good news is that they did provide those studios with a kind of fiscal sinew and nourished them with the money they needed to work a twenty or thirty-pictures-a-year release and distribution schedule. Change is the order of life; the mixture which is not stirred decomposes and where there is no strife, there is decay. We're in a volatile business and there'll be more change, a lot more change.'

In the 1960s Hollywood took Mr Valenti's rather odd aphorisms to heart; if the mixture decomposed it wasn't for want of stirring and if there was decay it was not for lack of strife. The children of the postwar baby boom had come of age, or certainly of cinema-going age, and it was to them and their slightly younger brothers and sisters that the industry began to address itself. Towards the end of the decade there was a marked increase in the production of films devised with the young in mind – *Bonnie and Clyde*, *The Graduate*, *Easy Rider*. These and their imitators, usually stories of rootless young people, anti-Establishment and alienated from society, seemed to strike a chord in what the industry regarded as the new "movie generation". AIP and Roger Corman had been making similar pictures, though on a smaller scale, even earlier and it became increasingly apparent that if a new audience was to be found it would have to be sought among the young.

Not that Hollywood had abandoned its dream of reclaiming the much longed-for family audience without a dogged struggle. In 1965 Fox, with Darryl Zanuck back in charge and his son Richard as head of production, made *The Sound of Music* and the enormous success of this, following the good business done earlier by Disney's *Mary Poppins* and Warner's *My Fair Lady*, persuaded the studio that the future lay in lavish musicals after all. What a mistake that was. *Dr Dolittle* with Rex Harrison, was a disaster that should have taught somebody a lesson but, no, all Fox seemed to learn from one flop was how to make another. Okay, the argument appeared to run, maybe the public doesn't want Harrison in a musical but, by Golly, it wants Julie Andrews, doesn't it? *Mary Poppins*, *The Sound of Music* – why, sure the public wants Julie Andrews. So Fox plunged the unfortunate woman into *Star!*, another disaster. If *Dolittle* did little at the box office this hardly did more. The studio shook its head gravely, fired a few menials, had a bit of a rethink and came up with another idea: maybe, it said, we were wrong about Andrews but not about musicals, no sirree, we just know the public is crying out for musicals. So listen, it said, we're talking Streisand now – how's about Barbra Streisand in *Hello, Dolly*? That's gotta be a hit. Wrong again. *Dolly* was another disaster and by 1970 the situation at Fox was so desperate that Darryl Zanuck was driven to the extraordinary measure of firing his own son, a move that cast a dark shadow over the future of the entire nepotism business.

So with not even sons, let alone nephews and sons-in-law, now able to rest easy in their executive offices ended the decade in which, as Bogdanovich put it, Hollywood died and nobody noticed. Perhaps at that point it had indeed reached its lowest ebb so far with the major studios losing, according to *Variety*, some 600 milllion dollars between them from 1969 to 1972 and the annual cinema attendance having dropped from around 4,060 million in 1946 to about 820 million. But there have been so many low ebbs that it is difficult to say with any certainty which was the lowest, though financially that time around the end of the 1960s might make a pretty strong claim. Artistically, however, worse was yet to come and from that point of view there can hardly have been any period much more dismal and low of ebb than the mid-1980s.

In the early 70s, however, there was something of a resurgence with the arrival of a new school of directors, among them Bogdanovich himself, Francis Ford Coppola, Martin Scorsese and the prodigy Steven Spielberg. Bogdanovich said: 'There was a new hope, a period there when everybody thought, Oh gee, it's going to start up again in another way.' And for a while that did seem to be a possibility. The films made by these new directors and the new stars, Redford, Hoffman, Pacino and such, were not perhaps remarkably original but they had a freshness of approach that was exciting because it seemed to look forward to a bright new future instead of back to the distant glories of the past.

In the end, of course, that future was not exactly what Bogdanovich and his contemporaries might have wished or predicted. But in the early to middle 1970s there was a renewed vigour in Hollywood film-making. Bogdanovich himself made *The Last Picture Show*, *What's Up, Doc?* and *Paper Moon*; Coppola contributed the two *Godfather* films and *The Conversation*; Scorsese made *Mean Streets* and *Taxi Driver*; George Lucas chipped in with *American Graffiti*; Clint Eastwood turned director to make *Play Misty for Me* and *The Outlaw Josey Wales*; and more veteran figures such as Don Siegel, with *Dirty Harry* and *Charlie Varrick*, Alan J. Pakula with *Klute* and Sidney Lumet with *Serpico* and *Dog Day Afternoon* were hitting mid-season form. This was, too, the decade in which Woody Allen, who is incontrovertibly one of the most significant figures of the contemporary cinema, won recognition as a comic film maker to rank alongside Chaplin with a series of pictures that ranged from *Bananas* in 1971 through *Play It Again, Sam, Love and Death* and *Annie Hall* to *Manhattan* in 1979.

I'm not suggesting that such films necessarily raised the art of the cinema to a new and higher level but at least they attempted to be original and for the most part seemed to assume that the audience was prepared to bring its mind along when it went to the movies. At the same time, however, other parallel and less beneficial forces were at work. In 1969 *Midnight Cowboy* had become the first X-rated film to win the Academy Award for best picture. The fact that it was a serious story, seriously told by a skilled writer (Waldo Salt) and director (John Schlesinger) tended to be overlooked: the point that impressed itself upon Hollywood was that the Oscar had lent respectability to movies that dealt frankly and openly with sex and from then on there was to be a plethora of such films, few of them of such calibre or reasonably high intent as *Midnight Cowboy*.

At the same time the deal-makers were gaining more influence than ever. For example, Creative Management Associates acquired so much kudos – and financial reward – by packaging films like *The Towering Inferno, The Sting* and *Dog Day Afternoon* that their chief executives Freddie Fields and David Begelman became heads of major studios. Packaging was therefore seen as the answer to all the industry's problems and was pursued so zealously as to reach ludicrous proportions in the mid-seventies when *Lucky Lady* took an entire year simply to cast because each of its three stars, Burt Reynolds, Gene Hackman and Liza Minnelli had the power of veto over the choice of co-stars. Also, of course, packaging did *not* prove to be the answer because *Lucky Lady* was an expensive box office failure as, too, were *The Fortune*, which teamed Warren Beatty and Jack Nicholson, and *Missouri Breaks* – Nicholson again, this time with Brando. Indeed Arthur Penn, who directed *Missouri Breaks*, is on record as saying that he should have shot the deal rather than the movie since it would have made a far more devious and thrilling story. Not that any of these disasters made much difference to the packagers. If Hollywood agents and lawyers are not involved in putting packages together they have no real raison d'être, hence more recent financial disasters such as *City Heat*, the deal-makers' attempt to revive the flagging careers of Clint Eastwood and Burt Reynolds by putting them together in a gangster caper, and the positively horrendous *Rhinestone*, in which Sylvester Stallone had the gall to attempt to sing duets with Dolly Parton. Just about the only criticism you could not level at this film (unlike *Samson and Delilah*) was that he had bigger tits than her but it was close.

Another significant factor in the early 1970s was the Vietnam War which, as the writer George Axelrod said, created 'a dichotomy between youth and middle-age'. If anyone was in favour of the war it was the middle-aged; the youth of America was increasingly opposed to it. Axelrod believed that it 'revolutionised the whole society

Above: After the gim-
micks Hollywood put its
faith in epics like *Ben
Hur* (Charlton Heston)
of which a critic said,
'loved Ben, hated Hur'
Left: And then there
were the musicals.
In *The King and I*
Yul Brynner ruled Siam
but not necessarily
Deborah Kerr

The hills – and the cinema box offices – were alive with *The Sound of Music*

Below: On stage the hero in *Cat on a Hot Tin Roof* was homosexual. In the film Paul Newman is briskly cured by Elizabeth Taylor of all that nonsense

and changed the nature of picture-making . . . Protest pictures came in.' They had come in, of course, with the likes of *Bonnie and Clyde* and *Easy Rider* and having come in they stayed in. And since their appeal was to the younger audience Hollywood began even more strenuously than before to aim its products at the twelve to twenty-five-year-olds. Adult protest pictures – the Watergate exposé *All the President's Men* in 1976 and Coppola's *Apocalypse Now* in 1979, for example – were still made but mostly the industry convinced itself that the future, if any, lay in gratifying the young. And when, by a process of trial and error, it discovered what the young appeared to want – space fantasy, horror, frenetic comedy and a seemingly interminable series of stories about teenagers growing up and trying to get laid – it set out to give them an almost unrelieved diet of the same.

In catering for these simple wants it was aided by the appearance on the scene of what have become known as the Movie Brats – the Lucases and Spielbergs, the very people whose earlier work had seemed to forecast a return to more adult movies – and in the early 1980s of the Brat Pack, a group of young actors and actresses including Emilio Estevez, Mollie Ringwald and Rob Lowe, who frequently work together and whose films are aimed almost exclusively at people of their own age – an audience in its late teens.

The two groups, the Pack and the Brats, rarely combine but between them and in their different ways they are, in varying degrees, guilty of what Peter Bogdanovich aptly calls "the juvenilisation" of the movies.

The times they are a-changing . . . In 1969 *Midnight Cowboy* was the first X-rated movie to win the Oscar for best picture

HOLLYWOOD TODAY

In 1974, said Richard Sylbert, an art director who was once head of production at Paramount, the industry was "reasonably healthy". *The Godfather* had grossed around 100 million dollars, *Shampoo* about 70 million. *Chinatown* in the region of 60 million. 'It was an industry in which the pictures that did make money were pictures about grown-ups in a grown-up world. But ... it's almost like there was a sign in 1974: there was a little picture made that was a huge success called *Jaws*. And it was the end of the grown-ups. From that moment on the seven major grossing pictures in the history of the industry were made by two guys – George Lucas and Steven Spielberg. What we hadn't realised, of course, was that there was this enormous audience out there, these kids. The whole culture became adolescent – and the grosses improved enormously.'

Sylbert was not especially critical of Spielberg and Lucas – indeed he referred to the latter as "the *real* Disney" – but others are. In assessing the state of Hollywood today the common practice is to lay all blame firmly at the door of the Movie Brats, with particular reference to Messrs Spielberg and Lucas.

Even other Movie Brats tend to do that, as witness the following conversation between myself and John Milius. We were talking about Francis Coppola, who is widely regarded as the very first Movie Brat and therefore guru to all the others, and Milius said that while 'Francis had a wonderful influence – he was the only one who really had power and tried to do something with it – the others have not been so ambitious at all.'

'By others,' I said, 'do you mean people like Steven Spielberg?'

'Uhuh. And George.'

'But what do you feel they've done that is so detrimental to the industry?'

He said: 'Well, I don't think that *Indiana Jones and the Temple of Doom* was pushing the limits of film. Or *Return of the Jedi* or whatever. I think they could make a lot more ambitious projects than they do ... I'm not sure this is really a conscious decision on their part: I think George and Steven make the films they really want to make but it influences everybody else.'

Ah, but in what way? Peter Bogdanovich, a director from the pre-Brats generation, said: 'There's a general juvenilisation of movies that's happened over the last ten years that's pretty scary. The other day somebody read a script that I was working on and said, "Oh, I get it: this is an adult comedy." I said, "What do you mean – that it's a comedy *for* adults?" He said, "No, no, no – it's a comedy *about* adults." Most of the comedies, the rest of the comedies, are about kids. I think a lot of things have gone wrong. Movies are far less complex in their structure and in their execution than they've ever been. Most movies seem to be very primitive today; it's been like a regression. Maybe it's just that this is a dry spell but I think the medium has become a bit decadent.'

In such an argument much depends on your definition of the word "juvenilisation". For instance, when discussing their 1986 hit *Top Gun* the production team of Don Simpson and Jerry Bruckheimer said, indignantly: 'Was *that* made for kids?' To which the only honest, though possibly impolite, response is a mildly astonished: 'Well, who else was it made for?' In truth that film fell clearly into a category of modern picture of which Richard Sylbert said 'the story's an excuse for the music'. Indeed, he went so far as to say of *Top Gun* that 'it's rock 'n roll in the sky', his theory being that the music soundtrack and sales thereof are just as important to the studios today as the film itself.

But even if you exclude *Top Gun*, support for the Bogdanovich argument is not hard to find. Over the last several years the vast bulk of Hollywood's output has been aimed at the young and the easily pleased: science fantasies, juvenile comedies and crude horror pix, most of them spawning an endless succession of sequels so that the cinemagoer is presented with a dismal vista of "Porkys" and "Police Academies". "Hallowe'ens" and "Poltergeists", "Nightmares on Elm Street" and more "Friday the 13ths" than you could find in a handful of calendar years. Decadent is not a bad word to describe such stuff.

But why should those who properly deplore such cheapjack product seek to blame Spielberg and Lucas for it? Quite simply because Spielberg and Lucas have gained hitherto undreamt of success at the box office by making films whose basic appeal is to young people. From *Jaws* to *E.T.*, from *Star Wars* to *Indiana Jones*, pictures which they have made either individually or together dominate the list of the world's most lucrative productions. And with a weary lack of imagination the rest of Hollywood has merely hoisted itself onto the bandwagon of their making on the principle that what worked once will work again so why beat your brains out trying to think of something new when you can clean up by imitating what Spielberg and Lucas have already done?

The fallacy here, of course, is that the films of said Spielberg and Lucas are the original and inventive work of highly gifted men; the films of their imitators are, on the whole, the work of barely talented hacks. No matter. Even the hacks are making money; money is what, *a priori*, the studios want; so carbon copies, however faint, of what has already proved successful are in much demand; and other, more serious, film makers who aspire to creating more serious films have a better chance of being shot on sight by the studio gatekeeper than of winning a sympathetic hearing and financial backing from the studio bosses. Consequently they tend to glare balefully in the direction of Spielberg and Lucas and cry: 'It's all their fault.'

But this is akin to killing the messenger who brings bad news. It may be regrettable that the films of Spielberg and Lucas are not films of deep intellectual content but they are put together carefully, wholeheartedly and without cynicism. They are, to say the least, honest films, trend-setting films, and it's most unfair to

George Lucas (left) and Steven Spielberg, blamed by many for the "juvenilisation" of the movies

And you thought it was safe to go into the water! *Jaws*, the film that brought "the end of the grown-ups"

find their creators guilty of the excesses of their unsought imitators.

At this stage, however, it might be useful to define and identify the Movie Brats a little more explicitly. Roughly speaking, they are the generation of film makers who were born during or just after the Second World War and came to prominence in the 1970s; a good many of them were film school graduates, the first such graduates to break through into mainstream cinema; and they differed from their predecessors, according to Haskell Wexler, in one significant detail.

'The directors who came around before,' he said, 'came in the main out of life. These people came out of film, their world was film. There's a sort of tail-chasing thing that happens with people who are fascinated by film from their youth and then go into film as a profession: the real world becomes the film world and the film world becomes the real world.'

Not surprisingly, John Milius did not agree with this, arguing that it was too easy an assumption which it probably is although, as with many sweeping statements, it seems to contain a large kernel of truth. Wexler also said: 'Television has been the strongest influence on the film industry. Television goes for the widest common denominator, television goes on the basis of computers, on the basis of polls – how can we get the most people to see the product? Who are the most people? So . . . who are the most people who buy tickets at movie theatres? These people [the Movie Brats] had their ears attuned to who the potential audience were – people of a certain age range, mostly younger people. So they [the Brats] began not so much with a tremendous urge to say something artistically, to express themselves or their innermost artistic feelings – they came, many times, to what they made on the basis of demographics, on the basis "What will bring 'em in at the box office?" '

He spoke without rancour; indeed he spoke as a friend and admirer of George Lucas for whom, as a favour, he photographed *American Graffiti* without a fee and for only a small share of the profits. At the time no profits were expected, since the studio had little faith in the film, and the fact that Wexler's points eventually proved so lucrative that they financed his documentary *Latino* did not, I am sure, influence him when he said: 'I love George Lucas: he's very honest and direct and a good friend,' or when he defended Lucas's right to make whatever films he wished. But he added: 'I just feel that *other* films should be made, too. Films should be made because people feel that something has to come out there, something has to be expressed and that a picture can still be good even if it doesn't reach 80 million people on the first day of release.' And because he also felt that thanks, unwittingly, to Lucas (and, of course, Spielberg) it was increasingly difficult to find backing for the kind of film that was not expected to reach 80 million people on the first day he could not regard the influence of the Brats as beneficial.

The point he made – that the Movie Brats came out of film and television rather than any experience of working life as most other people know it – is rather borne out, despite Milius' denials, by Steven Spielberg and Martin Scorsese. In his childhood, Spielberg said, he spent 'too much time watching TV because it was there. There was a gentle voice in the house. When my parents went out and left me with a baby-sitter, there it was – it became a third parent, I suppose. I think that's the way it is in

America today. Television is very influential and so many role models are cast by the blue flicker. It's not altogether healthy, depending on which programmes you watch, but I was influenced by it like any other of my friends and it became part of the American pop heritage.'

Scorsese, on the other hand, spent most of his formative years in movie theatres. He described himself and his contemporaries as "cine-literate" as opposed to men of earlier film generations who came from a literary or theatrical background. As a child he would rather go to a cinema than read a book and the same is true of Spielberg, who said: 'I don't read that much. I don't curl up with a good book. I like events: I like concerts, I like to listen, I like to see. I just never have developed the patience to open a thousand-page novel and put my feet up and dance through it.'

In this he is – regrettably, in my opinion – in harmony with his own generation and (since he is now forty-one) the generations that came after. And he – and they – might insist that this is perfectly reasonable since film, after all, is an audio-visual medium. But at its best it is also a literary medium. There are people who claim that if a film is visually dazzling enough it does not need a coherent story line but this is the intellectual masturbation of those who cannot handle plot, dialogue or characterisation. Besides, the great film makers of the past were men who read: they might not always admit it but they read, if only because they didn't have TV to stare at. And one reason why Peter Bogdanovich, for example, cannot be classified as a Movie Brat, even though he's the same age (forty-eight) as Coppola and only a few years older than Spielberg, Scorsese and the rest, is that he came to film making from journalism and movie criticism, in other words from a background of reading and writing.

The Brats came out of TV, out of film, out of film school. Coppola, Scorsese, Lucas, Milius, Gary Kurtz (the producer of *Star Wars*), Brian de Palma and many others gained film degrees from various universities, mostly in New York and California. Spielberg was different in that he did not go to college but spent his apprenticeship working in TV at Universal Studios. But unlike such people as Sidney Lumet and John Frankenheimer, who had also made the switch from TV to movies, he was not working in live TV but in TV films and it was his precocious direction of *Duel* when he was in his early twenties that brought him to the attention of the critics and enabled him to move effortlessly into theatrical film making.

It was around 1971 that these men of similar ages and similar backgrounds came together in Hollywood where they were all working, often in humble capacities, on various movie projects most of which, as Scorsese remembered, were in some kind of trouble. 'We'd sort of hang out together out of misery,' he said. 'We'd just sit down and complain and George Lucas would say, "This is the worst job in the world. I'll never do it again..."' Inevitably they influenced and advised each other – to such an extent that even much later, in 1977, when Scorsese was editing *New York, New York* Lucas would look at it and say: 'Marty, if the man and the woman walk away together at the end of the film it's gonna add 10 million dollars at the box office.' To which Scorsese would reply: 'Yeah, I know, but it just doesn't work for this story.' Therein perhaps lay the difference between them: Scorsese believed then, as he obviously still does, that it's what you want the film to say that is important while

Above: Martin Scorsese (here with Robert de Niro) said the Movie Brats would 'sort of hang out together out of misery'

Left: The combination of Spielberg and Lucas gave Harrison Ford one of the biggest hits of all time, *Raiders of the Lost Ark*

Lucas, an infinitely better businessman (give or take the awful disaster of *Howard the Duck*) clearly knew from the start that in the crap shoot that is the Hollywood movie industry the bottom line, as they say, is what comes in at the box office.

The true catalyst in all this, however, was Coppola who, with *The Godfather*, was the first to break through to the huge profits that could accrue from mainstream cinema. On the proceeds of that film, Scorsese said, 'he'd built an incredible screening room at his house in San Francisco and we'd go up there and look at all these foreign films . . .' In time this private screening room spread and grew into the Zoetrope Studios where Coppola reigned much like a Godfather himself, the capo of the Movie Brats. In John Milius' view *The Godfather* was the Trojan horse in which Coppola broke into the closed and cosy Hollywood society. 'He got inside the gates of the city and at night he came out and unlocked those gates for us to come in. We all owe a lot to him. I still think of him as Napoleon and myself as Marshal Ney.' Milius saw the creation of Zoetrope as a kind of rebellion. 'I often think of *Star Wars* where they're called "the rebel alliance" or whatever and I suppose we were the rebel alliance against the Empire of Hollywood.'

Well, there had been rebel alliances before – notably at the end of the 1960s when Bert Schneider (the son of the then head of Columbia), Bob Rafelson and Steve Blauner had formed BBS Productions and astonished Hollywood with such revolutionary movies as *Easy Rider, Five Easy Pieces*, Bogdanovich's *The Last Picture Show*, Jack Nicholson's *Drive, He Said* and Henry Jaglom's *A Safe Place*. All these were designed to break the allegedly safe but ultimately disastrous Hollywood mould of expensive musicals and so-called "family pictures". For a while BBS thrived but in the end the Hollywood Establishment overcame it. As one studio executive put it, Hollywood has a history of marching to false drums, of clinging to the coat tails of the last film that made a profit so that even the work of the innovators begins to look stale when it has been too frequently and indifferently copied. Eventually, the eager young innovators of BBS were absorbed into the system and much the same thing has happened to the Movie Brats, although Milius believed there was another and more basic reason for their decline from rebel alliance, poised to take over the industry, to defenders of the Empire.

'Greed,' he said. 'The rebel alliance turned out to be worse than the Empire. Everybody went their own way to seek an empire of their own. When they realised they could have an empire, they went crazy.'

Whether it was individual or corporate greed that overwhelmed them is difficult to say – individual greed for money or power, or the corporate greed of Hollywood studios and their financial backers who always wish to own whichever goose is laying this year's golden eggs. Maybe it was just success. As Brian de Palma said: 'I think one of the big problems is that we're no longer young directors. It's difficult for us to make movies that cost 2–3 million dollars any more because if you're used to building big sets and have all kinds of grand ideas about making films like David Lean used to make, you need money. So you're moving into a whole bigger game and you cannot make such experimental movies as you used to. You can't really go back.'

Or, as Lawrence Kasdan, the writer and director of such films as *Body Heat, The*

Big Chill and *Silverado*, put it: 'In Hollywood the damaging pressures of success may be heightened because it's such a public, high-stakes kind of game. The way people are paid is completely out of line with any sort of reality – there's no connection between your value to the world and what you're paid. Any teacher or social worker is doing just as viable work, probably more so, but won't earn in a lifetime what some lucky person who's made a hit will make in one year. So there's this massive dissociation from any reality. I think it confuses people. You tend to become defensive or you begin to believe praise, which is just as dangerous, and all these things bring you away from whatever pure impulse made you want to do the work in the first place. So then you begin to live differently, you have a different lifestyle and you think you *need* that kind of money to support it. In fact you do – you've created a situation where your decisions are no longer about what kind of film and art you want to make but what will be the best deal, what's your chance of making money, how can you get the most praise or Oscar nominations. You're likely to get into all these things which have nothing to do with the work. So, I mean, failure is more difficult to deal with, no question about it – but success is much tougher than people think.'

It is, of course, much too simplistic to say that making money is now the name of the game in Hollywood – it always was. But, as Kasdan said: 'The scale has changed so radically since *Star Wars*. It's really about ten years ago that studios and the conglomerates that were buying them – and still are – saw that they could make so much money on the right jackpot investment. Now a film is considered a failure if it makes a 20 per cent profit. It's absurd. If it's a modestly priced film with a modest profit, it's considered inconsequential and not worth doing. There's no way that good art can come out of an ethic like that.'

But then Hollywood doesn't want good art – it never did. What it wants is huge profits and it seized upon the Movie Brats as the people who could make them. And this the Brats have done. To give them due credit, most of them – especially Spielberg – are still inclined to make the kind of film they themselves would like to see in the cinemas but at the same time they stick to safe formulas and show little inclination to extend the boundaries of the medium. It's understandable – if you're handling budgets of 20 million dollars plus you can't afford to experiment, even if the studio would allow you to.

Some, admittedly, have compromised less than others. John Milius it could be said – and indeed he says it – has stayed true to his maverick beliefs. And though this could be because he has made less impact than his contemporaries, save with the gung-ho, anti-Russian, all-American *Red Dawn*, he says proudly: 'I've remained a rebel. I'm still in the hills of veritable Castro, waiting for my moment.'

Of them all, though, Scorsese is the one who has consistently enhanced his reputation with films that make no concession to current lucrative trends or are necessarily aimed at a mass audience. By and large his pictures are not blockbusters at the box office and for that reason he has more difficulty than most in raising finance. To make his latest film, *The Color of Money*, he and the star, Paul Newman, were obliged to put up their salaries as a guarantee against completion.

But in the overall disillusionment with the way the Brats have developed, or failed to develop, the biggest disappointment attaches to the comparative failure of Zoetrope and Coppola. Milius said: 'Francis would spend every dime that he could borrow. He was always in debt. And, of course, he bought magazines and financed bigger movies ... It was a very disorganised company ... There was a wonderful incident when a guy attempted to unionise Zoetrope. He said, "This is a film collective, we're all equal here," and he went up to Francis's office and Francis was a big liberal, you know, he believed in Communism and socialism and the Leninist and Marxist philosophies. And this guy said, "I want your desk for the people." And Francis said, "I have my desk – this is the biggest desk because I'm the biggest shot. Now get out of here." And that was that. He immediately reverted back to the Godfather and I loved him for it. People should be what they are. He's Napoleon, he can't help himself.' As Napoleon, Milius added, Coppola had 'a wonderful attitude, outgoing, daring, offending people, a threat that somehow shook the foundations of Hollywood. He loved that, he just loved it. And we knew he was immensely talented.'

But then at Zoetrope, as elsewhere among the Brats, came the gradual transition from offending Hollywood to *becoming* Hollywood. 'We were the first generation of film school people,' Milius said, 'fanatical about movies, grown up with movies; we could quote movies. The very thing that made us any good at all was a desperation, a kamikaze attitude. We didn't have a desperation for wealth, although a lot of these people ended up wealthy beyond the dreams of anyone in Hollywood then. But there was a desperation just to do anything, just to get any kind of work done, an absolute love of the idea when you had some work to do and were allowed to do it.'

But as the work became ever more outrageously successful a cynicism set in, if not among the Brats themselves then, in Milius's view, among their successors. 'Kids today,' he said, referring to the latest generation of young directors, 'sort of say, "Well, I'm gonna take the steps of Steven Spielberg and eventually I'm gonna have 100 million dollars." We didn't look at it that way. We didn't care what we did; we just dashed ourselves against the wall.'

Well, one hates to spoil his heroic image of his younger self but, in truth, dashing themselves against the wall is what the newer generation of film makers is still doing. It took Oliver Stone, the writer and director of 1987's most successful film *Platoon*, ten years of dashing himself against the wall to get the picture made. Almost every major Hollywood studio turned it down on the grounds that it was uncommercial and in the end it was the British-based Hemdale, later joined by Orion, an independent company, that put up the money. Nor was Stone's an isolated experience.

Even a producer like Richard Zanuck, whose track record goes back to *Compulsion* in 1959 and includes *Jaws*, has similar difficulties. His most recent success, and financially it was a very big one, was *Cocoon* and of this he said: 'It took four years of pleading and cajoling finally to get a green light. We suffered through three different heads of the studio. Fortunately for *Cocoon* and for us, the last head liked it, the three previous heads didn't like it. But we just thought, if we stick around here long enough the people who dislike it will be fired and we're liable to hit somebody who does like it. We kept going in and making the same speech in the same office; there was just a different person behind the same desk. We'd say, "I know you're not gonna like this. It's about old people and we've got Don Ameche and we've got Hume Cronyn," and they would say, "And we've got a door and you can leave because, you're right, we don't like this." And that's what we went through for four years, plus the entire studio was bought. I mean, not only had the people making the decisions changed three or four times but the company itself [20th Century-Fox] was bought by Rupert Murdoch. It's a miracle that the picture was made.'

In Hollywood today, as always, the men to hate are the men who run the studios, especially if you are, like Zanuck, an independent producer with no particular tie-up with any of the majors. But the men in charge now, he said, are not like the Mayers, the Warners and the Cohns. 'It's a very different breed. It's guys out of Harvard Business School, people with a kind of agent mentality, a packaging mentality. Very rarely does anybody who can say yea or nay to a project know anything about what he's talking about. These people haven't been schooled in production; they've been schooled in finance or economics or other things.'

What's more, as his four-year experience with *Cocoon* indicated, nobody seems to stay in charge for very long. And that, Zanuck said, 'proves to me that the system is wrong. See, they say, "Let's get people who are cost-conscious in there to run the studios," and that sounds very logical. But they're taking people who know about costs and putting them in positions where creative decisions have to be made. And the fact that, time and time again, these people only last a year or six months at every studio proves that the system isn't working.'

Once, he said, each studio had one man who could make decisions. 'Today you go before committees. They take surveys, they do market research, they do this and that and everybody including the cop at the gate reads the script and has an opinion and it's just an endless, frustrating thing. Then if they finally say, "Okay, let's go ahead if you can get X, Y or Z to star," you have all of that. Nobody's under contract any more so you have to go through all of those agents and business managers and advisers and psychiatrists and everybody else who's reading the script before they'll even send it to the star that the studio said they want in the picture. It's agonising, it's just teeth-pulling all the way. Nothing is easy, nothing is simple.'

Those who appoint the "cost-conscious" people are, of course, the multi-national conglomerates who between them now own all the studios except Universal, and opinion is divided as to whether their influence is beneficial or malign. Generally speaking, there is approval of the way in which the parent companies inject money into the studios; widespread disapproval when, as Brian de Palma said, 'the conglomerates get into the motion picture ends of their companies because when you're into real estate and soft drinks, the world of making movies is a whole different business'; and a fair amount of doubt about the frequent choice of businessmen to run the studios.

Even so, de Palma felt that the business was still run by people 'who have belief in the ability of certain film makers, of certain stars to create a product that will have a large audience appeal. And those guys move around from studio to studio. It's not like they vanish. The studio heads are constantly changing but they're very familiar faces; they haven't changed that much in the twenty years I've been in Hollywood.'

But why do they move around so much? Well, as the screenwriter William Goldman said: 'Being a studio head is a very, very difficult job, which they all fail at because the problem a studio head has is trying to predict public taste years and years down the line. Movies take two to three years, if they're lucky, from the time the screenplay is commissioned to when the film hits the screen and no one knows where taste is gonna be by then.'

If, after two to three years, the studio head has guessed wrong more often than he has guessed right he is immediately fired, probably to be replaced by somebody who has had a similar experience at another studio. It may seem a bizarre system but that's the way it works – at studio-head level failure in one place is usually rewarded by the chance to fail again somewhere else. Lawrence Kasdan said: 'Hollywood is chaos. There's no system, there's no agreement among the people in power – it's all chaos. They're just operating out of fear and ignorance.'

For that reason they cling doggedly to the belief that, despite mounds of evidence to the contrary, films need stars. 'They want what they think is protection,' said William Goldman. 'Stars give them a certain kind of security. They'll say, "Well, I've got a new Jane Fonda picture ... I've got a new Barbra Streisand picture ... I have a new Clint Eastwood picture." People think you're a big deal if you've got a Clint Eastwood picture. If you can say, "Well, I've got Eastwood," we'll know that the film will have some action and he'll be fine and it'll probably make some money. So they tell themselves that stars are basically a big plus, though Paul Newman once said that he felt he could only justify his salary if he was right for a movie and if he was not right he was no help to it at all. In other words, *The Color of Money* with any other actor would not have been the success it is no matter who that actor was because Newman was exactly right for it.'

So, all studio heads get fired because, in the end, they fail, not necessarily to make good films but to make money, though sometimes they manage to enjoy a fair run of success.

'Right now,' Goldman said, 'Paramount can't miss. I was talking to a producer, I said, "Who's so smart at Paramount?" He said, "It's not that anybody's smart, it's just their turn." And in a year what'll happen is that Paramount's movies will all be stiffs and Universal will be hot. It always changes.' And when it changes somebody will get fired.

In fairness, though, that faith in the efficacy of the star is not entirely misplaced. It's easier to sell a film to foreign and ancillary markets – video, cable TV and the like – if it contains one or two highly familiar names. The trouble is that stars add enormously to the production costs. Cannon paid Sylvester Stallone 12 million dollars to write and appear in *Over the Top* and he reputedly earned 15 million dollars for making *Rambo 3*. Now, admittedly, this is exceptional but there are many others who are paid smaller, but still mind-boggling, sums to ply their trade. 'In the late 60s,' Goldman said, 'they were paying the Burtons a million dollars to appear in movies. Now a top star – this is unbelievable – a top star in Hollywood, as we sit here in 1987, gets around 6 million dollars. That's what you pay if you want Dustin

Hoffman, that's what you pay if you want Robert Redford, that's what you pay if you want I don't know, Chevy Chase. You're talking 6 million dollars.'

In many cases, too, you are not only talking 6 million dollars: you are also talking a percentage of the gross profits. So if the film is a hit the star stands to make so much money that he probably never needs to work again. And that, in turn, pushes his price up because then the only way to entice a reluctant star back to work is to offer him even more unbelievable money than he was paid before. Goldman cited the case of Bill Murray who, he said, had made an enormous fortune from *Ghostbusters* and had followed this up with a serious role in *The Razor's Edge*, from which people stayed away in their droves. Possibly discouraged by this failure Murray had not worked since. 'But,' Goldman said, 'if Bill Murray would just do a comedy you and I would not be able to lift the amount of money they would pay him.' Well, a couple of days after this conversation Murray was discussing filming *Ghostbusters 2* for Columbia and though I have no idea how much money he was to be paid I'm quite prepared to believe that Goldman and I, even with Murray's help, would be unable to lift it.

The question that arises from all this is: how does an actor get to be in that enviable position where people are offering him unliftable sums of money merely to appear in a film? The answer is that nobody knows. Here's William Goldman again: 'The hottest star in America now, the number one star according to this poll that just came out – an annual poll of the theatre owners – is Tom Cruise. And you would say, Yes, that makes sense – *Top Gun*. In point of fact Tom Cruise had three movies in this calendar year: *Top Gun*, the number one picture of the year; *The Color of Money* which was a small success, a critical success but a small success; and a movie called *Legend* directed by Ridley Scott, which must have lost 30 or 40 or 50 million dollars. Now how can Tom Cruise be the top star in America when nobody wants to see him? They wanted to see *Top Gun*; they didn't want to see *Legend*. Nobody went to see *Legend*. I mean, it didn't open, to use that wonderful Hollywood phrase. But the fact is that *Top Gun* would have worked with Rob Lowe in it. *Top Gun* would have worked with any pretty kid. The people wanted to see the movie – don't ask me why, they did. They wanted to see the special effects with the airplanes. But we're looking for some other reason, some explanation. So we say, "Oh, Tom Cruise was the reason," but it's madness. Tom Cruise is now the number one star in the country having had one giant hit, one middling success and one giant flop. In the same year.'

You might well wonder why the studios go along with the mad inflation of star salaries. David Puttnam, indeed, has said that he will not do it. And yet it was Puttnam who negotiated with Bill Murray for *Ghostbusters 2* – because every studio needs at least one annual blockbuster, a film that will make so much money as to absorb the losses incurred on smaller, more serious and more ambitious projects. And even Puttnam, who has protested volubly about the insane amounts it now costs to make Hollywood films, has found himself locked inescapably into the system. William Goldman, one of the most intelligent people ever to work in Hollywood – which is probably one reason why he hasn't worked much in Hollywood over the last few years – said: 'Stars can be dangerous to a film, because sometimes you have to alter the writing to fit the star and in so doing destroy the movie, and they can be wonderfully helpful for it, if they're properly cast. If you're lucky enough to have a star in a part that the star is right for, it's gold.' But even if the star is not right he will still be cast as a form of insurance.

People, Goldman said, will say: 'Gee, this is a part that would be great for Jimmy Cagney, let's get Sylvester Stallone; he'll ruin the movie but we'll get him because if you get Sylvester Stallone the movie will happen.' Movies, Goldman said, 'are really about your next job. Everybody wants his next job and if you have a disaster – if you have a *Heaven's Gate* and you're Michael Cimino it's years before you're employable again and everybody wants to stay employed.'

In all this, though, I asked, in a situation wherein James Cagney is deemed replaceable by Sylvester Stallone without penalty does nobody actually care about the film? 'Within reason they care,' he said. 'Nobody wants to make junk; we all of us are serious.' Here, however, he paused before adding: 'That's too sweet a statement. Half the time it is junk. Nobody cares on *Hallowe'en 14* – they all know it's crap. But you would like a picture to have quality. You don't want basically to say to your family, "I'm making *Rocky 6*"; you know the only thing that's good about making *Rocky 6* is the money but it doesn't enrich your soul.'

Enriching the soul – along with the bank balance, naturally is, however, strictly the province of the film makers; it doesn't much concern the studio heads. The average studio-owning conglomerate is always happy if its films win critical acclaim and Oscars but it's even happier if they cause endless queues to form around the block. Movies are a business and anybody involved in the making of them overlooks that fact to his peril. In Hollywood you are what you earn, what you own, what you wear, what you drive and what you live in, no matter how you gained these things.

This may sound depressing but if your profession is the movies Hollywood, surely, is still the place to be. Or is it? If you're particularly successful or well-established like, say, Sidney Lumet or Kathleen Turner, perhaps not. For everyone else the answer is probably yes. Lumet has made only one of his thirty-odd films in Hollywood – *The Morning After*, which, perhaps coincidentally, is by no means one of his best even though it won Jane Fonda an Oscar nomination in 1987. He was particularly deterred from working there, he said, around 1967 when there was some talk of him directing *Funny Girl*. (In the end William Wyler got the job.) 'I went out there.' Lumet said, 'and we sat down at a budget meeting and there were thirty-two heads of department. That's clearly a crazy way to make a movie – and mind you these heads of department had tremendous power.' But, I suggested, even when he was shooting his films in and around New York the baleful influence of those thirty-two heads of department could still be felt. 'Yes,' he said, 'but the sheer physical distance discouraged them. They usually didn't like coming to New York – there were people in the streets and all those unpleasant things.' So he stayed where he was, making his pictures on comparatively modest budgets and keeping his head below the trenches.

Kathleen Turner lives in New York for different reasons. In the first place she is, in the Hollywood phrase, "hot", one of the most sought-after actresses in the business. Therefore she does not need to be permanently visible to be offered work. Besides, the whole of Hollywood, she feels, is 'oriented around the film business. But in New York we have so many fields of success – great minds, great personalities, great people in all kinds of fields and you have the opportunity to meet them and mingle with them, which is much more interesting to me than spending all your time within your own sphere. I mean, that's boring and it's constricting and you don't grow and you don't learn. I don't want just to be worshipped. I would actually like to be challenged so I would rather stay here in New York.'

Which is all very well if you happen to be Kathleen Turner, or Meryl Streep, or Jane Fonda and you are so heavily in demand that you can afford to live wherever you like, confident that the offers will continue to roll in. But what if you have not quite reached that stage? What if you are, let us say, Jamie Lee Curtis?

Miss Curtis, the daughter of Janet Leigh and Tony Curtis, is a very good young actress, a kind of thinking man's sex symbol of the 1980s. But despite personal success in such films as *Trading Places* and *Perfect* she is not – or at least not yet and not usually – the first choice for the better roles on offer. So for her Hollywood is the place to be, whether she likes it or not, and she doesn't seem to like it a great deal.

She said: 'This is where the work is. You want to be in movies, you have to be here. People have to know you're around, people have to see you.' But you do not merely have to be seen around – you have to be seen around looking magnificent every minute of the day. Miss Curtis doesn't enjoy that and very often spoils her own chances of being spotted by the right people because she will not play the game. 'I'm not a fancy person, I don't dress up a lot, I never wear make-up, so I won't go to any restaurants where I know I'm going to run into somebody from the business. I specifically avoid them, simply because I don't want to have to look great every time I go out. I don't want to have to look fab so that when they see you, they go "Oh, wow, oh she looks *fabulous*!" and then they hire you. I'm not saying that's the only way you get hired but a lot of it is as random as that, as somebody seeing you and saying, "Oh, I saw her yesterday and she looked great la-de-da-de-da . . ." '

It's a dispiriting prospect but how long can it continue? How long, indeed, can Hollywood itself continue when the cost of the *average* film made there is now, and depending on the estimate of the last person you spoke to, anything between 14 million and 18 million dollars? Jack Valenti, he of the elaborate phraseology, who should know the facts as well as anybody, said that the average negative cost of a picture made by one of the major studios in 1985 was 16.8 million dollars. 'If you add to that the advertising prints, promotion and distribution costs, the marketing costs, it's another 7 million to 9 million. So you're talking about 23 million to 25 million as the investment retrieval level.'

Which is indeed an alarming investment retrieval level, although David Puttnam put it even higher, estimating that the true cost of a film whose shooting budget was 15 million dollars would be at least double that, so that the real investment retrieval level – or, to put it another way, the time when somebody began to see a penny profit – would not come until 30 million dollars or so had been taken at

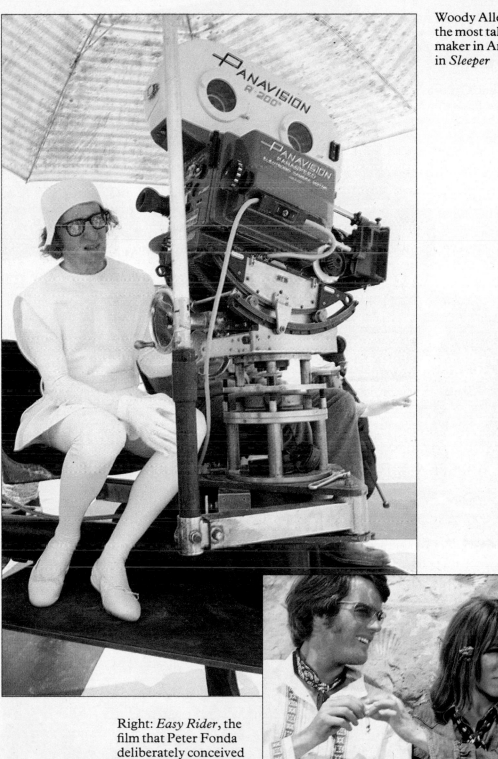

Woody Allen, possibly the most talented film-maker in America today, in *Sleeper*

Right: *Easy Rider*, the film that Peter Fonda deliberately conceived as an antidote to the anodyne *Dr Dolittle*

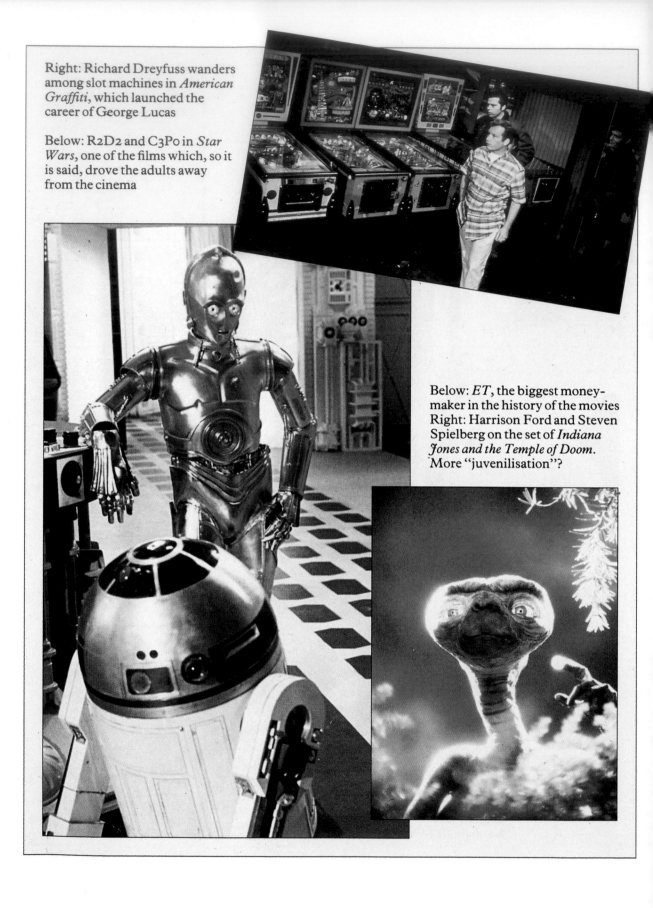

Right: Richard Dreyfuss wanders among slot machines in *American Graffiti*, which launched the career of George Lucas

Below: R2D2 and C3P0 in *Star Wars*, one of the films which, so it is said, drove the adults away from the cinema

Below: *ET*, the biggest money-maker in the history of the movies
Right: Harrison Ford and Steven Spielberg on the set of *Indiana Jones and the Temple of Doom*. More "juvenilisation"?

Michael Douglas and Kathleen Turner combining adventure with old-fashioned romance in *Romancing the Stone*

Above: *Ghostbusters* – Bill Murray, Dan Aykroyd and Harold Ramis. Right and below: Two examples of what Peter Bogdanovich calls "decadent" cinema? *Porky's* (right) and *Police Academy*. One sequel merely leads to another

Right: Kathleen Turner – here in *Peggy Sue Got Married* – already sufficiently in demand to be able to live in New York rather than Hollywood
Below: Jamie Lee Curtis, less fortunate than Kathleen Turner, here looking fabulous, though mostly she chooses not to

Two of the hottest names in Hollywood today – Eddie Murphy in *Beverly Hills Cop* and (right) Tom Cruise in *Top Gun*, 'rock 'n' roll in the sky'

Platoon, the biggest Oscar winner of 1987, heralding – dare we hope? – a return to more thoughtful movies

the box office. And there are still others who maintain that, realistically, you have to treble the basic production cost before the profits start.

Now this is perhaps acceptable if you have a *Top Gun*, a *Crocodile Dundee*, a *Golden Child* or a *Platoon*, all of which – regardless of merit or, in at least one case, lack of same – turned out to be virtually money-printing machines for the companies that released them. But most films are not like that, though the studios very much want them all to be like that – which is one reason why those studios are not greatly interested any more in modest films with modest box office ambitions. As Jamie Lee Curtis said: 'You make a movie now because of its ability to take 12 million dollars in one weekend. That becomes the goal.' Her own film, *Perfect*, took only about 5 million dollars in its opening week and was deemed a disaster.

What's more, marketing techniques are now so sophisticated that companies know after the very first public showing of a film whether it's going to be a success or not. One evening Miss Curtis was unusually – in Spago which, for whatever obscure reason dictates these things, is currently one of Hollywood's most fashionable restaurants and, seeing a producer whose film was opening later that night, said: 'Aren't you thrilled?' He said, No, he certainly wasn't thrilled because he knew in advance what the result was going to be. Because of the three-hour time difference the film had already had its first showing in New York that same Friday evening and it had not done well, which meant that the Saturday results weren't going to be good either. 'Basically,' said Miss Curtis, 'that movie was already a disaster – and this was opening night. You don't even get opening night any more: you know before the movie opens if it's going to do anything. It's hard, scary.'

But all this being so and it being a fact that most films lose money, how can production continue at that level and at that cost? The answer lies in the ancillary markets – the sale of the film to video, the airlines and the various TV outlets such as the networks, cable and satellite. David Puttnam said that in many ways these markets were now more important than the cinemas themselves but I think this is only true when applied to films of limited cost. A megabucks production – something like the 40 million-dollars-plus *Howard the Duck*, for instance – cannot hope to recoup its cost from ancillary sales: it desperately needs a strong run in the cinemas.

For anything much less expensive, however, the ancillary rights are crucial. Richard Sylbert said: 'When I started in this business, you made a movie for 4 million dollars that was no good, you couldn't give it away. It had no place to go. But suddenly television comes along and airlines come along. Now they have two more places that never existed before to lay off the movie. Then we get cable; then we get VCR. Cable has become a nearly 2 billion-dollar business in five years and the movies are only a 3 billion-dollar business. Now does that tell you something? You make a picture for 14 or 15 million, you have a very good chance to recoup a great deal of it.'

Furthermore, as Blake Edwards said, 'If you're reasonably intelligent about the project you're doing you can probably finance it up front on the ancillary rights.' And if you don't finance it all that way you can certainly attract a studio's interest in putting up the rest of the money if you can offer guaranteed sales to the ancillary markets. All of this, said Richard Zanuck, is 'critically important'. But he added a proviso: 'Bearing in mind that some of these avenues take away from the box office, it's not a pure addition. I mean, if somebody can go out and buy the cassette of your film, the cassette sales may look awfully good but you may be hurt in your theatrical exhibition sales. So it's not just a completely pure addition to the gross.'

At the moment, however, the ancillary markets do not seem to be having too deleterious an effect on the cinemas. The most successful year – financially – in cinema history was 1984 when 4.03 billion dollars were taken at the box office; the second most successful year was 1986 when the figure was 3.8 billion. In neither case, however, can we infer that more people were going to the cinema than ever before. The fact is that attendances were still considerably down on the peak years of the 1930s and 1940s and the additional revenue was simply the result of higher ticket prices.

Nevertheless, Hollywood and the major studios would claim now that they are healthy and they could become even healthier if they continue to buy back the cinema chains they were forced to relinquish in the late 1940s. Under the Reagan government the anti-trust laws have become sufficiently relaxed for the majors to start acquiring very large minority interests in theatre chains throughout North America. They acquire a minority interest so that they can never be accused of actually controlling the cinemas in the way they once did; but it is still large enough for them to have a great deal of influence on the way the theatres are run and on what films are shown there. Whether this will lead to the kind of block-booking that brought about the anti-trust decree in the first place remains to be seen but it will certainly mean a swifter cash flow for the studios. Richard Zanuck said: 'Studios don't get the money that's taken in at the box office for quite some time. But if they own the box office and the theatre they get it immediately – it's all going into the same pocket. That's a very big factor, I would think.'

So financially Hollywood appears to be in good shape. But never mind the width, what about the quality? Well, here the overall picture is less clear. Jamie Lee Curtis equates the current state of Hollywood movies with the current state of Hollywood architecture and she is in no bad position to comment because she is a child of the place. 'There's some sort of similarity between the big changes that have happened here architecturally and the movie business as a whole,' she said. 'Everywhere in the city right now you will see these little minimarkets that are nothing but cinder block and stucco and some sort of coloured rail and stained windows to make it look fake art deco. Well, that's the same thing as, I think, is happening with the architecture of Hollywood movies – so many of them are just sort of slapped together, cinder blocks with a lot of sprinkled glossy stuff to make them look real interesting. And that's fine for the immediacy of the experience but you don't remember them a year from now; they don't have any special value in your heart, they don't change your life like so many movies of the past have done. The whole place is collapsing, I think. It's a real scary time around here.'

Specifically, she was referring to what she called 'stupidity movies: movies that are made by stupid people from stupid scripts from stupid ideas and that are aimed at other stupid people. That's where the decay really begins.' Well, we can all draw up our own list of recent "stupidity movies". But she believed there was more to it than that. The current trend, she said, inspired by the 1987 success of the Bette Midler–Shelly Long film *Outrageous Fortune*, was for "women's buddy pictures". She said: 'Now the rage is, "Let's make movies putting two women together." Well, they'll do that until one of them becomes a failure and then they'll say, "Now we have to racially intermix them – so we'll put Chinese women in America." Okay, that'll be successful for one movie . . . It's this thought that you don't go for the material and try to produce something that is great and find the right actors for it – it's what's going well *now*. I'm up for a movie right now that was written for men and they're making it for two women. All of a sudden it's, "Any buddy picture you've got, can you make it for women? Oh, you can? Great!" '

That sort of attitude, of course, is not new: it's simply more intensified than it was in the halcyon days of the studio system. Hollywood, as Richard Sylbert put it, is 'continually re-inventing the wheel'. But perhaps over the years the size and variety of wheels it re-invents are diminishing. He said: 'There are four businesses to be in today that didn't exist in 1974, not in any way, shape or form. There's the Spielberg–Lucas business – anything from *Star Wars* to *Raiders of the Lost Ark*: terrific action adventures, the Saturday afternoon serial re-invented and done very well by film students, not by grown-up directors but by film students. The next business is the Stallone phenomenon – the completely patriotic, conservative right-wing, let's-go-for-it, we-can-do-it phenomenon. His pictures have probably brought in a billion dollars. Now, third, there's the serial, the sequel. We never had them before. People did remakes – remakes fail. Sequels don't fail because everybody knows what they're going to be about, all you don't know is the details. The next business to be in is anything that works and you could have it in any combination you wanted – John Belushi and Dan Aykroyd, or Aykroyd and Chevy Chase, or Chase and Bill Murray. Doesn't matter . . .'

William Goldman has a fifth category: the fish out of water movie. 'A fish out of water movie,' he said, 'is like *Beverly Hills Cop*, like *Crocodile Dundee* – it's a culture clash. Take a tough Detroit cop and put him in Beverly Hills, take a tough Australian alligator hunter and put him in New York City, take a tough Philadelphia policeman and put him with the Amish. You can have any combination and it may be a serious movie like *Witness* or a joke movie like *Crocodile Dundee*. *Back to the Future, Peggy Sue Got Married* – fish out of water movies and that's what's working right now, it's the craze out there.' He added, thoughtfully: 'It'll die soon.'

To be replaced, of course, by a new craze and one whose greatest appeal – as with Sylbert's "four businesses" – is to a young audience, whose importance is underlined by the fact that one of its cinematic shibboleths, the nineteen-year-old Molly Ringwald who, through no fault of her own, has not yet made a single film of any real merit, has already been featured on the cover of *Time* magazine, an honour which, in America, is akin to getting an OBE in Britain. 'Extraordinary,' said Goldman, shaking his head.

The corollary to all that, he thought – and this truly saddened him – was that 'the

Left: *Howard The Duck* aka Howard the Turkey
Below left: An example of "juvenilisation", no doubt, but one of the very best. Michael J. Fox and Christopher Lloyd in *Back to the Future*.
Below: The grown-ups version of *Back to the Future* – Kathleen Turner as Peggy Sue attending the high school reunion with her daughter, Helen Hunt, before being transported back to adolescence in *Peggy Sue Got Married*
Inset right: Jamie Lee Curtis: 'You want to be in movies, you have to be in Hollywood'

Paul Newman with Tom
Cruise in *The Color of
Money*. The film won
Newman the acting
Oscar he deserved and
failed to get for two
decades

great heroes whose work I adored – John Huston, Billy Wilder, Joe Mankiewicz, Elia Kazan, George Stevens and two or three others, Hawks, Ford – would all have been unemployable today. What movie in the last five years would John Ford have directed?' It's an exaggeration, of course – Huston, for instance, won an Oscar nomination in 1986 for *Prizzi's Honor* – but the point is still well made. Hollywood, as he said, is in a 'constant chase after past magic', after a repetition of what worked before, and what has most recently worked before is not the kind of film his heroes used to make, the kind to which you were required to bring your mind along.

He said: 'Steven Spielberg is an enormously talented director. I mean, he's just a dazzling talent. But thirty years ago I don't think anybody would have thought so because he would have been making pictures that were the second half of double features.' By this he meant that Spielberg's films are what he called 'kids' movies' and kids' movies were always the second half of the bill. He did not, he hastened to add, object to kids' movies as such but 'I would just like to have a film to see that was not insulting'.

The reference to Spielberg brings us back to where this chapter began. Does that mean that in the years since *Jaws* nothing has changed or will ever change? Oliver Stone took an optimistic view, suggesting that change had already taken place.

'There was a mass of inane movies about nothing, about kids but not even dealing realistically with kids' problems,' he said. 'But then about 1985, I think, the situation started to shift. There was a whole bunch of new independent companies coming in and because of the ancillary markets they were able to do their own distribution. And that made for a wider variety of selections. I don't think that *Blue Velvet* would have been made before 1985 or, for that matter, *Platoon*. These were made because of independent companies so maybe there's a shift in the wind back towards the 70s when there used to be a lot of this type of movie.'

Against that, however, it has been possible in almost any year to point to two or three, or even half a dozen, films of merit and serious intent and hail them as harbingers of a new, more adult era. But that era has still to dawn, though Richard Sylbert derived comfort from the failure of George Lucas's *Howard the Duck*. 'Dammit,' he said, '*Howard the Duck* is the beginning of something else. *Howard the Duck* is a 42 million-dollar failure, which means the people who knew how to do it don't know how to do it any more. Ten years have gone by. More. We've gone from 1974 to 1987 and they may have run out of gas. We're gonna see.'

Personally, I don't think they have run out of gas. *Howard the Duck* was Lucas's big flop; Spielberg had his with *1941* but Spielberg came back with even more monstrous hits than before and there's no reason to suppose that Lucas won't do the same. As Burt Reynolds said: 'They [the studios] always look for somebody who is the golden child, who has the touch. This guy makes movies that make money, or this lady makes movies that make money and if you are that person today, you can have the moon.' And Spielberg and Lucas, give or take *Howard the Duck*, are the current golden children.

But again the question arises: for how long can Hollywood continue the way it is? A recent, Oscar-winning film was budgeted at 25 million dollars and when that figure was broken down it was discovered that 6 million were earmarked for the leading man, 5 million for the leading lady, 1 million for the chief supporting actor and 3 million for the director. That left only 10 million for the below the line costs, in other words for the actual production of the picture. Can this possibly make any kind of financial sense?

Blake Edwards (who, incidentally, was not the director involved) thought not, although he admitted that much the same sort of situation had prevailed on some of his films. 'It's an imbalance,' he said, 'and that's wrong. But all the studio has to do is say, "Take less money. We'll give you a terrific deal on the back end so that if it's a success we get rich and you get rich. If it's a failure then you've made enough to pay your bills, we've made enough to pay our overheads but we all take a loss together." Now that's an over-simplification but if that proposition were put forward you would see movies coming back to some sensible budgets.'

Edwards reckoned that the average cost of a Hollywood movie in 1987 was 18 million dollars, a figure he found "terrifying". Something, he said, had got to be done because 'I just know that, by attrition, that 18 is going to become 19, is going to become 20, and it's going to be a house of cards. It'll just come tumbling down and out of the rubble we're going to have to resurrect ourselves. We're going to be the Phoenix. I hate to see us go through that process because it's painful, it hurts, but I guess we have to do it because we just don't learn our lessons. It's inevitable that eventually everybody's going to end up in the rubble and we'll be facing each other, you know, angry and dirty, but we're going to have to say: "Okay, now we got to make some kind of concessions here if we're going to go on making movies." We're going to have to think more about the sum total and less about the individual.'

All this, he thought, would happen later rather than sooner but 'it's on the way – it's very powerfully on the way'. Not surprisingly, though, few if any of his colleagues see the need for such dramatic remedies. For every pessimist about the future of Hollywood movies, you can always find an optimist.

The pessimists include Richard Zanuck who sees Hollywood today as primarily a television town where, because of costs and the unions' restrictive practices, the movies could 'shoot themselves out of business' Sidney Lumet pointed to declining cinema audiences and the growth of the cassette business and gloomily foresaw a day when movies were made strictly for TV and video consumption and film production became the equivalent of 'a small publishing house'.

By contrast Michael Douglas, who was both producer and star of films like *Romancing the Stone* and *Jewel of the Nile*, regarded the future 'with tremendous optimism, particularly with all the markets that are there. The person who creates a product is in the driving seat and I think that the creative entity has never been stronger than it is now or will be in the future.' And for Brian de Palma Hollywood 'is the place where you make movies and make deals to make movies. The hub of the industry is still in Hollywood because that's where most of the major financing and even the minor financing comes from. There's a tremendous film community there, a lot of talented people all in one town.'

Perhaps one day something like the scenario Blake Edwards put forward will have to be written or, if not anything quite that drastic, then at least there must surely be what Jack Valenti would call 'more fiscal discipline'. In 1987, indeed, David Puttnam was introducing more fiscal discipline into Columbia where he claimed that, by dint of refusing to pay inflated salaries, he had brought down the average cost of the studio's films to not much above 10 million dollars.

At the moment there is no real sign that other studios are planning to follow suit. On the contrary, Puttnam's outspoken criticism of the outrageous fees taken by stars, producers and directors has brought him considerable hostility from the film community. And there are still those – like Simpson and Bruckheimer, who make their films for Paramount – who protest that the figures quoted as the cost of the average picture are greatly exaggerated. The true figure, they said, was some way less than 10 million dollars. And if you take into account all the shoestring productions that are made by very young and aspiring film makers, this may well be true.

But we are not really talking about shoestring productions; we are talking about mainstream Hollywood movies and in that area enough people have expressed enough concern about the increasing size of the budgets to indicate that the film community's most urgent problem must be to bring costs down.

Assuming that is done, then the long-term prognosis could be that, yes, there will be changes – but there have always been changes – and that, yes, Hollywood will continue to be the hub of the industry and that, yes, the ancillary markets will become ever more important but the cinemas will struggle on. As William Goldman said: 'As long as kids want to get away from home, as long as they want to have a nice place to neck, as long as kids can't stand their parents, movies will exist.'

And that brings us to Hollywood's second most urgent problem, one in fact which people who regard films as something more than a mere business would regard as *the* most urgent: the content of the movies themselves.

The implication of Goldman's remark is that movies will exist only as long as kids want to see them and, by extension, it is frighteningly easy to see that as meaning that kids, and only kids, are the people for whom they will be made. It's a dire prospect and one that, surely, can please nobody. Like it or not, Hollywood is still the single most influential centre of film production in the world and, as of this moment, it is thriving financially, thanks mainly to "kids' movies". But no matter how much money it makes can it, for very much longer, continue to ignore the accusation that it has taken the most exciting new art form of the twentieth century and handed it over largely, if not indeed almost exclusively, to an endless exploration of the dreams, wishes, growing pains and masturbatory fantasies of teenage children?

INDEX

Figures in italics indicate black and white photographs; those in bold, colour plates.

Abbott, Bud, 111, 133, 262
Above Suspicion, 132
Adler, Luther, 167
'Adventures of Red Ryder, The' (series), 257
Adventures of Robin Hood, The, 297
Advise and Consent, 99
After the Thin Man, **124**
Agee, James, 139
Aherne, Brian, 114
Alamo, The, 253, 279
Aldrich, Robert, 224, 282
Alger, Horatio, 147
Alibi, 146
All About Eve, 48, 57, 89, 98, 137
All Quiet on the Western Front, 17, 22, 23, 29, 30
All the King's Men, 187
All the President's Men, 225, 306
Allen, Woody, 221, 284, 299, 303, **321**
Allyson, June, 37
Altman, Robert, 282
Alvarez Kelly, 280
Amarcord, 249
Amazing Colossal Man, The, 242
Ameche, Don, 43, 114–15, 140, 142, 316
American Graffiti, 302, 310, **322**
American in Paris, An, 296
Anderson, Gilbert M. (Bronco Billy), 252
Andrews, Dana, 139, 140, *141*
Andrews, Julie, 302
'Andy Hardy' series, 231, *238*
Angeli, Pier, 140
Angels Wash Their Faces, 155
Angels With Dirty Faces, 155, 162
Anna Christie, 22–3

Annie Get Your Gun, **270**, 277, 296
Annie Hall, 303
Anthony Adverse, 66
Antonioni, Michelangelo, 100
Apache, 273
Apocalypse Now, **198**, 225, 306
Appaloosa, The, 280
Applause, 17, 19, *21*
Arbuckle, Fatty, 78, 232
Arkoff, Samuel Z., 166, 242, 246
Arlen, Richard, 26, 27, 231
Arnold, Edward, 260
Around the World in 80 Days, 296, 299
Arsenic and Old Lace, 133
Arthur, Jean, 60, 133, 260
Asphalt Jungle, The, 98
Astaire, Fred, 130, **271**, 295, 296
Asther, Nils, 25
Astor, Mary, 10, 157
Astoria Studios, 18
At the Front, 129
Attack of the Crab Monsters, 244
Autry, Gene, 232, 235, 257, 260, 263, 264, **275**
Awful Truth, The, 240
Axelrod, George, 103, 303, 306
Aykroyd, Dan, **325**, 331
Ayres, Agnes, 86
Ayres, Lew, 23, 29, 30, 147

Baby Doll, 94, 98
Baby Face Nelson, 161, 163
Bacall, Lauren, 92, 191, **193**, 204
Back Street, 80
Back to the Future, 331, **332**
Bacon, Lloyd, 261
Bad Day at Black Rock, 112
Bad Men of Missouri, 261
Baker, Carroll, 64, 94, 95, 98–9
Balaban, Barney, 300
Bananas, 303

Bancroft, Anne, 104
Bancroft, George, 146, *150*
Band Wagon, The, 296
Bankhead, Tallulah, 80
Bara, Theda, 75, 77
Barry, Don, 257
Barrymore, John, 10, 28, 31, 44
Barrymore, Lionel, 44, 263
Bartholomew, Freddie, 34
Bataan, 117
Bates, Alan, 102
Battle of Midway, 117, 120
Baxter, Anne, 40, 48, 58–9, 64, 69–70
Baxter, Warner, **121**, 231
Beast of the City, 146
Beaton, Welford, 12
Beatty, Warren, 164, **199**, 226, 303
Beautiful Blonde from Bashful Bend, The, 137
Becky Sharp, 30, **268**, 297
Beery, Wallace, 26, 27, 33, 44, 146, 256
Begelman, David, 303
Belafonte, Harry, 206, 215
Bellamy, Ralph, 28, 30, 62, 237, 240
Bello, Marino, 161
Bells of St Mary's, The, 92
Belushi, John, 331
Ben Hur, 296, 299, *304*
Bengal Tiger, 237
Benjamin, Robert, 294
Bennett, Constance, 91
Bennett, Joan, 113–14
Benny, Jack, 133, 262
Benton, Robert, 164
Bergen, Candice, 222
Bergman, Ingmar, 249, 299
Bergman, Ingrid, 91, 92, 100, 116, 138, *158*, **194**, 261
Berkeley, Busby, 84, *87*, 130, 153, 295
Berkeley, Martin, 212–13
Berlin, Irving, 130
Berman, Pandro S., 65, 114

Bern, Paul, 43
Bessie, Alvah, 201
Best Years of our Lives, The, 47, 140, *141*, 142
Beverly Hills Cop, **327**, 331
Beyond the Law, 254
Beyond the Valley of the Dolls, 244
Biberman, Herbert, 201
Big Chill, The, 313–14
Big Combo, The, 102
Big Country, The, 278
Big Heat, The, 162
Big Jim McClain, 206
Big Sleep, The, 146
Big Trail, The, 234, 256, 257
Billy the Kid, 256, 261
Bioff, Willie, 184
Bird of Paradise, 84
Black Beauty, 235
Black Cat, The, 241, *243*
Black Fury, 179
Black Hills, The, 234
Blauner, Steve, 313
Blazing Saddles, 282
Blockade, 106, 181
Blonde Crazy, 153
Blonde Venus, 80
Blondell, Joan, 46, 59
Blood Alley, 206
Bloody Mama, 165–6
Blow Up, 100, **123**
Blue Angel, The, 24, 82, 98
Blue Dahlia, The, 140
Blue Velvet, 334
Bluebeard, 241
Body and Soul, 160
Body Heat, 313
Boetticher, Budd, 163–4, 254, 277, 278, 284, 285
Bogart, Humphrey, 27, 45, 46, 91, 115, 116, 117, *151*, 155, 156, 157, 167, 181, 183, 184, 191, **194**, 204, 231, 237, 261
Bogdanovich, Peter, 152, 157, 170, 247, 249, 252, 253, 264, 280, 286, 300, 301, 302, 306, 307–8, 311, 313
Bomba: the Jungle Boy, 235, *239*
Bond, Ward, 187, 215

Bonnie and Clyde, 162, 164, 165, 166, 167, 169, 176, 301, 306
Boone, Richard, 278, 282
Boorman, John, 162
Bordertown, 179
Borzage, Frank, 106
Boule, Pierre, 204
Bow, Clara, 24, 76
Bowery Boys, 235, 236
Boxcar Bertha, 248
Boyd, William, 260
Boys in the Band, The, 102
Bracken, Eddie, 63, 112–13, *134*, 136–7
Braham, John, 155
Brando, Marlon, 95, **124**, 140, 148, 168, 169, *173*, 195, 280, 291, 293, 294, 296, 297, 303
Brave One, The, 204
Breakfast at Tiffany's, 99, 102
Breath of Scandal, A, 216
Breathless, 235
Breen, Joseph Ignatius, 84, 85, 101, 104, 106
Brennan, Walter, 262
Brewer, Roy, 181, 182, 183, 184, 186, 187–8, 201, 206, 209, *210*, 212, 214, 217, 220–1
Bridge on the River Kwai, The, 204, 299
Bridges at Toko Ri, The, 214
Bright, John, 83–4, 148, 149, 180, 203, 222
Bringing Up Baby, 91, **121**
Briskin, Irving, 230
Broken Arrow, 264, 273, 276
Bronson, Charles, 103, 104, 171, 172
Brooks, Louise, 26
Brooks, Mel, 282
Brooks, Richard, 42, 65, 99, 100, 104, 139, 142, 161–2, 254, 273, 280, 285, 299
Brotherhood, The, 167
Brothers Rico, The, 162
Brown, George E., 184
Brown, Joe E., 262
Brown, Johnny Mack, 256, 257

337

Bruckheimer, Jerry, 308, 336
Brute Force, 161
Brynner, Yul, 296, *304*
Buck Benny Rides Again, 262
Buck Privates, 111, 133
Buffalo Bill, 262
Buffalo Bill and the Indians, 282
Burke, Billie, 44
Burnett, W. R., 146, 152, 156
Burton, Richard, 70, 182, 297, 317
Bus Stop, 98
Butch Cassidy and the Sundance Kid, 165, 256, **267**, 281, 282
Butterfield 8, 99
Bwana Devil, 297

Caan, James, 168, **195**
Cabot, Bruce, 25
Cagney, James, 36, *39*, 45, 46, **126**, 144, 146, 148–9, *150, 151*, 152–6 *passim*, 164, 166, 167, 181, 183, 184, **194**, 235, 237, 261, 319
Cagney, William, 235
Caine, Michael, 70
Calamity Jane, 277
Call Her Savage, 80
Camille, **56**
Cantor, Eddie, 11, 30, 205
Canutt, Yakima, 257
Capone, 249
Capone, Al, 144, 145, 146, 147, 149, 152, 153, 161, 184
Capra, Frank, *39*, 65, 112, 117, 129, 133, 142, 154, 291, 299
Captain Loves the Sea, The, 25
Captains of the Clouds, **126**
Captive Wild Woman, 230
Carey, Harry, Jr, 280
Carey, Harry, Sr, 252, 264
Carnal Knowledge, 102
Carradine, David, 283
Carradine, Keith, 283
Carradine, Robert, 283
Carroll, Madeleine, 106
Casablanca, 91, 110, 115–16, 137, 157, **194**, 233, 261, 299
Cass Timberlane, 89
Castle, William, 242.
Cat Ballou, 280
Cat on a Hot Tin Roof, 99, 299, *305*
Cat People, 237
Catch 22, 102
Cattle Queen of Montana, 277
Caught in the Draft, 111, 112, 133

Cazale, John, **195**
Chakiris, George, 246
Chalupek, Appolonia, 24
Chandler, Jeff, 48, 273
Chandler, Raymond, 137
Chaplin, Charlie, 23, 27, 28, 31, 110–11, **126**, 294, 303
Chapman Report, The, 98
'Charlie Chan' series, 235
Charlie Varrick, 303
Chase, Chevy, 318, 331
Chayevsky, Paddy, 300
Cheat, The, 75
Cheyenne Autumn, 253, 280
Chinatown, 172, 174, *176*, 307
Chisum, 281
Christie, Julie, 102, 103
Christmas in July, 136
Cimarron, 237, 256, *258*
Cimino, Michael, 175, 225, 283, 319
Cincinnati Kid, The, 216
Citizen Kane, 105, *108*, 136, 142, 170, 299
City Heat, 303
City Streets, 19, 22, 24
Clarens, Carlos, 167
Clarke, Mae, 148, 149, *150*, 240
Clift, Montgomery, 264
Clothier, William, 16, 17, 253, 254, 256, 284
Cobb, Lee J., 213
Coburn, Charles, 133
Coburn, James, 278
Cocoon, 315, 316
Cody, Bill, 235
Cody, Iron Eyes, 256, 273, 282
Cohens and the Kellys in Trouble, The, 230
Cohn, Harry, 58, 65, 66, 69, 161, 185, 212, 240, 254, 300
Cohn, Jack, 66
Colbert, Claudette, 46, 57, 81, 91, 132, *135*, 261, 296
Cole, Lester, 201, 204
Colman, Ronald, 26, 113, 132
Color of Money, The, 314, 317, 318, *333*
Color Purple, The, 7
Colorado Territory, 156
Coming Home, 225
Compulsion, 315
Confessions of a Nazi Spy, 106, 107, 110, 132, 185, 206, 237
Confessions of Boston Blackie, *109*, 230
Conte, Richard, 102, 139
Conversation, The, 302
Cook, Elisha, Jr, 92
Cooper, Gary, 19, 22, 26, 27, *60*, 62, 82, 111, 115,

187, 190, 251, 254, *258*, 260, 261, 262, 276, 277, 279, 284, 294
Cooper, Kenny, 257
Coote, Robert, 113
Coppola, Francis Ford, 143, 145, 164, 167, 168–9, 175, 225, 245, 247, 250, 302, 306, 307, 311, 313, 315
Coquette, 27
Corman, Gene, 248
Corman, Roger, 145, 163, 165–6, 244–5, 246, 247, 248, 249, 250, *250*, 301
Cornered, 137, 157, 187, 209
Costello, Dolores, 24
Costello, Lou, 111, 133, 262
Cotten, Joseph, 95, 132, 263
Cotton Club, The, 145, 164, 169, 175
Count of Monte Cristo, The, 178
Covered Wagon, 253
Cowboy Command, 262
Crawford, Joan, 44, 46, 48, **55**, 57, 59, 78, 81, 92, *108*, 117, 130, 132, 138, 183, 277
Cries and Whispers, 249
Crime School, 237
Cripple Creek Bar-room, 252
Crocodile Dundee, 331
Cronyn, Hume, 316
Crosby, Bing, 133, 296
Crosland, Alan, 30
Crossfire, 187
Cry of the City, 157
Cruise, Tom, 318, **327**
Cruze, James, 253, 260
Cry of the City, 157
Cukor, George, 82, 99
Culpepper Cattle Company, The, 282
Cummins, Peggy, 40, 41
Curtis, Jamie Lee, 7, 320, **326**, 329, 330
Curtis, Tony, 48, 94, **123**, 320
Curtiz, Michael, 110, 116, 155, 186, 261, 262, 297

Dakota Kid, 234
Dalton, Emmett, 254
Damaged Goods, 74
Daniels, Bill, 82
Danton, Ray, 163, 164
Darby, Kim, **266**
Dark Command, The, 262
Dark Horse, The, 153
Darling, 102, 103
Darnell, Linda, 41, **268**
Dassin, Jules, 157, 216
Daves, Delmer, 140, 264, 278
David and Bathsheba, 296
Davies, Joseph E., 186
Davies, Marion, 59

Davis, Bette, 46, 57, **61**, 92, 130, 132
Day, Doris, 94, 95, 96, 131
Days of Glory, 186, *211*
De Forest, Lee, 10
De Havilland, Olivia, 60, 202, 287–8
De Mille, Cecil B., 32, 36, 75, 76, 206, 217, 218, 219, 252, 253, 260, 261, 296, 300
De Niro, Robert, 169, 171, 172, *173*, **196**, **198**, 225, 248, *312*
De Palma, Brian, 152, 174, 175, 311, 313, 316–17, 335
De Wilde, Brandon, **266**
Dead End, 155
Dead End Kids, 236, 237
Dead Reckoning, 140
Dean, James, 163, 164, 165, 299
Death of a Salesman, 214
Death Wish, 103, **124**
Death Wish 3, 104
Death Wish series, 162, 170, 171, 174
Deep Throat, 102
Deerhunter, The, **198**, 225
Defiant Ones, The, 215
Derek, John, 167
Dern, Bruce, 246, *250*
Design for Living, 84
Destry Rides Again, 82, *259*, 261, 262, 263, 280
Detective, The, 102, 162
Detective Story, 162
Devil Dogs of the Air, 36, 107
Devil's Eight, The, 248
Diary of Major Thompson, The, 137
Dickson, W. K. Laurie, 9
Dies, Martin, 183, 184
Dieterle, William, 106, 110
Dietrich, Marlene, *21*, 24, 33, **54**, 80, 82, 86, 98, *210*, 245, *259*, 261, 263, 277
Dillinger, 160, 166, 249, *250*
Dinner at Eight, 44
Dirty Dozen, The, 248, 249
Dirty Harry, 170, 171, **195**, 303
Dirty Harry series, 162
Dirty Little Billy, 282
Disney, Walt, 187
Dive Bomber, 111, *118*
Dix, Richard, 16, 231, 256
Dmytryk, Edward, 70, 88, 132, 137–8, 157, 160, 180, 186, 187, 201, 203, 207, 209, 213, 221, 230
Dr Dolittle, 246, 302

Dr Ehrlich's Magic Bullet, 110
Dr Jekyll and Mr Hyde, 22
Dr Socrates, 231
Dodge City, 261
Dog Day Afternoon, 303
Dolorita's Houchi Kouchi, 73
Dolorita's Passion Dance, 73
Don Juan, 10, 30, **49**
Donahue, Troy, 94
Donen, Stanley, 296
Donlevy, Brian, *259*
Doorway to Hell, 147
Double Indemnity, 92, 157, *158*
Douglas, Kirk, 167, 216
Douglas, Melvyn, 85, 181, 205
Douglas, Michael, **324**, 335
Dragnet, 146
Dressed to Kill, 174
Dressler, Marie, 44
Dreyfuss, Richard, **322**
Drive, He Said, 313
Drums Along the Mohawk, 261
Duel, 311
Duel in the Sun, 95, 263, **265**
Dunaway, Faye, 164, 174
Dunne, Irene, 256
Dunne, Philip, 89–90, 115, 129, 178, 180–4 *passim*, 187, 188, 191, 192, 201–5 *passim*, 208, 220, 221, 294–5
Durbin, Deanna, 44
Dvorak, Ann, *151*, 152
Dwan, Allan, 234

Easter Parade, 296
Eastwood, Clint, 170, 172, **195**, 251, *255*, 281, 283, 284, 302, 303
Easy Rider, 222, 224, 246, 285, 301, 306, 313, **321**
Eddie Duchin Story, The, 296
Eddy, Nelson, 130
Edge of the City, 221
Edison, Thomas, 9, 252
Edwards, Blake, 329, 335
Egyptian, The, 296
Eisenstein, Sergei, 12, 260
Eisler, Gerhart, 189
Eisler, Hanns, 189
El Dorado, 279
Ellery Queen series, 240
End of the Trail, 276
Enforcer, The, 162
Epstein, Julius, 110, 116
Epstein, Philip, 110, 116
Escape, 111
Estevez, Emilio, 306
ET, 104, 308, **322**
Evans, Dale, **265**

Evans, Robert, 167–8, 169, 172, 174, 175
Execution of Private Slovnik, The, 216
Exodus, 216

Fairbanks, Douglas, Jr, 16–17, 26, 27, 28, 52, 113
Fairbanks, Douglas, Sr, 27, 28, 31
Faithless, 80
Fall Guy, 235
Fall of the House of Usher, The, 245
Farrow, Johnny, 237
Fashion of 1934, 84
Feld, Fritz, 16
Fellini, Federico, 236, 249, 299
Fessier, Michael, 230
Field, Sally, 104
Fields, Freddie, 303
Fields, W. C., 262
Fighting US Coast Guard, 234
Finian's Rainbow, 167
Fistful of Dollars, A, 281
Five Easy Pieces, 313
Five Graves to Cairo, 132
Five Star Final, 153
Flatiron Building on a Windy Day, The, 74
Fleming, Victor, 254
Fluegel, Darlene, 196
Flying Tigers, 117
Flynn, Errol, 45, 92, 110, 111, 115, 139, 140, 261–2, 297
Folsey, George, 18
Fonda, Henry, 62, 106, 136, 155, 156, 181, 246, 261, 262, 264, 275, 279, 284
Fonda, Jane, 104, 174, 224, 225, 319, 320
Fonda, Peter, 222, 245, 246, 249, 250, 285, 321
Fontaine, Joan, 35, 57, 92, 114, 115, 139, 140
Fool There Was, A, 75
Footlight Parade, 84
Forbidden Fruit, 76, 86
Force of Evil, 160
Ford, Glenn, 48, 157, 162, 222, 231, 284
Ford, Harrison, 312, 323
Ford, John, 22, 112, 114–15, 117, 118, 120, 129, 140, 142, 149, 218–19, 232, 234, 240, 252, 253, 254, 260, 261, 264, 273, 277, 278, 279, 280, 284, 286, 300, 334
Foreign Correspondent, 111
Foreman, Carl, 187, 203, 204, 276, 277
Forever Amber, 40–1, 268
Fort Apache, 264, 280
Fortune, The, 303

42nd Street, 130, 153
Foster, Jodie, 173
Four Frightened People, 296
Fox, Michael J., 332
Fox, William, 11, 75
Foy, Brian, 230, 231, 237
Francis, Kay, 231, 237
Frankenheimer, John, 311
Free Soul, A, 59, 80, 86
Freed, Arthur, 295
French Line, The, 98
From Here to Eternity, 99, 299
Front, The, 221
Front Page, The, 153
Fuller, Sam, 162, 240
Funny Girl, 319
Furthman, Charles, 146
Furthman, Jules, 146
Fury, 155, 179, 240

G Men, 154, **194**
Gable, Clark, 27, 28, 30, 41, 42, 44, 45, 59, 60, 62, 63, 67, 76, 80–1, 86, 91, 112, 142, 146, 212, 240, 241, 294
Gance, Abel, 13
Garbo, Greta, 15, 21, 22, 23, 24, 25, 27, 36, 44, 45, 46, 56, 59, 60, 81–2, 83, 91, 105
Gardner, Ava, 42, 68, 231
Garfield, John, 36, 71, 91, 140, 160, 191, 213
Garland, Judy, 63, 64, 191, 231, 238
Garner, James, 281
Garson, Greer, 44, 59, 63, 111–12, 113, 119, 132, 139, 241, 290, 301
Gaslight, 138
Genius, The, 216
Gentleman Jim, 92
Gentleman's Agreement, 187
George, Chief Dan, 282
Gere, Richard, 145
Gershwin, George, 130
Getting Straight, 222
Ghostbusters, 318, 325
Ghostbusters 2, 318
Gibson, Hoot, 253
Gigi, 299
Gilbert, Beatrice, 25
Gilbert, John, 15, 24–5, 26, 27, 62, 76, 81
Gilda, 157
Girl Climbing Tree, 73
Glasmon, Kubec, 149
Globus, Yoram, 247
Godard, Jean-Luc, 8, 164, 235
Goddard, Paulette, 130
Godfather, The, 148, 167–9, 173, 175, **195**, 302, 307, 313
Godfather II, The, 143, 167, 169, 302

Golan, Menahem, 247
Gold Diggers of 1933, 55, 84, 87, 153
Goldblum, Jeff, 283
Goldman, William, 7–8, 317–19, 331, 336
Goldstein, Manny, 232
Goldwyn, Samuel, 47, 63, 183, 296, 300
Gone With the Wind, 59, 105, 132, 168, 297
Goodbye Columbus, 102
Goodbye My Fancy, 57
Gorcey, Leo, 155, 236
Gould, Elliott, 222
Grable, Betty, 91, 92, 128, 131
Graduate, The, 102, 301
Grand Hotel, 44
Grant, Cary, 91, 99, 121
Granville, Bonita, 132
Grapes of Wrath, The, 182, **197**
Grayson, Kathryn, 298
Great Dictator, The, 110–11, 126, 185
Great Gatsby, The, 174
Great McGinty, The, 136
Great Northfield Minnesota Raid, The, 282
Great Train Robbery, The, 252, 255
Greatest Show on Earth, The, 296
Green Berets, The, 222, 223
Greenberg, Joel, 133
Greenstreet, Sydney, 92
Griffin, Wayne, 212
Griffith, D. W., 28, 31, 79, 145, 252
Grinde, Nick, 229
Guadalcanal Diary, 117
Gunfight at the O.K. Corral, The, 251, 278
Gunfighter, The, 276
Guys and Dolls, 296

Hackman, Gene, 303
Haig, Alexander, 226, 314
Hail the Conquering Hero, 134, 136
Hall, Huntz, 129–30, 139, 155, 236–7
Halliwell, Leslie, 48
Hallowe'en 14, 319
Hammett, Dashiell, 154, 156
Hangmen Also Die, 189
Harder They Fall, The, 65
Hardy, Oliver, 7
Harlow, Jean, 43, 44, 45, 81, 82, 146, 161
Harris, Richard, 282
Harrison, Rex, 302
Hart, William S., 252, 253
Harvey, Laurence, 102, 103
Hasty Heart, The, 212
Hathaway, Henry, 160, 284

Havana Rose, 234
Havoc, June, 205
Hawaii, 182
Hawks, Howard, 59, 93, 146, 152, 175, 237, 260, 264, 279, 284, 286, 334
Hayden, Sterling, 48, 206, 208, 211, 213
Hayes, Helen, 44
Hays, Will H., 10, 78, 80, 81, 84, 101, 105, 106
Hayward, Susan, 296
Hayworth, Rita, 157
Hearst, William Randolph, 178, 191
Hearts and Minds, 224
Heaven's Gate, 267, 283, 319
Hecht, Ben, 65, 79, 146, 152
Hecht, Harold, 294
Hellinger, Mark, 161, 162
Hellman, Lillian, 186, 212
Hellman, Monte, 245
Hello, Dolly, 302
Hell's Heroes, 18–19
Henreid, Paul, 132
Henry V, 90
Hepburn, Katharine, 46, 91, 121, 133
Here Comes the Navy, 197
Heston, Charlton, 170, 273, 282, 285, 291, 294, 296, 304
High Noon, 251, 256, 276, 277, 279, 299
High Plains Drifter, 283
High School Confidential, 242
High Sierra, 156
High Society, 296
Higham, Charles, 133
Hill, James, 294
Hill, Walter, 283
His Girl Friday, 240
His Glorious Night, 24–5
Hitchcock, Alfred, 99, 111, 294, 300
Hitler's Children, 132
Hoffman, Dustin, 102, 302, 317–18
Holden, William, 42, 208, 279, 281
Hollywood Canteen, 130
Hollywood Ten, 201–4 *passim*, 210
Home of the Brave, 187
Hondo, 276
Hoover, Herbert, 39
Hoover, J. Edgar, 154, 161, 205, 206
Hope, Bob, 93, 111, 112, 113, 133, 136
Hopper, Dennis, 222, 246
Hopper, Hedda, 187
Horse Soldiers, The, 253, 279
Hot Rod Girl, 242
House of Wax, The, 272, 297

Houseman, John, 129, 291, 295, 297
Hovic, June, 205
How Bridget Served the Salad Undressed, 73
How Green Was My Valley, 89–90, 182
How the West Was Won, 279
Howard, Leslie, 25, 44, 60
Howard, Trevor, 297
Howard the Duck, 313, 329, 332, 334
Hubbard, Lucien, 230
Hucksters, The, 142
Hudson, Rock, 37, 47, 72, 94, 95, 96
Hughes, Howard, 40, 47, 58, 59, 62, 92, 93, 137, 147, 152, 205–6, 263, 300
Hunt, Helen, 332
Hunter, Jeff, 94, 277
Hunter, Tab, 43–4, 62, 94, 95
Hustler, The, 297
Huston, John, 112, 115, 129, 137, 156, 174, 191, 192, 218, 282, 290, 291, 299, 334
Huston, Walter, 88, 146, 158
Hutton, Betty, 92, 131, 136, 270

I am a Fugitive from a Chain Gang, 179
I Married a Communist, 205, 211
I Was a Communist for the FBI, 206
I Was a Teenage Werewolf, 242, 243
I'm No Angel, 83
Immortal Mr Teas, The, 244
In Old Arizona, 253, 254
Ince, Thomas, H., 252
Indiana Jones and the Temple of Doom, 307, 308, 323
Informer, The, 261
Interference, 13, 51
Introduction to the Enemy, 224–5
Invasion of the Body Snatchers, The (1956), 236, 240, 243
Invasion of the Body Snatchers, The (1978), 243
Invasion USA, 200, 227
Invisible Ghost, 234
Invitation to the Dance, An, 296
Irma La Douce, 99
Iron Curtain, The, 206
Iron Horse, The, 253
Irwin, May, 73
It Happened One Night, 42, 81, 91

It's a Wonderful Life, 142, 299
It's Always Fair Weather, 296

Jackson, Donald, 209, 212
Jaglom, Henry, 313
Jannings, Emil, 23–4
Jaws, 168, 307, 308, *309*, 315, 334
Jaws 3D, 297
Jazz Singer, The, 7, 9, 11–12, 13, *14*, 23, 30
Jesse James, 261
Jesse James at Bay, 261
Jessel, George, 11, 30
Jet Pilot, 47
Jewel of the Nile, 335
Jezebel, 46, *61*
John and Mary, 102
Johnny Guitar, 277
Johnson, Ben, 281
Johnston, Eric, 189–90, 191, 192, 205
Jolson, Al, 9, 11, *14*, 30, **49**
Jolson Story, The, 30, 213
Jones, Buck, 252–3
Jones, Jennifer, 95, 132, *135*, 263, **265**
Juarez, 110
Julius Caesar, 290, 299·

Kael, Pauline, 104, 115, 251, 282
Kantor, Mackinlay, 140
Karloff, Boris, 230, 241, *243*, 245, 247
Karlson, Phil, 162
Kasdan, Lawrence, 313–14, 317
Katzman, Sam, 242
Kaufman, Joe, 106
Kaye, Danny, 47, 136, 191, 204, 205
Kazan, Elia, 94, 187, 213, 218, 334
Keach, James, 283
Keach, Stacy, 283
Keaton, Buster, 28, 31
Keaton, Diane, **199**
Keel, Howard, 296, *298*
Keitel, Harvey, 248
Kelly, Gene, 25, 295, 296
Kelly, Grace, 99, 276
Kennedy, Joseph, 41, 107
Kerkorian, Kirk, 300
Kerr, Deborah, 99, 290, 296, 299, *304*
Key Largo, 157, 162
Keyes, Evelyn, 36, 58, 65, 66, 191, 192, 221
Killens, John O., 215
Killers, The (1946), 161, 231
Killers, The (1964), 162
King, Henry, 261, 276
King and I, The, 296, *304*
King of the Underworld, 231
Kirk, Jack, 257

Kiss, The, 23, 73, 74, 77
Kiss Me Kate, 296, 297, 298
Kiss of Death, 160
Kitses, Jim, 277–8
Kline, Kevin, 283
Klute, 303
Klutz, Susan, 230
Knight, Patricia, 37
Knox, Alexander, 191
Koch, Howard, 110, 111, 115, 116, 186, 190, 191–2, 203, 205, *211*, 221–2
Kramer, Stanley, 69
Krims, Arthur, 294
Krims, Milton, 107, 185, 206
Kurosawa, Akira, 279, 299
Kurtz, Gary, 311

Ladd, Alan, 70–1, **266**, 276
Lady and the Monster, The (The Lady and the Doctor), 233, *238*
Lady Eve, The, 136
Lady for a Day, 154
Lady from Shanghai, The, 92
Laemmle, Carl, 31, 63
Lake, Veronica, 130
Lamarr, Hedy, 116, 296
Lamour, Dorothy, 130
Lancaster, Burt, 99, 224, 231, 273, 282, 294, 299
Lang, Fritz, 155, 157, 160, 162, 179, 218, 253, 262, 277
Lang, Jennings, 217
Lange, Jessica, 91, 104
Lansky, Meyer, 144, 161, 162
Lanza, Mario, 43
Lardner, Ring, 181, 203, 204, 216, 222
Lardner, Ring Jr, 190, 201, 203
Lasky, Jesse Sr, 19
Lassie Come Home, 231
Last Command, The, 24
Last Hunt, The, 285
Last of the Mohicans, The, 178
Last Picture Show, The, 302, 313
Last Tango in Paris, 102, **124**
Last Woman on Earth, The, 248
Late George Apley, The, 90
Latino, 310
Laughing Sinners, 59
Laura, 157
Laurel, Stan, 7
Lavery, Emmett, 190
Lawrence, Florence, 31
Lawrence, Marc, 206
Lawson, John Howard,

106, 178, 181, 186, 190, 192, 201, 209
Le Roy, Mervyn, 179
Lean, David, 313
Leech, John L., 183
Left-Handed Gun, The, 278
Legend, 318
Leigh, Janet, 40, 57, 58, 59, 62, 320
Leigh, Vivien, *60*, 71, 81, 95, 113, **127**
Lemmon, Jack, **123**
Leone, Sergio, 175, 281
Let Us Live, 155
Letter to Three Wives, A, 137
Lewis, Joseph H., 102, 103, 160–1, 234–5, 240, 241, 257
Lewton, Val, 230
Life and Times of Judge Roy Bean, The, 282
Lights of New York, 13, 50, 146, 230
Lindbergh, Charles, 11, 105, 107, 153, 183, 253
Line-Up, The, 162
Little Big Man, 224, 281–2
Little Caesar, 146, 147, *150*, 166
Little Man, What Now?, 106
Little Miss Marker, 154
Little Shop of Horrors, The, 245
Litvak, Anatole, 107
Livingstone, Margaret, 26
Lloyd, Christopher, *332*
Loder, John, *118*
Lombard, Carole, 112, 133
London, Jack, 208
Lone Star, 212
Long, Shelly, 331
Long Riders, The, 283
Longest Day, The, 129
Loo, Richard, *141*
Look into the Future, 242
Lord Jim, 299
Losey, Joseph, 203
Love and Death, 303
Love is a Racket, 153
Loved One, The, 216
Lowe, Rob, 306, 318
Loy, Myrna, 44, 91, 112, **124**, 154
Lubitsch, Ernst, 76, 89, 133
Lucas, George, 250, 302, 307, 308, *309*, 310, 311, 313, 331, 334
Luciano, Lucky, 144, 145, 161, 162, 164
Lucky Lady, 303
Lugosi, Bela, 241, *243*
Lukas, Paul, 107
Lumet, Sidney, 100, 300, 303, 319, 335

Lumière Brothers, 9
Lupino, Ida, 218
Lusty Men, The, 278

Macbeth, 234
McCarthy, Joseph, 162, 214–15, 228
McCoy, Tim, 235, 253, 276
McCrea, Joel, 111, 133, 262, 280
MacDonald, Jeanette, 45, 63, 130
McGuiness, James K., 187
McGuire, Dorothy, 138
McQueen, Steve, 279
Machine-Gun Kelly, 163, 166
McLaglen, Andrew, 280, 281, 284
McLaglen, Victor, 280
McLintock, 280
MacMurray, Fred, *118*, 132, *158*
Mad Doctor of Market Street, The, 234
Madigan, 172
Magnificent Ambersons, The, 237
Magnificent Seven, The, 279
Magnum Force, 170, 171
Malden, Karl, 94
Maltese Falcon, The, 92, 137, 156, 157
Maltz, Albert, 161, 201, 216
Mamoulian, Rouben, 17, 18, 19, *21*, 22, 24, 30, 81, 82, 88, 218, 297
Man Called Horse, A, 282
Man from Laramie, The, 277
Man is Ten Feet Tall, A, 221
Man Who Came to Dinner, The, 133
Man Who Shot Liberty Valance, The, 252, 264, 275, 279–80, 300
Manchurian Candidate, The, 103
Manhattan, 303
Manhunt, 132
Mankiewicz, Herman, 79, 146
Mankiewicz, Joseph L., 13, 16, 41, 44, 63, 66–7, 89, 90–1, 137, 179, 217–19, 240, 297, 299, 334
Mann, Anthony, 264, 277, 278
Mannix, Eddie, 212
Mansfield, Jayne, 62, 103, **122**
March, Fredric, 22, 140, *141*, 180, 181, 183, 184, 206, 214
March of Time newsreels, 185

Marshall, George, 261, 279
Martin, Dean, 279
Marvin, Lee, 278, 280, 282
Marx, Groucho, 296
Marx, Samuel, 25–6, 28, 33, 34, 43, 45, 63, 179–80, 240
Marx Brothers Go West, The, 262
Mary Poppins, 302
MASH, 224
Masque of the Red Death, The, 244
Massacre, 179
Mature, Victor, 296
Maupassant, Guy de, 261
Mayer, Arthur, 83
Mayer, Edwin Justus, 133
Mayer, Louis B., 24, 25–6, 33–7 *passim*, 39, 41, 42, 43, 45, 63, 65, 66, 67, 69, 81, 105, 106, 112, 178, 180, 184, 188, 190, 202, 206, 240, 289–90, 291, 300, 301
Maynard, Ken, 252, 253, 257
Mayo, Virginia, 47, 64, 140
Mayor of Hell, The, 237
Mean Streets, 166, 248, 302
Medium Cool, 224
Meet Me in St Louis, 130
Memphis Belle, 129
Men, The, 140
Menjou, Adolphe, 187, 190, 191, 217
Mercouri, Melina, 99
Meredith, Burgess, 139, 203
Meyer, Russ, 244
Miami Vice (TV series), 285
Mickey Mouse, 30
Midler, Bette, 331
Midnight Cowboy, 303, 306
Milestone, Lewis, 22, 30, 139, 147, 186, 297
Milius, John, 166, 170, 171, 172, 176, 226, 227, 248–9, *250*, 282, 285–6, 307, 310, 311, 313, 314, 315
Miller, Ann, 295
Miller, Arthur, 214
Miller, Dick, 245
Minnelli, Liza, 303
Minter, Mary Miles, 78
Miracle, The, 100
Miracle of Morgan's Creek, The, 136
Miranda, Carmen, 131
Mirisch, Harold, 235
Mirisch, Marvin, 235
Mirisch, Walter, 162–3, 235–6, 240, 242
Misfits, The, 98

Missing, 226
Missing in Action, 227
Mission to Moscow, 186, 189, 190, *211*
Missouri Breaks, 282, 303
Mr Deeds Goes to Town, 60, 65
Mr Smith Goes to Washington, 65
Mrs Miniver, 111–12, *119*
Mitchum, Robert, 139, 263, 279
Mix, Tom, 252, 253
Moby Dick, 299
Modern Times, 23, 111
Mogambo, 294
Monroe, Marilyn, 37, 71, 75, 82, 97, 98–9, 103, **123**, 131, 184
Monsignor, 182
Monte Walsh, 282
Montgomery, Douglass, 106
Montgomery, Robert, 44, 45, *112*, 187
Moon is Blue, The, 84, 93 4, 199
Moonstone, The, 235
Moore, Colleen, 76
Moore, Terry, 62
Moorehead, Agnes, 132
Moran, George 'Bugs', 144–5
More the Merrier, The, 133
Morgan, Helen, 17, 19, *21*
Morning After, The, 319
Morocco, 82, 86
Mortal Storm, The, 111
Motherhood, 74
Muni, Paul, 46, 146, *151*, 152, 179, 183, 231
Murder My Sweet, 88, 137, 138, 157
Murdoch, Rupert, 300, 316
Murnau, F. W., 240
Murphy, Eddie, **327**
Murphy, George, 187
Murray, Bill, 318, **325**, 331
Murray, Mae, 26
Musketeers of Pig Alley, 145–6
Mutiny on the Bounty (1935), 59
Mutiny on the Bounty (1962), 297
My Bill, 237
My Darling Clementine, 251, 264
My Fair Lady, 302
My Little Chickadee, 262
My Name is Julia Ross, 240
My Son John, 206
Myra Breckinridge, 102

Naish, J. Carol, **270**
Naked City, The, 157, 161
Napoleon, 13

Napoleon's Banner, 22
Nazi Conquest No. 1, 106
Nazimova, 111
Negri, Pola, *20*, 24
Negro Soldier, The, 129
Nelson, Ralph, 281
Nevada Smith, 280
Never on a Sunday, 99
New York City Lights, 24
New York, New York, 311
Newman, David, 164
Newman, Paul, 99, 100, **267**, 278, *305*, 314, 317, *333*
Ney, Richard, 112
Nichols, Mike, 102
Nicholson, Jack, 91, 192, 174, *176*, 245, 246, 247, 303, 313
Nicholson, James H., 242
Night After Night, 83
Night and Day, 130
Night Court, 153
Night Flight, 44
Night Nurse, 59, 81
Night Riders of Montana, 234
Ninotchka, 91
Niven, David, 25, 113
Normand, Mabel, 78
Norris, Chuck, **200**, 227
North by Northwest, 99
North Star, 186
Northwest Mounted Police, 261
Notorious, 138, *158*
Novak, Kim, 296
Now Voyager, 132
Nye, Gerald, 185

Oakie, Jack, 27, **126**
Oboler, Arch, 297
O'Brien, Pat, 36, 237
Odds Against Tomorrow, 215
Odets, Clifford, 181, 301
O'Hara, John, 182
Oklahoma!, 277
Oklahoma Kid, The, 261
Old Amarillo, 234
Old Man and the Sea, The, 294
Old Wives for New, 76
Oliver Twist, 235
Olivier, Laurence, 25, 71, 90, 113, 282
On the Town, 295
On the Waterfront, 162
Once Upon a Time in America, 175, **196**
One-Eyed Jacks, 280
One Flew Over the Cuckoo's Nest, 225
O'Neill, Eugene, 88
Operation Burma, 117
Ornitz, Sam, 201
Outlaw, The, 40, 75, 92, 93–4, 263
Outlaw Josey Wales, The, 251, *255*, 282, 283, 303
Outrageous Fortune, 331

Over the Top, 317
Ox-Bow Incident, The, 262, *275*

Pacino, Al, *151*, 168, 169, *173*, 174, **195**, 302
Pakula, Alan J., 225, 303
Pal Joey, 182
Palance, Jack, 276, 282
Pale Rider, 283
Pan, Hermes, 295
Paper Moon, 302
Parallax View, The, 172, 225
Parks, Larry, 30, 213
Parrish, Robert, 120, 129
Parsons, Louella, 47
Parton, Dolly, 303
Party Girl, 145
Patton, 167, 224
Pawnbroker, The, 100
Peck, Gregory, 95, 186, 191, *211*, 263, *265*, 276, 279, 296
Peckinpah, Sam, 280, 281
Peggy Sue Got Married, **326**, 331, *332*
Pegler, Westbrook, 184
Penn, Arthur, 164, 165, 166, 174, 176, 278, 282, 300, 303
Pepper, George, 186
Perfect, 320, 329
Pete Kelly's Blues, 162
Petrified Forest, The, 155
Phantom Lady, 157
Phantom President, The, 153
Phenix City Story, The, 162–3, 236
Pickford, Mary, 16, 27, 28, 31, **53**, 78, 294
Pinky, 178, 187
Plainsman, The, 252, 260
Platoon, 315, **328**, 334
Play It Again, Sam, 303
Play Misty for Me, 303
Poe, Edgar Allan, 244, 245
Point Blank, 162
Polanski, Roman, 172, 174
Police Academy, **325**
Polly of the Circus, 59
Polonsky, Abraham, 157, 160, 161, 172, 181, 183, 192, 201, 206–7, 208, 213, 215, 216–17, 219–20, 221, 227–8
Porky's, **325**
Porter, Cole, 130
Porter, Edwin S., 252
Possessed, 138
Postman Always Rings Twice, The, 91
Powell, Dick, 37, 88, 187, 209
Powell, Eleanor, 130
Powell, Jane, 94
Powell, William, 91, **124**, 154

Power, Tyrone, 111, 112, 261, 296
Powers, Tom, *158*
Prelude to War, 117
Preminger, Otto, 84, 93, 157, 160, 216
Prentiss, Paula, 102
Pretty Boy Floyd, 249
Price, Vincent, 244, 245, 297
Pride of the Marines, 140
Prizzi's Honor, 334
Professionals, The, 280
Prohibition, 164
Psycho, 294, 300
Public Enemy, The, 80, 146, 147, 148, 149, *150*
Purdom, Edmund, 296
Purple Heart, The, 139, *141*
Pursued, 263
Puttnam, David, 301, 318, 320, 329, 336
Puzo, Mario, 167

Queen Christina, 25, 81
Queen Kelly, 76
Quick Millions, 153
Quiet Man, The, 234
Quinn, Anthony, 36–7, 224
Quo Vadis, **269**, 296

Racket, The, 147
Rafelson, Bob, 313
Raft, George, 45, 64, 116, 145, 156
Raiders of the Lost Ark, *312*, 331
Rain People, The, 167
Rains, Claude, 116
Ralston, Esther, 16, 28, 35–6, *38*, 57
Ralston, Vera Hruba, 233, 234, *238*
Rambo, 104, 154, 228
Rambo: First Blood Part II, 226–7
Rambo 3, 317
Rancho Notorious, 277
Random Harvest, 132
'Range Buster' series, 262
Rank, J. Arthur, 234
Rankin, John L., 189
Rappe, Virginia, 78
Rare Breed, The, 280
Rathbone, Basil, 132
Ratoff, Gregory, 59
Raven, The, 245
Rawhide (TV series), 281
Ray, Nicholas, 145, 167, 278
Razor's Edge, The, 48, 58, 318
Reagan, Ronald, 116, 155, 186, 187, 188, 190, 201, 205, 206, 208, 212, 222, 226, 227, 261, 314
Rear Gunner, 107
Rebel Without a Cause, 164

Red Badge of Courage, 290
Red Dawn, **200**, 226, 314
Red Dust, 81
Red River, 264, 282
Redemption, 25
Redford, Robert, **267**, 302, 317
Redgrave, Vanessa, **123**
Reds, **199**, 226
Reed, Donna, 231
Reed, Oliver, 102
Reid, Wallace, 63, 78
Renoir, Jean, 129
Report from the Aleutians, 129
Return of Frank James, The, 253
Return of the Jedi, 307
Reunion in France, 108, 117
Revolt of Mamie Stover, The, 98
Revolutionary, The, 224
Reynolds, Burt, 303, 334
Reynolds, Debbie, 94, 279
Reynolds, Robert, 187
Rhapsody in Blue, 130
Rhinestone, 303
Rice, John C., 73
Rich, Robert, 204
Richardson, Tony, 216
Ride 'Em Cowboy, 262
Ride the High Country, 280
Rin Tin Tin, 253
Ringwald, Molly, 7, **306**, 331
Rio Bravo, 279
Rio Grande, 234, 264
Riot in Cell Block 11, 236
Rise and Fall of Legs Diamond, The, 163 4
Ritt, Martin, 157, 167, 221, 228
Ritter, Tex, 235
Roach, Hal, 7
'Road . . .' films, 133
Roaring Twenties, The, 144, *151*, 156
Robe, The, 178, 297
Roberson, Chuck, 188
Robinson, Edward G., 27, 45, 107, 110, 146, 148, *150*, 166, 167, 191, **197**, 204, 205, 206, 209, 213
Robson, Flora, 110, 111
Robson, Mark, 230
Rocky IV, *223*, 227
Rocky series, 104
Rogers, Buddy, 16, 17, 26–7, 33, 64
Rogers, Ginger, 130, 131
Rogers, Lela, 131–2
Rogers, Roy, 235, 260, 261, **265**
Romancing the Stone, **324**, 335
Romeo and Juliet, 44–5
Rooney, Mickey, 63, 88, 112, 231, *238*

Roosevelt, Franklin D., 83, 106, 110, 111, 112, 114, 120, 154, 180, 184, 186, 189
Roosevelt, Major James, 120
Rosie the Riveter, 131
Rossellini, Roberto, 92, 100
Rossen, Robert, 160, 186, 187, 190, 212, 297
Rotha, Paul, 12
Rothstein, Arnold, 144
Rowland, Richard, 31
RPM, 224
Ruggles, Wesley, 237, 256
Runyon, Damon, 154
Russell, Harold, 140, *141*
Russell, Jane, 40, 59, 75, 92, 93, 95, *96*, 98, 114, **122**, 263
Rutherford, Ann, 36, *238*
Ruttenberg, Joseph, 82
Ryan, Robert, 131, *211*, 215

Safe Place, A, 313
Sahara, 117
Saint, Eva Marie, 99
St Valentine's Day Massacre, The, 144–5, 249
Salt, Waldo, 225, 303
Samson and Delilah, **269**, 296, 303
San Francisco, 45
San Quentin, 237
Sanders, George, *109*, 132
Sandpiper, The, 182
Sands of Iwo Jima, **128**, 234
Santa Fe Trail, 262
Saris, Andrew, 240
Savage, The, 273
Scarface (1932), 80, 146, 147, *151*, 152, 166, 175
Scarface (1983), *151*, 174, 175
Schary, Dore, 42, 43, 81, 82, 202, 206, 214, 289, 290, 295
Schell, Maximilian, 245
Schenck, Joe, 31, 184, 185, 202
Schenck, Nick, 66, 184, 290
Schickel, Richard, 91, 283
Schlesinger, John, 303
Schneider, Bert, 224, 313
Schneider, Maria, **124**
Schulberg, B. P., 37, 65
Schulberg, Budd, 65, 69, 180, 207, 213
Schwarzenegger, Arnold, 19
Scofield, Paul, 282
Scorsese, Martin, 152, 164, 166–7, 171, 172, 248, 249, 250, 302, 310–14 *passim, 312*

Scott, Adrian, 187, 192, 201, 203, 209
Scott, Lizabeth, 138
Scott, Randolph, 47, 254, 277, 278, 280, 284
Scott, Ridley, 318
Sea Hawk, The, 110, 111
Searchers, The, 277
Seas Beneath, *118*
Secret Invasion, The, 249
Secret Six, The, 28, 146
Selig, William, 252
Selznick, David, 34, 48, 60, 132, 263, 295, 300
Sergeant, The, 102
Sergeant Rutledge, 279
Sergeant York, 111, 115, 185
Serpico, 303
Seven Brides for Seven Brothers, 277, 296
Seven Minutes, The, 244
Seven Samurai, The, 279
Seven Year Itch, The, 98 103
Sex Hygiene, 120
Shadow of a Doubt, *138*
Shampoo, 307
Shane, 256, **266**, 276, 283
She Done Him Wrong, 83
She Wore a Yellow Ribbon, 264, 280
Shearer, Norma, 26, 44, 59, 80, 81, *86*
Sheffield, Johnny, 235, 239
Shenandoah, 280
Sheridan, Ann, 71, 91, 92, 116, 237, 261
Sherman, George, 229, 232, 233, 234, 257, 260, 273
Sherman, Vincent, 67, 69, 209, 212, 231, 237
Sherwood, Robert, 140
Shootist, The, 282, 283
Showboat, 296
Shut My Big Mouth, 262
Sidney, George, 42, 45, 63, 67, 70, 71, 89, 291, 295, 297
Sidney, Sylvia, 19, 22, 23, 24, 37, *38*, 46, 67
Siegel, Bugsy, 161, 162
Siegel, Don, 161, 162, 163, 172, 240, 303
Siegel, Sol C., 230
Silberburg, Mendel, 202
Silverado, **267**, 283, 284, 314
Simmons, Jean, 296
Simpson, Don, 308, 336
Sinatra, Frank, 216, 224, 295, 296
Since You Went Away, 132, *135*
Sinclair, Upton, 179, 180, 208
Singin' in the Rain, 25, 296
Singing Fool, The, 30

Singing Outlaw, 234
Siodmak, Robert, 157, 160
Sitting Bull, *273*
Sleeper, **321**
Smith, Harold Jacob, 215, 216
Society Doctor, 240
Soldier Blue, 224, 281
Some Like It Hot, 98, **123**, 145
Song of Russia, 189
Song of Songs, 82
Song to Remember, A, 40, 71
Sorrel, Herbert K., 187–8
Soul of Bhudda, 77
Sound of Music, The, 302, 305
South Pacific, 296
Southern, Terry, 246
Southwest to Sonora, 280
Spacek, Sissy, 104
Spartacus, 216
Spellman, Cardinal, 92, 94
Spielberg, Steven, 7, 250, 302, 307–11 *passim*, 309, 314, 315, **323**, 331, 334
Spiral Staircase, The, 138
Spoor, George K., 252
Squaw Man, The, 253, 255
Stagecoach, 252, 256, 261, 263, 273, *274*, 282, 284
Stagedoor Canteen, 130
Stallone, Sylvester, **223**, 226–7, 284, 303, 317, 319, 331
Stander, Lionel, 177–8, 183, 184–5, 203, 206, 210, 216, 220
Stanwyck, Barbara, 59, 81, 92, 136, *158*, 277
Star!, 302
Star is Born, A, 25
Star Spangled Rhythm, 130, *134*
Star Wars, 104, 168, 286, 308, 311, 313, 314, **322**, 331
Steamboat Willie, 30
Steele, Bob, 235
Steele, George, 133, 230, 291, 297, 334
Stewart, James, 62, 112, 261, 264, 273, *275*, 277, 279, 284, 288, 291, *292*
Sting, The, 303
Stoloff, Ben, 230
Stone, Oliver, 315, 334
Storm Over Lisbon, 233
Story of GI Joe, The, 139
Strasberg, Susan, 167
Straw Dogs, 102
Strawberry Statement, The, 224
Streep, Meryl, 104, 320
Streetcar Named Desire, A, 95, *293*
Streisand, Barbra, 302

Strickling, Howard, 43
Strode, Woody, 279
Sturges, John, 278, 279
Sturges, Preston, 133, 136–7
Suid, Lawrence H., 117, 139
Sullavan, Margaret, 106
Sullivan, Francis L., 260
Sullivan's Travels, 136
Summer Holiday, 88
Sunset Boulevard, 42
Support Your Local Sheriff, 281
Susan Lennox, Her Fall and Rise, 59, 60
Sutherland, Donald, *243*
Sutter's Gold, 260
Swanson, Gloria, 28, 31, 32, 76
Sweet Bird of Youth, 100
Swing-Shift Maisie, 131
Sylbert, Richard, 307, 308, 329, 331, 334

Talmadge, Constance, 24, 31
Talmadge, Norma, 24, 28, 31
Targets, 247, 286
Taxi Driver, 171, 172, *173*, 302
Taylor, Elizabeth, 99, 231, *238*, 296, *305*
Taylor, Robert, 111, 117, 189, 190, 240, 261, 296
Taylor, William Desmond, 78
Teacher's Pet, 47
Temple, Shirley, 132, *135*, 154, 241
Ten Commandments, The, 296
Ten North Frederick, 178, 294
Tender Comrades, 131–2
Tenderloin, 24
Teresa, 140
Terror, The, 245, 247
Test Pilot, 45
Texas to Bataan, 262
Texas Rangers, The, 260
Thalberg, Irving, 44, 45, 59, 63, 178, 180
They Came to Blow Up America, 132
They Died with Their Boots On, 262, 281
They Won't Forget, 179
Thief of Baghdad, The, 27
'Thin Man' series, 91, 154, 156
This is the Army, 130
Thomas, J. Parnell, 189–92 *passim*, 201, 202, 204
Thomas, Olive, 78
Three Bad Men, 261
Three Comrades, 106
Three Days of the Condor, 172

Three Godfathers, The (1936), 240
Three Godfathers, The (1948), 240, 264
Three Little Words, 271
'Three Mesquiteers' series, 232, 257, 260
3.10 to Yuma, 278
Tierney, Gene, 92
Tiger Man, 238
Tiger Shark, 237
To Be Or Not To Be, 133
To Catch a Thief, 99
To Each His Own, 288
To Have and Have Not, 146, 157, **193**
Todd, Mike, 296
Todd, Richard, 212
Toland, Greg, 93, 120
Tomb of Ligeia, The, 244, 245
Tone, Franchot, 25, 183, 203
Top Gun, 308, 318, **327**
Topper series, 91
Torrio, Johnny, 147
Touch of Evil, *159*, 170
Towering Inferno, 303
Towne, Robert, 164, 165, 166, 169, 172, 174, 245, 247–8
Tracy, Spencer, 27, 43, 45, 89, 133, 153, 155, 294
Trading Places, 320
Traffic in Souls, 74, 143
Trevor, Claire, 261, *274*
Trip, The, 246
Trouble in Paradise, 84
True Grit, **266**, 281
Truffaut, François, 8, 164
Trumbo, Dalton, 132, 181, 190, 201, 204, 216
Tumbling Tumbleweeds, 257
Turner, Kathleen, 104, 319–20, **324**, **326**, *332*
Turner, Lana, 89, 91, 92, 231, *238*
Turner, Ted, 300
Turrou, Leon G., 107
Tuttle, Frank, 70
Two-Faced Woman, 81, 82, 85

Ulmer, Edward G., 240–1, 249
Ulzana's Raid, 224, 282
Under Fire, 226
Undercover Man, The, 160–1
Underground, 237
Underworld, 146, *150*
Underworld USA, 162
Union Pacific, 260–1, 274

Valenti, Jack, 101, 246, 301, 320, 336
Valentino, Rudolph, 76
Van Doren, Mamie, 37, 47–9, *72*, 92, 242, 247

Vera-Ellen, **271**
Vidor, Charles, 157
Vidor, King, 256, 260
Virginia City, 261–2
Virginian, The, 254, *258*
Vixen, 244
Voight, Jon, 224, 225
Von Richthofen and Brown, 249
Von Sternberg, Joseph, 82, 146
Von Stroheim, Erich, 76, 132, 233, *238*

Wagner, Robert, 37, 62, 64, 94–5, 295
Wagon Master, 264
Wake Island, 117
Wald, Jerry, 65
Walk East on Beacon, 206
Walk in the Sun, A, 139
Walk on the Wild Side, A, 99
Walken, Christopher, **198**
Wallis, Hal, 10, 11, 65–6, 104, 147, 291
Walsh, Raoul, 144, *151*, 156, 253, 254, 262, 263, 284
Wanger, Walter, 106, 202, 297

Warner, Albert, 10, 66
Warner, Harry, 10, 11, 66, 107, 185, 186, 190
Warner, Jack, 10, 12, 30, *39*, 45, 46, 57, 64, 65–6, 69, 106, 107, 110, 186, 190, 191, 201, 221, 231, 297, 300
Warner, Sam, 10, 11, 12, 13
Warshow, Robert, 282
Wasserman, Lew, 301
Way Down East, 79
Way of all Flesh, The, 23
Way West, The, 280
Wayne, John, 47, 59, *108*, 117, 120, **128**, 129, 140, 187, 188, 206, 215, 222, *223*, 232, 235, 256, 257, 261, 262, 264, **266**, 273, *274*, *275*, 276, 277, 279, 281–4 *passim*
Wayne, Michael, 222
Weiss, Hymie, 144, 145, 148
Weissmuller, Johnny, 235, 242
Welch, Raquel, 102
Welles, Orson, 136, 137, *159*, 169–70, 234, 237
Wellman, William, 139,

148, 153, 179
West, Mae, 44, 82, 83, 84, 87, 262
West Side Story, **272**, 296
Westbound, 47
Western Union, 253, 262
Westerner, The, 262
Wexler, Haskell, 216, 224–5, 226, 310
What's Up, Doc?, 302
Wheel of Life, The, 16
Wheeler, Burton, 185
When the Daltons Rode, 261
Where are My Children?, 74
Whiphand, The, 206
White Rose, The, 79
Who's Afraid of Virginia Woolf?, 100
Who's That Knocking at My Door?, 248
Widmark, Richard, 160, 172, 279, 280
Wife, Husband and Friend, **121**
Wilcoxon, Henry, 111
Wild Angels, The, 245, 246, 247, *250*
Wild Boys of the Road, 179

Wild Bunch, The, **266**, 281, *286*
Wilde, Cornel, 37, 40–1, 71, **268**
Wilder, Billy, 132, 137, 145, 157, 218, 300, 334
Will Penny, 282
Williams, Tennessee, 94, 100
Wilson, Donald, 214
Wilson, Michael, 204
Winchester '73, 264, 277, 291, *292*
Wings, 26
Winner, Michael, 103, 146, 171
Winters, Shelley, *292*
Wise, Robert, 215, 230
Witness, 331
Wizard of Oz, The, 105, **125**, 130, 297
Woman in the Window, The, 157
Woman of Passion, 24
Woman of the Year, 133
Woman on Pier 13, The, 205, *211*
Woman on the Beach, 189
Women in Love, 102
Wood, John S., 212
Wood, Natalie, 94, 277

Woods, Edward, 149
Wright, Teresa, 138
Wurtzel, Sol., 230
Wyler, William, 18–19, 129, 140, 155, 181, 191, 201, 218, 230, 278, 291, 319

Yank in the RAF, A, 111
Yankee Doodle Dandy, 131
Yates, Herbert, 232, 233–4, 235
Year of the Dragon, 175
You Only Live Once, 155
Young, Loretta, **121**
Young, Nedrick, 215–16

Zanuck, Darryl F., *39*, 40–1, 45, 46, 58, 59, 64, 112, 129, 139, 146, 147, 148, 149, 178, 185, 203, 262, 294, 296, 300, 302
Zanuck, Richard, 302, 315–16, 330, 335
Zinnemann, Fred, 17, 99, 140, 218, 230, 276, 277
Zugsmith, Albert, 170, 242
Zukor, Adolph, 19, 83

Most of the photographs in this book are stills issued to publicise films produced or distributed by the following companies or individuals:

AIP, AIP-Sunset, Allied Artists-Walter Wanger, Les Artistes Associes-PEA-UA, Charles Chaplin, Columbia, Columbia-Delphi, Columbia-Italo-Judeo, Columbia-Pando-Raybert, Edison, Charles K. Feldman-Elia Kazan, Samuel Goldwyn, Howard Hughes, Lucas Films-Universal, Paul Malansky-Ladd Co.-Warner Bros., MGM, MGM-Avon, MGM-Carlo Ponti, MGM-David O. Selznick, MGM-UA-Valkyrie, Mirisch-Seven Arts, Monogram, Omni-Zoetrope, Orion-Hemdale, Paramount, Paramount-Alfran, Paramount-John Ford, Paramount-Dino de Laurentiis, Paramount-Lucas Films, Paramount-Long Road, Paramount-Cecil B. de Mille, Paramount-Don Simpson-Jerry Bruckheimer, Paramount-Hal B. Wallis, Republic, RKO, RKO-Kenneth MacGowan, David O. Selznick, Melvin Simon-Astral Bellevue Pathe-Porky's Productions, Touchstone, Tri Star, Twentieth Century-Fox, TCF-Argyle, TCF-Campanile, TCF-El Corazon, TCF-Lucas Films, United Artists, UA-Michael Cimino, UA-Jerome Hellman, UA-Mirisch, UA-Robert H. Solo, Universal, Universal-EMI, Universal-Lucas Films-Coppola Co., Universal-Zanuck-Brown, US-Jack Rollins-Charles H. Joffe-Brodsky-Gould, Warner Brothers, Warner-Batjac, Warner-Embassy-Ladd-PSO, Warner Malpaso, Warner Seven Arts-Phil Feldman.

The Publishers apologise for any unintentional omission or oversight, and will be pleased to insert an appropriate acknowledgement in any subsequent edition of this book.

PICTURE ACKNOWLEDGEMENTS

BBC Hulton Picture Library/Bettmann Archive pages 14 (bottom), 15, 38 (right), 97, 150 (bottom), 210 & 298 (bottom); BBC Television back cover inside flap; Joel Finler page 266 (top left); The Kobal Collection front cover (left & right), page 14 (top), 20 (bottom) 21, 29 (top), 39, 49–51, 53–6, 60–87, 96 (bottom), 108 (bottom), 118, 119, 121–3, 124–8, 134–41, 150 (top & centre), 151–76, 193–7, 199, 200 (top), 238 (left & top right), 239, 243 (top right & bottom), 250–9, 265, 266 (right), 267, 268 (bottom), 269–72, 274–92, 298 (top), 304 (bottom), 305 (top), 306, 309, 312 (top), 321, 322 (bottom right), 324, 325 (bottom), 326 (bottom), 327 (top), 332 & 333; The National Film Archive pages 20 (top), 29 (bottom), 38 (left), 52, 96 (top), 108 (top), 109, 123 (inset), 198, 200 (bottom), 211 (top & bottom left), 223, 238 (bottom right), 243 (top left), 266 (bottom left), 268 (top), 293, 304 (top), 305 (bottom) & 322 (top); The Photo Source page 211 (bottom right); Rex Features Ltd front cover (centre), 312 (bottom), 322 (bottom left), 323, 325 (top), 326 (top), 327 (bottom) and 328.